New Zealand Votes

New Zealand Votes

The General Election of 2002

Edited by
Jonathan Boston
Stephen Church
Stephen Levine
Elizabeth McLeay
Nigel S. Roberts

VICTORIA UNIVERSITY PRESS

VICTORIA UNIVERSITY PRESS
Victoria University of Wellington
PO Box 600, Wellington

© Editors and contributors 2003

ISBN 0 86473 468 9

First published 2003

This book is copyright. Apart from any fair dealing for the purpose of private study, research, criticism or review, as permitted under the Copyright Act, no part may be reproduced by any process without the permission of the publishers

National Library of New Zealand Cataloguing-in-Publication Data
New Zealand votes : the general election of 2002 / edited by Jonathan Boston ... [et al.].
Includes index.
ISBN 0-86473-468-9
1. New Zealand. Parliament—Elections, 2002. 2. New Zealand—Politics and government—1996- I. Boston, Jonathan, 1957-
324.99304—dc 21

Cover photographs, from left:
The 'worm' records favourable responses by a sample of uncommitted voters to points made by Peter Dunne during a party leaders' debate on TV1 on 15 July 2002.
Helen Clark being questioned by John Campbell on TV3 on 10 July 2002 about what became known as the 'Corngate' saga.
'Paintergate': The picture that Helen Clark signed – but did not paint – for a charity fundraising event.
Bob the Builder (who inspired New Zealand First's campaign rhetoric) in front of Parliament and the Beehive.
From left to right, Peter Dunne (leader of the United Future Party), Helen Clark (leader of the Labour Party and Prime Minister of New Zealand), and Jim Anderton (leader of the Progressive Coalition) link arms after signing coalition and support-party agreements in Parliament Buildings on 8 August 2002.

Printed by PrintLink, Wellington

CONTENTS

Preface   9
    Jonathan Boston, Stephen Church, Stephen Levine,
    Elizabeth McLeay and Nigel S. Roberts

Overview of the Election

1. New Zealand Votes: An Overview   15
   Stephen Levine and Nigel S. Roberts
2. Going Early   28
   Stephen Church
3. Two Million Voters in Search of a Rationale   45
   Colin James
4. Leadership and the Campaign   59
   Jon Johansson
5. The Electoral Commission and the 2002 General Election   75
   Paul Harris

Party Perspectives: Tactics and Strategies

6. ACT III: ACT's Third MMP Election Campaign   87
   Tomas Kriha, Brian Nicolle and Graham Watson
7. The Green Campaign   98
   Cate Faehrmann
8. Oddity or New Paradigm? A Labour View of the 2002 Election   104
   Mike Williams
9. National's Campaign   111
   Tim Grafton

10	The New Zealand First Campaign *Brian Donnelly*	118
11	The United Future Campaign *Mark Stonyer*	123

The Candidates

12	Entertainment vs Education: Campaigning under MMP *Stephen Franks*	135
13	Being a Green Candidate *Nandor Tanczos*	140
14	A Red Jacket in Rangitikei *Margaret Hayward*	145
15	'Out of my Comfort Zone': Campaigning in Wellington Central *Hekia Parata*	150
16	Campaigning in a Maori Seat *John Tamihere*	156
17	Identity Politics and MMP: Political Correctness or Political Courage? *Paul Gibson*	161
18	Campaigning Disabled: A Perspective on the 2002 Election *Eamon Daly*	168
19	Window on Wairarapa: Georgina Beyer and the 2002 Election Campaign *Matt Lamason*	175
20	Choosing Candidates: Labour and National in 2002 *Rob Salmond*	192

Media Coverage

21	'Constructing Something from a Few Crumbs': A Journalist's View of the Campaign *Al Morrison*	209
22	News, Newszak, New Zealand: The Role, Performance and Impact of Television in the General Election of 2002 *Tim Bale*	217

23	The Party Vote, Populism and Political Advertising in 2002 *Claire Robinson*	235
24	'Read All About It!': Newspaper Coverage of the General Election *Janine Hayward and Chris Rudd*	254
25	All Over the Place: Billboard Battles in 2002 *Nigel S. Roberts*	270

The Results

26	Representation, Selection, Election: The 2002 Parliament *Elizabeth McLeay*	283
27	Consistent Patterns and Clear Trends: Electoral Behaviour in 2002 *Stephen Levine and Nigel S. Roberts*	309
28	Government Formation after the 2002 General Election *Jonathan Boston and Stephen Church*	333

Notes	361
References	375
Appendix 1: Coalition Agreement between the Labour and Progressive Coalition Parties in Parliament	387
Appendix 2: Agreement between the Labour/Progressive Government and the United Future Parliamentary Caucus	389
Appendix 3: Co-operation Agreement between the Labour/Progressive Government and the Green Parliamentary Caucus	393
Appendix 4: MPs in the 47th Parliament	398
Appendix 5: The Government	402
Contributors	407
Index	415
Contents of CD	424

PREFACE

*Jonathan Boston, Stephen Church, Stephen Levine,
Elizabeth McLeay and Nigel S. Roberts*

New Zealand Votes: The General Election of 2002 provides electoral interpretation in its chapters rather than in its title. The book offers perspectives from party officials and organisers, as well as from parliamentary candidates – some successful, some not.[1] The focus of the book is on campaigning, both nationwide and in individual electorates. Various chapters examine the role of the media, and of political advertising, on voter perceptions and electoral choice. The circumstances under which the election was called receive special attention. How New Zealand parties select their candidates, and with what results, form the basis for two contributions. The role of leaders in New Zealand's politics and election campaigning is a theme running through several chapters. As for what resulted from this election, this is considered from several angles: the composition of the new Parliament; the formation of a new coalition with its various support and consultative arrangements; and, through survey research, what it is New Zealanders thought they were accomplishing – and what they expected to happen – when they cast their votes as they did.

The book concludes with a set of materials that adds to its usefulness as a resource. These include the coalition agreement signed between Labour and the Progressive Coalition, allowing a new government to be formed; the agreement signed between that coalition and its supporting party, United Future; the subsequent accord agreed to by the coalition and the Greens; the members of the Parliament elected in the 2002 vote; and the members of the new government (comprising Ministers inside Cabinet, Ministers outside Cabinet, Parliamentary Under-secretaries and Parliamentary Private Secretaries).

Unlike its predecessors, both in New Zealand and elsewhere, the book is accompanied by a CD of video and audio segments from key campaign moments. This allows readers to see and hear for themselves many of the campaign events (such as highlights from debates and television advertisements by various parties) on which contributors comment. The result is a resource for students and scholars, both in New Zealand and overseas, whose value will increase as the 2002 election recedes with time and as memories of a campaign rich in incident and controversy fade. The radio and television extracts collected on the CD would otherwise become difficult to access in the future. The cooperation of the broadcasting authorities and political parties in making these materials available is warmly appreciated. In particular, we acknowledge with thanks permission received from Radio New Zealand, Television New Zealand, TV3, and the following political parties: ACT; Alliance; Christian Heritage; Green; Labour: National; New Zealand First; Outdoor Recreation; and United Future.[2] The credit for this initiative must go to Claire Robinson, whose suggestion it was, and her assistance in compiling the CD is gratefully acknowledged.

The book has its origins in a post-election conference held in Wellington at the Beehive (the Executive Wing of the New Zealand Parliament) on 27 July 2002. The theme of the conference was 'Campaigning Under MMP', and the conference was opened by the Speaker of the House, Jonathan Hunt, who had kindly allowed the participants to use the premises. This was the sixth successive occasion on which a post-election conference was held under the auspices of academics at Victoria University of Wellington. It was sponsored by two scholarly groups based at Victoria University, the New Zealand Politics Research Group, and the New Zealand Political Change Project. The principal organisers, Stephen Church and Elizabeth McLeay, were assisted by Janet Cockburn, administrative assistant to the New Zealand Political Change Project. She played a key role in organising the conference and seeing to it that everything went very smoothly on the day. Subsequently she displayed patience and persistence in assembling manuscripts and liaising with contributors. We have been grateful throughout for her efforts, both good-natured and a model of efficiency, and are delighted again to have the opportunity to acknowledge with thanks all that she has been able to do for us and for the Project.

The task of implementing editorial changes to the manuscripts was carried out by two administration assistants in the political science and international relations programme at Victoria University of Wellington. Amelia Bury skilfully and energetically put through the various changes to the manuscripts required by the editors, displaying an extraordinary ability to read and understand the notes scribbled on the text and in the margins (some of them scarcely intelligible to the editors themselves).

Amelia's departure from Wellington (at the end of her studies at Victoria University) came before the book had been finished. We are grateful to Holiday Powell for her assistance in processing the remaining book chapters. She took a keen interest in the book and learned things about New Zealand elections and politics that they never taught her in her native California.

Tina Barton (personal assistant to the head of Victoria University's school of history, philosophy, political science and international relations) made her own distinctive contribution to the book, particularly during the closing stages, assisting the editors with her mix of keyboard dexterity, research and administrative skills and unique vitality.

Anne Else assisted the editors by working through the chapters after initial revisions had been carried out. We are grateful to her for the many improvements in clarity and style she made to the manuscript. Credit for preparing the index goes to Ginny Sullivan. Victoria University Press gave this book its full support, and we are grateful to Fergus Barrowman and Sue Brown for their commitment and readiness to bring the manuscript swiftly to publication. In turn, Victoria University Press is grateful to the following organisations and individuals for permission to use their photographs on the cover of this book: Office of the Prime Minister; Gerry Keating; Mark Jennings and Kim Peacock, TV3 Network Services Ltd.; Trish Carter, Television New Zealand; and Phil Doyle.

The post-election conferences begun in 1987 have produced a series of books that have combined perspectives from participants and commentators alike. Their insights, coming so soon after the events themselves, have had immediacy and freshness. The frankness with which many of the participants have always been prepared to speak has also been apparent. The Victoria election studies series now includes a total of six books; the other five are: *The 1987 General Election: What Happened?*; *The 1990 General Election: Perspectives on Political Change in New Zealand*; *Double Decision: The 1993 Election and Referendum in New Zealand*; *From Campaign to Coalition: New Zealand's First General Election Under Proportional Representation*; and *Left Turn: The New Zealand General Election of 1999*. The first (1987) book, edited by Professor Margaret Clark of Victoria University's political science and international relations programme, was made possible by the Social Science Research Fund Committee. The 1990 and 1993 books were published in the Occasional Papers monograph series of Victoria's political science and international relations programme. The 1996 book was published by Dunmore Press. The 1999 and 2002 books have been published by Victoria University Press.

We are grateful for the support of these various entities – government, publishing and academic – over these many years. At the same time, we wish to acknowledge here, once more, the support provided to the New Zealand Political Change Project by New Zealand's Foundation for Research, Science and Technology (FRST). From 1995 to 2003, FRST sustained a commitment to a major collaborative research project by Victoria University scholars into the consequences for government and politics of New Zealand's change of electoral system. Over this period, as a result, the members of the Project – Jonathan Boston, Stephen Levine, Elizabeth McLeay and Nigel S. Roberts, and Stephen Church (from 1998 to 2002) – have been able to sponsor conferences; take part in international meetings, symposia and gatherings of one kind or another; offer lectures to the public and to community groups; and publish a large number of academic papers (and several books) on a range of interrelated and relevant topics. There has been widespread interest in MMP, both within New Zealand and overseas. Through FRST's commitment, we have been able to devote some effort to satisfying that interest, and it is fitting that we once again express our thanks to FRST for their confidence in us and our endeavours.

July 2003

OVERVIEW OF THE ELECTION

1

NEW ZEALAND VOTES: AN OVERVIEW

Stephen Levine and Nigel S. Roberts

The 2002 New Zealand election was the third to be held under the country's 'mixed' proportional representation system.[1] No longer a new electoral system, MMP – mixed member proportional – appears now to have become part of the fabric of a state that had formerly held its elections under first-past-the-post (plurality) rules for over 150 years.[2] In 2001, a parliamentary review of MMP required by statute (section 264 of the Electoral Act 1993) was completed. It left the system unchanged. The three MMP elections – 1996, 1999 and 2002 – have been free from constitutional crises. Even the 2002 early election created no apparent dilemmas for the Governor-General who was called upon to authorise it.

New Zealand's MMP elections have, as expected, brought to power coalition governments in a country previously accustomed only to read about the necessity for such contrivances elsewhere. Coalitions formed after the three elections have covered a wide range of the political spectrum. They have been on the centre-right: National-New Zealand First in 1996; the centre-left: Labour-Alliance in 1999; and somewhat closer to the centre: Labour-Progressive Coalition (supported by United Future and the Greens) in 2002. MMP governments have also comprised two of the four possible types of administration: multi-party majority (of seats in Parliament) and multi-party minority. To date New Zealand has not had a single-party minority government under MMP. As for the fourth possibility, a single-party majority regime – the norm under first-past-the-post (FPP) – this was within one party's grasp when the decision to go to the polls several months early was announced on 11 June 2002 by Labour Prime Minister Helen Clark.[3]

The Alliance and the early election

By contrast with New Zealand's most recent previous early election – the 1984 'snap election', called without warning (or consultation) by then Prime Minister Robert Muldoon – the move to an earlier than necessary election had been well signalled in advance by Labour. Neither the media nor the Labour Cabinet were caught by surprise. The public and the Opposition were not taken unawares either. Although it was not actually necessary for the election to be called – the government retained the confidence of the House – there was little objection raised about the development of a seemingly new convention in which early elections can be called almost as a matter of prime ministerial discretion.[4]

From a government that had been endeavouring to provide 'no surprises', this was a characteristically undramatic start to what was to become, at times, a lively and controversial campaign. The process began, perhaps unsurprisingly, with the spectacular collapse of the Alliance Party. Few other political movements disintegrate so comprehensively and so vividly as those on the left. The vitality with which they begin often deteriorates into vicious internal disputes. The inability of the Alliance's extraparliamentary leadership and grassroots membership to accept the constraints and conventions of Cabinet collective responsibility in the end made the party's presence as a coalition partner embarrassing, if not untenable.

Although clashes of personality and management style contributed to the break-up of the Alliance, matters came to a head when the party's leader, Deputy Prime Minister Jim Anderton, gave an ultimatum to wavering Alliance MPs and Cabinet Ministers, requiring them to accept the need to support government policy towards the US-led war on terror (specifically, the military campaign against the Taleban regime that had given shelter to the al-Qaeda terrorist movement in Afghanistan). While Anderton's requirement was accepted in the short term, the rupture within the Alliance over the issue never healed. Those opposed to government policy were unwilling and unable to subordinate their differences in the interest of party unity. Their outlook and actions meant that they could not, in practice, refrain from undermining Anderton and, by extension, the Labour-led coalition of which they were a part.

MMP was designed, in part, to offer smaller parties enhanced opportunities for the expression of political influence. In some ways, the system has functioned as intended. The larger parties have had to work within coalitions, while smaller parties have been able to gain a greater voice in policy development, either as members of a government or in support roles. But smaller parties have had to pay a price for such intimacy. Successful initiatives from government become associated in the public mind with the larger party in the coalition and with that party's leader, the prime minister. The smaller parties' experience of publicity from 1996 to 2002 often revolved around internal embarrassments, peculiar personalities and policy eccentricities. New Zealand First suffered in public esteem (and opinion polls) during its partnership with National after the first MMP election. A decline in the Alliance's standing was part of the backdrop to its disarray and ultimate disappearance. Winston Peters' depiction of Prime Minister Helen Clark as a species of black widow spider, devouring her mate after enjoying its services, was only the most lurid way of summarising the Alliance's overall predicament (*New Zealand Herald*, 23 July and 24 December 2002). A larger view of the matter is to suggest that neither the public nor the parties themselves have altogether adjusted to the new realities of multi-party Parliaments and Cabinets, the product of MMP. The Alliance was undone in part because much of the party never really thought of itself as part of government, that is, as part of the culture of government, administration and the exercise of power.[5] Conceived as an adversary to 'the powers that be', it remained, to the end, essentially an opposition party – opposed to the way things are, to the way power is allocated, and unable to accept that it was now among those who were responsible, part of a system that was to remain, in the end, substantially intact.

The scale of the Alliance's embarrassment at the polls was extraordinary. By the end of the campaign, with all the votes counted, a party that at its best had stood for a society committed to a fairer distribution of wealth and power had been eclipsed by the recently formed Outdoor Recreation Party, a group interested in little more than the maximisation of opportunities for hunting, shooting and fishing.

The prime minister had accused the opposition of impeding legislative progress through questions over the break-up of the Alliance and the continued presence in Parliament of its members. The Electoral Integrity Act 2001 seemed to require MPs who no longer represented the party under which they were elected to resign their seats. The Alliance MPs were no longer allied to one another, and it had been conceded that when an election was held, the faction led by Anderton would be competing as a separate party. Yet no MP resigned, and no formal steps were initiated that would have caused any MP to do so. However, as the asking of parliamentary questions on the subject was irrelevant to the progress of the legislative timetable (the questions were all being asked during 'Question Time'), it is difficult to view the prime minister's rationale for calling an early election as anything other than an attempt to make the best of a bad situation in Parliament, while exploiting her party's advantage in opinion polls.

The calling of an early election at a time when Labour's polling suggested that it could gain a parliamentary majority on its own produced little resistance from the media or the opposition. The Victoria University pre-election survey (see chapter 27) asked voters:

> Some people have said that the prime minister should not have held an early election, while others have said that she's justified in doing so. What do you think? Should the prime minister have waited and held the election in October or November, or is the fact that an election is being held now okay by you?

The results were highly favourable from Labour's point of view: 70 percent found the early election date acceptable. Voters from across the political spectrum were comfortable with the calling of the early election. Whether they intended to vote for Labour, National, or any of the smaller parties, voters showed they were unconcerned about the premature ending of the parliamentary session. This was not an 'issue' with voters, let alone one that the opposition could exploit. Apart from some initial complaints and criticisms, largely from National, the topic had little, if any, political traction.

Electoral redistribution

Each of the three MMP elections has been preceded by an electoral redistribution. With the party vote determining the overall distribution of seats, the precise boundaries of electorates are perhaps less significant than they were in the past. Nevertheless, electorate MPs are in the House to represent geographically defined groups of constitutents, and there remains an interest in these seats based on their representative function. When MMP was introduced, the number of electorates was reduced from 99 electorates in 1993 (under FPP) to 65 for the 1996 election. Three years later there were 67, and in 2002 there were 69. As a result the number of list seats declined, from 55 in 1996 to 53 in 1999 and to 51 in 2002. Those unhappy with MMP because of the role played by list MPs, who are alleged to be elected by 'no one', but simply according to the rankings chosen by party leaders and organisers, may feel some satisfaction in the gradual shrinking of their numbers.

At the same time, the MMP elections have been historic in bringing about the first-ever increases in the number of Maori seats. The four seats established in 1867 did not increase until the Electoral Act 1993 permitted them to fluctuate according to the numbers of Maori choosing to register on the Maori roll. The number of Maori electorates increased to 5 in 1996, rose to 6 in 1999, and rose again to 7 in 2002. As a proportion of the total number of electorate seats these incremental rises are far from insignificant. The four seats in 1993 were four out of 99, whereas under MMP the figures are five out of 65 electorates (1996); six out of 67 (1999); and seven out of a total of 69 electorates (2002).

These increases embody both continuity and change: continuity, as New Zealand has adapted its 'mixed system' to encompass its guarantees of indigenous parliamentary representation; and change, as MMP has allowed the system of separate Maori representation not merely to persist, but to grow. Yet the Royal Commission that originally recommended MMP suggested that because the new system was likely to lead to increased numbers of Maori MPs generally (as indeed it has), this would obviate the need for the separate Maori seats to be maintained (Royal Commission on the Electoral System 1986, pp.81–113).

Electoral administration and MMP

The administration of the 2002 election went very smoothly. There had been problems at the 1999 election, with dissatisfaction expressed over delays in the release of election night results.[6] In 2002, there were no referenda to be counted and the results were released very quickly. The high quality of New Zealand's electoral administration meant, perhaps ironically, that there were no media stories on it. The complaints after 1999 had continued long after the election had been held. In 2002, there was little evidence afterwards that the smooth running of the election had been appreciated. However, the Victoria University pre-election survey asked respondents for their views on the quality of New Zealand's electoral administration – its efficiency and integrity. It is clear from their answers that, even before the election had occurred, the public had a degree of confidence in the professionalism of New Zealand's electoral administration processes and personnel that would be the envy of comparable systems in most other democratic countries.

One question in the survey asked participants, 'How accurately do you believe votes are counted and reported in New Zealand?' More than 90 percent of respondents thought that the counting and reporting were either 'very accurate' or 'reasonably accurate'. Less than 1 percent of those polled – only 0.4 percent in fact – thought that the election results as they were reported were 'not accurate at all'.

Another question asked, 'could you tell me how much *trust and confidence* you have in the electoral system as a whole?' The results show that, when looking broadly at the electoral system, New Zealanders take a largely positive view: 72 percent of those polled had either 'a great deal' or 'quite a lot' of 'trust and confidence' in the country's electoral system. By contrast, only 3.7 percent had 'none at all'.

As usual, matters became less clear-cut once MMP itself was mentioned. The Electoral Commission would be gratified to know that survey participants were well informed about a basic feature, the party vote: 71 percent correctly stated that the 'party vote' determines the overall number of seats to which parties are entitled following an election. But there was much greater ambivalence about the virtues of MMP as an electoral system for New Zealand. Only 43 percent agreed with the MMP review committee's recommendation that no significant changes to the system were required, whereas 48 percent disagreed. A majority, 53 percent, thought it appropriate to hold another referendum on MMP; 37 percent were opposed; and another 6 percent thought that perhaps a referendum should be held, but 'not yet'. National voters were the most strongly opposed to MMP: nearly two-thirds disagreed with the parliamentary review's unwillingness to recommend major change, and they were also the group most strongly favouring another referendum.

New Zealanders' misgivings about MMP also continued to reflect concerns held by many about Parliament itself. Half of those questioned thought that MPs were 'out of touch' – this was especially the case among New Zealand First voters. The proposition that the size of Parliament 'should remain at 120 MPs' was rejected both overall (57 percent to 33 percent) and among nearly all groups of voters (the small group of Alliance voters excepted), with New Zealand First voters again being the most critical of present arrangements.

Voter turnout

Overall, MMP elections have seen a decline in voter turnout. This is somewhat counter-intuitive. Those who designed the electoral system argued that a more proportional electoral system would mean that because 'every vote counts', voters would have more incentives to cast a ballot even in what used to be described as safe seats, since their party vote would contribute to the overall result. At the first MMP election in 1996, the turnout of registered voters did, as expected, increase, from 85.2 percent to 88.2 percent. However, the 1999 election saw a decline in turnout of 3.4 percentage points, down to 84.8 percent. Nearly three years later, after a brisk midwinter campaign, the turnout was only 77 percent – a drop of nearly 8 percentage points. Although the size of the New Zealand population is continuing to grow, the number of people casting votes is gradually sliding down. The bottom lines of each section of Table 1.2 show turnout data for each of the three MMP elections.

It is easy, but unwise, to make too much of this. By international standards, New Zealand's level of voter turnout remains fairly high.[7] No one would suggest that a return to first-past-the-post would boost numbers: they might well drop still further. Voting is voluntary, although enrolment is mandatory (in fact no one has ever been prosecuted for not being on the rolls), and there is little support for changing this approach. To the extent that the level of voting participation is considered a problem, the Electoral Commission is already seeking, through its publicity and information campaigns, to boost public understanding of MMP and, by extension, public willingness to take part in MMP elections. New Zealand's parties have become more adept at using the latest technology – in 2002, for example, party websites were an integral part of their communication strategies. Attempts to involve younger New Zealanders and recent immigrants (the two groups least likely to take part) are also features of contemporary campaigning.

Political parties and candidacy

One measure of a system's 'legitimacy', and one of the ten criteria used by the Royal Commission on the Electoral System to evaluate electoral systems, is its ability to encourage and attract popular participation in its processes, not only through voting, but also through parties and candidacy. Table 1.1 gives the total number of candidates standing for electorate seats and on party lists in each of the three MMP elections. It also records the number of political party lists participating in 1996, 1999 and 2002. As it shows, in 1999 the number of electorate candidates and party list candidates both rose, and there was also a modest rise in the number of parties contesting

Table 1.1: Number of candidates and parties contesting the 1996, 1999 and 2002 general elections in New Zealand

	1996	1999	2002
Number of Electorate Candidates	611	679	593
Number of List Candidates	690	768	523
Total	1301	1447	1116
Total Number of Candidates*	842	965	683
Number of Party Lists	21	22	14

* The difference between 'Total' and 'Total Number of Candidates' reflects the fact that many individuals at each election were both Electorate and List candidates for their party.
Source: Electoral Commission 2002, pp.174–5; Chief Electoral Office 1997, pp.5–10; Chief Electoral Office 2000, pp.7–13; Chief Electoral Office 2002, pp.10–15.

the election. In 2002, however, all these indices of participation declined, along with the turnout. While some of this decline could perhaps be attributed to the early election, it is also possible that a greater sense of realism could be at work. Parties that might previously have almost routinely decided to nominate a full slate of candidates for the party list, regardless of the extremely slim prospects of those at the lower end getting any closer to Parliament than the public galleries, may now be becoming more realistic, by assembling a less than full complement of list candidates. The decline in overall numbers of electorate candidates also may show a greater sense of realism about electoral prospects under MMP. While initially there may have been a view that the system would open Parliament up to a vast array of parties and independents, it is now clear that there are still significant barriers facing newcomers.

Although MMP was recommended as a system that would be friendly to the aspirations of smaller parties, the three MMP elections have had little effect on the number, type or identity of parties represented in the House. The march towards MMP during the 1994–96 period had consequences for party stability and formation (Boston, Levine, McLeay and Roberts 1996, chapter 4). But despite appearances to the contrary, MMP itself has had little significant effect in this area. The 1996 election saw six political parties represented in the New Zealand Parliament: National, Labour, New Zealand First, Alliance, ACT and United. Three years later there were seven, with the additional party (the Greens) having re-emerged from its temporary home as a participating party within the Alliance.

The 2002 election left key elements of this picture unchanged. As before, seven parties gained representation; six of them were unchanged, and the Alliance was replaced by the Progressives, led by former Alliance leader and founder, Jim Anderton. The degree of fragmentation attributed by some to MMP has to a large extent been minimised; not only on the governing side, but among the opposition as well, a degree of stability has been achieved. In 1996, one other party, the Christian Coalition, nearly gained representation, falling just short of the 5 percent threshold, with 4.3 percent of the party vote; but since then, no other unsuccessful party has come anywhere near gaining representation.

The 2002 campaign

While the names and numbers of the parties in Parliament have changed very little, their fortunes have fluctuated dramatically. During the short 2002 election campaign, a government seeking to 'sleepwalk' not merely to victory, but to a majority, experienced not one rude awakening, but rather several. There were feisty interviews and prime ministerial walk-outs. Not since Robert Muldoon at his most withering has the New Zealand public seen a prime minister characterise an interviewer in such dismissive tones ('a sanctimonious little creep') (*Dominion Post,* 10 July 2002). Allegations of cover-ups (with one 'gate' following another), harsh words between former allies and friends (Labour vs the Greens, the Alliance vs itself), and the emergence of Peter Dunne and his United Future party on the back of a sudden success in a televised leaders' debate (and the return of the audience-response tool known in New Zealand as 'the worm' (see Sowry 1997, p.32)) all lent drama and intensity to the campaign. So did strong views from opposition parties on crime, immigrants and immigration, and Maori policy (particularly Treaty of Waitangi settlements claims).

The 2002 election took place in a country that was enjoying a degree not only of prosperity, but also of international recognition and acclaim. The first film of Wellington director Peter Jackson's *Lord of the Rings* trilogy saw the city claim to be the capital of 'Middle Earth'. New Zealand still held the America's Cup (with a challenge due to take place in 2003). However, the campaign and its backdrop encompassed serious issues. The war on terror and the events in Afghanistan were having an impact in New Zealand, as elsewhere. Although the focus of most election commentary was on 'popularity contests' – principally how Prime Minister Clark and National Party leader Bill English were faring against one another – the election had the potential to affect many more people than the party leaders and candidates gaining most of the attention.

The policy consequences of the 2002 election, like those of any other, will take some time to appreciate. Some of these belong to the genre of 'what if?' speculation. We will never know what might have happened if Labour had continued to coast towards a majority regime, or if Bill English's last-minute quest for victory had somehow ended in an improbable (but by no means impossible) four-party right-of-centre government, with English at the helm. Even identifying winners and losers can be a somewhat complex affair. New Zealand First narrowly escaped oblivion in 1999, surviving on the strength (if that is the right word) of its leader's 63-vote victory in his Tauranga electorate. Three years later, Winston Peters' at times virtuoso campaigning more than doubled his party's vote (although it still fell short of its 1996 level), increasing its seats in the House from five to thirteen. But was Peters a 'winner'? The strategy used to boost his party's numbers was an important element in his exclusion from even being considered as a partner of any sort for the Labour-Progressive coalition. Dismissed with an election-night grimace by the prime minister, he could look forward only to three years as the leader of an inexperienced New Zealand First caucus on the opposition benches.

The result

Table 1.2 gives the results for the three MMP elections held thus far. Elements of continuity with FPP remain intact. Nearly all electorate seats have continued to be won by National or Labour candidates. New Zealand First's brief capture of the Maori seats (in 1996) shows little sign of being repeated. Only a handful of seats have been won by candidates for smaller parties, and in every case these have been won by party leaders: Jim Anderton (Alliance in 1996 and 1999; the Progressives in 2002); Richard Prebble (ACT in 1996); Peter Dunne (United in 1996, 1999 and 2002); Winston Peters (New Zealand First in 1996, 1999 and 2002); and Jeanette Fitzsimons (Greens in 1999).

Most list seats are held by MPs representing New Zealand's smaller parties. This reflects their inability to win many electorate seats while at the same time capturing a sufficient proportion of the party vote to win representation in Parliament. In 1996, Labour and National together won

Table 1.2: The results of the 1996, 1999 and 2002 general elections in New Zealand

	1996							
	Party votes		Total seats		Elect votes		Elect seats	List seats
Party	#	%	#	%	#	%		
National	701,315	33.8	44	36.7	699,073	33.9	30	14
Labour	584,159	28.2	37	30.8	640,884	31.1	26	11
New Zealand First	276,603	13.4	17	14.2	278,103	13.5	6	11
Alliance	209,347	10.1	13	10.8	231,944	11.3	1	12
ACT	126,442	6.1	8	6.7	77,319	3.7	1	7
United	18,245	0.9	1	0.8	42,666	2.1	1	0
Christian Coalition	89,716	4.3	0	0.0	31,995	1.5	0	0
Legalise Cannabis	34,398	1.7	0	0.0	3,420	0.2	0	0
Others	32,134	1.5	0	0.0	56,342	2.7	0	0
Total	2,072,359	100.0	120	100.0	2,061,746	100.0	65	55

Turnout of registered voters: 88.2%
Eligible population-based turnout: 80.8%
Index of Disproportionality* (LSq): 4.36%

* The index of disproportionality (LSq) measures the overall discrepancy between the shares of votes and the shares of seats that political parties win in an election. The lower the figure, the more proportional the result – a perfectly proportional election would have 0.0 percent disproportionality. To put the data in this Table into perspective, the 17 first-past-the-post elections in New Zealand from 1946 to 1993 had an average index of disproportionality figure of 11.10 percent. For further information about the index, see Lijphart 1994: pp.57–62, 160–162.

	1999							
	Party votes		Total seats		Elect votes		Elect seats	List seats
Party	#	%	#	%	#	%		
Labour	800,199	38.7	49	40.9	854,736	41.8	41	8
National	629,932	30.5	39	32.5	641,361	31.3	22	17
Alliance	159,859	7.7	10	8.3	141,322	6.9	1	9
ACT	145,493	7.0	9	7.5	92,445	4.5	0	9
Green	106,560	5.2	7	5.8	86,157	4.2	1	6
New Zealand First	87,926	4.3	5	4.2	85,737	4.2	1	4
United	11,065	0.5	1	0.8	22,467	1.1	1	0
Christian Heritage	49,154	2.4	0	0.0	44,885	2.2	0	0
Future New Zealand	23,033	1.1	0	0.0	19,289	0.9	0	0
Legalise Cannabis	22,687	1.1	0	0.0	6,519	0.3	0	0
Others	29,586	1.5	0	0.0	52,555	2.6	0	0
Total	2,065,494	100.0	120	100.0	2,047,473	100.0	67	53

Turnout of registered voters: 84.8%
Eligible population-based turnout: 77.2%
Index of Disproportionality (LSq): 3.01%

Table 1.2 cont'd: The results of the 1996, 1999 and 2002 general elections in New Zealand

Party	2002							
	Party votes #	%	Total seats #	%	Elect votes #	%	Elect seats	List seats
Labour	838,219	41.3	52	43.3	891,866	44.7	45	7
National	425,310	20.9	27	22.5	609,458	30.5	21	6
New Zealand First	210,912	10.4	13	10.8	79,380	4.0	1	12
ACT	145,078	7.1	9	7.5	70,888	3.6	0	9
Green	142,250	7.0	9	7.5	106,717	5.4	0	9
United Future	135,918	6.7	8	6.7	92,484	4.6	1	7
Progressive Coalition	34,542	1.7	2	1.7	36,647	1.8	1	1
Christian Heritage	27,492	1.4	0	0.0	40,810	2.0	0	0
Outdoor Recreation	25,985	1.3	0	0.0	0	0.0	0	0
Alliance	25,888	1.3	0	0.0	33,655	1.7	0	0
Legalise Cannabis	12,987	0.6	0	0.0	3,397	0.2	0	0
Others	7,036	0.3	0	0.0	30,284	1.5	0	0
Total	2,031,617	100.0	120	100.0	1,995,586	100.0	69	51

Turnout of registered voters: 77.0%
Eligible population-based turnout: 72.5%
Index of Disproportionality (LSq): 2.53%

Note: Parties that obtained at least 1 percent of the party vote or at least one seat in any of the three general elections are included in this table. In 1996, the Christian Heritage Party and the Christian Democrats (Future New Zealand's predecessor) were part of the Christian Coalition.

Source: Electoral Commission 1997a: pp.18–19; Electoral Commission 2000: pp.60–61; Chief Electoral Office 2002: p.3; Electoral Commission 2002: p.174.

25 list seats; smaller parties won 30 of them. This was little changed in 1999: Labour and National again won 25 list seats, with smaller parties winning 28 (as noted earlier, the number of list seats fell by two at that election, reflecting the increase in the number of electorate seats). In 2002, owing largely to National's poor showing, Labour and National took only 13 list seats, whereas the smaller parties took 38.

Labour's success translated into its having more electorate seats and fewer list seats, shifting from 26/11 in 1996 (when it finished second to National) to 41/8 in 1999 and on to 45/7 in 2002. The National Party's fall from grace in 1999 saw its electorate seats drop (from 30 to 22) and its list seats correspondingly rise (from 14 to 17). Its very poor showing in 2002 left the party with only one less electorate seat (21), but far fewer list seats (only 6).

Labour's and National's joint share of seats fell in 2002 to its lowest proportion since the two parties began their competition with each other at the 1938 election. Only 62 percent of the party vote went to the two major parties. As a result, together they were able to win only 79 of 120 seats in Parliament – just under 66 percent of the total, their lowest combined proportion ever. Another way of looking at these results is to observe that under MMP, New Zealand's smaller parties have increased their combined share of the vote, allowing their membership in the House to reach record levels in 2002. In 1993, New Zealand's last first-past-the-post election, smaller parties won only four of 99 seats; in 1996, they won 39 of 120; and in 1999, they held 32 seats. The 2002 election brought smaller parties to a new high point of 41 seats in Parliament.

In broad terms, the story of this election is reflected in difficulties in choosing a title for this book. One possibility considered by the editors, *Early to the Polls*, reflected the unusual element of a government going for an early election without any particularly urgent constitutional reason for doing so. Another suggestion, *Back to the Centre*, was an attempt to suggest what New Zealanders as a whole wanted to achieve with their vote. If the point of the election was to put Labour back in (this time without the Alliance), *Labour Wins Again* sums things up; but this overlooks concerns about the Greens, and the emergence of Peter Dunne and United Future. *Steady as She Goes* was meant to focus on stability, but seemed rather ambiguous. *Left in the Lurch* tried to get across too convoluted a set of ideas to pass muster.

What these attempts underscore is that it is always difficult to discover any clear 'message' in the aggregation of ballot choices made by large numbers of people. In 2002, more than two million New Zealanders were able to organise their votes in such a way that Labour was able to win, but not by so much as to have a majority, while other parties elected to Parliament were each given opportunities to influence, consult, observe and oppose. Still other parties will retain identities and aims that do not really depend on elections or parliamentary representation: Christians can preserve and enjoy their heritage without winning a seat in the New Zealand Parliament, and outdoors enthusiasts can continue to use guns and fishing rods despite being unable to hit or hook an electorate.

2

GOING EARLY

Stephen Church

The most significant aspect of the 2002 election is that it was held early, an uncommon occurrence in New Zealand. The prevailing myth is that voters don't like early elections, encapsulated by that well-worn political aphorism 'turkeys don't vote for an early Christmas'. But based on the results of the only other early elections held in the post-war period, the evidence of voter backlash is equivocal. In 1951, the National Prime Minister, Sid Holland, called an election a year ahead of schedule, seeking a mandate for quashing a bitterly fought waterfront dispute. He improved his party's vote, and National stayed in government until 1957. In 1984, another National Prime Minister, Robert Muldoon, brought the election forward some months, arguing that National was in danger of losing its majority because of dissident backbenchers (despite the protestations of the MPs concerned that they would not bring down the government). The real reason was probably the country's rapidly deteriorating economic position, and this time National lost the snap election. So history gives no reliable guide as to whether voters are likely to punish the governing party for requiring them to vote early.

On 11 June 2002, Helen Clark became the first Labour prime minister ever to request an early dissolution of Parliament. Before examining the reasons behind the timing of the 2002 poll, the shaping of public attitudes, and the constitutional implications, this chapter surveys current thinking in political science on the phenomenon of early elections.

Understanding early elections

In many parliamentary systems, the timing of the next election is at the discretion of the government of the day, giving leaders the power to call elections at the most advantageous time for them, presumably when they expect to win. To date, political scientists have not delved deeply into the reasons for calling early elections. Some guidance may be found in the growing literature that examines the phenomenon of government termination in general. These studies tend to assume that any decision to change the government – whether it is the meltdown of a coalition, a realignment of parties in government, or calling an early election – is the product of a rational calculation by leaders regarding the relative benefits of these actions, versus maintaining the status quo. In the case of calling an election, it is assumed that a party implicitly trades off the benefits it currently receives in office against the prospects of winning a larger share of votes, therefore enhancing its chances of a further period in office.

However, calling an early election brings its own costs, even if it seems likely that the incumbent party or coalition will win another term. Mounting an election campaign is always a costly exercise for parties, and the potential for a new round of coalition negotiations sooner than expected can create difficulties for the continuity of a government's policy programme. But perhaps the most significant opportunity cost imposed by an early election is forfeiting the benefits of office that are available if the incumbent government were to complete its term. An early election effectively 'resets the clock' on the constitutionally mandated limit on the maximum length of a Cabinet's term. A government may win another term in office by going to the people a year early, but can it ever get that year back?

Recent studies have shown that governments are subject to a rising 'hazard rate' throughout their lifetime: that is, they are at greater risk of falling as their tenure wears on (Warwick 1994). According to Lupia and Strom (1995), the total benefit of office that a government can expect to collect over its life appears large at the beginning of the term, and as a result an early election will seldom look promising. But as the certainty of scheduled elections draws closer, the marginal value of a coalition to the parties in government declines, thereby reducing election-related opportunity costs. Diermeier and Stevenson (2000) find statistical support for the claim that the probability of an early dissolution increases as the government approaches the end of the constitutional inter-election period.

A number of other patterns emerge from cross-national studies. Countries in which the government can call an election at its own discretion appear to have more frequent elections than do countries in which early elections must be preceded by a vote of confidence (Laver and Schepsle 1996).

However, of this set, the electoral histories of those with three-year maximum terms reveal a distinct absence of early elections, and New Zealand is the prime example (Mackie and Rose 1991). The implication of a shorter term limit for the theory outlined above is relatively simple: a three-year term means that the point at which office benefits can be traded for future payoffs in the form of an increased vote share comes very late in the cycle. There is a much more limited window for opportunism, since it was not long since the last election, and therefore the experience of incumbency is still relatively brief.

There is a fairly limited body of specific research on the issue of election timing, but most studies (Cargill and Hutchison 1991; Chowdhury 1993; Reid 1998) focus on the idea of 'political surfing': that is, leaders simply wait until conditions are most advantageous before going to the polls. These studies assume that the electoral outcome is simply an expression of relative support for the government at the time the election is called (not to mention its performance during its time in office). However, according to Smith (2000), the timing itself influences the election result. The decision by a leader to call an election is based on an information advantage relative to voters about the future performance of the government. Yet in relying on these expectations to determine the attractiveness of immediate elections, governments may tip their hand as to what their information is. Thus Smith argues that the inference voters may draw upon hearing of an early election is that the government doubts its ability to continue producing good outcomes in the future.

In a survey of UK elections, Smith found that popular governments are more likely than unpopular governments to call early elections. However, governments with a large majority are less likely to go to the polls early, probably because they are in a better position to implement their preferred policies, and so may reap more utility from holding on to office. Conversely, those with only a slim majority, or minority governments, have a greater incentive to try to seek a working majority, and voters appear to reward them for doing so, perhaps seeing such governments as having a legitimate need to go to the nation (Kayser 2000). The later this happens the better, since voters regard popular leaders going to the polls late in their term as much less opportunistic than those trying to cash in on their popularity earlier.

Although the theoretical framework presented above appears fairly fragmented, the insights it provides can contribute to a better understanding of what caused the 2002 general election in New Zealand to be called four months early.

The official version

The statement by Prime Minister Helen Clark on 11 June 2002, announcing that the general election would be held on 27 July, neatly conveyed the government's justification for an early poll. It started with an affirmation of public satisfaction with the government and its programme, before acknowledging the division in the junior coalition partner, the Alliance.

In the second half of 2001, internal divisions within the Alliance surfaced publicly over the decision by leader Jim Anderton to back Labour's offer of New Zealand's military support for the US-led invasion of Afghanistan. This episode clearly signalled more fundamental differences within the party. Several of its MPs, party members, and the party's President, Matt McCarten, argued that they were being excluded from decision-making, and that the Alliance was not being assertive enough in pushing its own policies in government. To intensify matters, the Alliance's opinion poll ratings had sunk to very low levels as support for Labour soared, despite the constructive relationship between the two parties. Following a series of attempts by both factions to push the other aside, on 3 April 2002 Anderton declared his intention to quit the party and form a new political movement, with six other MPs, to contest the general election to be held later that year. Anderton planned to remain as Alliance leader as long as he had the support of a majority of MPs in caucus. To leave the party while Parliament was in session risked invoking the Electoral (Integrity) Amendment Act, which would require those who defected from the Alliance to resign from Parliament.[1] At the time, Clark stated that although there was a crisis in the Alliance, there was no crisis in government, since both factions continued to pledge their support. Indeed, as far as Parliament was concerned, the Alliance remained one party, and was still in government.[2]

The response of the Opposition, and the National Party in particular, was to use 'question time' on each sitting day to lodge relentless points of order challenging the legitimacy of Anderton as leader of the Alliance in the House. In attempting to obtain some formal recognition that he and other Alliance MPs had effectively left the party, National hoped to highlight the hypocrisy of the situation in light of the Electoral Integrity legislation, which both Anderton and Clark had strenuously pursued. At the very least, the Opposition hoped that the troubles within the Alliance would taint Labour's popularity. When the election was called, however, Clark was quick to blame these tactics for the decision, arguing that, while the troubles within the Alliance had not affected the functioning of the government:

> It is clear to me that that time wasting by the Opposition will continue to obstruct the passage of important legislation until an election is called. Little would be achieved by having Parliament sit for another two months. Indeed to prolong Parliament's sitting at this point can only further demean its public standing and enhance its unfortunate image as an institution which achieves little. In my view the will of the majority of New Zealanders is being thwarted and I intend to put that to the test (Clark 2002).

Clearly the prime minister was seeking to blame the Opposition for the early election. Although persistent, the attempts to hold up question time consumed an average of no more than 20 minutes of the House's time each sitting day. Even if accumulated over several months, it would be difficult to attribute these tactics to the fact that 94 Bills remained on the order paper at the time that Parliament was dissolved. The reliance on the Green Party had to some extent handicapped the government's legislative progress, given the need to consult with them over a range of issues. More significant than this, however, were the negotiations over the parliamentary process itself. The Greens would not agree to allow the government to take urgency,[3] and this evidently produced a level of frustration amongst ministers regarding their legislative programmes. Yet it could be argued that both National and the Greens were acting in the spirit of one of the key roles of Parliament, namely, to scrutinise.

The other reasons given for the election were rather understated. Clark mentioned twice that she was seeking a new mandate, and that in doing so:

> I am seeking the opportunity to form and lead a strong government. I do not believe that it is acceptable to New Zealanders to see small parties exercise a balance of power irresponsibly. This term our government has been strong and stable because that has not happened. I give full credit to Hon Jim Anderton for the emphasis he has placed on steady government and look forward to working with him again (Clark 2002).

The reference to small parties exercising power irresponsibly was not aimed at the Alliance, given the affirmation that this type of behaviour had not occurred under the 'stable' government of the current term. This comment was aimed squarely at the Greens, following events in previous weeks that had soured relations between the coalition and its support party.

On 22 May 2002, the Green Party's seven MPs simultaneously walked out of the debating chamber as legislation placing restrictions on genetic modification, including a temporary moratorium on field trials, was read for the third time. The Greens stated that they would bring down a future government that lifted the moratorium (due to expire in October 2003). Labour had known that the Greens would abstain on the vote, but not that they would use it as a platform to level an ultimatum. On the other hand, this may have been partly directed as a response to Clark's claim, at the Labour Party conference the previous weekend, that voters might welcome a majority government. The effect, however, was to give this argument even greater strength. The prime minister reacted by arguing that this was the 'kind of thing that brings small parties into disrepute' and that it was 'ridiculous to hold Governments to ransom over single issues'. She talked about 'small parties being the tail that wags the dog', mentioned 'Italian-style politics', and referred to the Greens' 'silliness'. Clark was also quick to provide the solution, as the episode would 'simply redouble my determination to campaign for two ticks for Labour', and that it was 'more momentum for a majority government' (*New Zealand Herald*, 23 May 2002; *Evening Post*, 27 May 2002).

Thus by the time the election was announced, it had already been flagged by the Greens as a referendum on GM, but for Labour it was effectively a referendum on MMP. Clark had been a vocal critic of the new electoral system prior to its introduction, but while in office she had deflated the prospect of major change to MMP during the review of the system by a select committee in 2000–2001. Now she had the opportunity to pull off an unexpected trick, a first-past-the-post result in an MMP election. This was an opportunity created in part by the actions of minor parties, but was given powerful logic by the popularity of the Labour Party and its leader.

What the government didn't tell you

In response to questions at the press conference announcing the election date, the prime minister said that Labour's sky-high approval ratings, which, she noted, appeared to have peaked, were not a consideration in deciding on a date. But even if this was 'as good as it gets' for Labour, then it is still difficult to see how its poll ratings could not have influenced its decision to

Figure 2.1: Labour Party ratings in public opinion polls, February 2000–June 2002

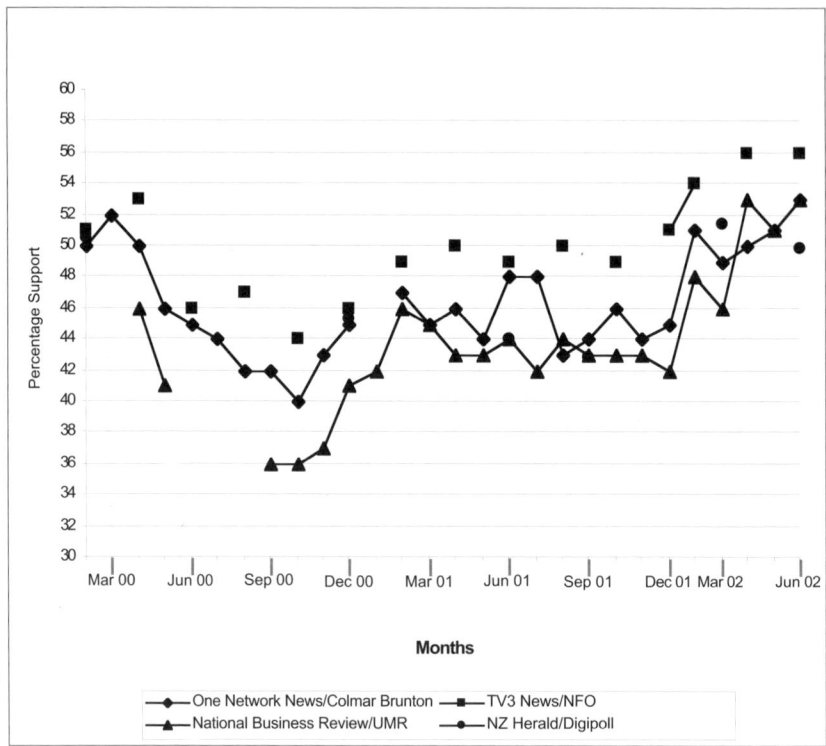

go to the people early. Figure 2.1 plots Labour's ratings for the four national published polls from March 2000 to June 2002. After building steadily throughout 2001, Labour was consistently scoring 50 percent in polls from April 2002, despite the problems with the Alliance. It is possible that Labour may have been afraid that its popularity might start to be affected by the difficulties its junior partner was experiencing, although in announcing the election, Clark revealed that she had been thinking about an early election since late March, before the Alliance divorce had become final. A longer lead-in to the election would have given the Alliance more time to organise, increasing the risk that it would glean votes from Labour. Anderton, on the other hand, was always going to be restricted by the fact that he could not start campaigning until the House rose, for fear of invoking the party-hopping legislation.

The other side of the equation, even in a multiparty environment, is the state of the major opposition party. National had replaced Jenny Shipley as leader with Bill English in October 2001, and the party also had a relatively new president, Michelle Boag. In his first campaign as leader, English would have to compete with Clark, who had already fought two elections at the head of the Labour Party. The less time he had to become established in the public eye as a potential prime minister, the better it would be for Labour. In the meantime, Boag's high-profile presidency was keeping the party in the news in an unflattering way. Internal party dissent was stimulated by her stated aim to 'stop the rot' by removing 'dead wood' MPs who were perceived to be under-performing, replacing them with new blood. There had also been the threat of scandal when, in May 2002, National was accused of 'laundering' large donations from private sources during the previous election campaign. This issue was ineptly managed by the party, and reminded voters of its big business connections, even though the accusations were not

Figure 2.2: National Party ratings in public opinion polls, February 2000–June 2002

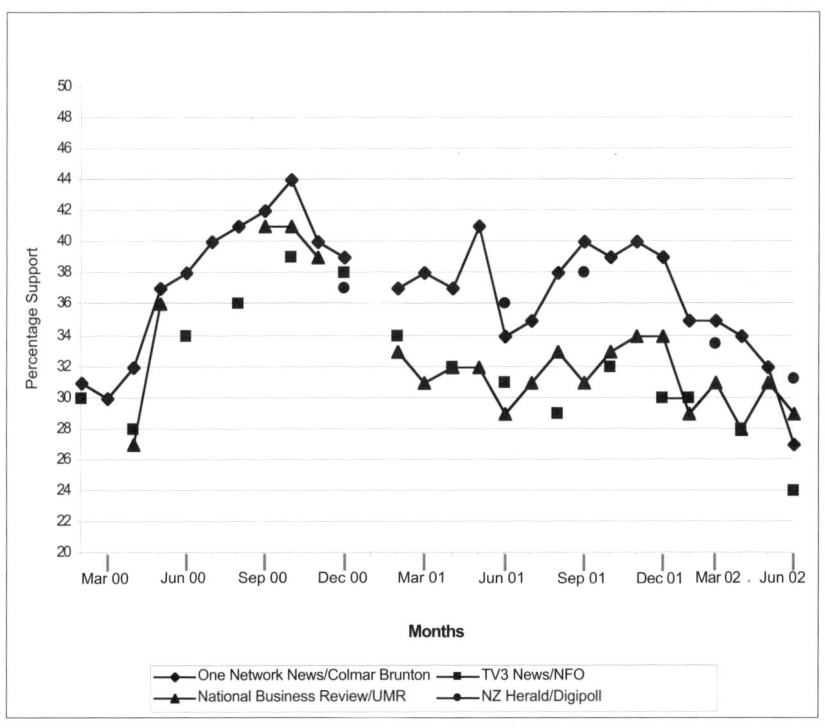

upheld by either by the Electoral Commission or the Serious Fraud Office. National also seemed unprepared to fight an election, bringing forward its policy announcements and candidate selection process only after the Alliance split. Above all, National's performance in opinion polls showed that it was unlikely to be in a position to lead an alternative government after the election. Figure 2.2 shows that by early June 2002, National was consistently dipping below 30 percent, less than its losing 1999 election result.

This 'acute relevancy deficit' (as one National Party strategist put it) began to have a self-reinforcing effect, as Labour was well aware. Apart from polling published by media agencies, political parties carry out their own research into the views of voters. UMR Insight is Labour's pollster, as well as conducting a regular poll for the *National Business Review*. A UMR poll commissioned by Labour in May found that 39 percent of National voters, seeing their own party in disarray, were willing to 'do the unthinkable' and vote Labour to keep the Greens out of government. This finding was leaked and mistakenly reported by other media as part of a *National Business Review* poll (*Evening Post*, 7 June 2002), but it supported anecdotal feedback from voters. The risk was that the motivation for National voters to switch could weaken over time, if Labour's support eased and a coalition partner became a necessity. Labour also used UMR to conduct qualitative research in the form of focus group work. Clark's comments, following the election announcement, that she had been getting 'quite a lot of feedback now about small parties stuffing up MMP, and I think MMP is on trial' bear the hallmarks of this kind of research. In particular, statements such as 'While people quite liked the representation and voice of small parties, they don't want vetoes bringing governments down' closely reflect the approach that UMR used in providing market research to the MMP Review Committee, when it tested both positive and negative attitudes towards MMP (see MMP Review Committee 2001, Appendix C).

Although Labour was seeking a parliamentary majority in calling an early election, this did not mean that it had to win 50 percent of the votes. MMP is not a purely proportional electoral system because of the threshold, which requires parties to win either 5 percent of the party vote or one electorate seat to be entitled to representation. At the 1996 and 1999 elections, 7.5 percent and 6.1 percent of votes respectively were cast for parties that failed to pass either of these thresholds. These votes are removed from the calculation of seats; this means that if, say, 5 percent of votes are 'wasted' in this way, then the seats are divided amongst the other parties holding 95 percent of party votes. In this case, to hold a majority of seats, a party would require only about half of that 95 percent of votes, i.e. 47–48 percent. Based on the experience of previous elections, and the likelihood that parties such as the Alliance and Christian Heritage would probably fail to win representation, Labour could expect that this proportion of the party vote would be enough to win a majority. Labour was not intending to govern alone, however, and the likelihood that Anderton would win his seat of Wigram effectively added another seat (or more, if the Progressives' party vote was sufficient) to the total. In other words, Labour might only need to win about 46–47 percent of the vote to achieve a combined majority without the help of the Greens, which gave it room to comfortably lose some support during the election campaign.

Labour had several reasons to believe that its support might well erode. There had been a longstanding dispute over secondary teachers' salaries that remained unresolved, resulting in widespread industrial action. Furthermore, Prime Minister Helen Clark was herself was under attack. In April it had come to light that she had signed a painting she had not herself created, to be sold at a charity auction. Just as the issue seemed to be dying down, on 10 May a member of the public made an official complaint to the police. When the date of the election was announced, the police still had not reported the findings of its inquiry, and the government went to the polls with the threat of an adverse ruling hanging over the prime minister.[4] Another factor in the government's calculations involved concerns that the economy was set to deteriorate later in the year on the back of a global slump. At the time, however, the economy appeared to be in reasonable shape, with unemployment down and the May 2002 Budget declaring respectable surpluses. If anything, this provided even more reason to send voters to the polling booths while they were reasonably content, at some risk of antagonising them, rather than waiting until the end of the parliamentary term for the economy to turn sour.

In making the decision to call an early election, Labour was surrendering another few months in office. Even if the timing was immaterial to the election result, when the tide eventually runs out on the government, it would have forfeited the opportunity to use the maximum time available to it. The trade-off was an opportunity to win another term, this time with a government majority, and unencumbered by a demanding support party. However, the government ran the risk that by going early it would appear to be acting opportunistically, hence the denial of a poll-fuelled decision, and the call for a mandate to install a majority government and avert minor party brinkmanship. In doing so, the government had to walk a fine line between identifying the threat to its stability, while denying that instability existed. Labour had won support in 1999 on a pledge that it would keep its word; this was at odds with a foreshortened term, unless that could be attributed to the actions of others. The success of this strategy would be sealed by the reaction of the electorate to the call for an early election.

A heightened state of readiness

An important feature of the decision to call an early election was the manner in which the idea developed in the public arena via the media, over a period of more than six months, from fairly wild speculation into reality. Indeed, to some degree the process exhibited the characteristics of a self-fulfilling prophecy. At other times it appeared to be a deliberate strategy on the part of the government to acclimatise the electorate to an acceptance that an early election was both necessary and desirable.

The possibility of an early election was first raised publicly in connection with the scheduled lifting of the initial moratorium on the release of genetically modified organisms into the environment, at the end of October 2001. The Greens threatened to withdraw support for the minority government if strict controls on GM were not imposed. Although the coalition subsequently decided to extend the moratorium until October 2003, Anderton warned the Greens that an early election would make Helen Clark's day. The continued ructions within the Alliance kept speculation alive, and the idea then began to develop a life of its own. For example, when Labour's Maori MPs expressed their opposition to GM during a caucus meeting in late October, Clark reportedly remarked that they could all be in for an early election at the rate they were going. Although it was a throwaway comment, National Party strategist Murray McCully read it as one of a series of signals from Labour that the party saw an early poll as a live option. When the *National Business Review* suggested in November that a projected slide in economic growth might lead the government to call an early election, Boag was quick to agree. Those in the business community with the PM's ear were also suggesting this option if the government continued to fail to advance its policy agenda, including GM and progress on a free trade deal with the US, both anathema to the Greens.

Labour's leadership gave some fairly mixed messages in response to the rumours, since at this stage they really were only rumours. When, on 14 November, National leader Bill English threatened not to back the government if it made matters such as GM, free trade agreements, or sending troops to Afghanistan into confidence issues, Deputy Labour Leader Michael Cullen challenged him to 'make my day'. Away from the theatre of the debating chamber, Cullen told journalists that he expected the government to run its full term, a message reiterated by the Prime Minister's Office the following day. In the early months of 2002 Clark was prepared to concede that the election could be as early as October, but she maintained that a decision was still months away. In the meantime, the Labour Party was moving towards a state of maximum preparedness. Its finances were in credit, its head office had called for tenders for its election year advertising, and the candidate selection process had begun in January and was expected to be finished by April. Up to that point, the prime minister could afford to deflect questions about the election with the response that it was not on her radar yet. However, two events were to force her to reveal more of her hand.

The first was the confirmation that the split in the Alliance was indeed terminal. Clark stated that she did not believe it was an issue for the government, since both factions continued to give it their support, and that it was certainly not cause for an early election. A One Network News/ Colmar Brunton poll released shortly afterwards showed that 71 percent were opposed to a snap election, with only 16 percent in favour. National's response was to welcome talk of an early election, presumably to underscore the idea that the government was no longer stable. Again, Cullen goaded English in the House by arguing that the Opposition never calls for an early election, to which his reply was 'why don't you call one!' (Parliamentary Debates 2002, p.15689).

Labour's position then seemed to become more equivocal, as its coalition partner came under increasing fire in Parliament. Clark maintained it was important that the government continue to pursue a steady course, on the grounds that there was no reason to do otherwise, but she let slip that 'nothing would give greater pleasure than to have an election next Saturday' (*The Press*, 22 April 2002). Labour Party President Mike Williams continued to entertain the idea, particularly if the Alliance infighting began to rub off support for the government, yet Labour's focus group work indicated that it was not doing it any harm. The election talk had also flushed out former Reserve Bank Governor Don Brash as a National Party candidate, and forced

National to release some policy ahead of schedule.

By the end of April, the media had moved on to speculation about the actual date of the election, identifying two alternatives: either late (27) July/ early (10) August, or mid-October. If this information had been obtained from government sources, then it suggests that Labour was still in two minds. Thus the question became not whether there would be an early election, but when. In her public utterances, Clark carefully refused to recommit herself to a late election – when questioned, she simply stressed that the government's first priority was to pass the Budget.

In the first week of May, a *Herald* Digipoll showed that 58 percent did not want the government to call an early election. National began to realise that its attacks could play into the government's hands. English changed tack to argue that the instability of the Alliance was no reason to call an early election, since 'embarrassment is no cause for an early election' (*New Zealand Herald*, 14 May 2002).

The second event that sharpened the issue of an early election was the walkout by the Greens late in May. The Greens subsequently placed ads in newspapers claiming that Labour was going to let GE out of the lab. Clark acknowledged that these kinds of actions gave rise to expectations of an early election. However, even on 10 June, the day before the election was announced, she made a point of avoiding speculation on the subject. Yet the public were clearly warming to the idea – a *Herald* Digipoll released the same day found 49 percent opposed to an early election, while 39 percent supported the prospect. A succession of newspaper editorials had called on the government to end the speculation, and business groups concurred, for fear that the uncertainty would flow into the commercial environment.

It could be argued that the government conducted a calculated campaign to soften up the electorate for an early poll. In view of the fact that Labour seemed prepared to take the Alliance meltdown on the chin, and assuming that it did not know of the Greens' intentions, it is probably more accurate to see the July election as one of a number of options that Labour was considering, depending on the circumstances. In terms of the official view, Clark's refusal to speculate and her statements about the need for stability tended to insulate her from suggestions that the eventual decision to go to the electorate was self-serving. If Clark had decided against going early, no one would have been able to say that she had ever said she would do so. At the same time, her position did not rule out an early election, so public expectations were hardly dampened by her comments. Unofficially, sources close to the prime minister were feeding journalists the scenario of an early election, indirectly generating a climate of expectation amongst the populace via the press gallery. In a circular fashion, the government's decision thus reflected decreasing public disagreement with the idea of an early election; the longer the speculation continued without categorical refutation by the prime minister, the more readily the public expected, and accepted, an early poll. The power of inevitability to create acquiescence is supported by the results of the Victoria University survey of 1,000 voters, taken in the final week of the campaign, which showed that 66.9 percent agreed with the timing of the election.

Constitutional implications

The decision by a prime minister to call for an early election is not as autonomous as one might assume, since, by constitutional necessity, it involves the Governor-General. The Queen, represented by the Governor-General, 'reigns' as a matter of law (under the Letters Patent last updated in 1983, and reaffirmed in the 1986 Constitution Act). However, the government of the day 'rules', in the sense that a prime minister who commands majority support of Parliament qualifies as a 'responsible advisor' to the head of state (Keith 1994, pp.30–31). The Governor-General must have responsible advisors at all times, and should act only on their advice, since the government is able to be held accountable at the polls or in Parliament for its actions (unlike the Governor-General, who is appointed). However, there also exists a series of residual 'reserve powers' left open to the Crown's discretion, including the power to exercise independent judgment on the appointment and/or dismissal of a prime minister, and on a prime ministerial request for an early dissolution of Parliament (Joseph 1993, p.591). The use of the Crown's reserve powers has atrophied as Parliament, but in reality Cabinet, has grown to dominate the decision-making process.

There are three different situations when a prime minister may request an early dissolution, distinguished by the degree of certainty regarding the prime minister's ability to tender advice. The first scenario may arise following an election, if parties find it impossible to form a workable government, in which case another election may be a final resort open to a Governor-General if it is clear that no government can be formed from the new Parliament.

The second occasion for an early dissolution is where a government decides to call a snap election while it retains the majority support of the House. In recent times in New Zealand, a single party majority government has twice requested, and received, an early dissolution from the Governor-General. In 1951, Holland's majority was never in doubt when he called fresh elections to seek endorsement for his government's handling of the waterfront strike. In July 1984, Prime Minister Muldoon requested an early dissolution four months before the scheduled election date because he could no longer count on the support of a majority of his own caucus, in particular National MP Marilyn Waring.[5] Although the Governor-General, David Beattie, might have been constitutionally correct had he refused a dissolution to a prime minister who admitted that he might not have the confidence of the House, the proximity of the scheduled election and the practicality of finding an alternative government among the existing members of the House[6] may have militated against such a decision. In any case, the election confirmed the government's lack of legitimacy, by installing the fourth Labour government in its place.

The third and most problematic scenario is a request for a dissolution when the Governor-General has reason to believe that a government no longer has the support of the House (e.g. through a defeat on a confidence motion, or the breakdown of a coalition). In these cases, if the prime minister does not immediately resign but instead requests a dissolution the Governor-General can refuse the request, provided an alternative government can be formed. This reserve power was first tested in 1872, before the advent of political parties, when Premier Stafford was defeated on a motion of no confidence and requested a dissolution. Governor Bowen refused, on the grounds that an election had been held recently and another one would have solved little, given the fluidity of Parliamentary groupings during that period. Stafford resigned and another ministry was formed.[7] The next occasion arose in 1877, when Premier Grey twice asked for a dissolution, yet still seemed to possess a majority. On both occasions he was refused. By his third attempt in 1879 Grey had lost his majority, and on this occasion the dissolution was granted. Thus, for the first time the right to go to the people was granted to a premier who lacked the confidence of the House. Thereafter, two more requests for dissolution by a premier were granted, to Atkinson in 1884 and to Stout in 1887. Both governments were defeated in the House before the requests were made.[8]

The fact that before 1879 a premier had three times sought and failed to obtain a dissolution, while in the next decade the same request was three times granted to governments without a majority, seems to establish a reasonable precedent that a Governor-General should accede to a prime minister's request. This was exemplified by the early dissolution of 1984, when the government's majority had perhaps been in some doubt.

The constitutional propriety of Clark's request for a dissolution in 2002 is much more certain. In fact, it falls clearly within the second category of dissolutions. There was no doubt that her government still commanded a majority in the House; the fact that it had just passed the first stages of its Budget underlines this point, which even the opposition conceded. In any case, there was no question that the Governor-General could have refused the request, since the Greens rejected calls from ACT to install English as caretaker, and National had appeared to support an early election when the matter had been raised in the House. This is not to say that a majority of parties supported the election, as the Progressives, the Greens and the Alliance all rejected the need for an earlier poll. But in such cases the prime minister holds the whip hand; as long as s/he is still a responsible advisor, the views of other parties on the matter of the election are theoretically irrelevant (unless they withdraw their support on the issue).

As for whether the reasons for the dissolution were valid, this is also technically immaterial to the Governor-General in cases such as this, where the prime minister commands a majority. If the government's majority had been in doubt, the Governor-General might have taken more interest in its justification for a dissolution, weighing this information against other factors, including the proximity of the scheduled election.

Conclusion

The decision to call an early election in 2002 seems to conform to what the political science literature would expect. In trading off the remaining four months of the term, Labour seized on stellar poll ratings to seek not only another term but also the possibility of governing unencumbered by an irksome minor party. A majority government could make the loss of several months in office worthwhile if it made it easier for the government to advance its legislation, and perhaps even increase its chances of a third term. However, the evidence of a rising hazard rate and New Zealand's comparatively short parliamentary term suggests that future early dissolutions that are not precipitated by a crisis will tend to be called late in the electoral cycle to achieve optimal time in office, as it was in this case.

Labour's decision seemed like a case of 'political surfing' – its support had hit the high tide mark and was built on a swell of opinion that it was a strong and responsive government. The government also had the luxury of knowing through its own market research that voters might be prepared to give it a majority, particularly in response to the actions of the Alliance and the Greens. Although the events of April–May 2002 did not make an early dissolution a constitutional necessity (paradoxically making the Governor-General's decision to assent to the request an easy one), a simultaneous campaign by Labour to defy the call for an early election officially, but tease the media with it informally, created a demand that would eventually be met by a prime minister perceived to be acting out of resignation rather than opportunism. However, in line with Smith's (2000) thinking, the government's stated rationale for the election also betrayed its worst fears, leading to the election being seen as a choice between FPP and MMP style government. In this sense, the timing of the poll did influence the result. Voters seemed prepared to accept Labour's desire for a majority as justification for an early election, but the tenor of the subsequent campaign caused many in the electorate to think again about whether this was actually a desirable outcome.

3

TWO MILLION VOTERS IN SEARCH OF A RATIONALE

Colin James

'They haven't settled down yet.' So said Barrie Leay, the National Party secretary, at the 1978 election, which decimated the National government's huge 1975 majority and slashed its vote by 9 percent to below Labour's. The same goes for the 2002 election.

The logic of the Clark government between 1999 and 2002 was consolidation. After the 1984–92 revolution,[1] there was a strong public desire for stability and moderation. Both in policy and in tone, this is for the most part what Helen Clark and her ministers supplied after 1999, and what set the scene of the battleground in the 2002 election.

This had two important effects on the campaign and the election. First, it assured Labour of leadership of the next government. Second, because the electorate reached that conclusion, many supporters of the National Party went in search of a vehicle to make their vote effective.

Tactics

In the hands of voters still learning MMP's levers, this search produced an amazing campaign and an equally amazing result. There had been a rule of thumb under FPP that the underdog major party made up ground during the campaign. In the 2002 campaign, the major underdog, National, steadily lost ground. MMP prompted many non-Labour voters to use their votes in ways they would not have chosen in an FPP election.[2] In short, *voter tactics were an issue*. They were much discussed among parties, in the media and by voters.

Time and again during the campaign, people of widely varying views and walks of life discussed with me – as though the election was a puzzle that needed to be sorted out somehow – how they could or should use their party vote. I have had similar conversations since election day. My usual reply was to ask: 'Why don't (didn't) you vote for the party that is nearest to what you believe in?' That was an MMP question, predicated on people voting for the party nearest their beliefs. The answer often was: 'But that might give me the government I don't want.' That was an FPP answer, predicated on people voting either *for* a government, or to block the election of – or to reshape – a government of which they disapproved. So there is some way to go yet before we have an election that we can pronounce to be the first truly MMP election, as some people did of this one.[3]

Moreover, the ethos among MPs themselves remains predicated on a winner-takes-all government. Minority government is now becoming the norm, and forms of non-coalition arrangements with supporting parties are being experimented with (an MMP phenomenon but also possible under FPP, as in the 1910s–20s). The chairing of select committees is being more broadly spread around other, including opposition, parties (an MMP phenomenon). However, the negotiations for support were still predicated on obtaining a majority to keep the government in office and allow passage of its programme. There is still little attempt in budget-making, policy development and legislating to broaden the parliamentary constituency for a proposed course of action beyond the numbers needed to get a measure through the House.

Whatever the tissue of pretexts offered by the government for calling an election four months early, the actual reason was to capitalise on benign polls – at the very least, to maximise Labour's vote, and preferably to obtain a majority, in combination with Deputy Prime Minister Jim Anderton's Progressive Coalition.[4] Part of the calculation the electorate then made during the campaign, quite independently of policy considerations, was whether an *absolute majority* was desirable if Helen Clark was going to exercise it – or indeed, at all. Clark attempted to counter this in her opening and closing television broadcasts, and at other times and in other ways, with declarations that it was a 'privilege every day to serve', but she and humility are not obvious or convincing bedfellows.

So one tactical conundrum pondered by many voters was how to ensure a Clark government, but not leave it unfettered. This played initially into the hands of the Greens, especially among those who wanted a government influenced by a party to Labour's left, but who discounted the Alliance as an option. But disunity got in the way: the Greens threw rocks at Labour over genetic modification (GM) and Labour threw rocks back, with some ferocity after the 'corn' affair, to which I will refer later. Disunity is usually punished: Labour in the late 1980s, National in the early 1990s, New Zealand First in the late 1990s and the Alliance in late 2001-early 2002 are recent examples. The open warfare between Labour and the Greens over GM may well have cost both parties votes among those who had thought of Labour and the Greens as a sensible government combination.

GM highlighted the difference between Labour and the Greens. That difference is part of the point of voting Green in support of a Labour-led government: to get more action on the environment and more commitment to 'free' and extensive social services, and to restrain Labour's enthusiasm for free trade and military alignment with the United States. But the difference was also the trigger for a different tactical conundrum mulled over by a second sort of voter: how to stop the Greens influencing a Labour government. Anecdotal evidence from as far back as mid-2001 suggested that many National voters were planning to vote Labour for exactly this reason.

For some National supporters, voting Labour was not difficult: two good economic years, plus some solicitous attention from the Cabinet's top brass to business and farming leaders, had softened antipathy and in some cases even generated warmth. Other National supporters had to hold their noses to vote Labour, yet still did so. Still others drifted off to New Zealand First. Others again found a merciful release from apostasy late in the campaign, when United Future emerged as an option. United Future and New Zealand First in fact explicitly campaigned as a mechanism to blunt the Greens. The United Future option incidentally had the added advantage of injecting a right-of-centre influence on economic and environmental policy, given leader Peter Dunne's generally pro-National voting record on those matters since 1996.

A third sort of voter wrestled with yet another tactical conundrum. This was triggered by dismay at National's performance, prospects, policy or campaigning. Judging by comments to me after the election and also by polling evidence, some went to ACT, some to New Zealand First, and some to United Future. Among the factors:
- Bill English's lack of credibility as an alternative prime minister (some saw Winston Peters as more credible);
- National at no stage was seen as likely to lead a government;
- National's policy was muddled and/or insufficiently firm on a range of issues from deregulation to stopping Maori claims and immigration;

- the campaign appeared amateurish and lacking in energy on the ground.[5]

Polls played a part in deciding tactics. They were a means whereby tactical voters, of whom there were a great many, could work out how to achieve their aim. The *Herald* DigiPoll post-election poll recorded 12 percent of all voters as saying polls had had a 'strong impact' on their party vote, while another 22 percent said they had had 'some impact'. Among those who voted for United Future, 11 percent said the first and 51 percent said the second, while 36 percent said they had made up their minds on election day or the day before. This indicates that the vote for United Future was essentially tactical (though this is a small subsample, and must be treated with care). Some 28 percent of Green voters said they made up their minds on election day, and another 3 percent the day before, while 31 percent ascribed some impact on their vote to the polls.

Leadership

The second issue to note is that of leadership. Because others, notably Jon Johansson (see this volume), know far more about leadership and its influence on voting, I confine my comments here to the attempt by both Bill English and the Greens to question Helen Clark's integrity.

In opinion polls, Clark scored high approval ratings and was far ahead of all others as 'preferred Prime Minister'. In a pre-election issues survey by Colmar Brunton for TV1, 58 percent agreed that 'many New Zealanders will vote for Labour because they like Helen Clark'. In TV3-NFO's matrix of characteristics, Clark consistently scored highly positively and was well ahead of English on every count. In part this may be put down to English's newness in the job: he became National's leader in September 2001, and is not the sort of charismatic person who makes an instant impact. But Clark developed as prime minister, adding an easy approachability in public to the authority and credibility she had established in opposition. Her campaign walkabouts resembled the progress of a respected and accessible monarch. English was equally approachable, but lacked authority.

English attempted to bridge some of the gap by questioning Clark's integrity in the wake of a police report, made public on 5 July, on a complaint about Clark's having signed someone else's artwork for auction for charity. This had surfaced in the media in April and had occasioned much mirth, though there was little evidence in polls that voters had marked her down for it – even though she merely apologised for an 'error of judgment' and did not own up to having done something wrong. It was that omission which prompted the complaint to the police, who found prima facie evidence of forgery, but not of such consequence as to warrant prosecution. English's attempt to exploit that police finding did not resonate with the electorate.[6]

What did resonate, at least temporarily, was an allegation by anti-establishment campaigner Nicky Hager in his book *Seeds of Distrust: The Story of a GE Cover-Up* – published on 10 July by the Greens' 19th-ranked list candidate, Craig Potton, but without the knowledge of the Green leadership – that Clark and the government had, in late 2000, covered up the planting of some GM-contaminated corn. In fact, stated officials on 11 July, there was no conclusive evidence that the corn was contaminated (reviews did not confirm an initial positive test, which may have been triggered by the presence of dirt). Nor, the officials said, was there evidence of a cover-up, only of muddle and incompetence among officials. There was reason to believe the officials: it was implausible that a one-year-old government (as it was at the time) that was intuitively suspicious of GM would cover up a finding of GM.[7]

Nevertheless, this incident may well have chipped away at Clark's reputation for integrity. Both Labour's and National's nightly tracking polls showed a 5 percent drop in Labour's support after 10 July (to 38 percent and 39 percent respectively, according to off-the-record interviews), from which Labour did not fully recover.

Perhaps more pertinently, both incidents displayed to the public another (understandable) aspect of Clark's public persona: overreaction to personal attacks, to the point of appearing to lose control. With respect to the painting, she threatened to sue English and any media which published his allegations; she withdrew the threats the next day. After the corn affair, she accused the Green leadership, which too readily accepted Hager's line, of complicity in his enterprise; she retracted the accusation for lack of evidence, after believable protestations of innocence by the Green co-leaders. Then on 21 July, when the Alliance published a poll purporting to show its leader, Laila Harré, surging into the lead in the Waitakere electorate race against Labour's Lynne Pillay (who in fact won), Clark said she doubted that there was such a poll; again, she retracted the next day.

A person not in control is a person not in authority. Her own demeanour, however sorely provoked (and she was sorely provoked), may have lost Labour votes. Clark's authority is a powerful plus for Labour, and any derogation from it is likely to diminish Labour's attraction to voters. Clark also lost good media time and space in sideshows which she did not start, but surely compounded. On 21 July, before her comment about Harré's poll, she had declared to a party rally in Wellington that she was going to push the government's positive record, ending her attacks on New Zealand First and the Greens of the week before. But TV1's 6pm television clips of her that evening and the following night were not of the government's positive achievements, but of her spat with Harré.

Media

This introduces another factor: the media. For around two decades, politicians have been using 'spin', stunts and manipulation to colour media coverage of campaigns. The media have become increasingly resistant to all this, and have countered with attempts to set the agenda and circumvent the manipulation. In this election the media's – and particularly television's – role in this ongoing cat-and-mouse game may have influenced votes. In particular, the corn affair and TV1's 'worm' – both media events – were significant vote-shifting events.

TV3's news presenter, John Campbell, recorded an interview with Clark on 9 July in which he put Hager's accusations to her as uncontested fact, without mentioning Hager or the book, and without prior warning of the topic, beyond that it was to be about GM. Clark had not been briefed about the incident and did not have the necessary information to respond to his questions. Also, TV3 did not run the interview until the next evening, after the book had become public, making it look as if Clark was refusing to respond to what had by then become public knowledge. Had TV3 – and, I have to add, the media in general – presented all sides of the corn story at the outset, the impact of Hager's allegations might well have been muted. This was a classic case, I think, of the medium becoming the message. Ethics matter, even when politicians are at their most devious and slippery. Ethics especially matter in an election campaign, when people are deciding the shape of their government and need sober and reliable information.

An arguably equally influential media event – this time TV1's doing – was the 'worm'. This was the recorded composite reaction of 100 uncommitted voters to comments by the leaders of eight parties in a 'debate' on TV1 on 15 July, presented as a line wriggling up and down as it recorded positive and negative reactions. The 'worm' was not shown during the debate, but an hour and a half later, accompanied by commentary by three journalists, including myself.

The worm's warmest reactions were for New Zealand First and United Future leaders Winston Peters and Peter Dunne. There was a rough logic in this: uncommitted voters only 12 days from election day were unlikely to be supporters of the well-defined, old-established parties, Labour or National, or of well-defined 'flank' parties of the far left and right, the Alliance, Greens, or ACT, which invite a specific commitment to a point of view. News stories the day after the 'worm' awarded Dunne a 'win'. United Future's poll ratings zoomed from less than 1 percent before the 'worm' to 8 percent in a *Herald* DigiPoll published on 20 July. As a middle-of-the-road advocate of 'balance' and 'common sense', Dunne became overnight a mechanism for moderate right-of-centre voters who wanted to ensure that Labour was not the captive of, nor unduly influenced by, the Greens.

Quite apart from these two events, Labour ministers fretted that the style of media coverage – by which they seemed to mean television coverage – obscured the 'real' issues, the ones on which Labour could expect support.[8] In defence, the media could point to the blandness of Labour's message. Its 2002 'credit card' of seven commitments was so unmemorable that when I invited two senior ministers to recite the list after the election, they could recall only one between them. Labour was so determined to avoid controversy in a 'business-as-usual' campaign that it forfeited media attention to what it did say.

Issues

So what were the 'substantive' issues? The number one issue recorded by the *Herald* DigiPoll was health, which was probably a negative for Labour, or at least not a strong positive. TV1 Colmar Brunton's pre-election issues survey rated a clutch of issues, including health, hospital waiting lists and mental health care number one, followed by another group involving violence, crime and inadequate penalties (another negative for Labour), well ahead of falling education standards. From these there was another long drop down to tax, superannuation, student debt, and the Treaty and alleged unequal treatment of Maori (again, all mostly negative for Labour).[9]

If these negatives for Labour were the issues, why didn't Labour do badly in the election? Because, I would argue, these 'issues' were in fact 'problems', and while problems are, of course, factors in people's voting, positives are also factors. And Labour had some positives, notably the economy. These arguably more than offset the problems.

Personal security

Dividing the 'substantive' issues into several groups, there was, first, a group of *personal security issues*. Top of these was the economy. Growth had been strong, unemployment was at a 13-year low, real wages were firm and household balance sheets were in good shape. There was also widening, though not universal, approval for the government's attempts to lift investment through research and positive interventions. In fact, though he did not make much of it, English said he would keep some of them, albeit refocused.

English tried to make something of the fall in export prices, and the consequent looming fall in farm incomes and slowdown in growth generally. But consumer sentiment remained resolutely high through the campaign. So did retail spending, especially on big-ticket items (though the pace of growth did begin to slow). Economic scare stories did not resonate.

In short, the economy was probably a big unstated positive for Labour. Some 65 percent told the TV1 Colmar Brunton pre-election 'issues survey' that the 'outlook for the New Zealand economy is very good'.[10] The obverse of that was that Labour could not get the media to run its claims of excellent economic management. While this was true, Labour's criticism was misplaced. First, a good deal of the good economic story was luck, not brilliant government management: it rained a lot, prices were high and a high American dollar kept New Zealand dollar returns from those prices high. Second, even if the media had carried Labour's claims, it is doubtful that they would have added anything to Labour's vote, because people knew without being told that economic conditions were good. The positive for Labour from the firm economy was probably fully built into its vote before the campaign began.

More relevant to the campaign were two personal security issues which are thought normally to work to Labour's advantage: health and education. To the extent that health was an issue, it was probably a negative for Labour. National claimed that its attacks on underfunding were scoring. But it was also probably only a small negative for a first term government that could claim to have increased funding and cut waiting times for operations.

National tried to make much of the secondary teachers' rejection of a pay offer and their obstruction of the introduction of a new pupil assessment system. But it is moot whether that worked against the government. Labour claimed that sentiment was moving against the teachers. In any case, the government and the union agreed to arbitration shortly before the election, taking the matter off the agenda.

Genetic modification was much more talked about and reported on. This is a personal security issue, because for most people it is a safe food issue. It was prominent in media coverage of the campaign for a number of reasons. First, part of the excuse for the election was that on 23 May the Greens had walked out of Parliament in protest at legislation setting a sunset of October 2003 on a two-year moratorium on applications for commercial release of genetically modified organisms (GMOs), declaring that they would vote to bring down any government that lifted the moratorium. The walkout provoked an angry and stinging response from Helen Clark. Second, the Greens made GM the centrepiece of their campaign, with scare ads that were classics of negative advertising. A third reason for GM's heightened media prominence was that on 3 July a new Sustainability Council, committed to a five-year moratorium, was announced. Each of its members had a high media profile. The council was headed by a former Federated Farmers president, Sir Peter Elworthy, and featured international movie star Sam Neill, former world squash champion Susan Devoy, and noted biochemistry professor Garth Cooper. A fourth reason for the GM issue gaining so much media coverage was the Hager book and the interview 'ambush' on 10 July.

In answers to two sets of questions, early and late in the campaign, the *Herald* DigiPoll found around a quarter of respondents wanted an absolute ban on release of GMOs. This was in line with the Greens' position. This sort of reaction encouraged the Greens to persist in an intransigent stance, and to hope for a vote above 10 percent as a result.

However, in the DigiPoll, around three-fifths of voters polled took the line of most other parties: they were in favour of strict controls, but not an absolute ban. Polls of 'important issues' never rated GM at more than about 10 percent, well below the more traditional issues. The DigiPoll found only 7 percent saying GM would 'absolutely' determine their vote, and only half of those said they would be voting Green.

In the event, GM may have boosted the Greens' vote, though, if so, not greatly. The Greens had been running in the 5–9 percent range for a year before the campaign. Moreover, the party's uncompromising stance may have cost the Greens votes among those who had been sympathetic to the Greens as an influence on Labour, but who had become worried that the Greens might prove too extreme.

GM may actually have obscured other issues from voters. In 1981, the National government's proposal for taxpayer-supported heavy industrialisation – 'think big' – was the biggest issue in the media, and was noted by voters as the biggest campaign issue, but it was not an issue they voted on. Its prominence, however, made it difficult for the government's opponents to raise other issues and have them reported.[11] GM may have had something of that effect in the 2002 campaign. Certainly, that is Labour's view.

More clearcut was the issue of violence and crime. In office, Labour had initiated legislation to lengthen sentences for serious crimes of violence, in response to a growing incidence of such crimes and rising public alarm. But one element of the new sentencing law made it possible for offenders to apply for release after only one-third of their sentence. Opponents latched on to this as going 'soft' on crime.

National, ACT and New Zealand First took a harder line on crime than Labour. Of the three, National was the least hardline; its promise of 'life means life' applied only to two or three murderers a year. ACT ran billboards promising tough sentences from well before the election. New Zealand First made it one of the three issues (along with the 'Treaty industry' and immigration) which it could 'fix'.

Cultural security

My second group of issues, *cultural security issues,* were probably negative for Labour. These were of two sorts: to do with the Treaty of Waitangi settlements and other supposed advantages or special concessions to Maori; and immigration.

National, ACT and New Zealand First all, in various ways, ran campaigns critical of the government on the Treaty – either of the length of time settlement of Treaty grievances was taking, now 17 years after the law change permitting them; or of supposed advantages for Maori over other citizens (sloganed as 'one law for all'); or – New Zealand First's preoccupation – the siphoning off of the spoils from the grievance negotiations process and outcomes by lawyers and others in a 'Treaty industry' and to leading figures in compensated iwi, rather than to ordinary, needy Maori.

Only New Zealand First added in immigration, drawing criticism not just from the left but also from ACT and United Future (which had, during 1996–99, merged with two small ethnic parties, one representing Asians and one Pacific Islanders). While New Zealand First leader Winston Peters was usually ethnically unspecific in his allegations that the country was being swamped with immigrants, at one point he talked of 'Asianisation by stealth'. This stung ACT leader Richard Prebble, who is married to a Solomon Islander, to accuse Peters of racism. Other liberals of both right and left expressed abhorrence. Clark declared that she would not work with Peters nor seek his support for a government she led.

Peters touched a nerve with some, especially older, people. No doubt some of those who flocked to him held racist views. But informal interviews with supporters suggested something more defensible: a fear, or at least a concern, that the cultural unity of their community was in danger of fragmenting. This same fear or concern was probably an important ingredient in drawing support to Peters on Treaty matters.

Liberals on both the right and left treated these fears during the campaign as in some way unclean, or even un-New Zealand. That denies their reality in the minds of the generally decent folk who hold them. A dismissive or contemptuous reaction by liberals is also unlikely to diminish the possibility that cultural security may become a major issue in future elections, as it has in Australia and in some European countries, including the quintessentially liberal society of Holland – where it is notable that the anti-immigrant party was led by a man formerly of the left.

Values

My third group of issues might loosely be called *values*. When the Labour-Alliance coalition came into office supported by the Greens in 1999, the three parties brought with them sets of values that seemed at odds with middle New Zealand, and were therefore potentially a limiting factor on the government's staying power. A number of public utterances by some MPs in the government's first year reinforced this perception – for example, proposing to ban cigarette smoking in bars; and Tariana Turia, a junior minister, alleging a 'holocaust' of Maori by British colonisers and their descendants.

Clark herself, purposefully childless, likewise seemed distant from ordinary folk, a member of an academic sisterhood. Proposals by backbenchers to legalise prostitution (Labour) and the moderate use of cannabis (Green) were said by opponents to be at odds with middle New Zealand's values.

But Clark proved adept at recognising and drawing back when the government or MPs were getting too far out of line with mainstream public opinion. Smoking in bars has remained.[12] Turia was countermanded: lest there be any doubt, a 'closing the gaps' programme designed to reduce social and economic disparities between Maori and the average population was renamed, and the phrase was expunged from government usage. By the time of the campaign, political correctness was effectively neutralised as an issue, except among those opposed to Labour and the left in any case.

To Labour's advantage, political correctness was overshadowed by another value position of which middle New Zealand did approve: Clark's repositioning of economic policy. During the 1990s, the electorate searched for a way of ending the Douglas/Richardson neo-liberal reforms. In 1990 it had replaced Labour with a National Party promising the 'decent society', but in reality preparing to continue the reforms. In 1993, without an alternative government on offer, the electorate opted for electoral reform. In 1996 it awarded New Zealand First the balance of power in the mistaken expectation, encouraged by Peters' public utterances, that New Zealand First would eject National from government. In 1999 – finally – Labour and the Alliance joined forces to present an alternative government. How weak National's mandate was for its policy stance can be gauged from its 33 percent average share of the vote in the three elections after it took power.

Clark's high-profile 'correction' or 'resetting of the compass' after 1999 resonated in part as a new set of values in policy. 'Moderate' replaced 'radical'; the 'smart state' replaced 'hands-off'. This was as much a matter of tone as of actual policy. However much Clark's personal values and the political correctness of her associates may have grated with middle New Zealand, the new economic and social policy values were very much in tune. In everyday life, the latter counted much more than the former.

So, at the risk of getting lost in the unmeasurable, I want to suggest that *tone* was a campaign issue, at least as a subset of values. It was tone that turned the 'worm' for Dunne. His repetition of 'common sense', coupled with his looking the part – as well as his two-handed answers, for example his support not just for tougher sentences, but for action on the causes of crime – appealed to reasonable uncommitted voters drifting in a Sargasso sea of absolutes from the other parties.[13]

Dunne injected two other values. One was a welcome for multiculturalism, which won as strong an endorsement from the 'worm' as Peters' anti-immigration declamations. The second was his emphasis on the family. This can be read as reactionary, even repressive, a return to an age of discipline, of women confined to the home and authority resting with the man of the house. In the context of United Future's evangelical Christian dimension, it was so read by many, including many in the media. It was notable that the only other party which made the family central to its platform was the fundamentalist Christian Heritage party.

But there is another way that 'family' can be read. This is well illustrated by the way Jenny Shipley, whose family seems from the outside to be genuinely well-knit, nevertheless always acknowledged as a minister and prime minister the co-existence of many other types of families. On this reading, 'family' encapsulates values of nurturing and mutual help. In early 21st century society, fragmented and fractious, with much of the responsibility for cohesion and assistance to the unfortunate, underprivileged and unloved apparently shucked off on to the impersonal apparatuses of the state, such 'family values' may have a subterranean appeal, as signifying stability and unity.[14]

Also as part of values, there was an issue of *extremism*. The great majority of the New Zealand electorate is non-extreme and even anti-extreme. Part of Helen Clark's success in capturing the centre – and National's plight in the campaign – was that her policies were a counterpoint to what large numbers of voters saw as ideologically driven neo-liberal extremism in the 1990s under National's rule. (Ironically, this cut the other way among some National-leaning voters, who thought that National had lost the neo-liberal plot.)

This also cut against the Greens. Labour attacked the Greens as extremists and, after the corn affair, this appeared to stick. As the *Herald* DigiPoll found, few were prepared to go out on to the Greens' GM limb. ACT, defending 7 percent, seemed to have taken this on board. In the campaign it attempted to present itself as less extreme. Whether it succeeded is a matter for conjecture. At least some of its vote came from National-leaners who wanted a sharper economic policy.

Conclusion

In an election as bizarre as that of 2002, how does one disentangle the influences on the result? I would sum it up in two parts: there was an underlying satisfaction with the government, a sense (underlined by poll findings) that the country was heading in the right direction, buttressed by good household balance sheets; and this was disturbed by two remarkable media events. 'Sleepwalking to victory' is no longer an option, it seems.

But there have been two interesting outcomes. One is a step nearer to a genuine MMP election and result. The third MMP election, while bizarre and still exhibiting hangovers from FPP, looked and felt more like MMP than the first two. So does the third MMP Parliament.

The second interesting outcome is the shape of that Parliament. Helen Clark's formation of a support arrangement with United Future from the centre-right has opened the possibility of a long-running left government – though an MMP minority, not an FPP majority. If she succeeds, MMP will almost certainly become embedded into the New Zealand political process.[15] If she fails . . . well, that is for the next election, whenever it might be.[16]

4

LEADERSHIP AND THE CAMPAIGN

Jon Johansson

Glendower: I can call spirits from the vasty deep.
Hotspur: Why, so can I, or any man; but will they come when you do call for them.

                        William Shakespeare, *Henry IV (Part I)*

Shakespeare understood that while any may call themselves a 'leader', mere assertion is no guarantee of support, let alone success. A committed following is therefore a necessary condition for those who would aspire to lead. For this reason, as party leaders vie for the favour of voters during the compacted period of an election campaign, a clear and compelling enunciation of purpose (via a campaign narrative) represents one of a leader's most persuasive tools in their attempts to mobilise voters behind a vision for the nation's future. Diagnosis is also crucial. A party leader must identify those unresolved problems, often linked to decisions made or not taken in the past, that are seen to be stifling the progress of the present. An accurate discernment of one's context is thus a key crucible of leadership efforts during any election campaign. Analysing party leaders' stated purposes and their understanding of the nation's context in 2002 provides the major focus of this chapter.

In any definition of leadership, *purpose* is closely related to the concept of *power*.[1] A New Zealand prime minister and their Cabinet bring to bear executive power to advance their policy agenda. Power is thus used in the service of whatever purpose or principles are acting as the government's lodestar. During an election campaign, however, power is necessarily de-emphasised, camouflaged beneath party strategy, the projection of personality and the presentation of issues. An example of this during the campaign was the prime minister's frequent refrain that it was 'a privilege to serve' the public. This phrase was designed to combat a perception –

fueled by her opponents – that Helen Clark's plea for an outright governing majority (albeit in coalition with Jim Anderton's Progressive Coalition Party) was a naked grab for power. Clark's leadership pendulum thus required an adjustment from its normal authoritative beat, in this case through a timely infusion of humility. The prime minister's comment also revealed the upheaval an election campaign creates for even an experienced, veteran leader in the ascendant position in which Clark began the campaign. It was also an issue of power – more specifically, her government's inability to exercise effective executive power – that the prime minister gave as her reason for calling an early election, and so the leadership implications of this decision need to be examined.

The nineteenth-century English writer, Thomas Carlyle, believed that his heroes – those 'Great Men' whom Carlyle rather exotically thought forged all of history – possessed a unique vision of reality, which he described as a 'deliberate illumination of the whole matter' (Carlyle 1841, p.136). Carlyle's view suggests a further overarching question to be considered in this chapter: namely, to what extent did leadership exhibited during the campaign, in its totality, offer the voting public 'a deliberate illumination of the whole matter'? An assumption underpinning this discussion is that the purpose of leadership itself is to act as a social adaptation tool. That is, leadership is a quality from which society can learn adaptive strategies that, in turn, can improve the quality of its choices in and about the future. This function of leadership could also be described in terms of cultural leadership, civil learning, public education or even 'teaching reality'. The extent to which this purpose was fulfilled in the 2002 campaign is also a primary concern of this chapter.

Leadership in context

A transcendent ideal such as the one Carlyle glimpsed must be properly tempered by the ruling realities of a six-week contest for political power, an election campaign which is itself embedded within a highly competitive multi-party system dominated by political party self-interest. An MMP election produces, as well as rational calculation from its participants, more Darwinian 'survival of the fittest' modes of behaviour. Parties seek either to maximise their strategic positioning for future political advantage, minimise their losses to preserve future viability or desperately reach for the MMP threshold triggers to maintain their political existence. Closely allied to strategy are tactics. Tactical battles occur on multiple fronts, across key demographic groupings as well as at national, regional and local electorate levels. Tactics are aided by technique, in turn facilitated by money. Sophisticated polling, image creation and presentational techniques are vital instruments in the positioning, refining and presentational practices of parties that can afford to employ them. Taken together, the contest of strategy, tactics and technique provide the thrust and counterthrust behind each leader's attempts to embody or defy the *zeitgeist*, the underlying spirit of the times that each party hopes either to reinforce or disturb.

Despite a widely held view that New Zealand election campaigns have become increasingly presidential in both nature and scope, it would be inappropriate to overemphasise the role of a leader and leadership in isolation from other important influences on electoral choice. The effects of wider political, historical and economic contexts provide a powerful influence over voting intentions. These contextual factors include global economic and security conditions; the historical ascendancy of certain political and economic ideas over others; identification with a party and/or with other social groupings; the performance and popularity of the government; and the quality of the Opposition. All these shape or reinforce existing perceptions before the first campaign event even begins the attempt to shift voter predispositions. These factors comprise the macro-environment surrounding an election. The immediate situation or trigger events that happen during a campaign also have an impact on voter preferences. Here the situational milieu is mediated by a constant interplay between cognitive and emotive aspects of public psychology. Issues such as immigration or 'corngate' – two highly emotive issues for some voters – compete alongside more deeply embedded cognitive tracks already established in the public mind. Strong perceptions of trust in Helen Clark and her Labour-led government for having kept its key 1999 campaign promises provide an obvious example.

Nevertheless, voter attitudes towards leaders can have a significant influence on their voting intentions, and this effect has increased since the advent of television in the 1960s (Bean 1992, p.156). This phenomenon can also be explained, at least in part, by the weakening bonds of party identification. The media has increasingly shifted its attention to the shallow reefs of opinion poll movements, political scandals and the surface personalities of the nation's political actors. Leaders, too, are strategically well placed to influence voters during the highly pressurised atmosphere of an election campaign. In 2002, Labour, National and New Zealand First all ran highly leader-centred, presidential style campaigns. Helen Clark, Bill English and Winston Peters were their respective party's chief vehicles for promoting and mobilising support behind their party's policy ideas, while at the same time seeking to project their perceived leadership strengths to help reinforce support behind their parties. Even those parties that de-emphasised their leader(s) in favour of the collective – such as ACT and the Greens – had their leaders fronting influential events such as the televised leaders' debates.

Finally, in all leadership phenomena the interaction between a leader and their potential followers is a dynamic one, not easily predicted. A leader's major role during a campaign is to persuade (even inspire), mobilise, reinforce and educate the public about its future choices. During the heat of an election campaign, a party leader performs another role, that of a *wild card* between the realm of ideas and the material conditions found at the time of democracy's triennial accounting. A leader can prove to be a tuning fork to the rhythms of the *zeitgeist*, or prove incapable of preventing wider, even historic forces from wreaking havoc upon their party's fortunes.

The July election: Prime ministerial government plus?

The twentieth century history of governments going to the polls early is well documented in New Zealand (see McLeay 1995, pp.27–28; Alley 1992, p.176). Conventional wisdom has pointed more towards the risks of forcing voters to an early poll than the potential rewards for doing so. New Zealand's three-year election cycle has seemed a natural barrier to the exploitation of momentary political advantage. A further disincentive has been public mistrust of politicians in general and, more specifically, an inclination towards electoral revenge if the public's ire has been sufficiently provoked. An opinion poll released on 10 June supported the conventional view. Some 58 percent of respondents thought the prime minister should 'wait until later in the year' to call the election, while only 26 percent thought Clark should 'call it now' (TV3 NFO Opinion Poll 2002, p.13).

What proved irresistible, however, was further confirmation of a trend that had been apparent for several months across all of the major polls.[2] Labour's lead over National continued to widen, as it had been doing since October 2001. Labour held a 32-point lead over National, and at 56 percent in the crucial party vote, the government's popularity had probably reached its zenith (p.4). On 11 June the prime minister sought and was granted an early dissolution of Parliament by the Governor-General, Dame Sylvia Cartwright.

Seeking dissolution is a prime ministerial prerogative. The power is available and it was used. It also succeeded, although only inadvertently, because political success was achieved by a different route from the one Clark asked voters to walk. Her desired majority coalition government was not achieved, but an unintended consequence of the collapse of National's party vote provided the prime minister – whose ambition is to lead a three-term government – with a strong strategic position entering her second term. The public did not punish Labour for going to the polls early.

Clark's success in avoiding public displeasure for calling an early election has consequences for prime ministerial decision-making, and the tension between prime ministerial as opposed to Cabinet government. A prime minister can have significantly disruptive effects on the political system, largely because of their pre-eminent strategic position within it (Johansson 2002a, p.374). These effects tend to be cumulative in nature. When viewed in this light, Clark has opened the door for future prime ministers – in concert with their colleagues and/or advisors – to choose to follow her path. If a government is committed to incremental change, requiring several terms to embed the principles and rationale behind its exercise of power, then the overriding political question becomes how best to win the time required to achieve its goals. Once a government allows such political considerations fully into its thinking, then managing the election cycle becomes merely another instrument, a means to its desired ends. It is also a rational act, although clearly one that carries significant risk.

If the prime ministership is viewed as a role of few formal powers – ones forged largely by evolutionary convention – then Clark's use of an early dissolution in 2002 has further moved the relative power of executive government in the prime minister's direction. If a prime minister is popular with the voting public, then that leader has a powerful weapon to use against opponents (in another party), friends (in one's own party), or simply as an instrument to be used when the political opportunity presents itself. Weller (1985, pp.4–5) identified six factors influencing arguments over prime ministerial government versus cabinet government,[3] but a prime minister's dissolution powers were not among them. While a tension will always exist between different power centres at the core of the executive, with outcomes shaped by the idiosyncratic nature of each prime minister and the group dynamic that develops, Helen Clark's early dissolution of Parliament has certainly broadened the scope and continued evolution of prime ministerial powers. The significance of her decision to go early may be judged in part by the frequency with which her successors repeat her use of the lever of what was an entirely discretionary dissolution.

Exploiting advantages: Leadership perceptions of Clark versus English

Going into the campaign, two powerful factors were advantageous in shaping the government's bid for re-election. The first was economic: there were good commodity prices, a favourable exchange rate for exporters, a 13-year low in unemployment and solid (if not spectacular) growth. As a result, the public seemed satisfied with the government's performance and generally optimistic about the nation's outlook. The second factor was the dominating presence of the prime minister. Clark bestrode the political landscape in a manner quite unlike any of her recent Labour predecessors. Although there have been parallels between Clark and Muldoon, the prime minister preferred comparison with Peter Fraser, 'who was known as a very strong Labour Prime Minister' (Sky News Leaders' Debates, 2002).

What strengths have underpinned Clark's leadership? First, there is an almost Lincolnesque quality to the perseverance that Clark has exhibited throughout her lengthy political career.[4] No stranger to setback, upset, or disappointment, Clark has survived and built a formidable well of experience to draw upon. Her astute political management has reinforced her authority, especially during crucial moments when it was placed most under stress (Gomibuchi 2001). More than any other prime minister in recent memory, Clark has continued to learn on the job. She has needed to, as an adherent to the centrist policy mix that social democratic parties have pursued in both the United States and Europe. She has also proven quite adaptable, even unexpectedly so. Her insight into the public mood has been astute, if not altogether original. Labour's pledge card in 1999 – borrowed from Tony Blair's winning 'New Labour' campaign – was stunningly successful in helping Labour reconnect with voters. By maintaining its fidelity to its explicit commitments, Clark's government was able to generate unprecedented levels of trust and goodwill from an electorate that had grown accustomed, over the preceding 15 years, to governments breaking promises.

With conditions so favouring the incumbent – it was always Clark's and Labour's election to lose – the 2002 campaign represented for Bill English a crucial opportunity to position himself and his National Party for a serious try at reclaiming power in 2005. Although National strategists blamed commentators for dismissing its chances in 2002, from the outset it was apparent that National was poorly prepared for an early election. Its policy development was in some cases incomplete, its positioning lacked clarity, and English had yet to penetrate the public consciousness. His 'fight for life' – the boxing match in which English took part to promote suicide awareness – certainly raised his public profile while also revealing his tenacity, but this media event was a somewhat belated attempt to showcase National's new leader.

Entering the campaign, English was judged inferior to Clark on every measure of leadership. For example, the TV3 NFO poll (10 June) showed that 85 percent of respondents thought Clark was a capable leader, compared with only 38 percent thinking English was. Respondents also believed Clark would be far superior to English in a crisis (85 percent, compared with 34 percent); that she had better judgement (71 percent, compared with 43 percent); and that she understood the problems facing the New Zealand economy (71 percent, compared with 55 percent). Given that National's traditional strength had been long been underpinned by perceptions that it was a better manager of the economy, this last category reinforced a dramatic shift created by a combination of good management and even better luck. Collapsing the 14 leadership questions asked by NFO pollsters into four categories – integrity, competence, and positive and negative image – revealed

Table 4.1. Leadership measures adapted from TV3 NFO opinion poll

Measure	Clark	English
Integrity	57%	35%
Competence	76%	43%
Image (positive)	62%	39%
Image (negative)	28%	35%
Positive measures	68%	40.25%
Negative measures	27.50%	34.33%
Net Positive rating	40.50%	5.92%

the leadership comparisons between Clark and English shown in Table 4.1.[5]

What Bill English needed most of all in the run-up to the election was the very thing Clark's decision to go early denied him – time. The early election contributed to National's collapse, its disarray exacerbated by the circumstances of a July campaign. Voters were ambivalent about English, and his party was inadequately prepared to compete against Clark and Labour.

Diagnosis and vision: The good, the bad and the godly

A leader's narratives – their stories – are a vital tool in their rhetorical arsenal (Gardner 1995, pp.42–44). These stories compete with each other in an effort to penetrate and convert the 'unschooled minds' of the many. Stories of identity are particularly compelling, especially during times of uncertainty or crisis. In the 2002 campaign, leaders' perspectives – incorporating diagnosis, purpose and vision – were offered at key campaign moments, during critical televised debates and/or interviews.[6]

Some campaign narratives were clearly more successful in mobilising voters than others, none more so than the one offered to potential New Zealand First voters by Winston Peters. After a quiet term in opposition, following the unedifying collapse of his coalition with National, Peters returned, suitably chastened but with a clear diagnosis of the country's ills. His troika of issues – immigration, law-and-order, and the Treaty 'grievance industry' – represented simplicity personified, even down to his jingoistic catch cry in which he promised audiences that he would 'fix it'. Peters also evoked a nostalgia for the past, remembering the nation 'as it once was when we were number one in the world, both in the economy and in social justice' (TV3 Leaders' Debate, 4 July). Underpinning Peters' narrative was the idea of security – personal security from violence, and economic security from being overrun by immigrants. His attacks on the Treaty also reflected a widespread belief that reparations for past injustices were taking too long, and that resources were not being fairly dispersed beyond a small Maori elite. The New Zealand Political Change Project's pre-election survey showed considerable support for Peters' view, with 63.5 percent of respondents agreeing with the proposition that the process of settling Maori claims had gone on for long enough and should now be discontinued.

At hand to reinforce his narrative was Peter's particular brand of charisma. During the major debates, his ready smile and frequent bursts of levity easily distinguished him from the general tone of seriousness swirling around him. Peters began the campaign by fiercely attacking the prime minister's call for an outright majority 'because they want to govern alone in a one-party state and that's why you need Winston Peters and New Zealand First, to stop their hidden agenda . . .' (TV3 Leaders' Debate, 4 July). In a key moment, also during that first debate, Peters defended the Green Party's position on genetic modification (GM), arguing from the high ground that it was the Greens' democratic right to express its position, however unconvincing he thought the actual policy was. The mix of vitriolic attack and democratic defence played well for Peters and his party.

The cult-of-Winston effect on his potential pool of voters underscores the importance of a close fit between a leader's story and their embodiment of it. Here Winston Peters stands out as a powerful messenger. With his history of railing against everything from corporate malfeasance to abuse of office, he has fashioned himself as someone who will take on the forces of privilege and the establishment. He is, in the tradition of his mentor, Sir Robert Muldoon, the champion of the 'ordinary bloke' (and, as well, the ordinary bloke's wife). The fact that Winston has a touch of the rogue about him only endears him to many voters.

Like Muldoon, however, Peters' narrative is not an inclusive one. It relies for its power on a capacity to single out specific groups of New Zealanders for scorn and exclusion, whether it is Asian drivers on Auckland motorways, or litigious lawyers growing rich out of the Treaty 'gravy train'. The 2002 pre-election survey confirmed among those expressing a preference for Peters' party that their most important reason for voting for New Zealand First was that 'Winston keeps them on their toes' – he 'stirs them up.' One might conclude, therefore, that Winston appeals to that strand of New Zealand political culture that maintains a basic *negalitarian* outlook towards symbols of wealth and power.[7] Peters and New Zealand First were rewarded for a highly effective campaign, increasing their share of the vote and number of seats in Parliament; but Peters did not achieve his more strategic objective, failing to become a potential coalition partner for Labour because of his stance on immigration and the Treaty. Yet the 2002 election provided another colourful twist in the ongoing political theatre that is Winston Peters' contribution to the country's politics.

The Labour campaign was a mixed success. The prime minister seemed intemperate throughout the campaign, especially whenever her or her government's integrity was questioned. At times she appeared to regard the whole business of campaigning as more of a hindrance than an opportunity. Yet despite setbacks, Clark still led Labour to an increased share of the vote, a feat rarely achieved by a New Zealand governing party. The prime minister can also enjoy from a position of comfort the view of a fragmented centre-right, leaving Labour strategically well placed to challenge for an historic third term in 2005.

Clark's narrative, deconstructed, was essentially a very simple one. It asked the voters to 'let us continue.' She first reminded voters that 'most importantly, I know we came to you, the voters, last election with a set of commitments and we kept our word on every single one of them' (TV3 Leaders' Debate, 4 July). Having provided strong leadership and direction, the prime minister urged voters to allow her to continue the progress already begun. Clark's narrative was certainly an inclusive one, even explicitly so. During the first leaders' debate, she concluded her personal vision by saying that she wanted a country 'in which every single citizen has a real and general stake'. Clark's views on the Treaty also emphasise the need to keep 'the best possible relationship between peoples' (TV3 Leaders' Debate, 4 July).

If the logic of the Clark government's first term was one of consolidation in meeting the demand from voters for stability and moderation, after the turbulence of the 1984–92 period (see chapter 3), there are limits to that kind of approach to political management. Consolidation can easily come to seem like drift if people do not see tangible improvements happening in and around their lives. An alternative view, taking into account Clark's ambition for at least three terms in government, would posit that the 1999–2002 period was one of preparation, with achievements to be delivered in succeeding terms. This view, however, might also come to seem like drift, especially considering that Labour's new set of election promises had neither the specificity nor the clarity of its 1999 pledge card.[8] If expectations are not met and the government is no longer perceived to be projecting a clear sense of purpose, then dissatisfaction will grow rapidly, both within the government and among the public.

This may then prove to be the prime minister's real test during her second term in office. Is there a clear-sighted vision which offers a rationale for Clark's leadership? Have her ambitions been satisfied? Clark might consider herself free from the normal electoral imperatives if she were to win a coveted third term. Then we might witness the full maturation of Clark's leadership for good or ill. A caveat to this view, however, seems warranted as a result of the evolving nature of Clark's relationship with the media. In some respects, the media provided a more searching test of Clark's leadership during the campaign than her political opponents were able to produce. For instance, in the major set-piece debates Clark rarely looked as if she was extended.

She was, however, frequently uncomfortable and angry that the media would not focus on issues of her choosing. Clark behaved in a distinctly bad-tempered fashion when she was forced into a reactive, defensive mode, especially when her virtue was challenged. Purposeful and decisive leadership can come to seem like authoritarian rule when a leader reacts negatively to criticism. That was Muldoon's eventual path, and it should serve as a warning to the prime minister.

National's campaign narrative suffered from its failure to offer the voting public a *mea culpa* for the way it governed between 1990–92 (Johansson 2002b). Jim Bolger made a serious error of judgment in permitting his finance minister, Ruth Richardson, to continue with neo-liberal reforms after these policies (and the manner in which they had been implemented under Labour) had been so utterly rejected by voters in 1990. Perhaps National's strategists believed that having spent three years out of government (1999–2002), there was no longer any need to revisit the past.

Successful political leaders strive to present a coherent and compelling narrative about their own place in their country's history (Skowronek 1997). Their 'story' describes where they have traveled from (their link to the past), where they are now, and where they intend going (their future direction). Viewed in this light, what was most noticeable about Bill English and the National Party during the campaign was their willful dislocation from their own past. It might not have been such a concern if previously committed National voters had not taken flight in such numbers. From the start of the campaign until the final votes had been counted, however, National's voting support only ever moved in one direction – down.

National was unable to offer the public a compelling vision of the future because it refused – or was unable – to present a coherent story about where it had come from, let alone where it was going. Bill English went so far as to decline the invitation to explain where on the political spectrum National was positioned, rejecting a considerable body of received wisdom in the process. English chose instead to respond that he did not find those sorts of labels 'useful'; or he would say that he was leading a 'new' National Party that had moved on from the debates of the 1980s; or he would say that you 'can't keep looking back' (TV1 Leaders' Debate, July 17). These answers were neither plausible nor convincing.

Finally, just two days before polling day, during the final leaders' debate between Helen Clark and Bill English, TV3's John Campbell asked English if he wanted to make a *mea culpa*. English used his stock defence(s), saying variously that National had 'taken it on the chin,' that it was 'not fighting the battles of the 1980s and 1990s' and, finally, that he 'was only looking ahead' (TV3 Leaders' Debate, July 25). The prime minister, by contrast, made the most of the dialogue, volunteering that Labour did not begin to move forward until after it had publicly expressed contrition for the 'wrongs of Rogernomics'. When asked, again, if he wanted to apologise for 'the wrongs of Ruthanomics', English finally said he wanted to 'turn his back on the dogmatic and narrow-minded attitude that came through in the policy and made New Zealanders feel threatened' (TV3 Leaders' Debate).

One element of the diagnosis for National's dismal showing in 2002 is that its implementation of further significant policy volatility after 1990 – in direct conflict with its then leader's vision of 'a decent society' – undermined its moral authority to govern, while at the same time corrupting much of the language surrounding the economic ideas and policies implemented under the mantra of Ruth Richardson's 'there is no alternative' (see James 1992, pp.281–283). During the 2002 campaign, therefore, Bill English could not escape the ghosts of National's past, try as he might. A good example of this phenomenon was in education, where English tried to label his party's policy 'self management'. Every time English would attempt to promote the term, either the interviewer or his opponent(s) would interrupt with the retort 'you mean bulk funding'. Language associated with the most doctrinaire phase of New Zealand's not-so-distant neo-liberal past has reached its use-by date.

The ACT Party was reported to have spent $1.6 million dollars on its campaign, the most spent by any of the parties. ACT's election result saw a near repeat of its 1999 return, allowing it to survive at least in part by attracting disappointed former National voters (at times with National's blessing, as in the case of Epsom voters).[9] The party de-emphasised its leader, Richard Prebble, in favour of a narrative that emphasised values such as 'zero tolerance for crime,' across-the-board tax cuts, and 'one rule for all.' ACT took the initiative on issues of personal security. With New Zealand First dominating immigration and ACT owning crime, National was unable to elicit any emotional impact from its mix of policies, which largely offered in small doses what Peters and ACT promised in abundance.

United Future's remarkable result revealed the significant impact the media can have during an election campaign. Peter Dunne took the same moderate line in 2002 that he had taken in previous elections. After hovering around the margin of error in every poll for an entire parliamentary term,

Dunne's measured performance on the *Holmes* 'worm' debate – followed by the even bigger story *about* the story of Dunne's performance – propelled United Future into Parliament, and a pivotal strategic position between Labour and National. Voters found in United the moderate supporting act for Labour for which they had been searching. Promotion of the family and 'common sense' attitudes represented an acceptable narrative for voters to embrace, especially after the early phase of the campaign had been dominated by the far more polarising debate over GM. A disturbing aspect of United Future's success, however, was the ease with which a political party was able to establish a firm presence in Parliament with little serious scrutiny by the media.

The Greens' disappointment with its election result, despite a modest rise in support, reflects its failure to achieve its own goal of 10 percent, let alone the 15 percent that co-leader Rod Donald had predicted early in the campaign. GM was the issue on which the Greens staked their campaign, but 'corngate' modified their most positive issue into a more mixed, problematic storyline. The prime minister's framing of the Greens as 'Luddites', and her refusal to accommodate a threatened Green veto over the future commercial release of GM, led many voters to turn to United or New Zealand First to find Labour a more suitable coalition partner. Stability arguments ultimately won out over the Green vision of environmental safety and sustainability. Interestingly, Green co-leader Jeanette Fitzsimons also proved to have quite a polarising effect on voters. The 2002 pre-election survey showed that when respondents were asked whom they would 'least prefer' as prime minister, Fitzsimons attracted the third highest response, behind only Richard Prebble and Winston Peters.

The Alliance's collapse left its former leader, Jim Anderton, at the head of a new political party, the Progressive Coalition. From that position he called voters from 'the vasty deep' to support him and his new political movement. But fewer and fewer voters came when he called. Fewer still came when the Alliance leader, Laila Harré, sought to summon up the spirit of the old left. And so Anderton – with his mixed narrative on behalf of stability and a moderately progressive critique – was able to return to Cabinet, a seemingly indispensable part of the minority coalition government formed to govern New Zealand after the 2002 votes were counted.

A vision of illusion?

One view of leadership sees leaders responding to adaptive challenges by reflecting the nature of the challenge back onto citizens (Heifetz, 1994). In this approach, government becomes something of a collaborative problem-solving exercise. Three distinct policy dilemmas – encompassing foreign and defence policy, superannuation and the Treaty settlement process – are seen as conforming to this conception. New Zealand's place in the world after 11 September 2001 is surely one such challenge, because the event itself represented such a significant 'ripple in history', and because choices made in response to this event can lead the nation to vastly different futures. Three questions, particularly, arise from September 11 to challenge our foreign and defence outlook:

- Does the prime minister's pre-September 11 assessment that New Zealand exists in an 'incredibly benign' strategic environment still hold true post-September 11?
- What benefits and costs accrue from the increasing divergence between the foreign and defence policies of New Zealand and Australia?
- What benefits and costs exist for New Zealand in maintaining its anti-nuclear posture?

An election campaign represents a small window where the increased attention of voters affords political leaders opportunities to educate the electorate about future choices. While foreign and defence policy cannot compete with perennial and more emotive issues such as health and education, an opportunity was lost in 2002 to hear a full exchange of views about what, if any, effect September 11 has had on major strategic questions that go to the very core of our identity as a people, and how we define ourselves in relation to the rest of the world.

A second policy dilemma, rarely discussed during the campaign, concerned national superannuation. Labour continues to build up its superannuation fund, with the intention of part-funding pensions for the demographic bulge when it reaches its peak in coming decades. National, by contrast, stated categorically during the campaign that when it returned to government, the fund would be redeployed and used instead to retire debt. The politicisation of superannuation policy thus remains the most distinguishing feature of discourse over the policy. The issue that requires a fuller public airing than it received during the campaign is whether the country can afford the luxury of such partisanship. Must party differentiation prevent sensible bipartisanship in a policy area that affects every New Zealander?

On the other hand, debate about the Treaty settlement process *was* a feature of the campaign. Parties on the right argued that the process should be brought to a swift conclusion so that the country could move forward, freed from the guilt of its injurious past. Parties on the left argued that the process of settlements was inherently important as a means of restoring justice and mana to Maori. From a leadership perspective, what is striking about this continued and narrow discourse is the extent to which the country is mired in the present. Perhaps the reason for this is that no political leader – neither Pakeha nor Maori – has offered an inclusive or compelling vision of a future New Zealand that has moved beyond where we now find ourselves. We cannot yet see a way forward.

Another way of looking at this is to draw attention to an alternative. An unusually vivid example of political rhetoric moving a nation forward by transforming its understanding of its own past, in order to create a more desirable future for itself, occurred in 1863, 140 years ago and only 23 years after the signing of the Treaty of Waitangi. Speaking at Gettysburg, in the midst of a civil war, to an audience gathered at a battlefield site where tens of thousands had died only months earlier in defence of competing national narratives, US President Abraham Lincoln used less than 300 words to give 'people a new past to live with that would change their future indefinitely' (Wills 1992, p.38). In his Gettysburg Address, Lincoln smoothed ambiguity by reinterpreting his country's past. Rhetoric (rather than process) might also help New Zealand elevate its impatience into something higher, something more adaptive for the future, since ambiguity would also seem to sit at the core of our own current understanding.

Conclusion

Leadership effects during an election campaign cannot be predicted with any certainty. In 2002, the campaign was itself initiated through a bold exercise of leadership. The prime minister weighed up her political situation, considered it favourable to her government's interests, and attempted to exploit it for maximum gain. In the end, she achieved only mixed success. Although voters did not grant Clark her preferred option – a parliamentary majority – they abandoned National in such numbers that the splintered right has put Labour in a strategic position that may prove even more advantageous next election – whenever that might be.

While none of the party leaders offered a vision for the future sufficiently compelling to transform the election and their own image with the public, some leaders – Peters, Clark and Dunne – developed narratives that resonated widely with the voting public. Less coherent narratives, such as Bill English sought to present, proved unpersuasive. While some leaders were able to exploit insecurities, ultimately this was not an election that represented a call for a change from Labour's basic policy direction.

The most disappointing aspect of the campaign was its inability to educate the citizenry about difficult or intractable policy dilemmas. This is ultimately a failure of leadership and, in a larger sense, of the democratic process. The heightened interest of voters during the six weeks of the campaign was not directed in any meaningful or adaptive way to problems posed by the new security environment post-September 11. Voters were also not educated by our collective leadership about the continued uncertainty surrounding the country's national superannuation policy. Leadership can be a force for social adaptation. The direction of race relations in New Zealand continues its difficult progress without any sense of purpose, and without an agreed national understanding that could better mobilise New Zealanders behind an idea that could serve as an instrument for national unity rather than division. Given these leadership failures, the public in 2002 was not given that 'deliberate illumination of the whole matter' that it needed and to which it was entitled. There is still potential in New Zealand for those who call themselves a 'leader' to provide a more compelling vision, one that could allow New Zealanders to adapt to old truths and new realities, in the context of a more mature and more profound understanding of what constitutes national leadership.

5

THE ELECTORAL COMMISSION AND THE 2002 GENERAL ELECTION

Paul Harris

The Electoral Commission maintains a state of readiness throughout the electoral cycle in case of an unexpected general election.[1] The level of that state of readiness and the detail of the contingency planning vary according to the political situation and the stage of the normal electoral cycle. For example, the political uncertainties before the first MMP election in 1996 meant a higher state of readiness – indeed, the Commission decided to begin its public education campaign on MMP somewhat earlier in 1996 than it might otherwise have done, because of the magnitude of the task and the fact that an early election would have limited the time the Commission had to run an effective campaign. There was a somewhat similar situation in August 1998, as questions were raised about the survival of the government, and whether the newly installed prime minister might wish to seek a fresh mandate. Although the Commission had contingency plans to cope with that situation, a general election at that time (particularly with a short period of notice and a brief campaign period) would have been held well in advance of the normal election period, and would thus have increased the risks for the Commission in carrying out its statutory functions relating to the election.

Because the 2002 election was held only a few months before the expected time of October/November, its timing did not cause too many problems for the Commission. With the exception of making the allocations to parties of time and money for election broadcasting (which were due to be released in mid-July), all the Commission's other preparations were on track to be completed by 30 June. The late passage of amendments to the Electoral Act in February 2002 meant that the Commission had to publish revised pamphlets and guides quickly, but the legislative changes did not affect the Commission's preparations for the general election to the extent that they had an impact on the other electoral agencies. There was the usual election-year heightened activity concerning registration of parties and party logos, and the July election meant that perhaps two or three parties decided they did not have enough time to gain registration before the writ day deadline.

Two of the Commission's statutory responsibilities that were most affected by the timing of the election were the allocation of election broadcasting time and money to political parties, and the public information campaign about MMP.

Election broadcasting allocations

The Commission certainly felt the impact of the announcement of the early election in relation to its election broadcasting responsibilities. The Broadcasting Act 1989 requires the process for making broadcasting allocations to begin eight or nine months before Parliament is due to expire, and specifies the procedural steps which the Commission must take before making the allocations. So in April 2002, the Commission had to begin the process of allocating to eligible political parties free or discounted time provided by broadcasters (including the time which Television New Zealand and Radio New Zealand must provide for parties' opening and closing addresses) and $2 million of public money for parties' election broadcasting.

Persistent media reports that the prime minister was considering calling an early election raised an issue for the Commission concerning the application of the 'early election' provisions in the Broadcasting Act. Those provisions come into effect if the writ for a general election is issued before the allocation process has begun, or before a certain point is reached in the allocation process. They fast-track the allocation process but, more importantly in the circumstances of 2002, they also change the criteria which a party must meet in order to be eligible for an allocation. Accordingly, the Commission sought advice from the Crown Law Office in late May 2002 on the application of the early election provisions of the Broadcasting Act, if an election were to be announced during the allocation process. That advice concluded that the early election provisions no longer applied in 2002, and the announcement that the election would be held on 27 July meant that three parties which had notified the Commission of their intention to apply for registration were not eligible for an allocation.

Secondly, the announcement of the election date in the middle of the allocation process naturally meant that parties were keen to know their allocations as soon as possible, so that they could plan their campaigns. By shortening the timetable after the hearings of parties required by law, the Commission was able to issue allocations of money and time for opening and closing addresses on 19 June, the day after it completed the hearings, a week after the announcement of the election, and six days before writ day, when parties were permitted to begin broadcasting their election programmes.

The 2002 election was the third for which the Commission had been responsible for allocating election broadcasting time and money. After the first MMP election in 1996, the Commission said that 'the current system of allocating time and funds to political parties for election broadcasting is unfair and unsatisfactory and the procedures required by the Act are very time-consuming, cumbersome and expensive' (Electoral Commission 1997, p.19). It recommended a fundamental select committee review of the election broadcasting regime. It repeated that recommendation after the 1999 election. That review has yet to occur.[2]

The result is that the law concerning election broadcasting is still contained in two Acts of Parliament (the Broadcasting Act and the Electoral Act) which are difficult to read together, are highly restrictive and confusing, and result in a minefield for parties, candidates and broadcasters. The fund provided for allocation to parties has not increased since 1990, despite increases in broadcasting costs since then, and despite the increase in the number of eligible political parties since the introduction of MMP. Parties which are not eligible for an allocation (even those likely to be in government after the election) cannot participate in the parties' opening and closing addresses (although they may be represented in some leaders' forums on radio and television). Since the law prevents parties from spending their own funds on buying radio and television time, an ineligible party is prevented from doing *any* radio or television advertising as part of its party election campaign.

To my way of thinking, such a restriction is undesirable and undemocratic, since it severely limits those parties' opportunities to choose how to present their policies to the public. Moreover it does so at the most significant point in the democratic process, when free speech and debate about parties' policies ought to be as open and as unrestricted as possible.

In my view, there needs to be a fundamental re-examination of the objectives of regulating election broadcasting, given modern communications methods, the changes to election campaigns brought by MMP, and the fact that limits on parties' election expenditure were introduced in 1996.

It may also be timely for the broadcasting allocation regime to be re-examined in a wider context. In 1986, the Royal Commission on the Electoral System recommended a transparent but 'modest' and limited extension to the public funding of political parties. While the Royal Commission believed that parties should meet most of their costs from their supporters, it recognised that there was a significant public interest in parties having the resources to develop sound policies, and then to communicate those policies to the public. It said (Royal Commission 1986, p.217):

> Our parties should be able to operate not just as electoral machines, but also as vehicles through which ideas may be discussed and sound policies developed. If and when elected to Government, political parties are expected to implement the policies and programmes developed when in Opposition. . . . If the parties' policies and programmes are inappropriate or poorly researched, either the quality of Government will suffer or the people may be denied the implementation of policies for which they voted. In view of the functions they are expected to fulfil, the incomes and expenditures on which our political parties operate are modest in the extreme. While it is no bad thing for them to be lean and hungry, political parties are too important to be left to starve.

There are many ways in which present public funding of political parties could be changed or extended. The Royal Commission proposed that parties should receive funding based on the number of votes each receives. In my view, the current fund which Parliament provides for allocation to parties for election broadcasting could provide the core of a system of state funding of political parties, such as that identified by the Royal Commission. A party would then be free to buy time for election broadcasting, subject only to the limit on its overall election expenses, and to a secondary limit on its election broadcasting expenditure.

Whatever the details of a new arrangement, it is my fervent hope that a fairer and more realistic election broadcasting regime will be consolidated in the Electoral Act by the time of the next general election.

Increasing public understanding of MMP

The Commission had planned to have all the media advertisements for its pre-election public information campaign on MMP completed by 30 June, in anticipation of an election at some time in the October-November period. Other information materials (e.g., pamphlets and resources for schools) were also due to be completed by the end of June. As the speculation about an earlier election increased, however, the Commission ensured that those preparations were completed well before an election was likely, and brought some items of expenditure forward into the 2001/2002 financial year. The Commission was also able to find additional funds to supplement funding for the pre-election campaign, which had not changed since the 1999 election. Although firm bookings for media time and space could not be made until the actual election date was known, our contingency plans allowed those bookings to be made as soon as the prime minister announced the election date on 11 June.

This was the third pre-election MMP information campaign conducted by the Commission, and, as before, it took place in parallel with the information campaigns conducted by the Chief Electoral Office and the Electoral Enrolment Centre. The Commission's experience of the previous campaigns in 1996 and 1999, coupled with periodic research into public understanding of MMP, allowed the Commission to refine the aims and methods of the pre-election campaign to complement its ongoing educational activities between elections.

The Commission's objective in 2002 was the same as in 1996 and 1999: to assist New Zealand electors to be sufficiently informed about their electoral system and parliamentary democracy to be able to cast an effective vote at the election. As in 1999, the campaign concentrated on reminding voters of three basic messages about the number of votes under MMP, the importance of the party vote in deciding parties' shares of all the seats in Parliament, and the threshold. The function of the party lists in topping up electorate seats was included in the Commission's 1996 media campaign, but was omitted from the 1999 and 2002 media campaigns, because it was regarded as of lower priority than the other three messages, and the funding for the 1999 and 2002 pre-election information campaigns was significantly lower than in 1996.

The Commission's 2002 campaign was short, running for 3–4 weeks before election day. It was aimed at the general population aged 18 years and over, and at the four particular target groups that have consistently been identified since Colmar Brunton's first benchmark research monitor for the Commission in 1994 as having lower understanding of MMP: people aged 18–24, women, Maori, and Pacific Island people. The Commission's brief to its advertising agency for the design of the media advertisements and basic pamphlets emphasised the need for simplicity, accessibility and appealing design, plus promotion of sources of more information (principally a toll-free number and the electoral website) for those who wanted more information about how MMP works. A fictitious ballot paper was used in visual advertisements and pamphlets to convey the messages about the number of votes and the critical function of the party vote. A second advertisement reduced the more complex message about the threshold to the barest minimum. All advertisements were pre-tested in focus groups drawn from the Commission's target groups.

The challenge to the Commission's media placement agency was to ensure placements of advertisements to reach all voters, but with particular emphasis on the Commission's target groups. Some media were used exclusively to reach particular target groups: particular radio stations to reach a younger audience, iwi radio stations, and ethnic newspapers. The Commission was also able to take advantage of the Chief Electoral Office's new EasyVote Pack to get MMP information mailed a week before the election to each of the 2.67 million registered electors. The Commission's total printing and insertion cost of doing so was just over $81,000 (excl. GST) – a very cost-effective communication, which received good feedback in the post-election research.

Other education and information activities ran in parallel with the media advertising. As might be expected, the number of public enquiries increases markedly during an election period; in July the Commission's small office received just over 1,800 telephone and written enquiries about electoral matters, an average of almost 79 per working day, and twice the number received in June. (Those figures do not include 6,445 enquiries to the Commission's toll-free 0800 number in July.)

In a non-election year, the Commission conducts one monitoring research survey on public understanding of MMP, usually in the October-November period. At the time of a general election, however, there are two phases to the Commission's monitoring research on public understanding of MMP. The first occurs before the Commission's public information campaign begins, and the second begins on the day after election day. Table 5.1 shows the main findings for the Commission's surveys from 1995 to 2002.

Levels of understanding of the number of votes and the threshold in 2002 were similar to those reached in 1999 (counting 'four' in 1999 as a

Table 5.1: Results of monitoring research on understanding of MMP, 1995–2002 (%)

	Nov 1995	April 1996	July 1996	Pre-election 1996	Post-election 1996	Oct 1997	Oct 1998	Pre-election 1999	Post-election 1999	Oct /Dec 2000	Oct /Nov 2001	Pre-election 2002	Pre-election 2002
Sample size	800	309	500	504	300	815	710	512	491	546	501	598	591
Methodology§	F	C	F	C	C	C,F	C,F	C	C	C,F	C,F	C,F	C,F
Two votes under MMP	58	82	79	88	97	76	61	76	66†	70	55	67	92
–party vote	31	75	72	85	95	78	62	77	90	75	66	74	91
–electorate vote	23	74	72	80	94	78	64	75	86	72	61	70	88
Party votes decide shares of seats	31	47	44	70*	77*	55*	47*	58*	70*	58*	49*	55*	79*
Threshold criteria													
–win 5% party votes	43	32	42	51	54	35	30	42	57	39	41	49	54
–win 1 electorate seat	33	24	46	36	38	28	31	31	43	35	32	34	42
–win either 5% party votes or 1 electorate seat	19	14	31	28	31	18	18	20	37	26	21	27	34
Party list tops up electorate seats	35	30	40	41	46	55	51	48	49	45	48	49	46

† An additional 22% stated they had four votes because, in addition to their two MMP votes, electors also had one vote in each of two Citizens Initiated Referendums (see Church 2000a).

§ Samples were drawn from those aged 17 years and over in 1995 and those aged 18 and over from 1996 on; C = computer assisted telephone interviewing (CATI); F = face-to-face interviews.

* Includes correct response from additional probe.

correct response for the number of votes). Understanding of the function of the party vote exceeded that reached in 1999, and was slightly higher than in 1996. (No doubt the Commission's information campaign was assisted by parties' election advertising, since most political parties now seem to realise that party votes decide parties' shares of all the seats in Parliament, and are therefore worth campaigning for.) Overall knowledge of the threshold did not increase to the same extent as in 1999; it is, however, possible that voters paid less attention to threshold matters in 2002 compared with 1999, because political polling during the election campaign showed that all of the significant third parties were likely to win at least 5 percent of the party votes, or would win an electorate seat. Knowledge of the function of party lists (which was not included in the Commission's media advertising) remained static.

The Commission's monitoring research in 2002 again showed lower levels of understanding of MMP among women, people aged 18–24, Maori and Pacific Island people, compared to the overall levels in the population as a whole. Table 5.2 shows the results of the Commission's monitoring research from 1999 to 2002 for each of those groups, covering their interest in politics and understanding of the basic elements of MMP.

Even though there was no significant difference between men and women in their overall interest in politics in 2002, there were again large gaps between males' and females' understanding of all of the basic elements of MMP. Although some of the gaps tended to narrow during the campaign, males' understanding of the function of the party vote was still 10 points higher than that of females (compared with 16 points in 1999).

There has been a marked decline in interest in politics among 18–24 year olds since the 1999 post-election survey, although interest among young people did increase between the 2002 pre-election and post-election surveys. It is interesting that knowledge levels among 18–24 year olds of the number of votes and the function of the party vote were higher than the percentage expressing some degree of interest in politics.

Although interest in politics among Maori declined during the campaign, the change is not statistically significant. Knowledge of the number of votes increased, as did knowledge of the function of the party vote and of both parts of the threshold.

Interest in politics among Pacific Island people increased during the campaign. The research found increases in knowledge of all three aspects of MMP, especially the number of votes and the function of the party vote.

Table 5.2: Target groups' understanding of MMP, 1999–2002 (%)*

	1999 pre-election %	1999 post-election %	2000 %	2001 %	2002 pre-election %	2002 post-election %
Extremely/very/quite interested in politics						
all respondents	74	81	73	74	71	78
women	71	79	74	66	70	78
18–24 year olds	62	79	66	47	39	53
Maori	67	75	74	62	73	66
Pacific Islanders	–	–	55	58	51	69
Two votes†						
all respondents	76	66	70	55	67	92
women	67	61	64	43	58	88
18–24 year olds	67	60	59	53	56	79
Maori	54	59	60	33	48	82
Pacific Islanders	–	–	34	16	23	70
Party votes decide parties' shares of seats						
all respondents	58	70	58	49	55	79
women	44	62	52	44	48	74
18–24 year olds	40	70	54	34	47	71
Maori	43	64	42	37	34	63
Pacific Islanders	–	–	20	16	19	58
Threshold – win either 5% of party votes or 1 electorate seat						
all respondents	20	37	26	21	27	34
women	11	27	17	15	18	23
18–24 year olds	9	32	20	15	19	20
Maori	10	21	20	18	11	26
Pacific Islanders	–	–	7	10	6	11
Party list tops up electorate seats						
all respondents	48	49	45	48	49	46
women	37	42	40	41	41	38
18–24 year olds	26	30	23	34	26	28
Maori	29	32	29	31	23	33
Pacific Islanders	–	–	12	13	9	16

* Samples were drawn from those aged 18 and over and included booster sampling of Maori respondents (from the Maori roll only in 2002). From 2000 the research included booster sampling of Pacific Island respondents using face-to-face interviews in households in areas with high densities of Pacific Island populations.

† In the post-election survey in 1999, an additional 22 percent of all respondents stated they had four votes. The additional target group percentages were as follows: women 24 percent; 18–25 year olds 17 percent; Maori 26 percent.

On the whole, these results are encouraging, particularly when considered alongside the lower turnout in 2002 (72.5 percent of the estimated voting age population, down from 77 percent in 1999). There were lower levels of informal voting in 2002, compared with 1999 (party votes down from 1 percent to 0.4 percent; electorate votes down from 1.8 percent to 1.3 percent), and the level of split voting in 2002 (39 percent) was higher than in both 1996 (37 percent) and 1999 (35 percent). All this suggests that most of those who did vote, as well as many of those who did not, had a pretty good grasp of the fundamentals of the MMP voting system by the time of the election – even if they did not appear to do so at the beginning of the Commission's campaign.

The Commission's experience of three electoral cycles under MMP shows that most voters (particularly those in target groups) do need a pre-election reminder of the basic principles of MMP. However, the effectiveness of such reminder campaigns is likely to depend on voters' interest in politics, on the salience of particular messages in the context of parties' electoral prospects, and on the resources available for the campaigns.

PARTY PERSPECTIVES:
TACTICS AND STRATEGIES

6

ACT III
ACT'S THIRD MMP ELECTION CAMPAIGN

Tomas Kriha, Brian Nicolle and Graham Watson

ACT has set records at every MMP election. In 1996, ACT became the first party to be elected into Parliament under MMP without any incumbent MPs. Two elections later, it is still the only party to have done so. In 1999, ACT became the first party to enter Parliament solely by clearing the 5 percent party vote threshold without winning an electorate seat, a feat repeated by both ACT and the Greens in the 2002 snap election. And in 2002, ACT became the first party to successfully campaign for the party vote only nationwide, and the only minor party to have increased its share of party votes at every MMP election.

ACT did this even though none of the three main media surveys had its average share of party votes, over the parliamentary term, above the 5 percent threshold.[1] ACT was described by many commentators as being the most effective opposition party, but supposedly having little or no electoral appeal. Some were even predicting ACT's demise. However, to paraphrase Mark Twain, reports of ACT's demise were exaggerated. During the course of the campaign, ACT doubled its poll support and polled well above 5 percent for most of the campaign.

Campaign strategy

The campaign took place in an environment dominated by a complacent mood favourable to the government, and by what we dubbed the *meta-campaign*.

Voters were generally content and complacent – for a variety of reasons, most of which had nothing to do with government policy – and had little interest in the snap election. Labour was polling well, while National was struggling to gain traction, after losing power following nine years in government and a recent leadership change. The media and, consequently, voters generally expected the election to return a Labour-led government of some form or another. This environment was challenging for ACT, because the media did not view it as being able to have much of an influence on the outcome of the election.

ACT was also adversely affected by National's polling slump, a point misunderstood by many commentators. Far from providing an opportunity for ACT to attract 'disaffected' National supporters, as some have claimed, National's misfortune made it all the more difficult for ACT to attract tactical votes from National supporters. It was not National's liberal supporters – those who are most sympathetic to ACT – that it was losing, but the floating voters of the political centre. These voters were more likely to be attracted to populist parties such as New Zealand First, United Future, and even Labour. Our own research showed that National supporters who considered ACT their second preference were more likely to stay loyal to National the worse it polled, realising that it would need every last vote.

As the campaign progressed, it became increasingly clear to us that media coverage was dominated by the metacampaign – the campaign about the campaign. The campaign proper is a contest between parties, their candidates and their policies. The metacampaign is a contest over and above that contest and is usually dominated by tactical considerations.

For example, a voter might be persuaded by campaign messages that National and ACT have the best candidates and policies. However, that voter might be persuaded by metacampaign messages to vote for United Future, in order to ensure that the inevitable Labour-led government has a more centrist coalition partner than the Greens. That voter was persuaded by tactical considerations over and above their actual preferences.

Some commentators expected tactical considerations to become less important under MMP. It is our view that tactical voting will occur in any electoral system in some form or another; representative democracy will inevitably confront voters with choices between 'the lesser of two evils'. Under MMP, tactical voting is emerging as a choice between parties or coalitions of parties. A voter may well make a rational decision not to vote for their preferred party if it is not a potential coalition partner or influencer. Instead, they might vote for the potential coalition partner or influencer that they dislike least, in order to move the likely coalition in the direction they prefer.[2]

In 2002 the metacampaign was dominated by the possible Labour-led governments that might result from the election. In the early stages of the campaign, Labour raised and dominated the metacampaign, casting it as a choice between a Labour majority government (dressed up as a Labour-Progressive Coalition coalition) or a Labour-led coalition government with the Greens. Labour raised this scare tactic to introduce the idea that National voters could influence the election outcome by voting Labour to prevent a Green-dependent government.

However, Labour soon lost control of the metacampaign, as tactical voters moved from both major parties to minor parties. They moved mostly to the two parties receiving the most media coverage at the time: New Zealand First and United Future. Both were presented as 'alternatives' to the major parties, as neither 'left' nor 'right', and as parties that could lead (or push) a Labour-led government down a more pragmatic centrist path than the walk in the wilderness the Greens were proposing. In the final fortnight, the metacampaign was cast by the media as a choice between a Labour-led coalition relying on the Greens, or United Future, or New Zealand First, or on some combination of the three. Given media attention on the metacampaign, it is no surprise that a third of voters voted for a successful minor party, the highest proportion under MMP so far.

Many issues that surfaced during the campaign – issues that appeared to be matters of policy on the surface – were in fact metacampaign issues. The continual resurfacing of genetic engineering, for example, was less about the issue of genetic engineering itself (which survey after survey showed was of little interest to voters) than about the viability of a Labour-Green coalition. Both parties had an interest in this metacampaign issue: Labour attempted to persuade voters it should govern alone, while the Greens attempted to convince voters that they were needed to keep Labour in check.

Unfortunately, ACT was largely irrelevant to this metacampaign, which proved so dominant to the election. ACT was not seen by the media as being in a position to affect the composition of any supposedly inevitable Labour-led government. However, ACT was able to establish its relevance through its own communications as an effective opposition party and as championing important issues that few other parties were taking up.

Electoral strategy

The party decided in May to contest only the party vote nationwide, despite coming within 2,000 votes of winning two electorates (Wellington Central and Epsom) in the 1999 general election. Our internal research showed that it might be possible, though difficult, to win either seat in the right circumstances. There was particular media speculation about whether ACT MP Rodney Hide would target Epsom.

The party was faced with two options: campaign as it had in the previous two general elections for the party vote nationwide, except for a 'safety net' seat in case it failed to clear the 5 percent threshold; or 'go for broke' for the party vote only nationwide. The decision was a difficult one and was reached only after much internal research and debate. The party's board decided on the second option for several reasons:

- ACT's two most high profile MPs would be freed to campaign nationwide and would not be required to spend time, effort and resources fighting local campaigns which they might not win.
- The same messages and materials could be used nationwide. This made communicating with commentators and voters simpler, cheaper and more effective.
- The large number of tactical ACT supporters in Wellington Central and Epsom who were prepared to give ACT just one of their votes would be freed to give ACT their party vote.
- We found that many voters saw a party entering Parliament by receiving more than 5 percent of party votes as more legitimate than those entering 'on the coattails' of an electorate MP, as New Zealand First MPs did in 1999.

Communications strategy

ACT's communications strategy was to promote issues perceived by potential ACT voters as our relative strengths, while leveraging off perceived strengths in the party's brand. Three key research tools were used to identify our strengths and monitor the success of the strategy:

- Two 'benchmark' surveys (in December 2001 and May 2002) with relatively large sample sizes;
- Six focus groups (each targeting a different ACT demographic);
- A daily tracking poll during July.

The object of this research was to analyse the 'ACT audience' rather than the entire electorate. The ACT audience was defined as those who either (a) already intended to vote ACT; or (b) intended to vote for another party, but considered ACT their second preference; or (c) would consider voting ACT. For example, the ACT audience covered 18 percent of those polled in our May 2002 benchmark survey: 4 percent intended to vote

ACT, another 5 percent considered ACT their second preference, and another 9 percent would consider voting ACT.

Our benchmark surveys and focus groups were used to investigate the ACT audience's view of the party, the leader and its policies. As with most public surveys, our internal research reflected the electorate's complacency, and the damage to National's position following its 1999 election defeat and leadership change. Our benchmark surveys found a large number of voters agreeing with statements that National had lost its way, that its policies were too similar to Labour's, that Bill English was a nice guy but a weak leader, and that ACT was a serious alternative to voting National.

By contrast, ACT was seen as active, honest, straight-talking, and with a clear message of promoting personal freedom. Interestingly, our target market overwhelmingly did not see a vote for ACT as a wasted vote – a welcome change from the previous two elections. But, crucially, 80 percent of the ACT audience believed that voting National was the best way to stop Labour getting back in, despite their low opinion of National's performance. This was a critical perception, given the prevailing expectation that a Labour-led government would be elected.

Unfortunately, ACT is still seen by many National voters as a 'tactical appendage' to National, rather than a force of its own. They see ACT as National's natural, but small, coalition partner. In general terms, they see ACT as different only in that it is more active than National, and that its policies are less like Labour's and more principled than National's.

Figure 6.1: The ACT audience's view of ACT

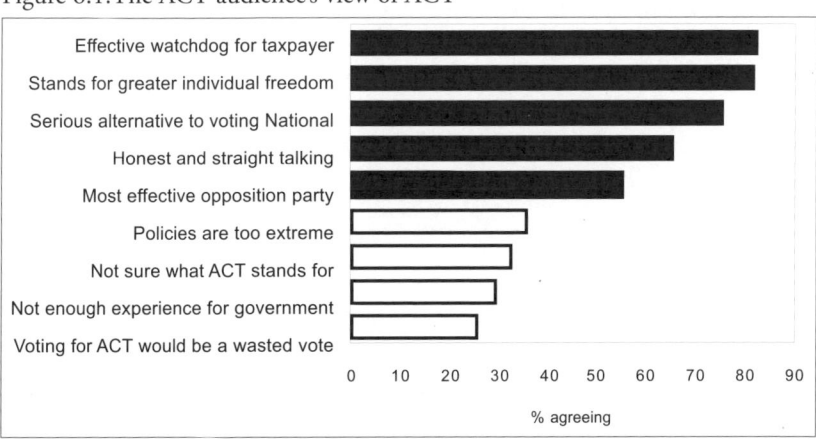

Richard Prebble outperformed Bill English on all statements put to ACT's target market – although obviously the ACT audience is *not* representative of the wider electorate. Richard Prebble was particularly strong on 'getting things done', on being 'upfront', and on understanding 'economic problems'.

Our benchmark survey in December 2001 had already identified health, education, crime and the economy as the most important issues to the ACT audience. Interestingly, most voters had little knowledge of parties' precise positions on most issues, particularly health and education, even though voters were very concerned about them. However, voters did perceive particular parties as having more or less concern for, or better solutions for, the problems in each issue. (Interestingly, health, as an issue, was not a vote winner for any party.)[3] ACT, for example, was clearly identified as being tough on crime, supporting lower taxes, cutting red tape, and opposing laws that discriminate on the basis of race. The ACT audience preferred ACT's positions on those issues well above those of any other party.

Our benchmark surveys showed that ACT was strongly associated with a hard line against violent crime well before the campaign started: 30 percent of the ACT audience already preferred its crime policy to any other party's; 86 percent agreed that ACT would get tough on crime; and only 7 percent disagreed with ACT's approach. ACT also had relative strengths in taxation, and with respect to its policy of one law for all New Zealanders, though not quite to the same extent as with crime.

ACT has for some time been modifying its image into that of a classical liberal party (in the European sense of a social and economic liberalism) and repositioning to increase its appeal to a broader audience. Our communications style has played a key role in this process, which continued as part of the campaign proper. We worked hard to broaden our electoral appeal by communicating our values and positions in a more user-friendly style, rigorously testing our hoarding messages and design in focus groups. All proposed messages and designs were put before focus groups and tested for interest, clarity and persuasiveness.

Evaluation

While ACT's tracking poll monitored the support of parties among voters generally, it was primarily used to monitor the size, demographics and opinions of the ACT audience. The ACT audience fluctuated from 8.9 percent to 28.1 percent, depending on the day.[4] Throughout most of July, the size of the ACT audience tended to slump at the beginning of each week, build during the week, and peak on weekends. It is unclear whether this is just a coincidence, or whether there was a weekly cycle, perhaps related to the weekly news cycle.

In the December benchmark survey, we discovered that while our existing supporters (at that time below 5 percent) were predominantly male, potential ACT voters had a much higher share of women. The proportion of intending ACT voters who were female rose dramatically in our internal polling, from 16 percent in December to 40 percent at the end of the campaign. This indicates that our campaign was particularly successful in converting women from potential ACT voters to actual ACT voters. Our research indicates that women were attracted by our position on crime, while polling and anecdotal evidence suggests that ACT attracted significantly more women in the 2002 election than it had in previous elections.[5] Coincidentally, ACT now has the highest share of women MPs (along with the Greens), despite not having a policy of 'affirmative action'.

ACT's tracking poll clearly picked up major shifts in party support generally: Labour plummeted after the 'corngate' scandal erupted, and whenever Helen Clark attacked the Greens (or any other minor party for that matter); the Greens tracked downwards throughout the campaign; New Zealand First tracked steadily upwards throughout the campaign; and United Future rose spectacularly after the first leaders' debate. (Given that few voters actually watched the debate, United Future's result shows yet again how influential media *coverage* of the leaders' debates – rather than the debates themselves – can be with floating voters.)

Campaign tactics

ACT was well prepared for the 27 July snap election by the time it was called on 11 June. To some extent ACT is always prepared for an early election because it continually runs issue-based 'off-season' campaigns in the field to build grassroots support and compensate for our lack of mainstream media coverage. Even so, field activity was progressively stepped up as speculation about an early election increased throughout the year. By the time the election was called, policies had been developed, pre-campaign research completed, strategy decided, and many of our tactics not only planned but already in the field.

ACT already had a high 'street-level' profile in late June. Commercial billboards were already carrying our distinctive yellow campaign messages around the country, and a good supply of similar hoardings was being distributed to electorates. A direct mail letter and survey on crime was being delivered to 700,000 households in our target market. ACT's leader was already in the middle of a nationwide speaking tour on crime, which was continued during the campaign and expanded into simultaneous North Island and South Island speaking tours.

Our challenge for the rest of the campaign was to communicate our messages to the ACT audience. Obviously, broadcast media are the most efficient and cost-effective means of doing so, but ACT, like other minor parties, is severely handicapped by regulations limiting broadcast advertising. ACT, even more than other minor parties, finds it difficult to obtain 'free media' (positive coverage in news stories), and broadcasting regulations prevent us from purchasing more television and radio advertising to compensate. By contrast, major parties receive the lion's share of both free media coverage and broadcast advertising allocations.

ACT strongly believes that parties should be able to purchase television and radio advertising within existing Electoral Act campaign expenditure limits. This would be a much fairer regime than the present one, where the amount of broadcast advertising each party receives is dictated by a statutory body and paid for by taxpayers. The present regime forces ACT to work harder for free media and work around broadcast media by communicating directly with voters through hoardings, direct mail and electronic media.

Mainstream media advertising

In the previous two elections, ACT entered a 'coverage desert' in the last fortnight of the campaign, when mainstream media coverage dried up as attention focused on the two major parties. In 2002, ACT deliberately concentrated advertising in mainstream broadcast and print media in the final 10 days of the campaign, to compensate for the anticipated drying up of media coverage. As it happened, ACT did enter a 'coverage desert' in the final fortnight of the 2002 campaign, but not because media coverage returned to the two major parties as it had done in the previous two elections. Instead it turned to other minor parties, particularly New Zealand First and United Future.

ACT's opening and closing broadcasts were used to showcase the ACT team. While the broadcasts made good use of the party's leader Richard

Prebble, they were not dominated by him – a marked contrast to the advertising of the two major parties. In keeping with our communications strategy, the remaining broadcast and most print advertisements were short and sharp issue-based messages, rarely featuring ACT MPs.

Free media coverage

ACT's lack of free media coverage – even compared with other minor parties such as the Greens and United Future – forced it to turn to an innovative visual free media campaign to attract attention. ACT ran a programme of daily media events illustrating campaign messages; these included a bonfire of regulations on the steps of Parliament, wrapping a Wellington restaurant in red tape, and highlighting our crime policy in front of Mt Eden Prison and in a frequently robbed dairy in Christchurch. Local party organisations proved instrumental in organising these events. The free media programme was a mixed success. It received good coverage on radio and in print media (particularly talkback radio and community 'give-aways'), but received less attention from television networks.

It is ironic that ACT received less broadcast media coverage than the Greens and United Future, yet it outpolled both of them in the election. This points to ACT's success in bypassing mainstream media by communicating directly with voters, both 'above the radar' (using publicly visible hoardings and billboards) and 'below the radar' (using direct mail and electronic campaigning).

Hoardings and billboards

Freed from running tactical campaigns in safety net seats, ACT was able to use the same hoardings and billboards nationwide for the first time. Both commercial billboards and smaller hoardings used the same messages and style, which were tested on focus groups during our pre-campaign research. The resulting signs gave ACT higher street-level visibility than most other parties in many urban areas.

The issue-based signs used simple but powerful statements – such as 'zero tolerance for crime' and 'a tax cut for every worker' – reinforcing core campaign messages. ACT was the only party to exclusively use issue-based hoardings that did not feature the party's leader. Chinese subtitles were also added to all billboards, reflecting ACT's growing constituency in this key demographic. The style of the signs was crisp and distinctive, featuring the bright yellow colour that voters are increasingly identifying with ACT. Yellow was first used (with great success) on hoardings during the Taranaki-King Country by-election in 1998, and was re-used during the 1999 and 2002 general election campaigns. It has proved so effective that our research shows that many voters now associate yellow with ACT.

Direct mail

ACT has relied heavily on direct mail to bypass mainstream media since its inception. We have found that our electoral success is often directly related to the quality and quantity of direct mail.

In 2002, ACT used both personalised (addressed to an individual voter) and householder (addressed to a household) mail. Personalised mail was targeted using information from the electoral roll; householder mail was targeted using census data at the meshblock level. The targeting used a complex formula of demographic characteristics based on our pre-election research, as well as our experience in past elections and off-season issue campaigns. Targeting aimed to identify voters with characteristics similar to the known characteristics of the broader ACT audience, not simply present ACT members or voters.

This targeting resulted in a core mailing list of 700,000 targets, which were hit repeatedly during the campaign. Those 700,000 targets received two mailouts on two core messages (crime and taxation) in the first two weeks of the campaign alone, and most received another three to four mailouts before the election. All 700,000 received a letter in the final week summarising ACT policies and asking for their party vote. ACT also used niche market mailouts, such as a letter in Chinese sent to over 30,000 households, a letter in Korean sent to 3,000 households, and 750,000 items sent to rural households in five mailouts. Some government ministers were also targeted in their home electorates with a provocative 'letter bomb' on crime.

All mailouts used response devices such as surveys to assist voter identification and assess their impact. One crime mailout alone received over 50,000 responses. Mailouts also included a copy of *Liberal Vision*, a broadsheet pamphlet that summarised our campaign messages in a style exemplifying the tone of our campaign.

Electronic campaigning

ACT has always been a keen user of emerging technology in campaigning. ACT was one of the first parties to use a website in a campaign, having one as early as the 1996 campaign. ACT is probably also the greatest user of 'fax attacks' (which are regularly used to target small businesses) and telephone canvassing. In 2002, ACT also trialled website banner advertising, webcasting[6] press conferences, chain emails, and even broadcast text messages to mobile phones. ACT supporters are keen users of technology, particularly the internet, and this allowed us to be the first, if not the only, parliamentary party to publish its manifesto in electronic form only.

Changing the landscape

ACT has now cleared the 5 percent party vote hurdle three consecutive times, each time by a greater margin. This has not been an easy task. In 2002, voters were generally content and expected the government's return in one form or another. ACT had little opportunity to affect the outcome of the election, while issues that it had successfully put on the agenda – such as crime and one law for all New Zealanders – had been adopted by other opposition parties. That ACT managed to hold its support, let alone increase it, was a remarkable accomplishment itself.

ACT has proved itself to be a permanent feature of New Zealand's political landscape. Even so, it might be unrealistic to expect commentators to stop predicting the imminent demise of the party, as they have for the eight years the party has been in existence. Whatever they may say, ACT has lived up to its reputation as a progressive campaigning party.[7] With over 7 percent of the party vote and nine talented MPs, ACT will continue to make its presence felt in Parliament.

7

THE GREEN CAMPAIGN

Cate Faehrmann

It's hard to describe what the 2002 General Election was like for the Green Party. Initially it was like a dream run, soaring in the polls and *our* issue being *the* main issue of the election. Then our run seemed to hit a hidden obstacle course and we had shots fired at us from all sides. Finally we appeared to drop the baton and just make it home stumbling across the finish line. At times we felt slightly exposed, under a media spotlight that we weren't entirely used to. Yet it was also heartening to know that this time around, we wouldn't have to rely on media stunts to make the news. We had already made it. Conscious that success breeds enemies, we were also aware of – though perhaps a little unprepared for – the hard hits we were to take during the campaign.

Campaign goals

The Green Party's goals for the 2002 General Election were defined in June 2000. A paper adopted at a party conference outlined them as:
- achieving at least 10 percent of the total party vote; and
- retaining Coromandel and coming a credible second in one or possibly two other electorate seats.

Our 'two-tick' campaigns in Nelson and Rodney were not a success, and have meant that the party will closely examine the worth of running for the electorate vote again, for the next election at least.

Realistically, we knew that we would have to fight mighty hard to keep Coromandel. We were also aware that we had to rely on Labour to give the not-so-subtle nod to their voters to give Jeanette Fitzsimons their electorate vote. However, it soon became apparent that the only thing on which we could rely on for Labour during the campaign was to keep us in the media spotlight, as we constantly tried to counter some of their attacks.

Throughout much of the campaign, it did appear that we might achieve our first goal of 10 percent of the party vote. The decision by our MPs in May to walk out of the House when the vote was taken on the Hazardous Substances and New Organisms (HSNO) bill made GE resurface once again as a prominent issue, particularly as the media could not stop talking about it. The polls were evidence that our principled stand had hit a chord with a public disillusioned with the often fickle nature of politics.

Campaign strategy

Our campaign strategy was influenced by the findings of a poll commissioned by the party earlier in the year on voter behaviour at the last election. One thing the poll showed that was of particular interest to us was the number of voters who voted Labour first and Greens second. Over 80 percent of people who put the Greens down as their second choice in 1999 had put Labour down as their first. Most of these respondents liked our policies and were concerned about the environment, but just couldn't seem to give us their vote.

Their reasons for this included:
- our perceived lack of influence;
- that we don't want to play too much of a role in government and that we just want to cause trouble;
- that we are a single issue party – in fact, in this case our single issue was not even the environment, but had been narrowed down to a party campaigning solely on GE;
- that we aren't serious enough and we're too flaky.

Predictably, during the campaign much of the media (as well as the other parties) played on these various misconceptions. Media headlines (all in the same paper) included 'Freaks and Loonies on Greens list', 'Cannabis High on Greens Agenda' and something that linked Greens and 'Stoned Kids', which still eludes me. Other parties raved about our extreme, Luddite, drug-pushing, ridiculous, anti-science, anti-business, single issue behaviour – in their literature, on their websites, at public forums and to the media. It seemed that one of our major strategies of breaking down the misconceptions about the Greens seemed to be up against everyone else's strategies of running riot with them.

As the poll findings indicated, we had decided to target the soft Labour voter. Just a month out from the election, we were still planning around a strategy that focused on adding value to a Labour-led government. Much of this was hastily thrown out the window, however, when the Green MPs walked out of the House over the HSNO bill. Surprising as it may seem to some, the walkout itself was never viewed as a major tool for our election campaign. The fact that this took place only weeks out from an election being called changed the political landscape for everyone, not least the Greens.

Initially, we were hoping to be able to inform voters about three things during the campaign: our people, our policies and our politics – quite a long shot for a snap election. Unlike some of the other parties, the Greens put a lot of effort into demonstrating what a great range of electable candidates we had on our party list. Before the list went public, there was a great deal of behind the scenes work to ensure that it met certain criteria based on gender, age, geography and Maoridom. This ensured that the end result represented a good range of highly skilled and experienced Green Party candidates. Perhaps more importantly, it also demonstrated that we 'walk the talk'. In this case, the party's long-held tradition of equal opportunity and democratic decision-making was put into practice, with 2659 eligible members being given the opportunity to vote on the party list.

We also aimed to highlight the achievements of our MPs, in order to signal to voters that we had been a supportive, stable partner to the previous Labour-Alliance government. Our message was going to be that we wanted to work with Labour, and add value to Labour, but that we would also work, to quote Greens' co-leader Rod Donald, to 'strengthen their spine'. This proved a little difficult after Helen Clark called us 'ridiculous' and 'Luddites', and a single issue party that was holding the country to ransom. And then she called the election.

As a result, much of our advertising attempted to explain our stance on GE to voters, while at the same time exposing how Labour's hardline stance was linked to big business interests. Our style of advertising attempted things which the Green Party had not tried before. We went for a new image. The style of our ads was urban and contemporary. Our messages were sharp and sometimes hard-hitting. Our audience was, we hoped, well educated and politically astute.

Granted more than $166,000 from the broadcasting allocation pool, the party was able to deliver its messages during prime time as never before. Always trying to do politics differently, an eight-minute slot for our opening broadcast was seized upon to ensure we stood out from the predictable party political deliveries. It opened with a stylised, futuristic setting some place overseas and a newsreader breaking a GE contamination story. Grabs of ads highlighted the clean, green paradise New Zealand had become in contrast to the polluted, virtual reality world of other countries. All of the Greens' MPs featured, as well as the then unelected Green MP Metiria Turei.

First time/young voters

We performed incredibly strongly in the special votes, getting 11.5 percent of the vote, lifting our overall vote to 7 percent and gaining an extra MP. This seems to indicate that we did something right in trying to reach one of our main targets – young voters.

Before the election was announced, we had released a drum and bass CD called the Green Room. This was a collaborative effort between the Greens, young New Zealand music artists and an independent label. Green MP Nandor Tanczos featured on the last track, its launch made the evening news, and it was the subject of mostly very positive reviews in countless publications across the country. We wrote the text espousing an 'eco nation' for the sleeve and had the Electoral Commission design a specially sized reply-paid enrolment postcard that was slipped inside each copy.

In a similar vein, and again with Nandor, we launched a 'Get on the Roll' campaign, making the evening news again. We had posters and stickers designed and had them pasted up in the larger cities. This particular method of a more underground style of campaigning continued right through to the last week, when we did another urban poster paste-up, featuring Nandor with the words 'Everything you do is Political'.

Our strong showings in both Auckland Central and Wellington Central indicated that these campaigns hit their target. It would seem, though, that no matter how appealing some of our campaigning was to younger voters, we are all still faced with the enormously difficult task of getting them out on the day to vote.

Direct mail

For the first time we delved into the serious politicking of direct mail. We mailed teachers our education policy, while nurses received our health policy

– to name two examples. Similar to last election, we produced a tabloid that went to more than one million households.

Overseas campaigning

The party ran two list candidates who were residing overseas, one in Sydney and the other in London. Our advantage of being a global party meant that the New South Wales Greens could assist us in our campaign. Their media skills and networks resulted in a two-minute spot on the SBS evening news for our candidate, as well as a few radio interviews on the popular government-owned youth radio station, Triple J. Our UK candidate spoke at a forum to which other parties had to fly their candidates, and sold our Green Room CD at a New Zealand music gig at which many of the artists on the CD were playing. We also stood out in the Maori electorates, averaging 10.7 percent of the party vote.

Policies

One of the more difficult tasks of the campaign was trying to get media coverage of our policies. We had planned for a series of policies to be launched by our MPs across the country, on such things as health, education, children, ecological tax reform, transport and animal welfare.

It started off positively, with the launch of our children's policy at the party's annual meeting, held before the election was called. There was a heavy media presence at this three-day meeting, due to interesting discussions about coalition negotiations and the GE moratorium, and the launch was favourably covered. Our other policy launches, however, lost out to the politics of elections. The increasingly presidential style of campaigning meant that unless one of the party's co-leaders was present at a launch, media attendance was scarce. When the co-leaders were there, the media were more often than not pressing for comments on whatever the current conflict was, rather than covering the launch in any detail. Or they were wanting to talk to Jeanette about GE.

Our campaign strategy didn't allow for Nicky Hager's book *Seeds of Distrust* being released in the middle of the campaign, though perhaps this was the baton that we dropped before the finish line. If it was, we didn't pick it up. What was for much of the public a very simple situation – that genetically engineered crops will be released commercially by the next government unless you vote to stop them – suddenly became a much more confusing issue. 'Cornfusion', as we lovingly dubbed it, reigned – in the media, in the public and within the party itself. The party did not know about the book, but we began to look as if we were doing what our voters despise – playing dirty politics. With the book's publisher, Craig Potton, a candidate on the party's list, how on earth did we not know about it? The GE issue became sullied. It was suddenly seen by some as simply a political tool, instead of an issue that made people take principled stands and fight passionately for them.

We certainly didn't know about the book when, in early July, a group calling themselves the Sustainability Council issued a statement that the moratorium should be extended by at least another five years. This seemed incredibly good for us at the time, though the group seemed to fade away and was silent during the two crucial weeks before the election. In contrast, the powerful Life Sciences Network ran a huge pro-GE campaign in the final week, running television commercials and full page ads in all newspapers.

We attempted to counter this by holding a GE Information Day the same day, mobilising hundreds of members to hand out a poster-sized information sheet detailing the reasons behind our stance on the issue. Our actions got some attention in the news that night, but so did a flyer put out by New Zealand First in Coromandel attacking the Greens.

In the end, we received 142,250 party votes – an increase from the 1999 election of 35,690 votes (33.5 percent more party votes than the previous election) despite an overall voter turnout that was down by 7.8 percent. This increase compares very favourably with Labour's party vote increase of 38,020, despite much more exposure and advertising spending. The Green Party is not an overnight success story. We've been around for decades and have parties in more than 80 different countries. Voters tend to come to us after they've thought long and hard about it! We don't perform politics based on populist notions, and we are not afraid to take stands that may lose us a few votes. Almost anywhere that the Greens have stood for elections around the world in the last five years, they have increased their vote significantly. We will continue to see this rise in support for the New Zealand Green Party, but we will need to be extremely well-prepared for the attacks that will ensue as a result.

8

ODDITY OR NEW PARADIGM?
A LABOUR VIEW OF THE 2002 ELECTION

Mike Williams

I repeatedly delayed writing this chapter in the hope that the fog of confusion would suddenly clear and the question that is in my title would be answered. This strategy has failed. I suspect that only subsequent elections will tell us whether the 2002 general election was a one-of-a-kind oddity or the formation of a new pattern in New Zealand politics.

The early election

The election was called early, overcoming our natural conservatism on the matter, as a result of several factors:
- the continuing mayhem in our coalition partner, the Alliance, which threatened to give Labour's opponents a platform to attack our moral authority to govern;
- the alarming wobbles on Wall Street, and the US economy in general, with their possible effects on the economic wellbeing of the country;
- the high level of support for the government and for Prime Minister Helen Clark, demonstrated in political market research over a sustained period.

Last and by no means least, we were encouraged by the state of readiness achieved by the Labour Party, particularly when contrasted with the obviously parlous state of the National Party.

Labour's strategy

Labour's approach was that of a successful incumbent governing party seeking a second term in office. The Labour Party's record in office was good, with the key economic indicators – employment, interest rates, business confidence and economic growth – all in positive territory. Voters expressed high levels of confidence in the country's future and in their own personal prospects, and Helen Clark's 'be yourself and tell it like it is' leadership style had engaged the public.

The party saw a danger in being seen to be resting on its laurels. Labour had been through an intense period of policy development, resulting in several kilograms of new and revised policy for the election. Our overall strategy was therefore to recognise that MMP elections are by definition 'presidential'. As a result, we sought to use Helen Clark's dominance in leadership to maximise Labour's party vote, by focusing on our success in office and on new policy initiatives.

The Labour Party went into the 2002 general election with the expectation that it would, sooner or later, come down to a two-cornered slugfest between the old adversaries, National and Labour. The campaign, which followed the announcement of the poll, turned much of the received political wisdom on its head. More mature analysis (and it remains much too early to attempt this) will need to accommodate and explain a number of apparent novelties and new phenomena.

The campaign

Election 2002 demonstrated that *campaigns do matter*. In the course of the campaign period, the voting population showed immense volatility. Labour went from a strong winning position at the outset of the campaign to one close to defeat with a mere ten days to go, and then back to a pivotal vote share by election day. National began as the weakened but clearly dominant force on the right. It went on to lose votes to virtually every other party as the campaign developed, recording its worst result ever.

Minor party support was equally unstable. The Green and ACT parties peaked towards the mid-point of the campaign and fell away badly in the second half, while United Future came from nowhere to pick up considerable support in that same period. New Zealand First replaced a nightmare run in 1999 with a dream run in 2002. It succeeded in picking up much of the populist right vote that neither ACT nor National could attract.

The unusual volatility that emerged during the campaign period was the result of the unique electoral atmosphere in which the campaign was conducted. The determinants of this atmosphere, in order of importance, were, first, the absence of the traditional 'major issues'. Issues surrounding health, education and the economy had been largely neutralised (with the exception of a showdown with secondary teachers). Election campaigns by definition cannot be 'issue free', so the vacuum created by the absence of these major concerns was partly filled by alternative issues, presented to the media by parties which sought to exploit them. These included genetic engineering, crime, immigration, and Treaty issues. It is worth noting that these 'campaign issues' hardly rated as public concerns in the months before the election was called.

A second influence was the historic weakness of the National Party. Virtually nothing went right for National, which had suffered a steady erosion of its support dating from the time of its leadership change. Unable to achieve internal party unity, Bill English proved to be an ineffectual campaigner. National had been unable to update its policies, and the party became the victim of tactical party voting, as a segment of its former support defected to Labour as an antidote to perceived Green Party extremism. To compound these problems, National's local campaigns were generally weak and lacked central direction. Where they existed, these campaigns seemed aimed at securing the electorate vote.

A third element was the perception that Labour could not be beaten. Even when Labour support slumped two weeks from the election date, the voting public still overwhelmingly believed that Labour would be the dominant force in the next government. This attitude, potentially disastrous for the Labour Party, apparently liberated some voters to search for other options.

None of these conditions would have produced the result on 27 July without an essential trigger. This was supplied by what became known as 'corngate'.

Corngate

The 'corngate' controversy was a pivotal point in the election campaign. It had an impact on nearly every party and undoubtedly affected the result. In the period before 'corngate', Labour was almost certainly headed for majority government or a result very close to it. In the time after 'corngate', the term 'majority government' became a dirty word and a portion of the electorate set out to find a coalition partner for Labour. There are few incidents in the history of modern democracy that have had such a profound effect on the course of an election campaign. Only the Zinoviev letter in the 1920s in Britain or the Petrov affair in Australia in the 1950s can offer adequate comparisons.

Researcher Nicky Hager's *Seeds of Distrust*, published towards the midpoint of the election campaign, was launched via a highly aggressive TV3 interview conducted by presenter John Campbell with Prime Minister Helen Clark. The central thesis of the book was that corn contaminated with genetically modified seed had been imported and repeatedly tested positive for contamination, before being allowed nevertheless to grow to maturity in three locations, after the government – up to and including the prime minister – had orchestrated a cover-up. The book launch was well-planned and well-organised, and the TV3 interview was followed up with the appearance of corncob stickers on Labour Party hoardings the next morning. Anti-GE campaigners dressed as cans of organic sweet corn began dogging Helen Clark in the days immediately following the book launch.

While there is much yet to be written on this sequence of events, there is probably now enough distance in time to make a judgement on why they were so devastating for Labour and how they altered the course of the election campaign. The key media outlets coopted for the book launch accepted the central thesis of the book without question. It seems that neither TV3 nor *The Listener* had the slightest doubt about the author's interpretation of events, and the science that underpinned this interpretation. At no stage does it seem to have occurred to the media organs that made the early running that Nicky Hager might be wrong. There was, however, a completely different, and innocent, interpretation of the incident that took some time to emerge. This was that a single sample had returned a positive test for GE contamination. This sample was taken from seed that had been decanted, mixed with talc for drilling, then rebagged and returned. This sole positive test probably arose from pollution that occurred during this process. Subsequent samples all returned negative results, and the government, after some initial confusion reflected in papers selectively leaked to Nicky Hager, reached the correct conclusion that the seed was not contaminated.

Compounding the absence of any doubt about the Hager thesis by the media involved in the book launch was the fact that the government took some time to answer the charges. The delay during this period allowed the impression that a cover-up had occurred to take root. Key documents that would have allowed the charges to be refuted were spread around a variety of sites and were often in storage. Many of the arguments which had been resolved to the apparent satisfaction of the government at the time of the incident had to be relitigated, including a highly abstruse debate concerning the nature (if any) of certainty in science. Those allegedly involved and to whom I spoke immediately after the TV3 interview had only a hazy recollection of the incident, if they recalled it at all. I found this very hard to reconcile with the book's allegations of an elaborate cover-up, but it obviously inhibited any rapid response.

The electorate was well aware of GE as an issue, and was therefore susceptible to it. The Green Party's parliamentary walkout in protest at the proposed expiry of the GE moratorium, and its practically single-issue anti-GE campaign – which included showing elderly American farmers apparently ruined by GE contamination of their farms – meant a higher level of awareness of the dangers of GE and a degree of knowledge about the alleged dangers of a release of GE organisms.

Allegations of cover-ups were devastating for Labour because they went to the heart of one of its key strengths – trust. The Labour Party, well aware that the electorate was cynical and mistrusted politicians, had consciously sought to rebuild voters' trust in politicians and in government. That is why the 1999 election policy promulgated by Labour was relatively modest in scope. It had to be achievable. In office the Labour-led government had repeatedly emphasised that it had, indeed, kept its word. The Clark approach *had* achieved something of a turn-around in public attitudes to politicians. Thus the allegations of a cover-up were terribly damaging, bringing back memories of past betrayals, both real and imagined. Following 'corngate', this electoral advantage was largely dissipated, leaving a gap for a party that would, in the memorable words of Australian Democrat founder Senator Don Chipp, 'keep the bastards honest'. It is arguable that into this gap the United Future Party sailed, unsullied by having no past.

The importance of the 2002 election to the parties

Shortly after the election, an old friend, resident in Crete, sent me a small clipping from a local newspaper which reported the 2002 New Zealand general election in one sentence. It reads (his rough translation):

> In New Zealand Helen Clark's left wing Labour Government was returned with an increased share of the vote in a general election in which the conservative opposition party collapsed.

This dehydrated version of events contains probably the two historically most important aspects of the election. First, Labour was returned with an increased share of the vote. Unlike the party's winning of a second term in

1987, its reelection in 2002 was accomplished while it remained true to its social democratic heritage. In this achievement, the Clark-led Labour administration clearly captured and reflected the aspirations and imagination of middle New Zealand. This general election also marked another step in the rebuilding of the New Zealand Labour Party as a dominant political force. It was gratifying to see much higher levels of local activity – particularly in provincial and rural New Zealand – than the party had managed in 1999. The quirky result in itself bodes well for the long-term health of the Labour Party. The minority coalition arrangement means that all but one of the members of the Executive are Labour MPs, offering priceless experience for a long-term Labour administration or a future Labour government.

The election was, of course, a singular disaster for the National Party, which now runs the risk of becoming merely one of three or four voting options on the right of the political spectrum. While Labour Party activists relish the thought of facing a Bill English-led National Party again in 2005, this must be a fond hope, as the true enormity of the 2002 general election result for the National Party finally sinks in.

Equally, the ACT Party managed only to spin its wheels while large chunks of the vote were up for grabs. Its leader made no impact in an environment where Peter Dunne managed to come from nowhere to a position of influence, and Winston Peters managed yet another self-invention. The opportunity was there for ACT, but Richard Prebble seemed unmotivated and, despite huge spending, made no impression. Look for a change at the top in ACT, particularly if polling shows the party to be below the threshold over an extended period. A dash of Peters-type populism courtesy of ACT MP Rodney Hide may well become irresistible.

In terms of issues, New Zealand First made the running until 'corngate' burst upon the campaign. It remains difficult, however, to imagine a post-Peters New Zealand First, and building a long-term support base on the ephemera of personality and populist issues is a dangerous strategy.

The Green Party missed a major opportunity to increase its political influence through its essentially single-issue campaign, which was undoubtedly responsible for the party's loss of its electoral insurance policy – the Coromandel electorate. The party's strategists seem to have taken some superficial market research on the issue at face value, underestimating the effect of their ultimatum on the GE moratorium. While attitudes to MMP are still forming among the voting public, it does seem now proven that bottom lines from minor parties are interpreted as the tail wagging the dog, and are counterproductive.

Some random personal observations

I have been involved in so many elections that I have lost count. I have never before experienced one where the main opposition party was regarded as almost irrelevant. This factor introduced a dynamic of instability into the campaign that was entirely unprecedented, and may have been the major influence on the overall outcome.

I believe that journalistic standards slipped badly at times during the campaign. I regard 'ambush journalism' as an unwelcome innovation that is likely to reduce the accessibility of our politicians, to the detriment of informed reporting. Some supposedly 'independent and impartial' commentators were anything but. On election night, one high profile 'journalist' was unable to disguise his jubilation at the early results, which he interpreted (incorrectly) as a defeat for the Labour-led government.

Helen Clark has the constitution of a bison. This was the most gruelling of campaigns for any Labour leader. She achieved a government re-elected with an increased vote share for the Labour Party while leading the country's administration. It was a remarkable achievement.

9

NATIONAL'S CAMPAIGN

Tim Grafton

The 2002 election campaign cannot be seen in isolation from the context of the 1999–2002 period. It was always going to be a tall order for National to win the 2002 election. The New Zealand economy was in pretty good shape from 1999–2002, as it experienced the best export conditions for decades. Historically, governments have been sacked only when the economy has faded into recession, or after at least two terms in office. These factors persuaded commentators early in the electoral cycle that Labour would win a second term unless there was a serious economic mishap. By 2002, this was received wisdom. So before the campaign began, it was never going to be easy to oust a popular, first-term Labour government that was riding high in the polls. Under these conditions, and with an MMP electoral system, it meant that voters who did not see National winning started to interpret the election as a choice between those parties best suited to hold Labour in check, possibly as a coalition partner.

If this was not a big enough challenge, National also had to profile a new leader, Bill English, and his plans for the future, to a largely content electorate, with that traditional strength for conservative parties, economic management, well down their list of concerns. The campaign therefore had several objectives:
- to promote a new and relatively unknown leader;
- to promote policy which had not yet been made public;
- to establish relevance in voters' electoral calculations.

All these needed to be achieved in the shortened time allowed by the snap election, and with fierce competition for media space from other parties during the campaign. Labour not only had an established leader, but as the incumbent it could let its record speak for itself, and was not under pressure to present a new set of policies. Neither was 'relevance' an issue for Labour.

Even with these advantages, Labour showed little strategic focus. It gambled at the outset on gaining sufficient support to govern alone. It tried to set the agenda as a choice between governing alone, or being held to ransom by the Greens over the GE issue. This proved disastrous. Labour shed over 20 percent of the support it enjoyed in early June over a few weeks. If Labour's total absence of new ideas for the future had come under greater scrutiny, the outcome could have been far worse for them. The collapse in Labour's support ironically had an adverse impact on National, by reinforcing the perception that Labour would need a coalition partner to hold it in check.

Opposition and the lead-up to the 2002 election

After nine years in government, adjustment by National to opposition following the 1999 election proved difficult. Few of National's 39 MPs had ever been in opposition. Most of those who had been had held only junior, backbench positions at that time. It therefore took time to develop an opposition culture, and to learn how to work effectively with vastly reduced resources.

The media were willing to believe the new government's frequent refrain that all problems could be laid at the feet of the previous National government. Until National had served a rehabilitation period – the best part of a term in opposition –there was going to be public resistance to what National had to offer. For these reasons, National was not able to move onto a strong campaign footing early in the electoral cycle. Even so, a number of successful campaigns were run on specific issues, such as against the Employment Relations Bill. The net effect, though, was that apart from a brief period during the latter half of 2000, National remained on or about its 1999 level of support of 30 percent for the first two years.

National changed its leadership in October 2001, as part of a difficult transition out of its lengthy time in government. National expected a presidential campaign, and was aware that the new leader, Bill English, would need 12 months to become known to the public, to put a stamp on the party, and to develop a suitable campaign style.

The change in leadership had no impact on National's poll ratings, because it was overshadowed by the events after 11 September 2001 and the continuance of a strong economy. By the end of the year, Labour had more than made up for its initial faltering reaction to the terrorist attacks by committing troops to Afghanistan in the war on terror. National finished 2001 polling in the low 30s.

The leadership change brought with it a consequential change in portfolio allocations, at a critical time in the policy development cycle. It slowed policy development, as new spokespeople took stock of their portfolios. It meant that by the time substantial policy was released, such as the economic policy in April 2002, it was only a matter of weeks before the election campaign. While a snap election meant that policy was released too late, the situation was compounded by plans to release policy after the May Budget. It was argued that a post-Budget release of policy would build campaign momentum for a spring election, and by then it would be impossible for National's ideas to be pre-empted by the government. The election date was announced less than four weeks after the Budget.

At the time of the leadership change, the 'right direction' poll – the one that asks people whether they think the country is moving in the 'right direction' – showed a strong rise, on the back of the government's reaction to September 11 and a further lift in the economy. By the beginning of February 2002, this strong rise in the 'right direction' poll led to a substantial lift in government support. This was reinforced in late March by the prime minister's visit to Washington and New York. Even so, National was polling in the low 30s until publicity about a Serious Fraud Office inquiry into party donations. That occurred in mid-May, when support dropped to the mid-20s, and never recovered above 30 percent. Early in the year, polling showed Labour held a strong lead on most issues as well as leadership. Research showed that most people, including a significant proportion of National supporters, felt that Labour had done enough to win the election.

Research and the campaign

National's research showed that voters did not want a change of government, but it also showed that they did feel strongly about some key issues where Labour was failing. Health, education and law-and-order were the top three issues. Labour also held a significant lead in leadership preference, which was hardly surprising, given National's new leadership and Labour's popularity.

National's strategy was to persuade people that by voting on issues of major concern to them, they could send a message to the government, and that voting National was the best way to send that message. The rationale was that this would enable them to vote against the government even though they did not wish to change it. If sufficient voters could be persuaded to vote on these issues, then Labour's support would fall and it was thought that National would be the principal beneficiary.

This strategy failed, partly because the message was communicated poorly by the campaign advertising in the early stages of the campaign, partly because the gap between National and Labour created a 'relevance' issue for National, and partly because the party's campaign failed to focus on the party vote.

Other parties which followed the strategy of focusing on voters' concerns and clearly applied them in the execution of their advertising, such as New Zealand First, enjoyed better electoral success. As these parties were also seen as potentially holding the balance of power, with National out of the picture, they became natural repositories for those who wanted to send Labour a message. By contrast, National's advertising in the early stages of the campaign focused on positioning the leader for a presidential campaign, at the expense of clear messages which reflected voters' concerns.

Nevertheless, as the campaign proceeded, the messages in media interviews, television debates and advertising focused more on the issues National wanted to run on. These issues were standards in education, a strong economy through backing small businesses, law-and-order, and the Treaty of Waitangi. Two of the top three issues for voters – education and law-and-order – were run. While National began the campaign behind Labour on education, there was a belief that a combination of the teachers' strike and Bill English's commitment to the issue would work in its favour. On law-and-order, we began the campaign with a lead over Labour, and research showed that people felt the 1999 referendum on tougher sentencing had been ignored by the government. Research also showed that voters did not believe National would fix their concerns about the health sector. Health thus became an attack issue, rather than a strong focus for policy promotion.

The economy (with particular emphasis on the costs to small businesses) and the Treaty were chosen as the other two main planks. Even though economic issues did not rate highly in voters' minds, small businesses were a large constituency that traditionally backed National and its values of enterprise. The Treaty was chosen because of strongly held views across the community about the time taken to settle historic grievances. The Treaty was an issue that crossed the political spectrum. Our commitments to close the book on historic claims and one standard of citizenship for all, we believed, were positive statements about the future of New Zealand.

On leadership, the gap between Bill English and Helen Clark closed, but not sufficiently to make any difference to the outcome. On one measure – having energy and new ideas – Bill English made large gains and beat Helen Clark. Through the campaign, National extended its lead over Labour as the party that would best encourage business and enterprise and address law-and-order concerns. National caught and passed Labour on education and the Treaty. Gains on law-and-order and education were particularly strong, and laid the grounds for development of a strong position in the future.

However, despite these gains, the real choices voters on the centre-right began to entertain were about the party that could best act as a brake on Labour as a coalition partner. The real battle for National was therefore one of relevance.

The campaign

The media chose to give the issues that were of most concern to voters a back seat to their main preoccupations – coverage of poll results, likely coalition scenarios, and the style of the various campaigns. 'Paintergate' followed by 'corngate' had a much bigger effect on the vote of the left than had been anticipated, but it also had the effect of making moderately centre-right parties more relevant. 'Corngate' and the subsequent Labour-Green fighting was a major factor in driving down National's vote, because it presented National supporters with a strong motive for tactical voting. It had been assumed that a lower 'left' vote would help National, because people would realise Labour could not make it on its own. This proved to be wrong. National had not done enough to retain the respect and affection of its supporters, who went out to fill the gaps National had left, and as a result helped Labour make the best of it.

By the last week of the campaign, it became crucial to pull back support from the smaller parties, or at least to stop further leakage. The sudden rise of United Future, from less than 1 percent to 7 percent over the space of a single week, took everyone by surprise and took a toll on National's support. In the final week, National floated the idea of a coalition of like-minded, centre-right parties, in an attempt to show that it was not a foregone conclusion that Labour would win. This was reinforced with the message that only a strong vote for National would address the main concerns voters had. It is possible that talk of a such a coalition only helped waning National supporters feel comfortable supporting minor parties of the centre-right. It is also possible that National might have done worse without this pitch to its supporters.

Lessons learned

National has learned from the 2002 campaign, and a second term in opposition is enabling it to position itself more strongly for the next election. It is moving onto a permanent campaign footing and is expressing more clearly what it stands for.

Many of the issues that were present during the 2002 campaign are likely to persist. Failings in core public services, particularly in health and education, are becoming more acute. National will force the pace by showing that it is better able to manage public services and tackle the causes of problems like crime. It won't pander to prejudices, but it will acknowledge anxieties in the community. Skill shortages and compliance costs are emerging as major problems for small businesses and New Zealand's ability to grow the economy. Other issues include rising crime, welfare dependency, the role of the Treaty of Waitangi, and some major infrastructure problems that will require large amounts of capital and legislative changes to fix.

It is no longer credible for Labour in its second term to blame the former National government for its own failings. Indeed, the bar has been set much higher for Labour to deliver, and it will be more difficult for the government to achieve its objectives because of the hand it was dealt by the 2002 result. Labour campaigned on the status quo, and has a mandate to do nothing more than that in its second term. The political conundrum it now finds itself in between the Greens and United Future will only reinforce this situation. The contradiction it faces is of its own making. By striking out against the Green Party, Labour is reliant on support from the conservative United Future. Yet if it wishes to make progress with a centre-left agenda, it is dependent on the Greens for support.

National is now able to walk out from a shadow cast by the 1990s. By 1999, middle New Zealand for various reasons had judged that National had lost its compassion and drive. It never really recovered during that decade from substituting a promise of a decent society for a period of radical reform, in response to what it had inherited in 1990 – New Zealand's deepest recession since the Great Depression. The party is now able to express what it stands for in terms of outcomes for mainstream families and communities, not just in purely economic terms. This will enable the party to respond to community concerns which have seen National's traditional supporters back other parties of the right. National's mainstream approach will reflect those concerns and will moderate the more extreme responses that will only divide communities further.

National has started to position itself once more as the party of property owners, small businesses and families. It will be able to release policy much earlier in the electoral cycle to promote low crime, ready access to good healthcare, great schools, jobs for people to be independent, more choices and opportunities, and a more tolerant society with one standard of citizenship for all. National's younger, fresher and experienced leadership will be a tougher match for Labour's leaders, who have changed little over the past 15 years. Defeat has also led the party organisation to undergo a major restructure that will better equip it to function in the MMP environment.

10

THE NEW ZEALAND FIRST CAMPAIGN

Brian Donnelly

'My pappy never had to kick my backside twice for making the same mistake.'
— Bill Clinton

In the 1999 election, the voters kicked New Zealand First's backside. So our campaign 2002 started early in 2000. We realised that the voters had kicked our backsides because of the perceived arrogance of some of our departed members – memories of 'dirty dog' sunglasses abounded – and that Winston Peters had almost lost his electorate because, since 1993, his time and energies had been tied up with establishing a new party, with campaigning for that party nationwide through three elections, and with his roles as Deputy Prime Minister and Treasurer during the first MMP government.

We set ourselves four goals. We had to re-establish credibility as a party and, as the visible side of the party, this meant credibility of the caucus. Our behaviour had to be impeccable and we needed to demonstrate constructive responsibility, both in the House and in select committees. That meant doing our penance without complaint and working hard in Parliament.

Secondly, Winston had to regain his reputation as an electorate MP in Tauranga. His presence at prize-givings, opening shopping malls and constituency work was to be given priority over other activities.

Thirdly, we had to carefully position ourselves. We predicted that as long as the economy remained buoyant and National remained in disarray, Labour would be the dominant party in 2002. We also predicted the demise of the Alliance and that they would have few, if any, policy wins. This prediction was confirmed by the body language of Alliance ministers during the pre-Budget months of 2001. That meant that Labour would have only one party to its left with which it could form a coalition – the Greens. Our strategy was to outflank the Greens.

One such opportunity for us was with the superannuation legislation. However, from the election point of view, GE was a more significant one. The Royal Commission's report was a godsend. Its well reasoned and balanced conclusions fitted very well with a centrist party such as New Zealand First. It allowed us not only to support Labour's subsequent legislation, but also to counter any excuse by the Greens that they were only supporting it because, without that support, the good bits would not get through.

From the first reading, we told the Greens that they did not have to vote for the legislation, because we would. The day they walked out I jumped for joy, because I knew that an irreconcilable distance had been put between the Greens and Labour. Labour was going to need another potential partner if they were to achieve their biotechnology strategy. They would not be able to dismiss us as a potential coalition partner.

Finally, we had one other deliberate element to our strategy: we assiduously listened. We listened to what people were saying. New Zealand First does not have the resources to do sophisticated polling like National and Labour. However, polling results can only give surface information. We tried to get below the surface – to the visceral level if you like – and we carefully analysed what we were hearing across the country.

By the beginning of 2002, we had narrowed the issues down to six. One was what might be called the Treaty of Waitangi issue. ACT had picked up the same issue, but their response was simplistic and aimed at the redneck element in our society. What we were picking up wasn't red-neckism, and we had to approach the issue from a far more sophisticated angle. Hence the series of oral questions we were asking in Parliament throughout the months leading up to the election. Only one journalist, Jane Clifton, seemed to have picked up on what we were doing. The vague, evasive and often contradictory answers we received from ministers made magnificent ammunition throughout the campaign, without putting down Maori. With no candidates in the Maori electorates, we virtually doubled our party vote.

We had early on made a decision that we would go for quality, not quantity, in our selection of candidates. When you're a party running at 2 percent in the polls, it's not that easy to attract people who are successful in their fields, who have an agenda reflective of the party's principles, and who are prepared to put up their hands. However, we stuck religiously to the quality principle.

The announcement of the date of the election caught us somewhat by surprise. We knew that the prime minister would have to call an early election, but we thought she would get the Budget and critical legislation, such as the Tertiary Education Reform Bill, out of the way first. While we had our general strategy worked out, the bread and butter stuff had not been sorted out. The decision to have me co-ordinate the campaign had been made only weeks before, and had come out of the blue. I had never been involved in a campaign at the national level before, and didn't know where to start. Nor had I been a student of national campaigns. The only educative experience I had had was attending the VUW post-election conference in 1999.

However, all the groundwork had been laid. We were going to run a very focused campaign aimed at two objectives: to win Tauranga, and to lift our party vote as high as possible. The campaign was going to be kept simple and focused on Winston. However, we had agreed on one other aspect for our campaign. We were going to inject a bit of humour, a bit of light-heartedness, a bit of fun: hence 'Bob the Builder'. We can thank the grandchildren of Graham Harding, head of our research unit, for that. We had unsuccessfully agonised for two years over a suitable campaign slogan. One day, just weeks before the election was announced, as we waited in the caucus room for Winston to arrive, Graham Harding came in enthusiastically proclaiming what our slogan should be. None of us knew what he was talking about. It is not that Graham Harding is an avid watcher of kids' television, but it seemed he had been made to sit down and join in with his grandchildren as they watched their favourite programme, and the jingle had stuck in his head. We loved it and it took off from there, but I'm sure Winston didn't know the origin of the slogan until after the campaign opening. However, we did manage to get photographs of him doing carpentry on a 'Habitat for Humanity' house in Kaitaia included in his Tauranga campaign brochure.

For our strategy to work, we had to get some traction in the polls and look like a viable counterfoil to the Greens. The decision to pare the six issues down to three was made in the week following the announcement of the election. Timing was critical. When Winston first demonstrated the three finger signal, he did so with his fingernails facing outward. I immediately recognised what would happen to billboards across the country with that image. One, if not two, of those fingers would have been whitened out. Winston turned his hand around and said 'What about that?' The rest is history.

As long as I live, when the 2002 campaign is mentioned, the image of a swan gliding smoothly across the waters will spring to mind. Underneath the water, invisible to the public, we were paddling like hell. We had a very small team to work with, the campaign was firmly controlled from the centre, and we had such a small budget that we had to make every dollar count. Detailed policy was promoted through the website and via the hand delivery of 100,000 copies of a summary booklet entitled 'YES WE CAN'.

We made the decision to launch early, not so much because we were fully prepared, but because we wanted to get our message into the public arena before the stage became cluttered by all the other parties. I think 'Bob the Builder' got us more publicity than our three issues, but we certainly showed that this was a party that, although bloodied, was not down. One of the issues we had identified was what might be referred to as moral issues. We believed that there was enough discontent among traditional Labour voters over issues such as prostitution reform, gay marriage and cannabis decriminalisation that there would be many who would give their list vote to a party opposed to these developments. The only time we played that issue was with the debit card. We had planned to release this the day after Helen Clark produced Labour's credit card. While we had the design all ready, we had not actually produced the card, and the machine had to go into overdrive to get it ready. While the debit card did not shoot us up in the polls, it certainly demonstrated that Labour was not going to sleepwalk its way to victory.

Our deputy leader, Peter Brown, ran what might be described as a subterranean campaign around these issues. However, at the level of the national campaign we stuck doggedly to the three we had decided upon. I believe that the meteoric rise by United Future in the polls in the last few weeks of the campaign indicates that our analysis that these areas were a matter of tenderness with a proportion of the electorate was accurate.

For the first few weeks of the campaign, our polling did not rise as we had thought it would. Nevertheless, informal feedback suggested something different. I believe Winston's performance in the first leaders' debate was a circuit breaker. The defining moment in that debate was when he supported the Greens' right to its policy position on GE on the grounds of democracy. In doing so, he lifted the debate to a level above the petty squabbling.

The one thing we did not predict – could not predict – was the power of the 'worm'. As I've said, we had already identified a tenderness in the electorate over the direction it perceived the government to be going in what might be described as moral areas. The 'worm' drew attention to a party which could be seen to satisfy their needs. However, the consequence of polls of 6 percent for United Future meant that the prime minister no longer needed us, and we saw her turn on us. The only time that we were tempted to add an extra component to our plan was when Labour went on the attack with some scurrilous advertising at the beginning of the final week of the campaign. In our view, these ads were in breach of the broadcasting standards. We took cognisance of what had happened in the last election, when Jenny Shipley had attacked the Greens, and their support had gone up. We assessed that these ads would do Labour more harm than ourselves, and it is to be noted how quickly they were dropped.

On the night before the election, I spoke to Winston on the phone about the three polls that had come out over the previous days. I said to him that I believed there was an extra 1 percent shift in our favour which would occur between what those polls were saying, and what election night would yield. The election results were, in the end, as I had suggested. We were back with 10 percent of the vote and 13 seats – the third largest party in the New Zealand Parliament.

11

THE UNITED FUTURE CAMPAIGN

Mark Stonyer

'Nine! Did someone say they have nine?'
Mike Hosking, *TV1 Election Special*, 27 July 2002

Perhaps the tritest rhetoric heard around political offices immediately after an election is: 'The campaign for the next election starts now'. After the 1999 general election, United New Zealand (as the party was then known) decided this was more appropriately reworded to 'If nothing happens next time perhaps we should pull the plug!' The party had survived the previous three years; its leader and sole parliamentary representative, Peter Dunne, had increased his majority in Ohariu-Belmont; and the party vote, although lower than in 1996, had been sufficient to avoid Dunne being an 'overhang' member. But the party had failed to make a significant impact with the voters, the media had all but ignored it during the campaign, and various strategies to gain voter support from targeted groups had obviously not worked.

At the party's first post-election board meeting, however, any feeling that there was a need to give up trying to establish a true centre party in New Zealand was quickly dispelled. While there was the inevitable navel-gazing, the general feeling was that we had survived. Anecdotal evidence suggested that some of our target markets were listening but, being somewhat cautious, they were waiting to see if we were staying 'on message'. These voters, mainly Asian new migrants, wasted no time after the election telling us to persist in our efforts, and we would be sure to gain more of their support in 2002.

The more immediate problem was one of profile. With the formation of the Labour-Alliance coalition, together with support for confidence and supply from the Green Party, there was no longer the need for the government to ask for support from United for majority on legislation and other votes. The obvious problem was one of maintaining Peter Dunne's media profile. Put simply, he was just another opposition Member whose vote didn't affect anything. As the term progressed, however, this perceived problem did not really eventuate. Local issues and a 'common sense' approach to major national issues proved enough to keep media interest at similar levels to those in the 1996–1999 parliamentary term. Arguably, this profile of Peter Dunne as a 'common sense' politician was to be of immense help to us later on during the campaign.

Early in 2000, the United New Zealand parliamentary office received an approach from senior executive members of another small party, Future New Zealand, seeking talks on matters of mutual concern and interest. This type of offer had been made to United's president by Future New Zealand prior to the 1999 general election. The United president had reported back then that a possible merger of the two parties had been discussed during these talks, but neither party could reach a satisfactory agreement to proceed much beyond these initial discussions.

An initial meeting was held between Peter Dunne, as leader of United New Zealand, myself, as party secretary, and David Brown and Anthony Walton, president and leader respectively, of Future New Zealand. Both parties recognised that our combined party vote from the 1999 general election would have been enough to have given us two MPs in the House if we had been standing as one party. Future New Zealand was anxious to point out to us that they had deliberately changed their name from the Christian Democrats to avoid being seen as a Christian party and to try to increase their support base as a secular party. Their policies, when examined beside those of United New Zealand, were found to be compatible and, in some cases, virtually identical. On the basis that our respective policies were not likely to be a matter of any contention, the board of United New Zealand agreed that the talks could continue.

It became increasingly obvious that the two parties not only had policies that were similar, but also were not too disparate in their core philosophies. However, Future New Zealand assessed that United's small 'l' liberal tag would scare some of its members, just as United New Zealand thought that Future's small 'c' Christian label would worry some of its membership. Without compromising either party's policy positions, it was felt that this would not be a problem if some other common 'branding' was used to present a new combined party to their respective memberships. The one glaringly obvious point of commonality between the two parties' policies was the need to secure future social and economic security for the New Zealand family. This theme was to become the genesis of the entire election campaign.

Talks continued between the two parties, consultations with the respective memberships were carried out, and an agreement was finally reached in early October 2000 to form a new party – a coalition between United New Zealand and Future New Zealand, to be known as United Future New Zealand. One immediate casualty was the United New Zealand president, Mike Sheppard, who decided to resign from both the presidency and the party. Sheppard was the only dissenting voice among the board and, under the deal being brokered, he would have been deputy president of the new party had he remained.

The new party was launched on 16 November 2000 at the Sheraton Hotel in Auckland. The party was registered with the Electoral Commission as a separate party in its own right, and plans were made to establish branch organisations. Throughout the following year, the party set up a network of regional organisations. Auckland became a particularly strong region, with six sub-regional branches including an ethnic branch focusing on the interests of the new migrant populations. Part of the responsibilities of these regional organisations was to identify, at the earliest stage possible, suitable candidates to put forward in electorates for the 2002 general election. This plan was also aimed at building up grassroots support and helping to identify a volunteer force to assist with electorate campaigns during the upcoming election.

Late in 2001, a small campaign committee was set up in Wellington. Headed by the party leader, Peter Dunne, this committee began the detailed campaign planning for the 2002 election. Various people, from party officials to advertising consultants, were drafted in when needed, and all the major decisions needed at this time were made by this committee. In February 2002 a weekend meeting of the key regional personnel, board members and candidates was held at the Wairakei Resort Hotel just north of Taupo. Workshops were held to develop campaign strategies, mainly for electorate campaigns, with the rationale being that an effective local electorate campaign was the best way to enhance the party's share of the list vote. It was clearly understood by all that realistically there was only going to be one person winning an electorate seat, and that was Dunne, in Ohariu-Belmont. Experience from both United and Future New Zealand showed, however, that where a candidate stood in an electorate, the number of list votes gained could, potentially, be doubled, compared with those electorates where there was no candidate. This 'mini-conference' also provided an opportunity for all those attending to be invigorated and motivated to the levels of enthusiasm necessary for an effective and undoubtedly tough campaign. It was generally held that this conference was a success, but there were some rumblings that not enough notice had been taken of the ethnic and Maori voter potential.

Fundraising started in earnest, aimed especially at the corporate sector, and visits to senior executives were organised. A major fundraising effort also commenced with an appeal to the party's membership. With these activities, plus the ongoing weekly planning meetings, it was decided by the board that the party should prepare its advertising campaign. The theme of the family was well entrenched in the party's thinking, and it was this theme that would not only guide all the ongoing policy development, but would also be the major branding for the campaign.

In the past, United New Zealand had used the small boutique agency, Cognito, and its creative head, David Collinge. Collinge had been involved in every election campaign since 1987, with both Labour and National, and in 1999 he had designed United New Zealand's advertising, had overseen the production of its opening and closing addresses and television advertisements, and had produced the copy for all the print advertising. Collinge had one or two meetings with the group, and in April the board decided to put the advertising contract up for competitive tender. Cognito and one other boutique-style agency were asked to make presentations to the board, after I had briefed each of them on what the board saw as our political position, our theme for the election, and the possible constituency we thought we could attract. Both agencies made their presentations a month later. One agency simply didn't get it. Their presentation was all about the 'Peter Dunne' factor and his 'safe seat'. It aimed to educate the voters on the way MMP worked, and the need not to have to cross the 5 percent barrier with Peter winning his electorate seat. They acknowledged that I had briefed them on the importance of our chosen theme of the 'family', but the advice they gave to us was that this was too difficult to express as a coherent and saleable political theme. Collinge's presentation, on the other hand, showed a good understanding of our desired positioning. He had developed several themes whereby every policy issue could be defined as a 'family' issue. This was also an idea that the deputy leader of United Future, Anthony Walton, had been working on with the team for some time.

We had decided that some sort of direct mail approach should be used, but were reluctant to do the standard 'A4 folded DLE' style brochure. Collinge came up with a very attractive alternative in the form of a small credit card sized booklet, hard glossy covered, that would open out into a large poster style pamphlet. It was different, tactile and had obvious potential to stand out as something completely different from all the other party literature. Some initial development work was done, but the early election made it impossible for us to proceed with it. The booklet was to have been produced in Australia and freighted to us. Time constraints and expense saw us drop this idea. United's parliamentary unit then put a six-page policy booklet together that used the 'family' as its theme. This allowed us to meet the immediate need to have something we could send to candidates and to give out to potential voters.

Eventually we did produce a different product. A 20-page A6, three colour, staple bound booklet was planned, scripted and printed within a fortnight of the election being announced. As the number of candidates grew and the demand for material increased, it was this booklet that proved to be one of our most useful aids. It opened with an introduction to the party and the leader, followed by a brief explanation of the value of a vote for United Future, and a statement about why the Greens must not be allowed to be the government's coalition partner. There were then 16 pages of policy, all of it expressed as bullet points, showing what the problems were in each policy area and then our solution to these problems. It finished with another message reinforcing the danger the Greens posed to the country and a membership application form was inserted at the back of the booklet. The booklet was entitled *The Hard Facts*, with the sub-heading 'We Want New Zealand to Be The Best Country In The World In Which To Raise A Family . . . Again'. This little publication was enthusiastically received by the party and the candidates. In total, 340,000 copies were printed and distributed. It was smart-looking, the right size to distribute and keep, and it explained the party philosophy and policy in a clear, innovative and practical manner.

Throughout April and May, there was a steady stream of applications for candidacy from party members. Rumour and speculation on when the election would be called were rife, especially around Parliament, with a range of dates being proposed. When the prime minister announced on Tuesday 11 June that election day would be Saturday 27 July the party was in a good position to begin campaigning in earnest.

For some time it had been apparent that interest in the party was on the increase. There had been continuous requests for policy information, for the names of possible electorate candidates, and for spokespeople's contact details, from organisations and individuals. These early and ongoing requests were something that the party had not experienced in previous elections, even in 1996 when there had been six MPs standing for re-election under the United banner. Something was afoot – we just didn't know exactly what. Information from other parties' private polling seemed to indicate that our level of voter support had risen throughout the year and was hovering around 1.5–1.7 percent. Feedback from the corporate sector confirmed the high regard it held for the party's leader, Peter Dunne, and his message emphasising the need for stable government seemed to strike a chord with voters who were motivated to contact the party. The climate of disorder that surrounded the Alliance break-up inevitably helped us.

From the Tuesday that the election was announced, the volume of requests for information skyrocketed. The parliamentary unit, tiny by comparison to those run by other parliamentary parties, soon became inundated with requests for policy information related to the election. The full-time staff of three plus a part-time intern worked virtually seven days a week right up to election day. The objective was to answer all these questionnaires and individual requests for information. Given the resources available, this was a huge task, but we estimate that around 99 percent were answered by the time of the election. The most notable aspect of this election, compared with previous ones, was the dramatic increase in email traffic. During the three days after the Holmes 'worm' debate, the United office received over 1,000 email messages. Added to the deluge of all the other requests and messages, this placed the office under some considerable strain.

In the weeks leading up to nomination day, the board worked swiftly to fill the positions for electorate candidates. Initially, the board had thought that somewhere between 40 and 50 candidates would be an exceptional result for its efforts. As it turned out, the request for candidates was enthusiastically received by the eligible members, and the party ended up with 63 electorate candidates, 61 of whom also stood for the party list.

The critical difference from previous elections that became apparent during the campaign was the result of our efforts earlier on to establish strong, functional regional organisations. An itinerary for the leader was planned at the start of the campaign, but we now had more requests for visits to areas outside Wellington than Peter Dunne could physically attend.

The regions were able to organise events and media coverage for visits from the leader and, during the last two weeks of the campaign, from the party's deputy leader, Anthony Walton. Walton had been out of the country for all but the last two weeks of July, fulfilling prior commitments, and he had decided not to stand for Parliament because of the lack of time he could devote to the campaign.

Peter Dunne was insistent that the national campaign plan must allow time for him to run his usual effective local campaign in his home electorate of Ohariu-Belmont. Compared with previous elections, however, there were only a handful of 'Meet The Candidate' meetings organised this year. The party had previously commissioned UMR-Insight to run a local electorate poll, whose results were released by the party in May. This poll and a further one taken by the same pollsters during the campaign showed that, even with a National candidate standing for the first time since 1993, support for Peter had remained constant at 55 percent. The election night result confirmed this, with Peter taking almost 58 percent of the electorate vote. Labour's candidate received 20 percent and National's a mere 13 percent. One interesting aspect of the results was that Labour won the party vote with 37 percent, with National receiving only 24 percent. Significantly, this electorate is, according to the last official census, the wealthiest electorate in the country.

Aside from the usual hoardings and direct mail brochures, we also placed a large outdoor hoarding at the bottom of Ngauranga Gorge, the main route north out of Wellington, and the entrance to a large part of the electorate. It was a simple, easily understood message: a photo of Peter, the party logo, and a two-word slogan: 'Common Sense'. The campaign continued at a hectic pace. One thousand hoardings were designed, manufactured and distributed across the country; the brochure went into several reprints to keep up with demand; and rosettes and bumper stickers were produced and distributed as the demand for information from the parliamentary office kept increasing.

The Electoral Commission had determined the share of the broadcasting advertising we were being allocated to be $75,000. The scripting and filming of the television commercial and the opening and closing addresses proceeded, with the leader's diary subject to rapid change as television production facilities became available. The production for all the television and radio products was carried out in the studios of a local regional television station, Wellington TV. It was decided that all the television products would follow a common theme and style. Internally, they became known as the 'no bullshit' approach. They were shot on a plain white background, Peter talked direct to the camera, and there was a minimum of on-screen copy, although a logo was on screen continually. Three one-minute advertisements were shot, all with a common 40-second 'outro' and with three different 20-second 'intros'. With $15,000 spent for three weeks of intensive advertising on the three-station Radio Rhema network, aimed specifically at the Future New Zealand Christian constituency, and a further $5,000 each for local television in Wellington and Christchurch, there was only $50,000 left for free-to-air national television.

In previous years, United had used 15-second advertisements, but it was felt that these were too easily 'lost' in the clutter of all the other advertising in any particular time slot. The decision to make 60-second advertisements was a gamble, but it appeared to pay off. Twenty slots were booked for the last week of the campaign, with a fair percentage being for peak-time viewing. Feedback from these advertisements showed they had achieved at least critical acclaim. Given the limited resources of Wellington TV, production values weren't as high as we would have preferred, but the end result was overwhelmingly better than expected.

The other major television event was, of course, the notable Holmes 'worm' debate. The first television leaders' debate was actually a Bill Ralston-hosted show on SkyTV on 2 July. This debate went almost completely unnoticed by the rest of the media, although the team felt that Peter had done very well in it. On the evening of 15 July, a small group of supporters gathered at Avalon studios in Lower Hutt, outside Wellington, to participate as part of the audience for what was to be the first of three televised debates with party leaders to be shown that week. Peter had arrived before most of the support crew and was ensconced in a spartan changing room at the end of a long corridor in the bowels of the building. A small entourage consisting of Peter's wife Jennifer, his younger son Alistair, myself and my wife was ushered down to this room. The five of us stood around or squatted on the hard vinyl-covered benches for over an hour and talked about anything other than the impending debate. The mood was remarkably light, the only mild anxiety being the lateness of the call to go into the studio. Watching the debate on the in-house television screen from the much more palatial 'Green Room' that had been used by National's leader was an interesting experience. The National people sat quietly, looking rather glum; the Alliance personnel chatted throughout; and the ACT group held furtive conversations that prompted much activity during the ad breaks, while they ran up and down the corridor seeking cell phone coverage. By the end of the debate, it was clear that Peter had done well. His debating skills were obvious, and the messages he projected, although not noticeably different from any he had delivered during the previous two election campaigns, were enthusiastically enough received to have several of the other leaders, including the prime minister, agreeing with him.

Later that evening, when the analysis of the 'worm' was discussed on the follow-up programme, it was clear that our initial thoughts on Peter's performance were confirmed. This began the most extraordinary fortnight of the entire campaign. Massive media coverage of Peter's taming of the 'worm' had him experiencing rock star-like status. Everywhere he went he was recognised as a leader of a party that was going places, one that stood a serious chance of success at the election. United candidates were overjoyed that campaigning had become so much easier, literally overnight. Polling announced on the night of the debate from TV3-NFO had the party registering at 1.6 percent – enough to return two Members to Parliament, and well on the way for a third. A further one-on-one debate with Kim Hill on the Thursday night of the same week also went very well. After savaging Winston Peters and giving Richard Prebble a particularly hard time, Hill virtually purred through the 20-minute interview with Peter Dunne. The last of the debates was another live panel debate, with all the party leaders except Clark and English. It was interesting to note the change in the rhetoric of the other party leaders, as they all scrambled to include frequent positive messages on the importance of the family in their presentations. Holmes seemed somewhat distracted throughout most of the show, and it lacked the direction and spark of Monday's event. It still went well for Peter, and the team then spent the weekend speculating on the possible outcome of the *Herald* poll due out the following Monday. On Sunday night, Peter was rung by a *Herald* reporter asking for his reaction to their next day's announcement of a poll for United Future showing us with 6.6 percent support. A rather rhetorical question really!

The week had concluded with the news that the party website had recorded 85,000 'hits' from Tuesday to Friday. We had made only one direct public comment on the 'worm' debate during the week, and that was a press release suggesting the media should allow wider debate to balance their new obligations in election campaign coverage. This seemed to prompt a furious response from Christian Heritage Leader Graham Capill, who burst into print with accusations of media bias against him and his party. Capill also tried to mount a smear campaign against Peter personally, based on his somewhat incorrect assessment of Peter's previous voting record. Our response to this attack, long expected by us, was generally to ignore Capill, and neither to debate nor defend the accusations in public, but to answer individual queries directly.

The last week of the campaign went by in something of a blur. The website was hurriedly upgraded to include the biographies of the top 20 candidates on the list, and media attention continued unabated, while the polling on the Thursday before the election on both TVNZ and TV3 put party support at 4 percent.

It is difficult to pinpoint exactly what we did that was so right for this election. Peter Dunne and his public presence were obviously the key factors in the party's success. His message was simple and timely, but not greatly different from the message he had delivered in previous elections. Obviously, his participation in the widely publicised Holmes debates allowed him to spread his message to more voters than ever before.

The significant factor in the whole campaign was probably best summed up by our advertising guru, Dave Collinge, when early on in the year he had emphasised that political campaigns are unlike any other type of advertising campaign. No one has to spend any money expressing their preference when it comes to voting, no one is at all certain of any outcome when they vote, and there is no obvious immediate satisfaction of needs when people vote. Collinge's frequent refrain was that, 'We should just treat the voters as real people with real concerns and speak directly and plainly to them'. Perhaps that was what Peter Dunne did. For United Future New Zealand, those concerns are all about the family.

THE CANDIDATES

12

ENTERTAINMENT VS EDUCATION: CAMPAIGNING UNDER MMP

Stephen Franks

Being a candidate in Wellington Central was enormous fun. I hadn't expected that at all. In fact when I was first asked (and initially declined) to be a candidate about nine months before the 1999 election, the campaigning seemed to be the least desirable part of a rather unattractive package. I saw it as something that just had to be done to get to do something more interesting – namely, to represent a business/classical liberal constituency in Parliament. But certainly this time the campaign was fascinating.

I met interesting people all over the country. They were decent, concerned people. The people who come to ACT political meetings are not a normal sample of the population. Many are self-starters, people who feel successful and are impatient about failure in politicians, in government and in individuals. People who come along to political meetings generally, instead of watching sport or the soaps on television, are probably not normal. Certainly I found interesting questioners at all election meetings, including Wellington meetings for all candidates. They seem more serious, more substantial, and much better informed than their neighbours. They are interested in where the country is going. So they want to talk about serious topics. At election meetings they can be serious without feeling that they will be seen as 'nerdy' or weird. And they're also very concerned. A lot of them come along, even if they are not the party faithful, because they are anxious about the future of the country. They're worried about the issues I'm worried about.

Volunteers

I also found campaigning humbling. People put in hard work for no pay on tasks they would normally have to be well paid to do. They did this despite reservations, not necessarily 'believing' in all that I or my party stood for.

Most were realistic about the inevitability of compromise for their pet causes. Those who are not realistic tend to criticise, but don't do the work. So campaigning can be an uplifting experience, because you are mixing with makers and doers more than with takers and whingers, even though the latter are present in force at meetings.

Fundraising

Fundraising is the hardest part of campaigning. You know that in hindsight some resources will be seen to have been misdirected. Mistakes are inevitable, but you have to encourage people to help get the message out nevertheless. You know it is vital. And it is important to have to raise money. You have to justify your efforts to the contributors. Once people have contributed, they feel more entitled to be blunt with you. They feel they can make suggestions and complaints with less apology.

The domination of television

This election was a little different for me. Last time I was a relatively unknown candidate except in law and business circles. Accordingly, there was no reason for television to pay any attention to me. I have had to come to terms with the fact that television is far more powerful than anything else. Two and a half years experience as an MP shows me that carefully written articles and fully reasoned argument are all immaterial compared to fifteen seconds on television. I am very aware that even my family rarely have a clue what I've said on television, or what the issue was, but they know whether they liked me or didn't like me afterwards. They know whether they thought that I won – came off well or not. So television is where it's at.

I found television's importance disturbing. Most evenings I had meetings or was travelling, so I rarely saw it, but voters constantly talked about what they had seen. When I did catch it, there were parts of debates or interviews that I could scarcely bear to watch. It was so superficial. After participating in the debate on law and order, which Mike Hosking compered, I received a lot of adverse comment. People don't come up to the candidate and say 'you're a wanker', but in this case they came up and said things like 'it was ugly', 'you weren't as bad as [X] but I didn't watch all through' or 'that was a pretty horrible session' or 'I didn't learn anything out of it though you were much better than [Y]'. And I think that was unnecessary.

Mike Hosking did a session of about the same length of time on the Treaty of Waitangi two years ago. He chaired it very well. He made sure that people addressed the issues and cut them off when they were just going on. He gave everyone a chance to get their viewpoint out, with penetrating questions. In the countdown to that television law and order debate, someone said, 'How will you be running this? Will you set the times, will you lead into the next issue?' Hosking said, 'Oh, no, we want a bit of vigour in this. You'll have to come in over the top of each other. If you want to get heard, you're going to have to make yourself heard.' The unedifying result was absolutely predictable. I think all of us there then could predict exactly what was going to happen, and it happened. I compare that kind of slogan shouting with what I think can be done with political debate. The US presidential debates can be a model, but we don't need to look far for higher standards. As noted, the Waitangi Day debate two years earlier was a good exploration of the issues. I hope that television looks at the way it came out of this election and runs the coverage of the next election very differently. It could reduce the dopey beauty parade character of it.

As a candidate you miss a lot. I didn't see many of the televised debates. Because I was out at meetings all the time, I never saw my own party's television advertising, other than the campaign opening. So I don't know what it was like. Perhaps a real aficionado would have had someone video it. But the comments that came back showed how vital those scheduled debates and presentations were. If you are wooden or you are not a good competitor in the beauty parade, I think it is always going to be hard. My guess is that all the parties will have taken the lesson from this campaign that they are going to need spokespeople who can seem more appealing. This could drive a rush for candidates who are more bimbo-ish or ditsy or whatever is a better word for telegenic. Many will be told to 'retrain', to learn to appear more pleasant and attractive.

Policies vs personality

As a party, of course, ACT spends a lot of time on policies and issues. Our members tend to be dismissive of anything else as style over substance. But the election was not about policy, at least as far as I could judge from the kinds of questions and comments I received, such as, 'I can't stand [X] but [Y] seems nice, fair, tough, on top of things etc.'

Perhaps it's a little unfair to feel the resentment I did about the absence of focus on policy. Perhaps policy really wasn't relevant to the decision that people were making, once it was clear that Labour was going to win again. That was clear to me from the moment I saw the *National Business Review* poll several months before the election. It was a poll of satisfaction with your job, your boss, your suburb or town, and your income. There were very high levels of satisfaction – around or over 90 percent on many measures. With that level of satisfaction, I didn't think there was much chance of a change of government. Once that is decided, ideological issues or debate are not really very important to the election outcome or to most people. People can feel free to vote on whims, because they won't change the overall outcome.

Politics as entertainment

Television chose to cover the election as a presidential campaign and as entertainment. It was very irksome. I had put at least a year and a half into getting what I believe was a defensible crime and justice policy. We had the political high ground on those issues, but I wanted to earn and claim the moral high ground. I knew I had the research on our side. Instead, television focused on the politics of the crime and justice debate, not on any policy merits – as if it were simply a struggle between left and right, or harsh and gentle.

Labelling in the political spectrum

With seven parties in Parliament now, maybe we will see some increasing sophistication. It is wearying, and a depressing indication of low quality in New Zealanders' education and knowledge of the world, and of history, to be always tagged at candidates' meetings as the 'extreme right'. That was a 'fair game' strategy for our opponents, but for journalists to keep using it is just ignorant. Most of what I was saying on crime and justice is what British Prime Minister Tony Blair has been saying. If you go to Blair's website, you will find much tougher things on education and crime than anything ACT has said. To be tagged as extreme right wing when we can place most of our policies in the centre of the Republican Party and in a number of non-extreme European parties is very irksome. It is something I guess that we have to live down. What we believe is that we are a flexible liberal party.

There is no other competition in this country for the label 'classical liberal'. Our policies – privatisation, welfare reform, tax reform – are mainstream. Colour blind law was once mandatory and it is still mainstream. I hope that next time – at the next election – our candidates will be placed in a spectrum which better reflects the spectrum of politics that most of the world sees. Unlike Labour in Australia and Britain, and the Democrats in the US, the New Zealand Labour Party shed its right wing to ACT. In those overseas countries, the 'right of the left' took control. New Zealand has cut that spectrum in half. Here the remnant left camp masquerades as 'centrist'. Poorly informed commentators describe people in that remaining left side as though they are most of the normal spectrum. A more intelligent debate would use more accurate and precise language. I hope that we will get that more intelligent, more informed debate at New Zealand's next general election campaign.

13

BEING A GREEN CANDIDATE

Nandor Tanczos

I have to say that I enjoyed this election campaign. One of the very early decisions we had to make was whether to run a 'two tick' campaign in Auckland Central, or just go for the list vote. The Green Party nationally had an important strategic decision to make about where to run 'two tick' campaigns.

We decided not to run a 'two tick' campaign in Auckland Central for a number of reasons. First of all, of course, it would have meant taking on Judith Tizard, the sitting Labour MP, and there were questions about what that would mean for our relationship with the Labour Party. Another point was that you have to be clear when going for an electorate seat that you actually want the job. After going to Coromandel and seeing how hard Jeanette Fitzsimons had to work in the electorate on minor local issues, and the way that took her away from core Green concerns at a national level, I wasn't sure that I did. There was also the rumour that the Alliance's Matt McCarten would run for Auckland Central as well. We thought that it would be interesting to sit back and watch the scrap take place, but that was not to be. I was a bit disappointed about that.

So in the end we decided not to run a 'two tick' campaign in Auckland Central. Perhaps the main consideration was the recognition that my own constituency is really not a geographical one. I see my constituency very much as young people, and those people who have been alienated from the political system. So a lot of my campaigning was done not in Auckland Central but all over the country. I travelled to the south, north, east, west, and in the middle, and campaigned hard all over the place. I did spend the final week of the campaign in the electorate, and bits of time during the campaign, but a lot of the time was spent on the road. How to best use that time was the crucial question. I remember when I was in Wanaka, learning to snowboard, I really had to think whether that was productive in terms of the campaign. By that time we had already made the six o'clock news, and I figured that being seen on the slopes would pick up more votes than hassling people in cafés with Green Party leaflets.

I think that my favourite part of the campaign was going around the East Cape. We drove from Wairoa round to Whakatane and visited a number of small communities along the way. The comments that other candidates have made about the amazing people you meet along the way are absolutely true. Campaigning took me to a part of New Zealand that I do not get to see very often, and that many decision-makers never get to see at all. This is important if we are going to try to understand what the real issues are for those people – people who are really struggling, and who live in a kind of poverty that most of us have no idea about. The election was a chance for me to see what is going on and actually to meet some of the amazing people in Aotearoa – to go up to the occupation at Te Kuri o Paoa (Young Nick's Head), for example, and meet the people there who were putting themselves on the line for something they really believe strongly about.

We had a public meeting in Waimana which was amazing. I was told that it was the biggest political meeting that they had ever had in Waimana – there were about 80 people and they were all bush people, which was pretty amazing by itself. This was quite different from the usual party political meeting, but once again it was really awesome to have the opportunity to engage with them in political discussion. These are people who think very deeply about the issues facing them and their communities. At the heart of it is their demand for constitutional change and the recognition of their tino rangatiratanga as affirmed in Te Tiriti o Waitangi.

One of the things that I am always very careful about is what I actually say when asking people to vote for the Green Party, or to vote for any party, or to get involved in elections. One thing I am very clear about is that the answer to people's problems isn't in voting for the next government. Solutions to people's problems will come from the community. Of course we all know that, but it is important to not be trying to con people, to throw them a line which says 'vote for me and I'll solve your problems'. We have a duty to explain to people about how the political system works. There is an incredible amount of ignorance about how politics works in our country. Most people have no idea how a law gets made. So just giving people basic information about how the system works is a responsibility that I think MPs have. People are quite capable of understanding it if they are given information in language that they are familiar with. I think that is a big part of campaigning.

As I have said, I was targeting the young and the alienated. The Green Party used a number of different media to do that. Our CD, for example, was launched just before the election was announced. We were looking to find ways of breaking down the barriers between 'politics' and real life, because there are a lot of people, particularly young people, who do not relate to any kind of politics at all. Politics means old white guys in suits to them. So we were trying to say that politics is really about what happens – everything you do in your life is political, and politics affects you every day of your life. The CD was about that – that was the central message. People liked it – in fact the first 1,000 copies we burned sold out, and we had to burn another load. It ended up as the number two best-selling record in a couple of record shop chains.

The CD did not have 'Vote Green' in big letters on the front of it. We had Green Party logos in place, but they were subtle. People are used to reading subtle messages, particularly the audience we were aiming at with the CD. We also had the 'Get on the Roll' poster, which again was very much about encouraging young people to enrol, because of the massive lack of enrolments in the young population. One of the biggest challenges for the Greens is getting those people who do support our policies to get enrolled and to vote. But there is also a greater purpose. More participation is a good thing in itself.

The other major tool was the 'Everything You Do is Political' poster. This followed on from the campaign we ran in Auckland Central in 1999, which had featured a poster in the last couple of weeks with a kind of stencillated picture of me and the caption 'Put the Dread in the House'. Someone suggested that this time we go with 'Put the Dread in the House Again'. Well, been there, done that, we thought, so we ended up taking the new caption from my spoken word track on the CD. I think the poster worked pretty well, although one of the criticisms – and I put the blame on myself – was that we didn't have 'party vote' in large enough lettering. Once the posters were up, I realised that when you drove by, you couldn't read 'party vote' clearly enough.

I have to agree with Stephen Franks' points about the 'law and order' television debate run by Mike Hosking. It was truly shocking. It was a deliberate set-up in fact, because it was an essentially unfacilitated debate where the one who shouted the loudest got heard. Actually, before we went on, what we should have done was to get together and say let's take over the programme and run it our way. Although with Winston Peters, Phil Goff,

Matt Robson, Stephen Franks and myself there, it might have been hard to come up with an agreement.

There are two things about that programme that really do concern me. One is that when a debate is set up on that basis, you don't have a chance to challenge the assumptions that underlie the questions. Unless you are just dealing with sloganeering, you need to have an opportunity to do that to make sense. So having the opportunity for the spokespeople to say their piece, even for just a few minutes, is vital for any kind of real discussion. The other thing is that there's a public perception that politicians act like kindergarten children. While for many of us that is often true, I don't think that it's true of all of us and it's not true of us all of the time. So what you do by setting up a debate in that fashion is to reinforce the image that politicians don't know how to behave civilly. The fact was that in that debate, you either shouted over everyone else or you didn't get heard. And if you don't get heard, you get criticised for not taking part in the debate. In my opinion it is detrimental to our parliamentary system for the media to deliberately organise forums to generate that perception. That's not saying that we shouldn't be shown when MPs behave childishly, but I don't think the media should deliberately generate a wrong impression by the way it sets the format.

While on the media, I have to say that I was intensely frustrated over the media coverage of the launch of our justice policy at the proposed Ngawha prison site. We had television cameras up there, they took lots of footage, we had a really good interview, and it was a good launch, with lots of local people turning out to support our call for a ban on prison building. It was quite an awesome event. Right at the end of the interview, the journalist said to me, as an aside, 'by the way, England has just re-classified cannabis, what do you think of that?' 'Well, it's part of an international wave of cannabis law reform; it's bound to happen', I replied. Of course, that was the only comment that was used. So the coverage showed all these people holding signs up saying 'no more prisons', 'Hands off Ngawha' and the like, and me talking about cannabis. It looked bizarre but, more seriously, it was totally misrepresenting.

I do think that the cannabis issue was an important one for us. I think that the Green Party made a major mistake in terms of our cannabis policy, because we didn't go out and explain to people what it actually is. As a result, we saw United telling blatant lies about the policy without challenge. For example, United said that our policy is not family friendly. Of course, I would say that anyone who supports prohibition, supports the murder that results from it, supports cannabis being sold in our high schools, supports increasing cannabis abuse in our population and all those things resulting from prohibition has no right to be talking about family friendly. So I think we made a mistake in not getting out and explaining clearly what our policy is and why we need cannabis law reform, if we are going to solve some of the problems that we face with drug abuse in Aotearoa today.

The last thing I will say is that I was quite astounded by the good result we had in Auckland Central, given how little time I actually spent there. I think that we had strong visibility in Auckland Central because of the fantastic team of people that did the hard work in the electorate. I have to acknowledge the awesome work done by the local branch, which worked independently and freed me up as a candidate to travel around the country, while they continued to do the letterboxing, stalls and all those kinds of things. We had a really good result in Auckland Central: we came second for party votes, and we beat National, which was quite an achievement; and there was quite a good result for me in the electorate as well.[1] It will be interesting to see where we go in the future.

14

A RED JACKET IN RANGITIKEI

Margaret Hayward

The Rangitikei electorate is unique and I came to love it. It is one of the largest electorates, extending from the northern suburbs of Palmerston North up beyond Waiouru, so there was a lot of ground to cover in a short time. It's diverse: there are the suburban areas of Palmerston North, then small towns like Marton, Hunterville and Taihape, and the Defence Department clusters of airforce families at Ohakea and army families at Waiouru. Rangitikei was held for three elections, from 1978, by the Social Credit leader Bruce Beetham, who was something of a hero in Marton, where he had lived in a large house called Linden Hall. But traditionally, National has won the Rangitikei electorate with about a 6,000-vote majority. In 1999, however, it was won by the National candidate, Simon Power, with only a 300-vote majority. His vote was low, partly because he was an unknown National candidate, and the Labour Party had a strong young male candidate standing against him. In addition, the previous National MP had been particularly unpopular, so those circumstances made the electorate seem almost marginal.

I soon realised that it wasn't marginal, however, because when Labour called for nominations for the 2002 election, no one came forward. This caused some concern. Rangitikei couldn't be the only electorate without a Labour candidate, so I was asked if I would allow my name to go forward. Alex Stewart, the Labour Regional Council chairman, was both encouraging and persuasive. I was living at Te Horo in the neighbouring Otaki electorate, and as I had always wanted to find out what it was like to be a candidate, I said, 'Yes, but what about my age?' That was taken on board and the deadline for nominations was extended to try to get someone younger. No one volunteered. I was 61, and one of the first things I was asked by the *Rangitikei Herald* was my age. I said I didn't think it was relevant – a person's experience and ability were more relevant. The editor said that might be so, but they needed to know my age. It was a matter of public interest and their policy. And thereafter I was the only candidate for whom they kept putting the age. Every time it would be 'Margaret Hayward comma 61 comma'. The only good thing about it was that I turned 62 during the campaign and I never told them. . . .

By the time of the election, Simon Power was already ranked thirteenth in Parliament by the National Party, and so had done fairly well in only two and a half years. He had a very likable personality and people were drawn to him. He had built up quite an efficient organisation and had employed a top public relations executive for the campaign. He also had three attractive offices throughout the electorate: one in Palmerston North, one in Marton, and one in Feilding in the Square beside the town's information centre, which was later a polling booth – a wonderful site. And he also had a horsefloat with two large hoardings pasted to it, which his organisation moved strategically around Feilding. My office was my little Daihatsu Charade.

I chose to live in Marton because I liked the town, and also because the local Labour Party consisted of two branches, one in the northern suburbs of Palmerston North and one in Feilding, so there was no Labour presence in Marton. My strategy was simple and two-pronged. I moved to Marton in April and decided that I had to get to know people in the outlying towns first. Then, nearer the election, which I had thought would be about October, I would spend most of my time in the areas with the larger populations: Feilding and the three suburbs north of the railway line at Palmerston North. The second part of the strategy was to emphasise that Rangitikei needed an MP who was going to be in government and could effectively promote regional development for Rangitikei. Simon Power was going to get in on the National Party list anyway, and so I wanted to emphasise that this was Rangitikei's opportunity to have two MPs representing them in Parliament, one in opposition and one in government.

In May I had great fun going around the beach areas, Tangimoana and Himatangi, and the gumboot capital, Taihape. I enjoy meeting people and I knocked on doors to discover what was concerning people – mainly local issues, such as the council cutting down trees without public consultation, high rates, and culverts that flooded, rather than government policies. I also seemed to have the fortuitous knack of knocking on the doors of people who wrote community newsletters and thus were able to contribute political news.

There were other issues in Rangitikei – the lack of jobs and, of course, the grounding of the Skyhawks at nearby Ohakea. In response I enumerated the extra millions spent by the government in modernising the defence force, and I pushed the government's policy of strong regional development and job growth. The announcement by Mark Burton, as Minister of Defence, that the Ohakea runway was to be upgraded to the same level as Auckland airport, so it could also be used as a cargo hub by civilian planes, was timely. But locals were sceptical.

The few active Labour Party members were marvellous. Former Labour MP Jill White gave advice based on her experiences in three election campaigns. The campaign manager, Renetta Dennis, a retired school principal who volunteered when there seemed to be no one else, was awe-inspiring, both with the work she motored through and with her infectious good humour. She had been campaign manager when Jill White won the Manawatu seat in 1993, and she expertly managed everything, from writing two-minute radio scripts to gamely digging holes for electoral hoardings while up to her knees in mud. Most of the Labour Party members in the Rangitikei were over 70 and they were willing workers, but a campaign in July when it rained every day was not the ideal time to ask them to be out putting pamphlets in letterboxes. They did do it and I thought they were absolutely courageous.

I had arrived in the Rangitikei electorate thinking we could have a campaign committee where each person convened a small team of helpers to look after one aspect of the campaign. But given that there were few and that most were elderly, this was not possible. Even the youngest member – who was a journalist working for a radio station, and who we had hoped would be our publicity convener – was unable to help. Her employers objected to her being a member of the Labour Party during an election campaign, and she had to resign.

With the shortened campaign, there was very little time for fundraising. We did have a large attendance at the fundraising dinner to launch the campaign, thanks mainly to the local National Party's interest in hearing the reminiscences of the guest speaker, Wairarapa MP Georgina Beyer, and some loyal Wellington friends. However, I was extremely fortunate in being in an electorate that had funds already available, because of some wise investments made many years ago by the Feilding Branch. The treasurer Bruce Wilson, Renetta and I worked out a budget, we paced our spending and we came out on target. As a new candidate, I was surprised to learn that the electorate had to buy the huge posters for hoardings and pamphlets from the Labour Party's Head Office, even some that were fairly generic, such as the mock ballot paper. But they did supply, free, the posters for hoardings featuring Helen Clark and the party's policy pamphlet. Advertising on radio and in the local newspapers proved very expensive, but was vital because of the shorter election campaign.

This brings me to the candidate's day. I got up at 6 am and finished about 2 am. In the evening, when I returned to the apartment after a busy day, there were usually small articles to write – for newspapers such as the Marton *District Monitor* or the Tangimoana *Coastal Capers* – and nearly a hundred emails to answer. I had a rule that at 2 am I refused to open another email and went to bed.

One of the things I did throughout the campaign was to wear a red jacket – which is now looking a bit shabby – because I was from outside the Rangitikei electorate. Nobody knew me and I thought it might give some subliminal message. People might realise that anyone wearing bright red probably had something to do with the Labour Party.

Being a rural candidate offered many new experiences. I was invited to visit piggeries, helped feed 5,000 happy free-range organically raised hens (which almost got me over my bird phobia), and spent hours at stockyards. Being a candidate meant having your face staring down at you from hoardings, a genuinely surreal experience. But one hoarding cheekily on the gate of Linden Hall, Bruce Beetham's former home, gave even local journalists a chuckle. Other memories are of retiring Labour MP Judy Keall, just before her horrendous car accident, showing me how to introduce myself to people in supermarket carparks. I had to choose the moment they raised the boot of their car to stow their groceries and timidly (Judy said it should be more assertively) offer them my pamphlet and introduce myself. With the more direct Judy we were never asked to leave, but the three times that Renetta and I, very nicely we thought, approached people, we were ordered off by management. Nor could I imagine myself part of a small cavalcade, trawling suburban streets in a Range Rover decked with balloons, signs and a loud-hailer, proclaiming over and over again: 'Hello. This is your Labour candidate Margaret Hayward. Remember: vote Labour, vote Hayward, this Saturday.'

If I stood again, I would probably live in the biggest centre of population and I would try to put together a more measured media campaign. Some of the media did produce wonderful articles, better than I could write for myself. In one interview, where I boldly stated that if people wanted a say in government they should vote for me, the journalist wrote, 'and she said that without any malice at all towards the six other candidates'. Quite right. At our joint meetings the candidates all got on well. In fact I felt we were all trying to 'out-nice' each other. It's very hard to attack people who are being very nice to you. So it was a bland campaign, and although working hard and long hours, I felt I was 'sleepwalking to defeat'.

I put as much into the campaign as I possibly could and I made some wonderful new friends along the way: adventurous, determined elderly folk and a few enthusiastic, helpful young ones who came from Palmerston North, Wellington, Upper Hutt and even Hamilton to help in the last days. Although Simon Power won the electorate vote, it was extremely rewarding to see that in what had been a blue-ribbon National seat, Labour won the party vote for the first time – and by almost 2,500 votes.

15

'OUT OF MY COMFORT ZONE': CAMPAIGNING IN WELLINGTON CENTRAL

Hekia Parata

Participating in this election campaign has been the most exciting, positive experience I've had in a while. I thoroughly enjoyed myself. Clearly the icing would have been on the cake if I had won. I was interested in Margaret Hayward's saying that the candidates in her electorate were almost competing with each other to be nice. Ours were not quite like that, but I think we were all very respectful of each others' particular view and so it was enjoyable for me. Deciding to stand for Wellington Central created a number of challenges, because there were a whole range of uncertainties that came together, a bit like the tectonic plates that are currently sitting under the Pacific Ocean.

First of all, I was new to party politics. Second, National had not had a candidate in Wellington Central at the last election. In 1996 we had had one, but he'd been hobbled,[1] and so there was not a lot of electorate infrastructure to be working with in Wellington Central. And the third thing was that although I had lived and worked in Wellington for 20 years, it was never in the context of it being an electorate. The Wellington I knew was 'the public service' or 'the business area' I had worked in, or 'netball' with my children. I hadn't ever perceived it as an electorate. So all these things were new to me. I also went into it on the basis that the election was probably going to be in October. I was selected the week before Christmas in December 2001, so it was hard to know what was going to happen in less than seven months. It was a very intense period. But I had originally anticipated, as I think many New Zealanders had, that it was going to be in October. In the event, there were only six weeks to campaign from the time the prime minister announced the election date, and I had started campaigning only four weeks before that. So the whole campaign was only ten weeks.

I found all through the campaign that I was bumping up against rules, protocols and practices, things that everyone just knew about, except for me. One of the things about the election date being earlier rather later was that there was a $20,000 limit on how much you could spend in a campaign, and that forced us into being self-auditors all the time. Anyone who knows me knows that I have a penchant for spending. I love it. And so my attitude was, 'if that's what we need, let's just get it', and I had to be constrained from doing those things. One of the big challenges for me was getting my profile known, because of course no one is going to vote for someone they don't know – someone who has a particularly awkward name – and so in my case, I had to get over the awkwardness of my name. I didn't want to go through a whole election campaign with people mispronouncing my name – being constantly called 'Haki' or 'Hekaya' – because that is really diminishing. Coming up with the notion of 'who the heck is Hekia' was helpful on two levels. It helped people to pronounce my name, Hekia, but it also helped people to think that I was a fun sort of person, which I have occasionally been known to be. I had to get my profile up, because while I knew a lot of people who knew me, they didn't constitute 40,000 eager voters, and so I had to get people to know me. And that was one of the things that was always an irony in the way the media covered me, because they would always profile me with the words, 'the high profile candidate Hekia Parata'. But high to whom? Was it the voters who were in Wellington Central? And this is another funny thing: everybody I knew, either on a personal, friendship basis, or as relations or people I worked with, didn't live in Wellington Central. Can you believe it? They all lived in Khandallah, or Johnsonville, or over in Seatoun Heights or whatever. And they didn't have enough time to move, which shattered their undying commitment to our relationship. So getting my profile known was my big challenge.

I was very well treated by the media in all forms – the print media, radio and television. I received coverage mostly by accident rather than design. One of the lessons I learned early on was how difficult it was to get the media to cover you. I was getting a very favourable response from people on The Terrace and up Lambton Quay and I thought 'that's all very well, but how will everyone else know that I was the first out there?' So I rang up *The Evening Post* and *The Dominion* – of course they've merged now – and said, 'I'm out here, come and take a photo'. That's the other thing you have to get used to: just transparently begging people to give you coverage, and that's not something that I was used to. And they came down and took a photograph and when they didn't show it that night, I rang up like an intolerant client and said, 'You came and took a photograph and it's not in this evening's edition.' And the guy said, 'Well that's a decision the editor makes, not you.' 'Oh, well, is he there?' And then the next day there was one of [Wellington Central Labour candidate] Marian Hobbs holding out a puny little sign somewhere I couldn't recognise, and one of me graciously handing out pamphlets in Woodward Street!

I happened to be in conversation with a reporter a bit later and I said, 'How come you were able to put it in once Marian was out there?' 'Oh well, balance, you've got to have balance in the campaign.' So I said, 'What's the definition of balance? I'd like to know so that I can observe it all the way through.' 'Well, you know, it's one of these things that waxes and wanes, so you try to give equivalent coverage to everyone.' 'So, in effect, you'll be punishing me for initiative.' 'How does that work?' 'Every time I have a great idea, and I'll be thinking of great ideas all the time, I've got to wait until Marian copies me before I can get coverage.' And she said, 'Well, when you put it that way, it doesn't sound very fair.' I said, 'Is there another way to put it?' 'Well, this is just the way we do it.'

Anyway, I learned that you needed to try to work with the media in order to get the media to work with you. This didn't mean to say that I approved of the things they did all the time. For instance, I learned that if there were cameras around, you can't be caught looking bored even when you don't think they are pointing at you. This results in you having a grimace, which I got caught with a couple of times.

Raising my profile meant going from the 'micro' to the 'macro'. It meant rebuilding our electorate infrastructure here. We had a three-way race in Wellington Central. While my selection had been a popular choice, I was still a new member of the party, as I had only joined the National Party in August 2001, so I had to spend time ensuring that the traditional parts of the party felt comfortable with me. I was committed to doing that because the party, like any organisation, has a culture of its own, and one of my strong views is that if I want people to come to know the Ngati Porou culture, then the respectful thing for me to do is to understand the thoughts and practices of other people, so that was one of the things I set about doing. But it did mean I learned not to be as argumentative, I suppose.

I was disappointed at the superficiality and low level of debate at candidate meetings. I expected to be challenged intellectually more, ideologically and philosophically or on principles. I expected to have substantial debate about the direction of New Zealand, about our future as a nation, about what the distinct philosophical differences were between the parties putting themselves up before the voters. I expected my competence to be adjudged by people who might want me as a representative. But hardly any of the candidates' debates were interested in any of those kinds of things. I came to realise that it was just like student politics, which I had a skirmish with back in 1980, when I ran for President of the University of Waikato student union (and where, as an aside, the McGillicuddy Serious Party got started). One of the things I experienced there that also occurred a little in this election was that there were really two types of campaigns going on. One was the overt public campaign, and the other was a kind of subterranean subtext. At Waikato it had been much more transparent: 'Don't vote for her, she's Maori, she'll bring black power onto the campus.' In Wellington Central I discovered the subtext going around was: 'she's really a closet Maori independence sovereignty person. Don't vote for her because she'll have two police systems, two justice systems', and so on. We can hardly afford one. Why would we have two? And so I learned to start setting people up to ask me those questions, so I could give those types of answers. People would then have no excuse for continuing on with those sorts of ideas that weren't true.

I loved it. I loved the human contact stuff. I loved being able to quickly write letters. I hated that none of my letters to the editors ever got published. I hated that and I wondered why, so I handed them out to two people who were my closest friends and they said they were too complicated. You've got to read the letters to the editors and you'll see that they are simple and they take a position. In mine, I was composing them like a summary policy paper. That's my background: definitions, the issues, the rights and wrongs, why and so on. The letters were always too long, too complicated, and as a result they never got published.

We got together a really good group of volunteers. I'm really proud of the campaign we ran. I campaigned to win, obviously. There were things that I found quite hurtful. You have to grow a thick skin, because you get gratuitous remarks made by people about you – people you don't even know who say things about you, and you think, 'Have I met that person? No. Well, don't be naïve. You're now in the public arena and they can say things about you whether they are true or not.' And so I learned to grow a bit of a thick skin.

It was an intense campaign. We raised the money that we needed. We got very close to what would have been the limit if we had had an audit carried out, but we knew every cent. It was ridiculous. We knew how many A4 black and white leaflets, cut into three, had been handed out, at what location and at what time, so that we would have all the trails of transparency, seeing that we didn't get to $20,000. I wanted to go right to $19,999.00, but as my campaign manager was my husband, Wira Gardiner, he was used to my profligacy and wouldn't hear of that, so it was constrained.

There were other funny little things. I went over and campaigned in every part of the electorate and people said, 'What! You went to Newtown?' 'Yeah.' 'Huh, that's a Labour stronghold.' 'Well,' I replied, 'people could be making up their minds.' There is a little shop in Newtown, near Nairn Street, by the hospital. That area is all in Wellington Central. I can tell you that is a very eclectic community. There were Alliance, there were Greens, there were Labour – no ACT. I went into one antique shop and said, 'Hi, I'm Hekia Parata and I'm the National Party candidate for Wellington Central and I'm . . .' He said, 'Get out of my shop.' I said, 'Pardon.' He said, 'I'm bloody Labour through and through. Now get out of my shop.' And I said, 'Well, sir, you're entitled to your political allegiance just as I'm entitled to civility.' And I turned round to walk out. 'Oh, well, come back then.' I was really taken aback to be yelled at when I was carrying out the democratic process.

Campaigning is very testing on relationships, but it also bonds people. When I didn't win on election night, I knew that there wasn't one further thing I could have done – not one. So I moved on pretty quickly. And I'm a competitive person. I know the ups and downs of going into a competition. I knew I hadn't won. My husband told me rather earlier, I felt, than he needed to, that it was likely that I wouldn't win. He pulled me out and said, 'You're going to have to think about conceding.' And I said, 'Oh go away.' I said, 'Aren't you watching television? They're only at 21 percent of Wellington Central and it's only . . .' That's another thing, how analytical it all is: you know, booth by booth, whose booth was this and all those kind of things.

In the end my husband was right. All the Wellington Central candidates had run a very honourable campaign, so I didn't feel bad about going over to congratulate and concede to Marian. Our party – the National Party party – was far better than the victory one at Marian's: you'd have thought I'd won! We had a great time.

And then, after all that, to have political commentator Al Morrison lead me astray! That night, because I had been so focused on winning the constituency seat, I hadn't given any thought to the list result, because my own particular personal code was accountability. You have to be accountable to specific people, not some abstract group of people, and so I was really committed to winning Wellington Central. The list, to me, was a backstop, so not winning Wellington Central was really the key thing for me. And the fact that National's result meant that the line stopped above my name was all right with me. And then I get this false hope in the form of this sophisticated, analytical person, advising the public on radio how they should interpret the results. And he said to me, on the radio, 'No, no, I think you're going to make it.' And I said, 'Oh, Al, I love you.' He said, 'We're on air.' And the question was, would I still love him in the morning – because National came up short and so, no, I didn't win.

This experience has been, really, a very positive one for me. It forced me to go out of my 'comfort zone' in so many ways. It made me realise that there is a lot of work to be done on creating in New Zealanders a willingness, and an energy, and an interest in understanding and knowing about politics and how it affects people personally. I don't think we have enough of that. And so this six-week campaign was great. I really enjoyed it. Next time I'll run a perfect one. I'll be back.

16

CAMPAIGNING IN A MAORI SEAT

John Tamihere

Tamaki Makaurau, the seat I represent, is unique. It is the only entirely urban Maori seat. This marks a big change from 1999, when I won the Hauraki seat that included large rural areas. Despite the unique nature of my seat, I can offer some insights on campaigning in a Maori electorate that may have a more general application.

Campaign dynamics in a two-vote system

The reality of modern election campaigning is that the focus is on the party leadership. Unless you do something amazing, an MP campaigning in a local electorate is not going to get much coverage. So our job is really to keep grinding away as part of the team approach. This is only my second election campaign, and both have been under MMP. While I was never a candidate under the old system, it occurs to me that campaigning must have changed somewhat. Running in a safe seat, I had the good fortune of not having to fight very hard to hold it.

So my role in the election became focused on seeing that the party vote for Labour remained high. The problem I faced was ensuring that voters did not split their votes. Given the dominance of the Labour candidates in the electorates, this was a problem faced by many of my colleagues. While voters were clear that they wanted their local Labour candidate, they seemed determined to experiment with the party vote. In fact, if the share of electorate votes, rather than party votes, had determined the share of seats in Parliament, Labour would have been able to form a single-party majority government. In addition to keeping up the party vote in my own electorate, I also had a key role to play in encouraging Maori around the country to get out and vote for Labour. In this respect, I focused on the 15 seats in Auckland where there are anything from 2,500 to 6,000 Maori on the general rolls. It was very important for me to support my colleagues by campaigning in those areas.

The role of the Maori seats

From time to time, politicians question the need for the Maori seats. I am a great believer in debating our institutional arrangements. This can help to build confidence in our institutions and develop a better understanding of differing viewpoints. I also accept that there may come a time when we no longer need the Maori seats, but that time has not arrived yet. What disappoints me is the way some politicians see the Maori seats as an easy way to score cheap political points.

The same can also be said of issues to do with the Treaty of Waitangi. An important part of my campaigning was to change the focus on Treaty issues away from the negative 'preferential treatment' debate that seems to dominate so much of the discussion. Instead I try to encourage New Zealanders, both Maori and non-Maori alike, to celebrate the progress we are making in resolving Treaty grievances.

Many countries are going through similar processes as they build nations out of colonies. The process we are working through is not easy, but we are doing very well. To date we have settled 12 significant claims, excluding fisheries, at a cost of $370 million. We have agreed on at least broad dollar values with another eight at just less than $200 million. I would like to have seen more claims settled by this stage, but each of these settlements has reconciled multiple grievances. The money spent is not insignificant, but we need to put it in context. In the last decade governments have had to spend $600 million on bailing out the Bank of New Zealand and $840 million on Air New Zealand. I would say that we have satisfied justifiable grievances at a pretty good price. We are courageously facing up to matters of history that many might like to forget. The Treaty does not grant preferential treatment to either of the parties to it. It reserves some matters to Maori, while guaranteeing the right to equality of treatment and to just, sincere participation in our nation.

As I travel around my electorate, what gives me greatest hope is the attitude of our young people. They are setting the benchmark for a great nation that recognises, tolerates and respects the best from Maori culture, without ever being intolerant or disrespectful of anybody else's. As this generation and their children take on leadership roles in this country, the time may come for us to think again about whether we need Maori seats. For now, however, the seats play an important role in guaranteeing strong Maori representation in Parliament. Without them, I am sure that we would see the development of a separate Maori party as the necessary vehicle for representing Maori interests in Parliament. While I acknowledge that there are those who strongly advocate the need for such a party, I am sure that it is better for New Zealand that we have strong Maori advocates within the various political parties.

The Maori seats are also important to Maori representation in government because they crystallise the extent to which Maori are supporting the government. Some colleagues may argue that 'our women's branch has pulled in half the women's population; therefore we want half the seats in Cabinet'; as a Maori MP I am able to say that we won *all* the Maori seats. This should translate into representation in Cabinet and the wider Ministry. The current Executive has the highest proportion of Maori in New Zealand history. In addition to Parekura Horomia and myself in the Cabinet, there are two Ministers outside Cabinet, as well as one parliamentary undersecretary. Each of these Ministers is an electorate MP representing a Maori seat.

The challenge of low turnout

There is not a lot of information on why Maori vote on the general roll as opposed to the Maori roll. This is something that deserves greater attention from those interested in electoral behaviour in this country. One thing we do know is that turnout is traditionally very low in these seats. In Maori seats, getting the vote out can be quite challenging. This is something we need to keep working at. The turnout in my seat was low. It was 70 percent in 1999. This time it fell to 54 percent, the lowest in the country. In my view, the major cause of this low turnout was the lack of any real competition for the Maori seats, and the fact that Maori voters were very comfortable with our performance. This election was very different from 1999. At that time, the seats were up for grabs, with Mauri Pacific, New Zealand First and Independent incumbents, along with strong independent candidates. The clean sweep of the seats by New Zealand First in 1996 had broken the link with Labour, so there was much more robust campaigning going on to see whether Labour could win them back.

In 1999 we did regain the seats. From the high ground of holding all the

Maori seats, we proceeded over the next two and half years to introduce a series of programmes targeted at improving the position of Maori. That made it very difficult for anyone really to challenge us in the Maori seats. Hugely important to the strengthening of Labour's hold on the Maori electorates was the start of these 'for Maori by Maori' initiatives. Maori have grasped the opportunity to develop our own answers to the need for better education, health and social outcomes. For example, there are now about 650 kohanga reo, 59 kura kaupapa, three wananga, and at least 141 health providers in operation throughout the country. These are now significant businesses with almost $200 million in assets. In addition, there are many runanga that operate social services. Urban Maori organisations play a strong role in these areas, especially in Auckland. These organisations are being helped to grow through the 'for Maori by Maori' funding provided by the Ministries of Health, Education and Social Development. In the year ended June 2001, the Ministry of Health paid $135,698 million to Maori health providers, and $10 million for the Maori Providers Development Fund. In the year to June 2000, the Ministry of Education allocated $66.7 million to expenditure targeted solely at 'Improving Outcomes for Maori'. This is very significant and must be seen as a real source of opportunity. The investment in Maori communities and follow-on effects on skill development can provide a huge stimulus to Maori economic development — perhaps even more so than engagement with commercial assets.

The success of such policies was coupled with a lack of competitive opposition. We did not have anyone out there trying to hunt us down. We tried to get radio debates going on the iwi network, but opposition candidates would not take part. We tried to invite them to our campaign meetings, but that did not work either. In general it was very hard to engage with alternative candidates. This in turn meant that it was very hard to convince voters that it was important for them to get out and vote.

At the same time, National was running a strong campaign to strengthen its position with Maori. When Bill English took over the leadership, he said that National needed to change its image to survive a 'browning population'. His strategy, which included relegating Georgina Te Heuheu from a caucus ranking of eight to 13, did not work, and National's percentage of the vote in the Maori seats dropped by 27 percent in the last election. While National's failure to announce a Maori policy in time for the election probably did not help, the net result was that they took some of the anxiety out of the election in Maori communities. While Maori were never going to vote for National in large numbers, they also did not have the fear of National policies that they have had in the past.

How can we improve voter turnout? Getting voters involved is very important, and we will try to work on that. One initiative I tried this time involved telemarketing (or telepolling). Over the last 10 days of the campaign, we called 4,500 families to try to get them out to the polls. We also set up a range of groups working in the community trying to encourage voting. I do not think many MPs in general electorates need to put this level of effort into getting out the vote. Unfortunately the turnout on election day did not reflect the amount of energy and time we put into it. So I do not have an answer to the problem of low turnout. Hopefully we will find that this election was an anomaly. Even so, we clearly have to do a lot more thinking about how we can improve turnout in the Maori seats.

17

IDENTITY POLITICS AND MMP: POLITICAL CORRECTNESS OR POLITICAL COURAGE?

Paul Gibson

The MMP environment has successfully transformed a House of Representatives in which women and Maori were noticeably underrepresented into one where Maori appear in significant numbers, where women are in positions of greatest power, and where other voices are for the first time being heard. As a result, our House of Representatives has become a more representative body.

Prior to MMP, first-past-the-post delivered candidates who reflected a managed geographical mix. The theory was that communities were more in touch with their own needs and knew who best could represent them. Today's society is made up of many different types of communities, however, and geographical community is becoming less important.

Individuals belong to a matrix of communities. For me, the most important and distinct community to which I belong is the disability community. I write from the perspective of a disabled candidate in the 2002 election, as a person who has represented disabled people in non-government organisations as well as both disabled and non-disabled people in other settings.

Does the move from managing the diversity mix on a geographical basis only – with the addition of some Maori seats – to managing the diversity mix of geography, gender, ethnicity and sexual orientation mean that Parliament's capacity and competence is being compromised? Can institutions charged with collective decision-making responsibilities be rendered dysfunctional by the 'tunnel vision' self-interest of identity politics? Is 'identity politics' about political correctness or political courage? Is the principle of selection by merit compromised by the rise of identity politics?

These debates are simmering within society, and also within the New Zealand Labour Party. Leading up to the 2002 election, Labour looked at the different communities that make up our diverse society and endeavoured to select a party list that would better reflect that diversity. When Labour was selecting its list candidates, Eamon Daly, an academic, information and communication technologies ethicist and wheelchair user, and I, a disability consultant, Braille user by necessity and bike user for fun, stood for the list. We did so on the basis that the 20 percent of the population who are disabled in one way or another (according to 2001 census figures) needed to be represented. A branch of disabled people within the Labour Party had been established; a presentation had been given to the Labour Party's annual conference; and a comprehensive guide on practical and strategic ways to recruit and include disabled people within the party had been produced. Eamon Daly gained the number 53 spot on the list; going by the polls at the time of selection, he had about a 50–50 chance of getting into Parliament. I, on the other hand, was number 60 on the list, and felt secure in the knowledge that come post-election day, I would not be having a celebratory drink at Bellamy's.

The disability rights movement

Candidates openly and proudly stating that they are there to represent disabled people reflect the rise of the disability rights movement, an international revolution of considerable significance. We disabled people have traditionally been defined and analysed in terms of medical deficits. We have learned, however, from the struggles of other groups seeking greater equity, who have been disadvantaged by the way society has been constructed. We have redefined ourselves and now look to claim a part in a society that wishes to value and celebrate diversity. In that sense disabled people have moved away from a medical model, with its focus on deficits and cures, and towards a social model, which separates out two different concepts: impairment, the inherent differences that disabled people have, which may have negative, neutral and positive aspects; and disablement, the discrimination and barriers faced by people with impairments. These barriers include inaccessible information, services and environments, as well as discriminatory attitudes and the inequitable distribution of resources. Discrimination may be practised by individuals as well as by society as a whole through its systems and structures.

In New Zealand there was a time when gaps in educational attainment, employment status and socio-economic status separating men and women, Maori and non-Maori, were seen to reflect inherent qualities in the different groups. Decision-makers have now recognised that it is the structure of society that creates these gaps, not inherent inferiority, and that political action is required to close them. What limited evidence there is available suggests that the biggest 'gaps' in our society are between disabled and non-disabled people, but the societal conversation or the political energy directed towards closing these gaps has yet to occur. The grasp of disability issues by decision-makers at a conceptual level is weak, and at an instinctive level it is even weaker. People still don't instinctively see our under-representation in society as a political issue. We – disabled people – are regarded as inherently inferior.

Most political parties of the left and centre-left take a stand against some forms of discrimination; others they leave to the conscience of the elected Member of Parliament. Why is one form of discrimination – racism, for instance – any less acceptable than any other? Discrimination based on physical impairment – disablism – is, or ought to be, no less indefensible. However, many of the bio-ethical issues that have an impact on our lives as disabled people are seen as conscience issues, rather than as matters of party principle. Perhaps this is a hangover from the days when most political issues were able to be placed conveniently on a one-dimensional left-right continuum. For a party wanting to be a long-term government, political pragmatism wins over political courage in the short term.

But there is hope for the longer term, for a start has been made. The disability rights movement has had an impact on the political context in New Zealand. *The New Zealand Disability Strategy: Whakanui Oranga Making a World of Difference* was released in April 2001, after extensive consultation. The main barrier reported by New Zealand's disabled people was the attitudes of others. The consultation process endorsed the social model framework; this was supported and became government policy. Gary Williams, Chief Executive Officer of the Disabled Persons Assembly, representing disabled people on the day of the launch of the strategy, said, 'The strategy is our Treaty.'

The 2002 disability campaign

I hated the campaign. I passionately believed in what I was doing, but to go out and sell myself as the best vehicle for the collective values of disabled people made me feel like the stereotyped self-promoting power-hungry politician that everyone hates. I have had enough experience campaigning in the past, winning elections to become President of the Victoria University of Wellington Student Association and President of the Disabled Persons Assembly. I thought that I might get used to it with time, but not yet. Supporting two electorate candidates was more enjoyable and less isolating than being the lowly list candidate.

I set up an email network of those wishing to hear about Labour's disability campaign and the disability manifesto. Eamon Daly and I organised a few accessible meetings around the country where we endeavoured to cater to everyone's needs. The feeling of all meetings was very positive and very supportive. Disabled people were excited to see openly disabled candidates carrying a political flag on their behalf. Too often, political decisions are made by others about disabled people without our input. 'Nothing about us without us' has been a rallying catch-cry. Ruth Dyson, Minister for Disability Issues for most of the previous term, was seen as understanding the needs of the disability community and doing a great job. Labour appeared to be the only party doing any active targeting of the 22 percent of the voting age population with a disability. Prominent among the issues raised was access to the political process. This includes deaf people not having political telecasts captioned, as well as those of us dependent on alternative formats missing out on the masses of pamphlets, policies and other information available to the general public. This became a particular frustration to me. A busy party machine in full election battle cry couldn't let all its candidates know what the policy was. The second casualty of war is human rights.

There was much discussion within Labour about targeting not just the 'swinging voters', but also the non-voters as well. International research suggests that disabled people are over-represented among those who don't vote, and perhaps in New Zealand comprise the majority of people who do not vote. But the Labour Party was not able to translate this research into resources to support a well-targeted campaign. The needs of disabled people are diverse and barriers to our inclusion in the political process are many, but all are surmountable, given political will. The trend internationally is for 'third way' politics to be driven by the views of focus groups managed by statisticians who haven't heard that 22 percent of the voting age population are disabled people. Most of these people are excluded from the focus group process.

I wrote a 'disability sector' manifesto for Labour, with input from others, broadly stating the basics of what needed to happen for disabled people in the next three years. It ran to about 40 pages. The Labour Party Policy Council hacked and burned it down to two pages, and it was released three days before the election. Other issues which came up during campaign meetings and in the original 40-page disability manifesto were the value of our lives, bio-ethical rights, the right to go to school alongside our non-disabled peers, the right to a minimum wage and holidays, our representation in government agencies, and lack of equity depending on cause of impairment.

Identity and community and disabled people

The disability community can be discussed in several ways. Disabled people are us – individuals with impairments, inhabiting this society. The disability community includes families, whanau and unpaid carers. The disability sector includes the organisations providing specific services to us. The new disability politics puts the voices of disabled people in the lead, followed by families, then service providers. This is turning the traditional hierarchy on its head.

Disabled people include those with physical, sensory, psychiatric, intellectual, learning, age-related or other impairments; long-term illnesses; stigmatising conditions or difference; or anything which the other equity groups don't pick up. Impairment may be visible, but is more often invisible. It may be acquired through accident, illness or congenitally.

Historically there have been impairment-based communities. It is only recently that there has been the evolution of a broader community. In an attempt to achieve a more unified political voice, there has been the debate again about specific representation – merit vs identity – within disability. Unfortunately, we have our own hierarchy within disability. In the leading disability organisation, the Disabled Persons Assembly, there has been an active recruitment process of under-represented impairment groups into executive positions. People with intellectual impairments, for example, have struggled in the past to have their voices heard. This is not through any lack of strategic leadership ability from their leaders, but through the prejudice within broader society being reflected within the disability community. I know individuals with intellectual impairments who would do a better job of representing their constituency than the majority of current MPs. I can't see them getting into Parliament without identity politics becoming even more specific. Identity politics makes hierarchies more transparent.

The 'identity, community and pride' debate has long been led by the deaf community, describing themselves in terms of being a distinct culture rather than in terms of a deficit or medical model. During a conversation I had a few years ago with a leader in the deaf community, I learned that in New Zealand Sign Language the signs for assimilation and for inclusion are the same, unless there is context in which it is required to contrast them. This is probably based on the deaf community's experience of being included as being merely one of assimilation. The broader disability community has tried to redefine inclusion as something very distinct from assimilation. Inclusion is about partnership, recognising both commonalities and differences, and allowing both commonalities and differences to flourish. Partnership also requires an awareness of inherent power differences, be they based on numerical supremacy, better access to resources or other factors. Assimilation doesn't promote difference or recognise that power and might are not necessarily right.

Conclusion

Ironically, the latest MMP election's new list entrants are predominantly male. It now seems difficult for members of major parties to get new members into Parliament on the list. It is easier to get there representing a geographical community.

Identity politics has not taken political courage. It is a matter of necessity for any party wishing to be truly 'representative'. It does, however, take a lot of managing.

Is Parliament ready to meet the needs of disabled people? My experience suggests not yet, but they must be met. Margaret Wilson, a highly talented and openly disabled person, though not an activist in the area, was thrown immediately on her entrance into Parliament into the heart of politics, a seat in Cabinet. Even with her high profile leading position, she has not had her basic needs as a disabled person met.

Internationally, faster progress on disability issues is being made where a government has specific seats for disabled people. The 2002 Labour disability campaign marked real progress, and the first step on the way to better things to come. Identity politics has stirred up the debate further among disabled people on identity, community, pride, and taking a lead ourselves. In the future I would be hoping that all other political parties will actively compete for the disabled voter. This would be less likely to occur, and the issues mentioned previously would be less likely to be raised, in a non-MMP environment, including STV, which I can't see delivering for disabled people. A major benefit of identity politics I have experienced is the beginning of valuing of a much undervalued group, and the impact that this has had on previously undervalued individuals.

The second major benefit of identity politics is the raising of disability issues from the perspective of disabled people, before the majority swamp the issue with mediocrity and with a lack of interest. One example of an issue that was 'hot' in the pre- and post-election debate was the issue of selective abortion (as distinct from the polarising issue of abortion, 'pro-choice' or 'pro-life'). We can look overseas and see countries where parents decide to abort selectively on the grounds of gender. Without passing judgement on the parents, we recognise from here in New Zealand that this is a result of a society that values men far more than it does women. In New Zealand it is unethical to selectively abort on a gender basis. But we allow selective abortion on the grounds of impairment. What does this say about the way our society values disabled people? What impact must this have on the identity of disabled individuals?

The personal is the political. For me personally, I like being blind. I couldn't have said this while growing up, when I was unable to separate my inherent difference from the discrimination I experienced. Would I take the miracle cure? This is a valid hypothetical question. No, I wouldn't. I am happy with who I am. But there is no valid hypothetical question, 'What would life be like if I were me but not blind?' If I were not blind I would not be me – just as if I were not male I would not be me. I believe I am the sum of both my genes and my collective experiences. My partner, who has an acquired impairment, and an identity pre-impairment, as well as an acceptance of her new identity, would take a cure, but recognises that more resources should be directed to supporting, not attempting to cure. She states that she is a better person, and has more to contribute to society, and is contributing more, than if she had remained a non-disabled person. We are, at time of writing, pregnant for the first time. We have both a sense of excitement and awe at the task that lies ahead. We are well positioned, practically and emotionally, to bring a loved child with an impairment into a world which, as a result of our efforts, will be more inclusive and affirming of her identity. And if she is non-disabled, we will love her anyway!

18

CAMPAIGNING DISABLED: A PERSPECTIVE ON THE 2002 ELECTION

Eamon Daly

This chapter is a brief account of one candidate's list campaign during the 2002 New Zealand general election, an account just like any other except for one material difference – the candidate happens to be in a wheelchair. This fact shaped major aspects of his campaign.

Before I outline the structure of this paper, I want to indulge in a little social commentary. As little as 20 years ago, an article such as this might have been headlined 'This is the story of a courageous young man afflicted by a severe disability who is defying the odds and "having a go" at politics'. Even now, there remains a latent tendency for the public and the media to paint a picture of the tragic individual attempting to overcome seemingly insurmountable odds in pursuit of some ordinarily unattainable goal. But that is not to say that attitudes have not improved in 20 years, for they have in many ways. Moreover, not only have attitudes improved (and attitudes are pivotal in enabling other improvements), but so also have education, employment and participation outcomes. Needless to say, these improvements come with the obligatory caveat that more still needs to be done.

Candidate selection

At the beginning of 2002, I had been back in the country for just over a year, after spending the previous three years engaged in postgraduate research at the University of California at Berkeley. Immediately prior to my time there, I had completed a Master's degree at the University of Canterbury, and cut my political teeth as the Labour candidate for Ilam in the 1996 general election.

Upon returning to New Zealand, I set about reconstructing and consolidating my position within the Labour Party. This involved, among other things, heading the establishment of the first and only disability-orientated party political branch in New Zealand – the nationwide Kirk Branch of the Labour Party. As a result of these efforts, I began 2002 as the current and inaugural Chair of the Kirk Branch, executive member of the Canterbury Labour Regional Council, Avonhead Branch delegate to the Ilam Labour Electorate Committee (LEC), and Kirk Branch delegate to the Christchurch Central LEC. I had by then already signalled my intention to run as a list candidate, and I was about to embark on an initial lobbying phase.

As election year unfolded, the Labour Party held electorate and list candidate selection meetings in each of its six regions throughout the country. Region Five (the Northern South Island, and the region in which I live) held its Listing Conference in March. It was with a mixture of humility, great relief and exultation that I was elected to the fourth position on the Region Five List, this being the first position not held by an incumbent Member of Parliament. Unfortunately, that high position was not subsequently properly translated into an accordingly high position on the final Labour Party list, and I eventually found myself at number 53 – high enough to have an outside chance of being elected, but low enough to render such a result unlikely.

Regional party work

Also during this time (March and April 2002) I was elected to several other positions within the Labour Party, including Chair of the Regional Party Vote Committee and Deputy Chair of the Canterbury Labour Regional Council itself. The latter role, albeit somewhat influential, existed independently of the election campaign, whereas the former involved arranging and chairing regular meetings during the campaign for the region's candidates, campaign chairs, and various other centrally involved party personnel. The primary purpose of these meetings was to coordinate efforts to target the party vote on a regional basis, and they had a secondary purpose of campaign-specific information and communication sharing. This information-sharing capacity was greatly enhanced by my setting up a regional campaign Yahoo Group for that purpose.

Alongside this regional party work, I was beginning to construct ideas for my list campaign, and assessing how it might beneficially interact with a nationwide disability sector campaign. The task of a list candidate is to campaign for the party vote, and it assists greatly in that regard to have access to a readily identified constituency. As a person with a disability, I had access to such a constituency, and it was only logical that I should target it. Much of my list campaign, therefore, was run within a nationwide disability sector campaign, and as such most of what is written here refers to this combined campaign.

The disability sector campaign

Plans and possibilities
Having decided to run a nationwide disability sector campaign, I wrote to the Head Office of the Labour Party with a proposal and request for funding. I viewed any campaigning on disability issues as being divisible into two areas: that which ought to be part of an inclusive central campaign, and that which is properly constitutive of a sector campaign. Examples of initiatives which, in my view, fell within the former category included promoting a disability perspective in print, radio and television advertising, producing the policy manifesto in alternative formats, and producing a leaflet which detailed proudly Labour's achievements in government for people with disabilities, also to be produced in alternative formats.

At the time I sent in my proposal, we (Labour Party members with disabilities) were in many ways already conducting a disability sector campaign. We were spreading the good word through our networks; liaising with and informing list and constituency candidates regarding interaction with the disabled community; and providing advice and feedback to ensure harmony between policy committee and sector draft manifesto sections, the disability sector draft manifesto, and the New Zealand Disability Strategy. We were also taking our message to the media, and with considerable success – until the commencement of campaign proper, that is; but more on that later.

The proposal for a disability sector campaign entailed holding meetings in the five main centres of Auckland, Hamilton, Wellington, Christchurch and Dunedin. The format for these meetings was to be one of trumpeting Labour's record of achievement in general, and for people with disabilities in particular. I expected to have policy information available by way of information packs in alternative formats, including the disability issues leaflet referred to earlier, and a video detailing Labour's achievements, with the

Minister for Disability Issues, Ruth Dyson, narrating. Each meeting was to be very well publicised, with invitations being sent to all relevant disability-related organisations in the area. It was envisaged that relevant ministers (especially the Minister for Disability Issues), local MPs and local candidates would be involved where appropriate and where possible, including Prime Minister Helen Clark for the Auckland meeting. In addition, local and nationwide media were to be contacted by way of media releases, noting the participation of ministers, MPs, and other candidates where applicable.

The proposal met with unanimous approval, but the accompanying request for funding was only partially successful. Accordingly, we had to adjust our plans to accommodate the reduced budget, with Dunedin being the only location casualty. A combination of limited funds, limited hands and limited time resulted in further cuts to the original proposal, including the disability issues leaflet and the Ruth Dyson-narrated video detailing Labour's achievements. In their place we had a large supply of generic policy leaflets, enrolment forms, membership forms and pledge cards. Armed with this material, our own knowledge of already implemented Labour Party policy, and our informed ideas for the future, fellow disabled Labour candidate Paul Gibson and I set off on our disability sector campaign 'road trip'.

On the road
We first flew into Auckland, where we had hoped to secure the services of the prime minister to open our disability issues forum. But we had known for about a week that she was unfortunately not available, so we tailored our media release accordingly. I arrived in Auckland several hours before the forum, as I was to be interviewed on the disability issues show of one of Auckland's community access radio stations. The interview went very well, but it was subsequently accidentally erased before being broadcast, necessitating a second interview over the telephone. The disability issues forum itself was held later in the day, and it too was very successful. Over 40 people were in attendance, with a wide range of disability types represented. Paul Gibson and I delivered well-received presentations, which were followed by a lengthy question-and-answer session. Much of the feedback was positive, but not all, and we were given the firm message that although Labour was doing some things right, it was largely in a competitive vacuum and much more needed to be accomplished.

Having successfully completed the Auckland leg of the sector campaign, we headed for Wellington, and it was at this point that the wheels came close to falling off the cart. Actually, they did in a way, except that in this case the 'wheels' were in the form of a heavy-duty fuse, and the 'cart' was in fact my power chair. Upon arrival in Wellington, I found that my power chair had no power. A short inspection revealed that it was missing a fuse, and several telephone calls later I had ascertained that the ground crew at Auckland Airport had dropped the fuse on the tarmac. Given the scarcity of such power chair fuses, it was extremely fortunate that it was found intact. I still faced the prospect of no power until the next morning, when the fuse was to be flown from Auckland to Wellington on one of the first flights. I contemplated issuing a media release critical of air travel conditions for people with disabilities, but decided against it, lest it give ammunition to those with prejudices who believe someone with such a major disability is too frail to be in Parliament.

The forum in Wellington followed a similar pattern to that of Auckland, with the only disappointing note being the small number of attendees. But what was missing in terms of quantity was more than compensated for by the quality of and positions held by those who did attend. As was the case for all fora, members of the deaf community were notable for their presence, and the sign language interpreters I had arranged proved indispensable. At the completion of the Wellington forum, I flew to Christchurch, while fellow candidate Paul Gibson remained in Wellington.

While I had been away from Christchurch, others on my campaign team had emailed, phoned and faxed almost the entire spectrum of disability-related organisations in the Christchurch area to invite their members to the disability issues forum. This widespread invitation had the desired result, and again over 40 people were in attendance. Unlike the previous fora, in Christchurch we had the obvious drawcard of the Minister for Disability Issues, Ruth Dyson, giving the main address of the meeting, followed by a brief introduction from me. Given the presence of the minister, the concluding question-and-answer session predictably revolved around (mostly legitimate) dissatisfaction with government-related services.

Following the Christchurch forum, the disability sector campaign road show moved to Hamilton, where I was involved in two election meetings over and above the disability issues forum. The first of these was in fact a cross-party meeting on disability policies, involving constituency candidates from most of the recognised political parties. I was invited to give details on Labour's disability policies, which was a little difficult, given that they had not yet been released. I did have some information, however, and that combined with my being the only candidate with a disability gave Labour a level of credibility beyond the reach of the other parties present.

The Hamilton disability issues forum I had already organised was also a success, with approximately 40 people attending. This meeting had the welcome additional support and involvement of Dianne Yates and Martin Gallagher, the Labour MPs for Hamilton West and Hamilton East respectively. Having the MPs there was of immense value, as they were able to answer many of the questions specific to Hamilton. Almost immediately following the forum, we attended a shorter meeting at the premises of the deaf society in Hamilton, where I briefly reiterated Labour's record and asked for the support of the deaf community, both on election day and, following that, in building the disability sector within the Labour Party.

The Hamilton leg of the disability sector campaign was perhaps the most personally rewarding, as well as being the most successful in terms of audiences reached. I found it rewarding because it was late in the overall campaign, and I was able to argue what I believed to be the superiority of Labour Party policies at a number of different meetings. Moreover, I realised that I had retained in memory considerable policy detail, and it became clear to me that I was a valuable part of the Labour Party campaign effort.

Again, as with Auckland, the only downside to the Hamilton meetings was airport related. I arrived at Hamilton Airport to find that Wellington Airport was closed all day due to bad weather, and as a result I was forced to stay overnight at a nearby hotel. My flight the following day was delayed, causing me to miss my connecting flight to Christchurch. Such delays were not exactly helpful in the final week leading up to the election, but I took some comfort in knowing that high profile candidates from other parties were experiencing similar fates.

Campaigns and campaigning – an assessment

Looking back at the disability sector campaign, I am pleased to note that overall, the disability issues fora were well attended and very productive. It was especially gratifying to have in attendance people from most disability groups, including those in leadership positions. Also in attendance were key people within the private and public sector. This cross-sectoral representation created opportunities for information exchange and facilitated immediate answers to questions. It also resulted in opportunities for ongoing collaboration and communication between the sectors.

Media releases were frequently distributed throughout the campaign, some designed to advertise upcoming disability fora, and some to comment on other events or releases. Media releases met with considerable success before the campaign proper was underway, but with considerable failure subsequently. It seems to me that this disparity in reporting was not due simply to a difference in the overall number of political media releases, and that an additional factor was that people with disabilities are still dealing with some media 'perception' problems based on stereotype and prejudice. If this is indeed the case, disability sector campaigns and individual campaigns by people with disabilities will need to find practical ways to combat this problem.

Despite these problems, I rate my 2002 list campaign and the disability sector campaign as being considerably successful. Each benefited the Labour Party over and above the primary aim of increasing Labour's party vote. For example, we increased the number of active members in the Kirk Branch, as well as identifying key people to build the Labour Party disability sector in Auckland, Hamilton and Wellington. In the final analysis, therefore, it seems to me that we ran an excellent campaign with limited resources and limited time.

With 20 percent of New Zealand's population having a long-term and non-trivial disability, a sector campaign targeting people with disabilities has the potential to reach meaningfully over 700,000 people directly affected, and many others indirectly affected, such as partners, family, friends and associates. A concerted, well resourced and well organised campaign for the votes of people with disabilities has hitherto not been attempted, but given the numbers of people affected by disabilities, such a campaign clearly offers a substantial potential dividend in terms of increasing the party vote. The 2005 general election will provide us with another opportunity to raise issues, promote policies and appeal for support from the disability sector of our society.

19

WINDOW ON WAIRARAPA: GEORGINA BEYER AND THE 2002 ELECTION CAMPAIGN

Matt Lamason

In 2002, after her first term in Parliament, Wairarapa incumbent MP Georgina Beyer was re-elected to Parliament with a healthy majority. Wairarapa is the largest electorate in the North Island, since boundary changes in 1996 merged it with what was the Pahiatua electorate, and it provides an interesting study of an electorate that has undergone significant change in the last 25 years. Along with growing diversity of culture and an economy which would be the envy of some rural regions, the political landscape has moved from being a National stronghold to a Labour 'safe seat' in the space of only one election. This chapter highlights some of these changes, and the part they played in what was a calm and comfortable 2002 victory for Labour.[1]

The changing electorate

The electorate now called Wairarapa has undergone extensive change since it was first established as an electorate in 1860 (see McRobie 1989, p.32). What used to be a geographically isolated region, known for its introverted and at times backward rural characteristics, has in the last 25 years been transformed into a vibrant economic area proudly sporting diverse cultures, a booming tourist and wine industry, and an active civic life.

Historical accounts of Wairarapa are quite typical of any rural region around New Zealand over the same period, although Wairarapa has some distinctive characteristics, due to its geographical layout. One short account describes some of these characteristics:

> Wairarapa is a distinct, a separate region – cut off by high mountains from the Capital yet close enough to feel a special affinity with Wellington its principal trade outlet. But because it was cut off, Wairarapa had from the

beginning its separate development, and that meant a development of special characteristics which have particular significance for the men, women and children of the district (Bagnall 1976, p.vii).

Other accounts of early Wairarapa describe how the physical isolation of the region also had a psychological impact on its inhabitants. McWhinnie's thesis covering the social history of Wairarapa outlines two different perceptions. One account, from a government-funded survey in 1968, makes the following assessment: 'The isolation of the region in its early days would certainly have done much to foster a feeling of clannisheness among its inhabitants. Isolation is normally broken down by improved communications and tourism' (see McWhinnie 1995, p.71).

A more anecdotal account from a local interviewee gives a more vivid perception of the sense of isolation:

> [Masterton is] twenty or thirty years behind. I would say it's in a whole time warp of its own . . . You go back there and you can't believe that people say the things they're saying sometimes. They seem to have no idea about what is happening in the world, politically, financially, or the effects it is going to have on New Zealand at all (McWhinnie 1995, p.71).

However, take a drive through the region in 2002, and it is apparent that Wairarapa is not what it once was. The 8-kilometre railway tunnel through the Rimutakas connecting the region with Wellington, and recent upgrades on the Rimutaka Hill road, have made Wairarapa the new lifestyle choice for many Wellington city workers. From encountering rural townships characterised by gumboots and agricultural stores, city goers are now just as likely to enjoy a well-made latte in the main street of Masterton or Greytown as they would in the centre of Wellington.

Along with social and cultural change, the region has diversified and improved economically. The main industry of the region is still agriculture, with 24.4 percent employed in the agriculture, forestry and fishing sector, compared with the national average of 8.4 percent (Parliamentary Library 2002, p.9). However, Wairarapa is now most commonly associated with a burgeoning wine and tourist industry, hosting major events such as the Martinborough Country Fair, the largest of its type in the southern hemisphere, running twice in two months, and attracting up to 30,000 visitors for each event.

The Masterton Business Enterprise (MBE) Report of 2002 also makes a point of showcasing the diversity of its industry, citing the internationally acclaimed pinot noir wines of Palliser Estate, through to newly established global information technology (IT) companies such as Marconi Online (MBE Incorporated 2001). Furthermore, the Regional Economic Development Strategy 2002–2007 (Go Wairarapa 2002), also run by the MBE and coordinating with central government regional development, is an example of the impressive amount of research that is going into developing the Wairarapa.

Finally, economic improvement can be seen from the rise in employment and GDP growth in the region. In the period 1995–2000 employment growth and GDP were roughly 2 percentage points lower than national averages (MBE Incorporated 2002, p.1). Data from the 2001 census show the current proportion gainfully employed at 61.3 percent, slightly higher than the national average (Parliamentary Library 2002, p.8). Alongside the change in Wairarapa's social and economic areas, a profound change in the political landscape has occurred.

Past incumbents, a National Party stronghold

Wairarapa has traditionally been a National Party stronghold. A brief account of the political history of the seat shows only brief windows of power held by Labour in the last one hundred years. One excerpt from a 1970s historical account of district politics recounts the shift in power from liberal and conservative parties:

> The play for a decade was with the liberals on the issues of concern to the small farmers but, in time, some administrative confusion and dilatoriness on the rental problem (of housing), with examples of what could be recouped from a sale of the freehold, linked with an inevitable boredom by the electorates with the party in power, led to the conservative-reform revival which was to dominate Wairarapa from 1911 for almost 25 years, until the 1935 Labour landslide (Bagnall 1976, p.315).

Following 1935, Labour enjoyed only ten years holding what was then the Masterton electorate (it had been Wairarapa North until 1887). After National regained Masterton in 1943, and then the amalgamated Wairarapa electorate after the 1946 boundary change, Labour won the seat only three times in 13 elections – in 1969, 1972, and on the back of Labour's landslide victory in 1984. Following the very marginal election of Wyatt Creech for National in 1987, Labour was not to regain the seat until the second MMP election in 1999.

When Labour regained the electorate through first-time MP Georgina Beyer in 1999, it was not purely through her own personal popularity. First of all, Creech, who had been a popular MP for four government terms, decided not to stand as a candidate in 1999, effectively removing the strongest competitor. Creech instead opted to go on the National Party list, due to the demands of his ministerial portfolio: 'I made sure Wairarapa didn't miss out because of my Cabinet portfolio. But when I thought the workload became too great and I thought I couldn't represent the people of Wairarapa, well, I became a list MP' (Rowe 2002, p.3).

Secondly, in 1996 the boundary of the Wairarapa electorate changed to incorporate the adjourning northern Pahiatua electorate. The MP for Pahiatua, then Minister for Agriculture John Falloon, retired, leaving his fellow party member with a greatly expanded Wairarapa electorate for his final term. Therefore when Creech stood for the list in 1999, with Falloon also gone, the void left by these two strong MPs opened the door for a change, one which Labour took up whole-heartedly.

Changes to the electoral boundaries and their effects

The body governing boundary changes is the Representation Commission. In accordance with the Electoral Act of 1993, New Zealand electorate boundaries are subject to change every five years, after the national census. This automatically triggers the work of the Commission (McRobie 1989, p.10). Change takes place in an attempt to make sure all electorates are equal in size, that is, having more or less the same total population as each other. As a mandatory requirement of the Representation Commission, the fixing of the boundaries is based on equal population, and attempts 'to reduce to a minimum the possibility of boundaries being gerrymandered in favor of one particular candidate or party' (ibid).

McRobie's compilation of boundary changes compares electorates from 1853 through to 1987, and outlines some of the implications of the various boundary changes. The electorate boundaries of Wairarapa first came into existence in 1860, extending on its East boundary from the base of the Rimutaka Ranges on the south coast, 175 degrees longitude, north through to the Manawatu Gorge. The northern boundary stretched east to west from Woodville to the coast at Cape Turnagain. Since 1853, Wairarapa's boundaries have been substantially altered four times. They were first changed in 1881, as mentioned above, where Wairarapa was split into North and South, with a boundary separating the major population centre of Masterton from those towns south of it. The boundary changed again in 1887, with Wairarapa North being renamed Masterton. However, the two changes up to 2002 produced the largest shifts in boundaries, resulting in the north-bordering Pahiatua electorate being joined with Wairarapa in 1996, and the electorate being extended further north in 2001, to encompass an east coast stretch of land from Cape Turnagain to its most northern point, from Waipawa to the east coast (Dick 1960, p.33).

The changing size and layout of electorate boundaries has had the following effects. First, electoral redistribution has implications for electors and their connection to their MP. McRobie states that, 'Traditional links between MP and constituent are still regarded as important by both . . . Frequent redistributions are, therefore, likely to disrupt this identity' (McRobie 1989, p.19). This problem conflicts with the Electoral Act's requirement for equal distribution of population numbers in electorates. The Act's provision for this is that 'communities of interest' must be taken into account, so as to retain electoral stability. However, the two requirements tend to be at odds with each other, with this being most evident in dense urban electorates.

Second, it has implications for parliamentary candidates. Changes in a boundary may strengthen or weaken an MP's constituent power base. From as early as 1881 in the Wairarapa, the changing electorate boundaries have had significant effects on electorate campaigns and outcomes. H. Bunny, the incumbent for Wairarapa from 1865–1881, was ousted by W.C. Buchanan in 1881, when the electorate was split into Wairarapa North and Wairarapa South. For the local newspaper at the time, one of the main reasons for Bunny's defeat was the fact that the alteration of the boundaries meant that he had two other areas, Gladstone and Flat Point to incorporate into his electorate (Bagnall 1976, p.319).

Third, an enlargement in an electorate boundary may increase the responsibilities of the incumbent MP. McRobie adds that, 'Even after the announcement of new boundaries an incumbent MP must maintain existing services to the constituents who elected him or her.' This was the case for Creech when the addition of the Pahiatua electorate in 1996 required extra attention, but not at the expense of his original constituency.

What seems to be most pertinent to Wairarapa therefore is the sheer size of the electorate, posing challenges both in adequately campaigning in such a vast area, with differing political cleavages, and in being successful at representing the whole electorate. Despite this being the largest electorate in the North Island, Labour in 2002 had only two electorate offices and two electorate secretaries. The large area covered by the electorate has brought particular challenges for both the incumbent MP, who must attempt to represent the whole electorate, and for candidates attempting to canvass all the electorate's members.

The effects of MMP and split ticket voting

If changing electorate boundaries have had an effect on the political landscape of the Wairarapa, so too the change to a proportional representation system is becoming an increasingly important element of campaigning in the region.

Before MMP, the constituents of Wairarapa generally[2] had only two choices when it came to choosing a candidate: National or Labour. Traditionally, this would have meant choosing a candidate typical of the rural farming region that was Wairarapa's principal characteristic. MMP has changed the face of candidates and campaigning, and has increased minority party participation in the campaign. Furthermore, with the number of electorates under MMP reduced from 99 to 65, and the introduction of party lists, voter volatility has been stimulated, with high levels of split ticket voting.

The election of Labour MP Georgina Beyer was a major change from the political traditions of the Wairarapa. Under the FPP electoral system, it is highly unlikely that Beyer would have been elected. There are two main reasons for this. First, although National had lost its strong candidates with Falloon retiring and Creech going on the party list in 1999, the fact that Beyer was a new Labour candidate standing in what was a safe National seat would not have augured well for success. Second, because FPP tied voters to their party loyalties, voting for a candidate such as Beyer on her personal merit would not have been a likely option because of her affiliation with Labour.

The increase of smaller parties and broader representation of the population is another feature of MMP in Wairarapa. In the third MMP election of 2002, a total of nine parties and candidates were standing in the electorate. Further demonstrating the representativeness of MMP was the strong standing of women in the campaign. Two of them came to dominate the media spotlight, due to their strong personalities.

Another feature of campaigning under MMP in Wairarapa is the use of list and electorate MPs. The Royal Commission on the Electoral System recognised that under FPP minority representatives were unlikely to be elected to Parliament, because parties would tend not to select candidates for constituency seats who were not 'widely acceptable' to the electorate (Royal Commission on the Electoral System 1986, p.15). The party list, a new method under MMP, generally assures that a more representative sample of MPs makes it into Parliament.

List candidates do appear to be playing an important role in Wairarapa. On the one hand, while Wyatt Creech was no longer technically accountable to the people of Wairarapa, his standing on the list nonetheless provided local constituents with yet another port of call when their electorate MP was not accessible. During the 2002 election campaign, Labour list candidate Denise MacKenzie was able to provide campaign assistance to incumbent MP Georgina Beyer.

A study by Johnston and Pattie of the 1996 MMP election shows that voters can opt to vote by either a strategic or a psychological model (Johnston and Pattie 1999, p.167). Both models can be applied to the way voters behave in Wairarapa. The psychological model applies when a voter with a strong attachment to one party votes 'straight', giving both ticks to the same party. The strategic model is used when a voter gives their party vote to their first preference, and then uses their candidate vote 'strategically' to support or harm the chances of another. This is split ticket voting.

A factor contributing to split ticket voting in the Wairarapa electorate was the strength of competing candidates in the campaign. Where there is no competition in an electorate, the incumbent is likely to gain both votes, unless they have developed a reputation for being a poor constituency representative. An example of this in Wairarapa was the way in which Merepeka Raukawa-Tait attracted the third highest number of electorate votes, despite the fact that very few people would have voted for the Christian Heritage Party (CHP). As a strong candidate in her own right, despite her party affiliation, Raukawa-Tait proved a strong alternative for voters who were 'shopping around' with their candidate vote.

General issues facing Wairarapa

Transport and health have been among the more salient issues in Wairarapa in recent times. As the incumbent from 1987 to 1999, Wyatt Creech had his work cut out for him: 'One [issue] was the hospital, and the other was access to Wellington. Maintaining the rail link was important and at various times there were threats to the service' (Rowe 2002, p.3).

With the closure of public hospitals now distant in most residents' memory, and the $13.7 million road realignment between Kaitoke and Te Marua approved, issues in the Wairarapa region now tend to be related more to business and economics. With the expansion of businesses and local industry, one of the biggest issues now is the shortage of a skilled work force. Because of this, there has been a greater focus on building links between the education and business sector at all levels (MBE Incorporated 2001, p.11).

The incumbent MP: Background and rise to power[3]

The change of Wairarapa's MP from conservative National parliamentarian Wyatt Creech to Georgina Beyer, apparently the world's first transsexual MP, was a transition that could not have been more dramatic or unexpected. Beyer's rise to prominence had quite humble beginnings. From the underworld of prostitution and the dancing club scene, Beyer first became involved with the electorate as a drama tutor employed by the Carterton community centre. Having been exposed to the rejections of society in her early years, Beyer had an understanding and concern for the people of Wairarapa at the grassroots level which was to become a feature of her life as her public responsibilities increased.

During the early years in the Wairarapa town of Carterton, Beyer became involved in managing the government's new Training Opportunities Program (TOPS), which attempted to get people off government benefits and back into the workforce. Working at the ground level in the Wairarapa enabled her to see at first hand the effects of government policy on local citizens. For instance, during 1991, when Ruth Richardson's 'mother of all Budgets' was released, beneficiaries felt the pressure. Beyer has summed up some of these effects:

> I was working with those people whose quality of life was directly affected by the government's savage benefits cuts. It seemed like overnight the Wairarapa economy had a few million dollars taken out of it. The effect of this was that beneficiaries couldn't afford to pay their rent. In small communities like Carterton, homeless people began sleeping in outhouses and empty carriages at the rail yards (Casey 1999, p.125).

As Beyer's proactive stance in the community gave her more public attention, it was not long before she was in the running for the 1992 local body elections for the Carterton District Council. Beyer's campaign platform in 1992 was, as in 2002, focused on representing the local people. However, despite running a strong campaign and failing to win election by only 14 votes, it was not until 1993, through a by-election, that she took up her first position in public office as a local government councillor. A reflection on this appointment made later in her maiden speech to Parliament highlights her motivations in standing for the Council: 'I was welcomed into that community and given opportunity in it, and I felt an obligation to reciprocate by some form of service to help others' (Beyer 2000).

Beyer's commitment to her locality and her ability to speak on behalf of others eventually led in 1995 to her appointment as the mayor of Carterton. It was at this point in her public life that her media appeal in New Zealand began to skyrocket. Being touted as the first transsexual mayor in the world was not something that could be lived down easily. During these times, there was a fear that she would be overly presented as a transsexual public figure, and not as a serious politician. Following an interview at that time with Ian Fraser, she remarked:

> I was a little disappointed that Ian got caught up with talking about my life. I had wanted to talk about my political aspirations. This was to be the nature of many of the media interviews I was to have. There was an unhealthy interest in my sexuality. I often wondered whether it would overshadow my political aspirations (Casey 1999, p.148).

Georgina Beyer's political aspirations were by no means overshadowed when in 1999, under MMP, she became the Labour MP for Wairarapa, coming in with the largest winning margin Labour had ever achieved in that seat.[4] In her maiden speech to Parliament, which was delivered without speech notes, she outlined that her primary reason for standing was to be a representative for the Wairarapa community. In general, she appears to prefer being in the electorate with her constituents, rather than being tied up with parliamentary business in Wellington. For this reason, she decided not to seek re-election for a second term. However, after the announcement had been made, according to her it was a group of Grey Power constituents in Dannevirke who tipped the scales in favour of her standing again (Beyer 2002).

Beyer's change of mind was not, however, received favourably by all members of the public. Interestingly, one of her strongest critics was the person who first signed her up as a Labour candidate. Peter Teahan, a former chairperson for Labour in the Wairarapa electorate, said in *The Dominion* at the time of her change of mind that he was tired of her indecision, stating, 'In my opinion she has not represented the members of the Wairarapa Labour Party, or the Wairarapa. Her priorities have been elsewhere' (Langdon 2002). When asked how she felt about her decision to stay on for another term, Beyer's response was that it must have been the right one, given the successful outcome: 'I had the fortitude to change my mind in the face of public ridicule and they [her electors] stood by me in the election'. However, Beyer is mindful that such public criticism is not healthy for her reputation: 'You don't dilly-dally too much. Once you may be forgiven, I have had my once' (Beyer 2002).

The campaign: Implications of an early election

For the Labour campaign committee in the Wairarapa, the early election had no real downsides. One of the members of the Labour Electoral Council (LEC), when asked about the impact of the early election date, responded by saying, 'I don't think it mattered. I never got the feeling that people were saying that she [Helen Clark] shouldn't have done that' (Patterson 2002). What was of particular concern, however, was that given Labour's strength in opinion polls, electors might not come out to vote. Indeed, holding the election in the middle of winter was not expected to encourage voters to come out and support their party. In view of the weather and voter apathy, on the actual day of the election one of Labour's biggest tasks in Wairarapa was driving older or frail people from their homes and down to the polling booths, a service that Labour has traditionally carried out through its party faithful.

The calling of an early election by a prime minister whose party is polling well at the national level is unlikely to put an incumbent government MP under much pressure. This was not, however, the case for the other candidates. In this respect, the most notable instance was the withdrawal of National candidate Koro Mullins, who stepped down after his son was charged with burglary and driving charges. The replacement candidate, Ian Buchanan, was chosen at the beginning of June, putting him on the back foot for launching an effective campaign (*Wairarapa Times-Age*, 5 June 2002, p.1).

The candidates and their campaign strategies

There were nine candidates standing in the Wairarapa electorate. These included Bill Henderson (Progressive Coalition), Sarah Millington (Greens), Edwin Perry (New Zealand First), Gerald Tait (Alliance), and Frank Owen (United Future). The Greens' candidate stood to draw attention to the GE issue that was being played out in the wider national campaign. Also drawing attention to particular election issues, namely crime and Treaty issues, was the New Zealand First candidate. The other three candidates had little appreciable impact on the campaign.

Also of interest, but of little consequence, was the campaign run by ACT candidate Ian MacFarlane. A publisher, editor, journalist and photographer, MacFarlane had a particular interest in the maintenance of the Wairarapa railway. As a relatively unknown candidate, he was the only ACT candidate to stand solely for his electorate, turning down a place on the ACT party list, and wishing instead to be elected 'as a person' by his fellow citizens (*Wairarapa Times-Age*, 9 July 2002, p.5). His quaint campaign jingle highlighted his commitment to the rail service; it went, 'Let's stop wringing our hands and start ringing bells.'

The real battle for Wairarapa was between the incumbent, Labour's Georgina Beyer, National's Ian Buchanan, and Christian Heritage's Merepeka Raukawa-Tait. Buchanan is a Wellington regional councillor who was ranked at 29 on the National Party list. Buchanan had also sat on the Wairarapa Catchment Board for six years prior to becoming a Wellington councillor (*Wairarapa Times-Age*, 5 June 2002, p.1). He ran a fairly straightforward campaign typical of a conservative National candidate.

High polling Merepeka Raukawa-Tait, the past CEO of the national organisation for Women's Refuge in Wellington, ran a strong publicity campaign incorporating the past All Black rugby player Michael Jones into her material. Her message was a tactical one, asking people to vote against Labour and to 'support Merepeka'. CHP campaign manager Adam Owens stated: 'Effectively, Wairarapa will get three MPs because Georgina Beyer and Ian Buchanan are both getting elected off the parties' lists anyway (Campbell 2002).

For Beyer, the campaign was aimed equally at the party vote and at her electorate vote: 'Our campaign was constant and consistent and simple, vote Labour, two ticks for Labour, very simple' (Beyer 2002). The simplicity of Beyer's campaign was its strength, building on the support that she had developed over the prior three years as MP for Wairarapa. Behind the scenes there was not much strategising going on in the Labour campaign committee. The committee began campaign planning only six weeks out from the election, a fact quickly picked up by the local newspaper, which ran a caption next to the billboards of National, the Alliance and the Greens asking, 'Where's Labour?' (*Wairarapa Times-Age*, 26 June 2002, p.1). Starting late, however, was not seen as a problem for Labour; it was perhaps even a benefit. Long drawn out campaigns place a heavy burden on a campaign team; most of Labour's were retired Wairarapa residents. Furthermore, there tends to be a decline in public interest if a campaign is too long.

Most campaigns in the Wairarapa are fought between National and Labour. In 2002, however, Beyer considered that there was very little contest: 'As far as the competition goes, there wasn't really a great deal at the end of the day. Ian Buchanan was on the back foot' (Beyer 2002). According to one member of Labour's campaign committee, it was not that the competing candidates were necessarily of lesser calibre; instead, there was a lack of strategy and poor organisation. Giving reasons for this in an interview, the committee member observed:

> I think Ian Buchanan was not a bad candidate. It is hard campaigning against people with a high profile, because people look at the personalities or the profiles of the people, not what they stand for. Merepeka was a threat to Georgina because of her high profile. But I think Ian was a more credible vote but a lot of his failing was that they did not run a strong campaign . . . Merepeka made the mistake of concentrating on Masterton and not doing the northern regions (Patterson 2002).

Election issues in the campaign

Issues arise on the national agenda during an election campaign, and then to some extent get played out at the level of the local campaign. This occurred in Wairarapa as well. Colin James' comments on the aftermath of the 2002 general election identified some key 'substantive' issues (see chapter 3, this volume).

The first of these concerned 'personal security', which focused in part around GE. For most people, GE was a 'safe food' issue. As a national issue, GE seemed for a while to become dominant, obscuring other election issues. In the Wairarapa campaign, however, GE did not appear so significant. In the two months of election coverage by the *Wairarapa Times-Age*, there was only one political article relating to GE.

Another issue raised nationally was violence and crime. On this a traditional vote-winning issue, National, ACT and New Zealand First all campaigned strongly for harsher sentences and a harder line on criminals. This issue did spill over to the Wairarapa, with Raukawa-Tait making the most of the attention gained. When Sensible Sentencing Trust member Garth McVicar came to the Wairarapa during the campaign, Raukawa-Tait was the only candidate to be visited. This type of issue exposure was very important for Raukawa-Tait's campaign.

A third substantive issue playing out in the campaign concerned the strength and health of the economy. This had the effect of bolstering Labour support, since the Wairarapa economy had improved and appeared healthy. This also seemed true for New Zealand as a whole.

The results: 'Red all over'

The 2002 results make it clear that the Wairarapa electorate is no longer a National stronghold. Even the northern areas of the electorate that were newly included following the 2001 boundary changes produced high yields of Labour support. The spectacular downfall of National Party support nationwide undoubtedly made a large contribution, with Labour picking up many disillusioned National supporters.

As Table 19.1 shows, Beyer was re-elected in 2002 with a comfortable majority. Her 6,372 vote margin over her National Party opponent was more than twice her 1999 majority (of 3,033). However, despite a record enrolment in the electorate, the number of votes cast for electorate candidates in 2002 was only 30,661, well down on 1999, when there were 32,545 valid votes.

Another equivocal feature in Labour's win was that its party vote in the Wairarapa actually went down – from 11,897 in 1999 to 11,867 in 2002. Although this was only a slight difference, the result may have been due to a lack of campaign intensity on the part of a Labour Party confident of victory.

The high number of votes gained by Merepeka Raukawa-Tait exemplifies just how much personality and intense campaigning can reap positive results. Beyer stated that she 'sympathised with Ms Raukawa-Tait whose profile she felt may be tarnished by the failure to win the seat' (Sharpe 2002).

Table 19.1: Electorate and party votes in Wairarapa in the 2002 New Zealand general election

		Electorate vote		Party vote	
		#	%	#	%
Beyer, Georgina	Labour Party	13,572	44.26	11,867	38.37
Buchanan, Ian	National Party	7,200	23.48	7,678	24.83
Henderson, William	Jim Anderton's Progressive Coalition	223	0.73	498	1.61
MacFarlane, Ian	ACT New Zealand	625	2.04	1,770	5.72
Millington, Sarah	Green Party	861	2.81	1,827	5.91
Owen, Francis	United Future	617	2.01	1,735	5.61
Perry, Edwin	New Zealand First Party	1,552	5.06	3,605	11.66
Raukawa-Tait, Merepeka	Christian Heritage Party	5,852	19.09	891	2.88
Tait, Gerald	Alliance	159	0.52	311	1.01
	Aotearoa Legalise Cannabis Party			178	0.58
	Mana Maori Movement			5	0.02
	NMP			3	0.01
	ONENZ Party			32	0.10
	Outdoor Recreation NZ			525	1.70

Electorate votes			
Total Valid Electorate Votes	30,661	100.00	
Majority	6,372		
Informal Electorate Votes	264	0.85 (percentage of all Electorate Votes)	

Party Votes			
Total Valid Party Votes	30,925	100.00	
Informal Party Votes	121	0.39 (percentage of all Party Votes)	

Subsequently Raukawa-Tait and Christian Heritage leader Graham Capill had a very public falling-out over the party's failure to make gains.

The effects of MMP post-campaign

Incumbent candidates may fail to build up the party vote, since it can be argued that they do not benefit from it personally. In a sense, any party votes that a successful incumbent electorate MP attracts go only towards getting other list MPs into Parliament (see Ganley 1997, p.108). It would seem fitting that list MPs should perhaps devote themselves to their colleagues during campaign time, as a form of goodwill, but also to help their own election chances.

A related outcome of the somewhat unexpected collapse of the National Party during the 2002 campaign, was that the allegedly 'safe' list seat of Ian Buchanan was not quite high enough to pull him into Parliament. Despite the changes brought about by MMP, a list candidacy, even one relatively highly ranked, is no guarantee of a seat; and when it comes to the electorate race, if a candidate does not make sure that they are known and that others know what they have been doing, they can have little hope of getting into Parliament.

Another observation made of the 2002 general election that affected the campaign in the Wairarapa electorate has to do with a 'presidential' style of campaigning. By this is meant the prominence given to the leaders of the main parties by the media. This contrasts with more traditional election campaigns, where real electorate issues can be raised and grappled with as candidates conduct a dialogue with voters. When asked if there was any noticeable difference between the 1999 and 2002 campaigns, one of the members of Georgina Beyer's campaign committee noted:

> You don't hear local issues. You want your candidate to be elected, but if you want to involve people . . . the presidential style moves away from that. People turn off, they don't want to know about it (Patterson 2002).

Instead of local issues such as health, education and the economy, other influences such as the 'worm' and GE may hijack issues of greater personal concern to the public. If the media obscure the 'real' issues for a local community, this may reduce the likelihood that electors will engage with the political process. Declining election turnouts in recent years in New Zealand are testament to this.

New roles for the second-term MP

The career path of politics can be an insecure road to travel. For Georgina Beyer, the decision to stay on for another term could have been rewarded with additional privileges and promotions – or, depending on how the straws of promotion were drawn, she might have remained unchanged in her parliamentary status. As it happened, the position of Deputy Speaker in which she was interested was not given to her. Disappointing though this was, Beyer acquired the responsibility of chairperson of the Social Services

Select Committee, and was also appointed Deputy Chair of the Law and Order Select Committee.

When asked if much had changed for her since the election, Beyer responded by saying that her new responsibilities did not take much extra time away from the work that is most important for her, namely, that of her electorate. 'It [chairing the Social Services Select Committee] balances well as a promotion of not compromising my electorate work too much' (Beyer 2002). A second term in Parliament following a reasonably uneventful and unchallenging campaign basically involves getting back down to business, and improving on the public services for her electorate.

If one thing changed for Beyer after 2002, it was the diminishing attention given to her by the national and local media. Paradoxically for a politician, the MP is glad about this change:

> I am not covered [in the media] as much as last term and I am grateful for that. I've enjoyed the growing anonymity that I am getting because I have work to do . . . I would rather get caught doing things that have substance. Too easily I could have been a media MP with no substance; but I see it the other way round, substance first (Beyer 2002).

Conclusion

The 2002 election campaign has allowed for a window on the Wairarapa electorate, offering insights into a number of changes that have taken place in the electorate. Some have been physical, enabling the region to throw off its isolation and develop into an attractive tourist destination. Some have been social. Where people were once perhaps as closed-minded as the mountains that encircle its southern regions, diversity and enterprise are now hallmarks of a region that is presently home to many skilled workers and is creating jobs for more. Some of the changes have been political. The redrawing of electoral boundaries has resulted in Wairarapa becoming the largest electorate in the North Island. The change to MMP in 1996 continues to alter the way constituents in the electorate vote for their MPs and their government. The 2002 election took place within this changing social, economic and political environment. One of the main features of the campaign was the strong position that has come to be held by the electorate's incumbent, Georgina Beyer. She provides an example of an MP who has journeyed with her electorate, from a time of economic hardship to a new position of security and growth.

The 2002 campaign brought with it the surprise of an early election. For the incumbent candidate and the Labour Party, there were tangible benefits. With the government taking a 'steady as she goes' approach to almost everything it did, the campaign of its Wairarapa incumbent tended to follow suit, with a stable, successful and low-key result. Despite the relatively quiet victory, there were some interesting cross-currents, with the results achieved by the Christian Heritage candidate showing how deft voters are becoming at split ticket voting. But in the end, the wooing of Wairarapa by Georgina Beyer remained the main story in an election held in the small towns and communities just north of the New Zealand capital.

20

CHOOSING CANDIDATES: LABOUR AND NATIONAL IN 2002

Rob Salmond

This chapter is about candidate selection, which is an important part of the political process because it represents the expression of the parties' personnel preferences to the electorate-at-large. It is partly on the basis of these expressed preferences that the electorate makes its final electoral choice. If one set of candidate selections is better than another in a given situation, the choice of selection procedure can have an impact on a party's ultimate electoral performance.

New Zealand's 2002 election is a good context in which to study candidate selection for two reasons. First, the election was the third under MMP, New Zealand's new German-style 'personalised' proportional representation system, which replaced the previous first-past-the-post system. This allows us to see whether the methods of candidate selection used by parties, which have not changed in character since the electoral reform, are better suited to proportional representation (PR) systems – including mixed-member systems such as MMP – or to those using single-member districts. Second, the 2002 election saw the two major political parties in New Zealand, Labour and National, approach candidate selection with two very different goals: the president of the latter was trying to reform its parliamentary team, while Labour was seeking a renewed electoral mandate for essentially the same group of parliamentarians.

The analysis in this chapter is limited to the National and Labour parties. They are the two biggest parties in New Zealand politics, and by far the oldest. These two parties are, therefore, a different kind of entity from all others, with mature regional and local structures, long-standing incumbents, and the other trappings of 'major party' status (see Duverger 1954). This is important for candidate selection, because the mass-nature of these parties creates a larger number of internal constituencies that make claims on the candidate selection process. The fact that all other parties currently represented in the New Zealand Parliament still have the leader that they had when they first gained legislative representation increases this difference in institutional maturity.

No 'hard data' exists about candidate selection in New Zealand, except for its outcomes. Political parties shroud the process of candidate selection in secrecy, so as to preserve (as far as possible) the appearance of absolute solidarity once the slate of candidates is announced. Given the paucity of publicly available data, this chapter examines candidate selection in New Zealand primarily via interview material gathered during August and September 2002, following the 27 July election. Interviews were conducted with 12 prominent figures in the Labour and National parties, including the presidents of both parties, two successful parliamentary candidates, five unsuccessful candidates, and two senior party advisors.[1] Some follow-up interviews were also conducted in April 2003. In order to encourage frankness and confidentiality, individual interviewees are not identified as the source of particular remarks or quotations. Only through this type of interview can we start to unravel the web of informal deals and lobbying which lies behind the formal institutional processes of the two parties.

The secrecy surrounding candidate selection in New Zealand is not unique. In other developed democracies, party leaders (or small sets of insiders) also determine their party's candidates behind closed doors, without direct reference to the voting public (Gallagher 1988, pp.237–238). The details of their deliberations are often kept secret forever, and the lack of impartial information has made research in the subject difficult. Indeed, candidate selection has been called 'the secret garden of politics' (Gallagher 1988).

The electoral context

Under MMP, over half (currently 69) of the 120 seats in Parliament come from single-member districts, with the remainder coming from party lists. Voters have two votes, but the overall composition of the House of Representatives is determined solely by the 'party' vote, which is, in effect, aggregated over a single national district (i.e. the country as a whole). In the post-reform period (one of comparative instability in the New Zealand political landscape), there have been eight political parties, along with a number of independent MPs,[2] represented in Parliament. Only two of these, the National and Labour parties, have ever exceeded 20 percent of the vote, and these parties have done so in each of the three MMP elections. The district and the list selection procedures for both these parties are analysed in this chapter, mainly with reference to the 2002 election.

The early election caused all parties to run abbreviated election campaigns, and meant that many parties had to bring forward their candidate selection procedures from their originally scheduled dates. Both parties under scrutiny here, however, managed to go through all of their constitutionally mandated procedures.

Labour put forward a very 'status quo' set of candidates, with very few seriously contested constituency selections, and the incumbent MPs appearing almost in caucus ranking order at the head of the party list. This was due in part to a belief in the party's hierarchy that the electorate-at-large was generally satisfied with the government's performance since it was elected in 1999, and therefore that a 'steady as she goes' attitude to all aspects of the election campaign would reap rewards.

National, on the other hand, made a conscious attempt to present a fresh image to the public. It had lost the 1999 election after spending the previous nine years in office, and many of the 'old hands' from that government, some of whom had lost much of their individual popularity in their electorates, had been returned in 1999 via the party list. Some sitting MPs were defeated by non-incumbent challengers in constituency pre-selection for 2002, while others were given low list rankings, so that a group of newcomers, in the main favoured by then party president Michelle Boag, could be given electable positions.

The election returned Labour to power, although in a slightly different coalition arrangement, and handed National its worst election result ever. Some of the criticism of National centred around its list rankings and internal acrimony over selections.

Formal institutional procedures

Labour

The Labour Party's candidate selection rules are codified in the party's constitution. The party list selection procedures had to be created for the 1996 election, New Zealand's first under MMP, but the local constituency selection procedures remained basically the same as those used under the old single member district system.

Labour constituency selection meetings are presided over by a committee of six: three direct delegates from Labour Party headquarters, one or two delegates from the local Labour committee (depending on the size of the party at the local level), one delegate elected from the floor at the meeting, and one vote on the basis of a poll of those party rank-and-file members present at the special selection meeting (NZLP 2001, s.238). Following presentations from each nominee, the selection committee conducts its meeting and reaches its decision in private. The record of votes and of the poll of party members are never made public.

Labour's list selection is a more complicated two-tier process. The first selection process takes place at each of Labour's six regional Annual General Meetings in election year. Policy remits, position motions and election of local party officials are also dealt with at these meetings. Votes in the selection process are awarded according to an individual's status as a Member of Parliament, as a member of the Labour Party's New Zealand Council, as an elected member of a local authority, such as a city or regional council (one vote per person), or as a representative of various local organs of the Labour Party (one to four votes, depending on the status or membership of the party unit) (NZLP 2001, s.254). Each region ranks a given number of candidates, based on the proportion of the New Zealand population that lives within the region. A total of 120 candidates are ranked by the six regions (NZLP 2001, s.257).

At each of the regional meetings, candidates for the list nominate themselves for a particular position on the regional list. Sometimes there is no competition for particular spots, due to pre-arranged deals between delegates that will be discussed below; but when list spots are contested, the delegates decide by an exhaustive ballot on the list spot in question.[3] This exhaustive ballot requires a candidate to receive 50 percent +1 of all available votes in order to be granted a particular list spot. If no candidate receives the required votes on the first ballot, the lowest polling candidate is dropped from consideration and a second round of voting takes place. This process is repeated as required until there are only two candidates remaining, at which point one of them will necessarily receive over 50 percent of the available votes (NZLP 2001, s.258). After every five selections, the regional conference must pause for an 'equity review' to ensure that it 'fairly represents tangata whenua [Maori], women, men, ethnic groups such as Pacific Island peoples, age and youth' (NZLP 2001, s.259a). The ranked regional lists are published. This process is almost identical to that used by all major parties in Germany (Roberts 1988, pp.100–102), except that the elites of the regional party are less intrusive in the meetings in New Zealand than they are in Germany. This is probably because there is no national-level aggregation of lists in Germany, making the regional process much more important than it is in New Zealand. In Germany, separate lists are presented in each of the *Lander* (States), and list seats are awarded on a *Land*-by-*Land* basis following the election.

The second stage of the Labour selection process is a single meeting of a nationwide moderating committee, consisting of four senior officers of the party executive, three representatives of the parliamentary caucus, two members of the Maori policy committee, sixteen representatives of various nationwide constituencies within the party, and seven representatives of the party's regional executives (two representatives for Auckland and one each for the others). The first two places on the list are reserved for the leader and deputy leader, and the same exhaustive ballot structure for single list place as used in the regions is also used at the nationwide level for the other places. Like the regional meetings, the moderating committee pauses after every set of five selections to review the equity (across all the same cleavages as above, but also in terms of geography) of their selections. The votes themselves, and the deals that precede them (see section below), are kept secret.

National
The formal selection institutions in the National Party follow a broadly similar pattern to Labour's, although there are some important differences in the details. The electorate candidate selection process follows the same basic structure as in the Labour Party, namely a formal meeting with candidate presentations, followed by secret deliberations by a selection committee. The membership of the selection committee, however, is very different from that in the Labour Party. Each local (i.e. suburban) branch of the party is entitled to one delegate to the electorate selection committee for every 15 branch members (NZNP 2000, 112(b)). Should the number of delegates from the local branches to the electorate selection committee not exceed 60, the regional chairperson of the National Party may nominate 'top up' delegates to take the number of delegates to 60. Given that the total number of financial members of the National Party is not more than 7,000, then even the laxest definition of 'member' will require many top-up delegates in almost every electorate. There is no representation on the committee for the party's head office, and furthermore there is no guarantee

that the regional chairperson will act according to the wishes of the party's headquarters when nominating top-up delegates. Thus the formal procedures in the National Party give far less power to the centre than in the Labour Party.

National's selection process for the party list is, like Labour's, a two-tier process that starts at the party's regional meetings, and then moves to a national moderating committee. The rules are codified in the party's constitution. Each delegate (there are ten per electorate) is entitled to one vote in the regional list ranking process (NZNP 2000, s.149). Voting is by a single preferential ballot for all places on the regional list. Unlike Labour Party practice, the regional lists are never made public. Both of these elements are substantially different from the usual process in Germany. The National Party practice of considering all list places together in a single ballot may be especially telling in allowing more unintended consequences to surface than in the more deliberative systems – using a separate ballot for each list place – used by German parties and by the New Zealand Labour Party.

A nationwide moderating committee undertakes the second stage of the list selection process in both parties. In National, this committee comprises the five regional chairpeople, along with four other delegates from each region, the president, the parliamentary leader of the party, and five other representatives from head office. The top two spots on the National list are reserved for the leader and deputy leader of the parliamentary party. For places beyond the third, the committee 'shall have regard to the ranking of regional nominations and the need for balance across the totality of candidates representing the Party for both Constituencies and the List' (NZNP 2000, s.153(c)). All deliberations other than the final ranked list are kept secret.

The key differences between the parties in terms of their formal selection institutions are four-fold. First, there is no formal role for the head office of the National Party in local constituency selections, while the head office of the Labour Party holds almost half the votes on all local selection committees. Second, the regional list ranking process is iterated in the Labour Party, but is done via a single ballot in the National Party. This allows Labour delegates to update their preferences based on results high up the regional list, whereas National delegates do not have that opportunity. Third, representation on National's list moderating committee is heavily skewed towards representatives of the regional branches of the party, whereas representation on Labour's committee is skewed in favour of representatives of head office and other nationwide constituency groups. Fourth, Labour's formal processes are more proactive than National's in ensuring gender and ethnic balance in the list selection process.

Culture, claims and counterclaims

National

National's institutional arrangements stem from a positive belief on the part of party members in transparently democratic processes as far as possible. Indeed, all of the interviewees from the National Party pointed out that their party's processes, compared with those of their main rival, the Labour Party, were much more democratic.[4] This preoccupation with democratic process has gone so far, however, as to lead one National Party observer to think that the process was 'too bloody democratic if you ask me'. This sentiment was expressed in less colourful terms by two other National interviewees. The party believes that it should operate essentially as 69 autonomous units in the constituencies in the day-to-day running of party activities. These constituencies join together – but retain their electorate affiliations and interests – when deciding on nationwide matters such as list rankings.

The relative transparency and representativeness of the formal institutions do not, however, preclude strategic maneuverings and back room deals. While the party president has no formal power in constituency selections, s/he is able to strategically encourage candidates to either stand or stand aside in order for a desired outcome to eventuate. In 2002, for example, it appears that Michelle Boag (party president during the build-up to the election) strongly encouraged Dale Stephens to stand in Wellington Central so that the 'anti-Hekia Parata' vote was split between Stephens and Annabel Young (a long-time hopeful for the seat), thereby allowing Parata – a known favourite of Boag's – to gain the nomination, which she duly did. Stephens' incentive for this deal was the (informal) backing of Boag to run for selection in the neighboring constituency of Ohariu-Belmont. Stephens ended up as the candidate for this seat. While this 'deal' was never written down, two National Party sources independently detailed this agreement, and its existence was not denied by other sources that were asked about it.

Similar questions exist about Boag's successfully counseling Ian Lupton to drop out of the race in the Auckland seat of Waitakere, a race that eventually saw John Key beat incumbent (and Boag antagonist) Brian

Neeson. If Boag, as president, was able to exert influence over local races by strategically encouraging candidates to run or not run, can it really be said that local races are free from central party influence?

Further evidence of the fear of the influence of National Party central office comes from the Auckland seat of Tamaki, where incumbent Clem Simich – a known political enemy of Boag – brought forward his candidate selection meeting immediately on hearing the news of Boag's election to the presidency of the party. The selection process was completed before Boag had been in her new job for two weeks, whereas normal scheduling would have seen the Tamaki selection occurring at least three to four months later. If Boag could not exert influence over local selections in Tamaki, there would have been no reason for Simich and his constituency committee to shift the date for candidate selection so suddenly.

Of Michelle Boag's reputation for strategic maneuvering in the candidate selection process, one National Party interviewee said:

> So I was wondering what to do, and then the phone rang. It was Michelle, and I thought 'oh-oh – what's going on here?' You don't get any free phone calls from Michelle.

The practice of selecting the National Party's list is also not as transparent or democratic as the institutional arrangements would suggest. Most National Party interviewees agreed that the primary motivation on which voters act in regional and nationwide selection meetings is not the desire to build the best overall list, but rather the desire to get one's 'own' candidates as high as possible on the list under consideration. Thus the regional meetings become not a test of the candidates' relative electoral appeal, but rather of the comparative persuasive and deal-making powers of the leaders of each electorate's delegation. Similarly, the nationwide selection meeting, dominated as it is by regional representatives, becomes a loose quota-based system for placing people on the list. Given these considerations, it appears that the National Party operates from, in Schattschneider's (1942) terms, a weaker party base and structure than the Labour Party.

At the regional meetings, this motivation led voters from particular electorates to come to bloc-voting agreements against candidates from other electorates who were seen as threats to their own constituency's candidates. Of the four Wellington regional National Party candidates interviewed, three believed that there had been a significant degree of bloc-voting directed against them, while all disputed the bloc-voting claims of the others.

Interviews with other National Party officials appeared to confirm that some bloc-voting did take place. For example, local committees in the Wellington regional electorates of Wellington Central, Mana and Rongotai all selected non-incumbent women with significant publicity from other fields as their constituency candidates and list nominees. Given the party's comparatively conservative stance on women's representation, it appears that delegates to the Wellington regional conference decided that each of these candidates was a threat to the chances of the other two. One National Party interviewee confirmed that some electorate delegations appeared to have picked their favourites or dual favourites among these three new female candidates, and then systematically bloc-voted the other candidate(s) down on their preferential voting ballot. This bloc-voting at the regional level has been cited by more than one National Party observer as one of the reasons for the poor final list ranking of Glenda Hughes, National candidate for Rongotai, and high profile ex-police officer, sports psychologist and Commonwealth Games athlete.[5]

At the nationwide list selection meeting, in which 25 regional representatives and seven others turn the five regional lists into a single nationwide list, a similar motivation to get the best places for 'one's own' candidates seems to be very powerful. While the non-regional members of the committee do not formally have any people of 'their own' to protect, they are powerless to prevent a loose quota-system being developed by negotiation among the remaining 25 members. Table 20.1 shows the distribution of list places for each of the five regions over the first 50 places of the National Party list, split into blocks of ten places (the same method of division as used by the National Party committee):

Table 20.1: Regional representation on the National Party 2002 list

Region	1–10	11–20	21–30	31–40	41–50	Mean
Auckland	3	2	5	4	4	3.6
Central North Island	2	1	2	3	1	1.6
Wellington	1	3	1	1	4	2
Canterbury	3	1	1	1	1	1.4
Otago/Southland	1	3	1	1	0	1

Despite some small exceptions, the pattern of regionally based representation on the final party list seems clear. National Party interviewees cited further evidence from within the selection committee room that the regional quota system was a powerful force. Chris Finlayson, the Wellington regional party chairperson, had succeeded in getting three candidates into the sought-after and controversial places ranking from 11 to 20. Moreover, two of the three were not incumbent parliamentarians. When Finlayson attempted to gain more than one place in the 21–30 and 31–40 brackets, he was informed by representatives of other regions that he had 'had his turn', and the candidates he was pushing would need to wait. Those candidates were finally given four of the five slots between 46 and 50, none of which were realistically electable.

This result came despite the fact, agreed on by almost all National Party interviewees, that the Wellington region had put up a 'bumper crop' of high-quality candidates, many of whom were not currently MPs. In an election where elements of the party loyal to Michelle Boag were making every attempt to reform the party's personnel, the Wellington region appeared to have done its job spectacularly. Any credit the region got for this, however, was overridden by the desire on the part of the national list selection committee for fair representation for each of the party's five regions. Thus the meeting appears not to have produced the best list of candidates in the eyes of the committee members, but rather the best list possible given substantial informal constraints. One interviewee put it this way: 'We say we're a meritocracy. How are we merit-based when the system is based around quotas?' Said another: 'Our party doesn't practice democracy – it feigns democracy.'

Labour
The Labour Party's arrangements are based on a different culture, one that values coordination from the centre rather than the simple aggregation of distinct sub-parties.[6] As a consequence, the party's central office has a far greater degree of authority in every step of the process in the Labour Party than in the National Party. Indeed, the Labour Party's procedures led one non-partisan observer to suggest that Labour was 'putting the "centralism" back into "democratic centralism"'.

Again, however, this ideal-type view of the party's internal procedures should not be taken at face value. It is true that nominees of the Labour Party's central office account for almost a majority of those available at selection meetings, thus requiring the local party to be both activist and united (a rare combination in a mass party) to defeat them. Despite this institutional advantage, on rare occasions Labour's central office is defeated. For example, the selection of Judy Keall for Otaki in 1993 was a blow to the central party office. Then Labour Party president Michael Hirschfeld's hopes of getting Brian Brooks selected for Wellington Central in 1999 were dashed when the local members came out strongly in support of Marian Hobbs. The overall pattern of evidence, however, suggests a strongly centralised constituency selection process.

The pattern of influence works the same way in the Labour Party's list selection process. In the first round of selections, the multi-round nature of the process works to the advantage of incumbents, because of the culture which has emerged to avoid contested elections when at all possible. Thus most of the bargaining over the list placements at the regional level takes place before the meeting starts. Incumbents are far more likely to have name recognition in the party, and a strong group of local party members acting as delegates to the regional meeting, than non-incumbent candidates. This, coupled with the leadership's declared wish to have (almost without exception) the sitting MPs at the head of the party's list, creates strong formal and informal pressures for delegates to regional conferences to behave in a particular way. While it is early to make definitive judgments, with only three elections having been held under the new system, delegates have thus far been very willing to accommodate the wishes of incumbents and the leadership.

The influence of central office is magnified further at the nationwide selection meeting, where regional bodies of the party have only seven votes. While grassroots members are able (through delegates) to rank their region's list candidates, they seldom stray from the rankings that the party's headquarters appears to have wanted. The comparative lack of regional representation on the national committee (seven members, as opposed to National's 25) means that central office (which controls the rest of the committee) is generally able to nominate a list almost as they please. This allows them more actively to balance the list in terms of gender and ethnicity than the National Party can. Again, the central office does not get all of its way all of the time, but it does get 90 percent of its way 90 percent of the time.

Consequences and conclusions

There are two sets of inferences that can be drawn from the evidence uncovered in previous sections of this chapter. The first concerns the role that particular candidate selection procedures may have played in the 2002 election in New Zealand (especially with reference to the National Party). The second deals with the broader comparative question of the impact of candidate selection procedures on electoral outcomes.

In the first case, it seems clear that internal disharmony within the National Party hindered its ability to field its potentially best slate of candidates in the abbreviated 2002 election campaign. Certainly there were other factors that worked against National, such as a popular incumbent government and a larger than usual number of parties making strong claims on the centre-right vote, but internal disharmony played more than a trivial role in National's election disaster. The question then becomes: what caused this disquiet within National?

Part of the answer appears to lie in the candidate selections, especially at the party list level. Acrimony came from various quarters of the party over three aspects of the list selection process:
- the perceived maltreatment of some incumbents;
- the fact that a leader inevitably provokes controversy when making attempts to reform while lacking many of the necessary institutional tools;
- the use of a regional quota system that led to candidates in higher quality regional fields being placed further down the list than they felt they deserved.

The groups who would have felt most annoyed by these aspects of the selection process were multi-term incumbents not friendly to National Party President Michelle Boag, grassroots party activists adhering to stated party policy on the proper role (or lack thereof) of party headquarters in candidate selection, and disgruntled candidates from the Wellington region.

Certainly the first and third groups were vocal in criticising aspects of their own party's campaign and performance immediately after the election. While the behavior of the second group is not known, it is plausible that at least some of these conservative activists switched their votes from National to the ACT, New Zealand First, or United Future parties, all of whom were competing for votes from the centre-right. The election results, in which all parties of the centre-right except National increased their support from the start of the campaign, while National's fell dramatically, are entirely consistent with this inference.[7]

It would be fair to conclude, therefore, that the moderately decentralised (that is, highly decentralised in name, but less so in reality) candidate selection process used by National had negative electoral repercussions for the party in 2002. Had the party's list selection process not emphasised and elevated disagreements between already disparate regional units, then the tension may not have reached the public's consciousness. And had the informal tension between the centre and the regions, and between the various regions, been absent from the media coverage of the election campaign, it would have been easier for National to present a united front to the voters and to gain additional votes.

The second set of inferences, in relation to the broader comparative study of candidate selection systems, is far more tentative than the first. This is because this chapter is focused on a single country, and within that country on only one election and two parties. However, the information in this chapter raises two interesting points on which later comparative studies might attempt to elaborate. First, and non-controversially, this study provides further confirmation of the general conclusion in the existing political science literature that selection procedures do matter to a party's electoral performance. Although non-controversial, this finding should further strengthen belief in current theories of the importance of 'the secret garden of politics'.

Gallagher (1988, pp.258–261) finds that a nation's electoral rules do not affect the degree of centralisation in the candidate selection systems of parties in that country. The second and more controversial conclusion of this chapter, however, is that perhaps political science should also ask whether a substantial degree of centralisation helps a party to organise a party list in a proportional representation system in a way that preserves its image as a united front, and therefore aids its election chances. This question has not yet been rigorously examined in the literature on candidate selection, and the experience of the parties in New Zealand suggests that centralisation may indeed be helpful. While the evidence thus far can be interpreted only in a tentative way, the question is of great interest to one group that is a major 'consumer' of political science: democratic political parties.

Afterword

In April 2003, the National Party held a Special Conference to consider changes to the party's rules as recommended by a Strategic Review. A number of the changes related specifically to the party's candidate selection procedure, while others dealt with the position of National Party President, both of which have been major focuses in this chapter. This brief afterword outlines the changes, and comments on their likely impact on the party's candidate selection procedures in future elections.

First, and most importantly, the National Party will now allow its president to be chosen by a nine-member Board of Governors, whose membership includes the leader and one other member of the parliamentary wing of the party. This procedure significantly limits the ability of the president to challenge the parliamentary leader on personnel or strategic issues, because the president is now partially dependent on the leader for their institutional position. It appears that the parliamentary leader is now the only person with the institutional power to engage in wide-ranging personnel reform. The leader's dependence for their own position, however, on the parliamentary caucus constrains the leader's ability to reform the parliamentary wing of the party. Thus the reforms in this area serve further to entrench the position of caucus incumbents.

Second, the National Party has made three rule changes that will have an impact on candidate selection at the electorate level. A new minimum membership fee of $5.00 may help prevent attempts to pack a local party selectorate with personal friends and family just prior to an electorate selection meeting. Some interviewees believed that such a strategy was (unsuccessfully) employed by Brian Neeson after he learned that he was being challenged for selection in Waitakere. The new requirement that local electorate selections use a progressive (that is, exhaustive) rather than preferential ballot structure makes it much more significant for a candidate to win selection when they do not hold majority support, but that majority support is split between two or more rivals. Thus this requirement renders the strategic entry deal brokered by Michelle Boag in Wellington Central for the 2002 election mostly ineffective. The new rule that small electorate organisations (with less than 200 members) will have candidates selected for them by the new nationwide Board of Governors takes power away from the electorates and the regional chairpeople (who, under the previous rules, would have been responsible for providing top-up delegates), and relocates that power at the centre.

Third, no significant changes were made in relation to the party list selection procedures. In the above two areas, there appears to be a concerted effort at centralising power within the party, making the lack of action in this area somewhat surprising. The preferential ballot for the party list at the regional conferences and the regionally dominated list ranking committee were both retained. Thus the potential for bloc-voting at the regional level and loose regional quotas at the national level remains. Both of these elements were identified earlier in the chapter as partial causes of the acrimony within National over the party's list selection.

The changes to the National Party's rules in 2003 have closed many of the loopholes that allowed strategic maneuvering at the electorate level, weakened the office of party president vis-a-vis the parliamentary leader, and retained the regional domination of the selection procedure for the party's list. These changes are likely to further enhance the incumbency advantage enjoyed by party MPs, and thwart almost any attempt at large scale personnel reform. Earlier in this chapter, a problem was identified with the National Party's structure: a reforming leader could did not, under the old rules, have all the necessary institutional tools to engage in effective reform. The party appears to have solved this problem by removing many of the remaining tools, and putting in place lines of accountability which ensure that outspoken reformers will not be able to gain selection as the party's president. In the words of one interviewee:

> Important checks and balances on the power of the parliamentary leader have been removed. . . . What you're seeing is a political party at its darkest time reforming itself from a weak base. These are defensive reforms: reforms without aspiration.

MEDIA COVERAGE

21

'CONSTRUCTING SOMETHING FROM A FEW CRUMBS': A JOURNALIST'S VIEW OF THE CAMPAIGN

Al Morrison

The 2002 election campaign began with the view firmly established in the voters' collective mind that Labour was going to form the next government. The two key things feeding into this were that Labour had done a good job of managing the economy in its first term, and that in any case National did not present itself as a viable alternative.

There was a view within National, most vigorously articulated by MP Murray McCully, that in fact his party had been written out of the campaign by political journalists who had decided the poll results should reflect the final outcome. His criticism reached a new level with the first of several polls suggesting that a good number of National voters anticipated a centre-left win, were not uncomfortable about that, and were considering shifting their vote to Labour to ensure that the Greens were blocked from influence. Mr McCully criticised the way that I reported the first poll to identify the trend, as well as the fact that the poll question was asked at all, insisting that it created and/or led the trend.

Leaving aside these arguable points, there is no doubt that the growing mood in Labour's favour was both prolonged and solid. By the end of the first week of the campaign, Labour had sailed through with these assumptions intact, the prospect still alive of it being in a strong, if not majority, position in government, and the campaign shaping up in line with its strategy that 'boring is good'; that stability and the status quo was what the public was seeking and what only Labour could deliver.

The image crumbles

In the following two weeks, the image crumbled. For whatever reason, the police chose to release their report of a high-level fraud inquiry into the prime minister's signing of a painting done by someone else to raise money for charity. It was accompanied by, in my experience, an unprecedented release of supporting evidence and inquiry notes. The report, in its presentation by none other than the police commissioner himself, and in its totality, reflected badly on the prime minister. The essentially trivial saga of an ill-considered attempt to aid a charity was elevated in importance and cloaked in respectability by the police inquiry into a pedantic complaint of fraud.

What upped the ante severalfold was the issue surrounding a crop of corn allegedly contaminated by genetically engineered seed that had been allowed to mature and be harvested for human consumption. In essence, the issue was more about government behaviour and actions over the contaminated corn than about the corn itself. Labour deflected the issue, first to news media behaviour and then to the Greens' behaviour over the saga. Basically it went like this. On day one the story conjured an impression that the Labour-led coalition had not told the public, or even all ministers or caucus members, the full story. The perception of a cover-up was reinforced by the government's extraordinary silence for the best part of the first day the story ran. Polling indicates that Labour lost some 5–6 percent overnight and never recovered.

The night before the story broke (engineered to coincide with the release of Nicky Hager's book *Seeds of Distrust: The Story of a GE Cover-Up*), TV3 presenter John Campbell had interviewed the prime minister around the topic. He clearly had full knowledge of, but made no reference to, the upcoming launch of the book. The prime minister complained that she had been ambushed, and TV3's treatment of the story became a distraction and point of government counterpunch.

Radio New Zealand first ran the story at 9 am the next morning, coinciding with the release of the book (the publishers embargoed it, fearing an injunction). My story further fed the government's anger. In retrospect, I should have been more careful to describe the book's statements as allegations, or given the government a reasonable time (about three hours) to respond alongside the breaking of the story. The book itself was soundly based. Officials later agreed that its facts were largely correct, but took issue with the interpretation. Official papers later released were consistent with the thrust of the book. But my initial coverage left an opening for the government to move away from the substantive issue and create a distraction in the election-charged environment in which it broke. This led to the government parties arguing that journalists did not understand the difference between confidence and tolerance levels. Had they done so, they would have realised there was no cover-up because there was nothing to cover up. The government created further distraction by focusing on the fact that a Green Party candidate, Craig Potton, owned the company that published the book.

Labour's attacks on the Greens (which extended beyond the issue itself to a wholesale slamming of the Greens as an unreliable coalition partner for the centre-left) were accompanied by a dive in that party's support, from around 12 to 7 percent in the polls. For the centre-left, it was a 'lose-lose' situation.

Options for Labour

After all this, the view that Labour would lead the next government remained, but from a considerably weaker position than appeared likely at the outset of the campaign. There was a mix of constituencies at work. There was the inherently conservative vote that anticipated a Labour win and was not greatly bothered by the prospect, but did not want Labour dependent on the Greens. There was a fractured left that was disenchanted and homeless in the wake of the Alliance break-up. It was wondering how to ensure that Labour would not be able to govern alone, and was looking to the Greens. Then there was a bunch of undecideds still playing around with 'Labour majority versus Labour dependent on other parties' – but if dependent on other parties, which one(s)? Labour's attacks on the Greens had thrown doubt on what had previously been seen as a viable centre-left bracketing. Labour and the Greens emerged almost as sworn enemies rather than respectful friends, and a good distance away from a reliable working relationship. This extended the voters' search for a party to couple with Labour in government. As the mood shifted from Labour being able to govern alone – either outright or with Jim Anderton's party, which in effect amounted to the same thing – so the focus on the right mix of minor parties to discipline Labour in a government of checks and balances sharpened.

The GE corn issue had focused unwanted attention on the Greens, but the party also lost support on two other counts. Some disliked the way they intended to exercise the balance of power if they got it, being prepared to bring the government down if it removed the moratorium on GE field trials within the term as promised. Others just found them too hard an ask, as the spotlight shone on the Greens' ever-growing package deal. Voters were asked to support Green environmental policies alongside opposition to the war on terrorism, decriminalising cannabis, a suspicion of trade deals and conventional economic growth, a seemingly radical Maori policy, and so on.

New Zealand First remained an option, as Winston Peters ran a clever campaign that whipped up the anti-immigration, and in particular, anti-Asian sentiment. But this came at a price, as the other parties distanced themselves from his extremism and the xenophobic vote it attracted. So voters got the message that neither Labour nor National would govern with New Zealand First, and it was consigned to the role of a significant, permanent oppositional party.

A market gap appeared and grew, and United Future filled it. Peter Dunne's message of stability in government, family values and common sense policies – and his influence in entrenching the conservative end of a Labour-led government – was made, almost literally, in heaven, and the voters grasped at it.

And that is where the election settled. It left Labour grumpy that the prize of governing alone had been snatched away, and angry with the news media for its primary role in the betrayal – at least as Labour leaders saw it. During the height of the election campaign, one Labour leader 'accused' several news media outlets of being too fair in their coverage, the point being that the fairness was artificial. The media had created a level playing field on which Labour, National, and the minor parties were to get an equal share of the playing time, and be treated as if it were a competition between players of equal strength, skill, experience and success. There was a deep irritation in particular that the news media were calling Helen Clark the 'Labour leader' rather than the prime minister, and that what had gone before in Labour's successful first term in office was swept aside. Labour argued that the playing field was not level, and that the polls showed the voters had overwhelmingly endorsed it as a good government headed in the right direction and deserving of a second term in the face of a weak opposition. It argued that the news media failed to reflect that in its coverage, and give it fair credit for its achievements in government.

Labour believed that journalists took a strong and deliberate editorial position and set out to make sure that it would not be able to govern alone. It believed that those journalists primarily responsible did so by shifting the focus to minor parties, and treating the two main parties with equal disdain and disrespect. It was a view forged in the heat of a very bruising election campaign that the prime minister regarded as the dirtiest in living memory. The level of anger died down after the campaign, but the post-election relationship between Labour's leadership and the political journalists was considerably more tense as a result.

Issues to ponder

That heightened professional tension is no bad thing. There was a feeling among some on both sides that familiarity was breeding contempt. But the campaign left the news media with some issues to ponder. MMP has made the notion of balance particularly troublesome. The basis on which you decide to include or exclude parties in coverage of a specific issue, or in such events as the leaders' debates, is arguable, because the grounds on which a decision can be based are varied. Is presence and/or size in the previous Parliament a fair guide? Should current polling determine the extent of coverage? If so, what do you do with a party such as United Future, that jumps from less than 1 percent at the start of the campaign to around 7 percent by the final week?

My own view is that elections are a 'green fields' exercise on a level playing field in which all players seek a fresh mandate. They must all therefore be treated equally, in a game where the rules are arbitrary and open to the referees' interpretation. If election campaigns are not clean slates, but rather a point in a seamless political process, then fresh judgements at the outset of the campaign are not justifiable. It is an interesting argument with significant implications for the news media and the way that campaigns are to be approached.

The news media, and the political parties, are becoming increasingly aware of the difficulty of running a party vote campaign. The local electorate campaigns of the old first-past-the-post system were relatively easy for a party to contest and for the news media to cover. But in the 2002 election, only one constituency campaign really mattered, and that was in Waitakere. It mattered only to the extent that the Alliance leader Laile Harré appeared to have some chance of winning the seat, thus keeping her party tenuously alive. The rest of the potentially significant constituencies – Tauranga, Coromandel, Ohariu-Belmont, and Wigram – had either become irrelevant or had arrived at predictable outcomes well out from election day.

So how do you run a national campaign for a party vote? Three elements dominated the 2002 campaign. First, the political parties' campaigns were leadership-driven and designed around mass-audience (mainly television) exposure. That meant creating photo opportunities and sound bites. It was a campaign that produced little material for in-depth reportage. The leaders were whizzed from place to place for quick-fire meetings, often made up of ticket-only party faithful. Even the walkabouts, which rarely produce much of substance, were rapid and carefully managed. There were few genuine public meetings. Journalism is usually a matter of taking a slice of bread from the loaf. This campaign was about constructing something from a few crumbs.

Second, the polls played a significant role. The tracking of support as it swirled around as never before was fascinating. The polls were the only reliable way to track the changing public mood. When United Future burst into recognition, the polls gave the news media a new focus. But the focus on polls also created problems, particularly in Waitakere, where the Alliance made public what was no more than one night of a rolling poll of typically well below 200 voters a time. The result was offered as evidence of Laile Harré edging Labour's Lynne Pillay out. The Engineers Union, who employed Ms Pillay and had promoted her as a candidate, waded in with its own poll to counterbalance with results that showed the opposite. The *New Zealand Herald* also created problems by issuing electorate polls that compared candidate names in some cases with party names only in others. The news media has some serious thinking to do about polls and their use.

Third, the television leaders' debates played a large part in the campaign. The format of leaders at lecterns in set pieces controlled by television stars in front of stacked audiences seemed past its 'use by' date. Efforts were made to inject new approaches: one-on-one interviews, and panels grilling a procession of leaders. In addition, the notorious 'worm' made (in my view) a welcome comeback. It is at least an attempt to inject an uncommitted voter's opinion into debate, and to deliver on the principle that elections are for voters, not politicians. But arguably 'the worm' is too influential, given the difficulty of getting it right in terms of its being a valid measure of anything meaningful. Leaders' debates are likely to become an increasingly influential feature of future election campaigns, and the news media need to think about new and better ways to present them. Certainly the major parties were left feeling grumpy about the formats and standard of debate, and there was a determination by them to take greater control next election and be prepared not to take part unless they had an influence.

A most elegant outcome

The standout feature of the 2002 election campaign was the lack of nationwide debate around the big policy issues. Potentially, engaging the parties and voters in debate over the important questions of policy is a way of dealing with the nationwide party vote campaign. But despite efforts, debate over policy did not fire in this campaign. Health barely figured; even the depleted services at Kaitaia were corralled as issues, presenting almost as a welcome local issue that deflected from saturation election coverage. ACT had one of the most interesting health policies of the campaign – that any citizen assessed as needing treatment who had not received it within a prescribed period of safety could have the treatment carried out by the private sector at the state's expense. But this radical and interesting notion did not spark debate and ACT did not pursue it. Nor did education issues fire. In fact, Bill English came in for criticism for sounding like a broken record on the teachers' dispute, and for his resurrection of old National policy planks as the answer to better schools.

There were three notable issues that the parties chose to push. Immigration was, in the end, left to Winston Peters, because even somewhat sympathetic parties like ACT found his extreme views offensive, and that had the effect of scaring off genuine debate. Treaty of Waitangi issues surfaced, with the right wing parties arguing for time limits to settlements, and the left wing parties arguing against them. The issue did not fire and did not appear to move votes. The third issue around which the parties created a lot of noise was the need for tougher sentences. The market was crowded on the right, as the parties competed for the title of which was prepared to lock up the most people for the longest time. The left did not take this debate on, instead attempting to argue that it had satisfied the public thirst for tougher punishments. There was no rigorous policy debate on the effect of tougher sentences on prevention; or on how you resolve the practical problem of communities screaming for more prisons, but unwilling to host one in their own neighbourhood; or on the cost-benefit aspect of the approach. It was not policy debate so much as sloganeering. As for the economy, ACT emphasised a tax cut for every worker on its billboards but said little about it otherwise. National had little to offer beyond the resurrection of past policies – privatising ACC, modest tax cuts at the top and, for business, labour market reform yet again.

It is interesting that post-election, Labour in particular was critical of journalists for not promoting policy debate, because Labour itself constructed its campaign around its record in office, rather than new policy initiatives. In fact, many news media outlets did prepare and run copious material designed to spark policy debate. But it was a campaign dominated by Labour asserting that it had earned the right to a second term in the face of a successful first one. In the absence of any viable alternative, the voters bought the line, but increasingly looked for the checks and balances of fettered power, as MMP allows them to do. What they delivered was a most elegant outcome.

22

NEWS, NEWSZAK, NEW ZEALAND: THE ROLE, PERFORMANCE AND IMPACT OF TELEVISION IN THE GENERAL ELECTION OF 2002

Tim Bale

The American social critic Walter Lippman once observed with characteristic pessimism that the media was 'like the beam of a searchlight that moves restlessly about bringing one episode and then another out of darkness into vision'. Politicians, he claimed, 'cannot do the work of the world by this light alone. They cannot govern society by episodes, incidents and interruptions' (Lippman 1922, p.229). Increasingly, however, they have to. Everyday politics is now an essentially mediated activity: getting anything done almost depends on it being so dull as not to attract attention, or so headline-grabbing that it demands public action. Elections, however, occupy an odd place in this scheme of things. On the one hand, they are largely fought out on television – a platform where, in New Zealand at least, notions of public service have long taken second place to commercial realities. On the other, those who fight them continue to expect that same platform to accord the four week contest we call the campaign a protected status that has no place in a world where – due to legislation which they themselves were responsible for passing – the dollar rather than democracy is king.

Inevitably, this demand that, at least once every three years, politicians be allowed to lay out their wares free of 'episodes, incidents and interruptions' clashes with the right of the electronic fourth estate to push its own product to people whose tastes it claims to know best. Clearly the result will not be an absolute victory for one side or the other. A reasonable trade-off is the best that can be hoped for. But this begs a question that deserves an answer, even at the risk of being accused of hopelessly high-minded naiveté and, worse still perhaps, siding with the politicians. Is a reasonable trade-off really what we have?

Democracy disdained?

Television coverage of the 2002 campaign was just like television coverage of the 1996 and 1999 campaigns – only more so. Election coverage made up about a quarter of the news on the two main channels, with the state-owned broadcaster (TV1) and its commercial competitor (TV3) all but crowding out their limited discussion of policy issues and party programmes with a focus on campaign strategies, speculation on who was winning (the 'horse race' aspect), and post-election coalitions.[1] This will come as no surprise – but also precious little comfort – to those who believe that the role of the media during elections is essentially to let voters know where parties stand on the issues that the public routinely say they most care about, such as health, education, the economy, and law and order.[2]

New Zealand television's supposed failure to do what idealists (and even some national newspaper editors) still consider to be the media's democratic duty reflects its reluctance to fully suspend what are essentially commercially oriented news values for the duration of the campaign. This is as understandable as it is predictable: the news, after all, is at best 'a workable compromise between the economic need of news organisations to attract and hold their audiences and the polity's need for a public forum' (Patterson 2000, p.264). Given that television news and current affairs already devote disproportionate time to elections, in spite of the fact that politics is a turn-off for a substantial portion of its audience, it may be too much also to expect the medium to abandon its notions of what does and does not constitute a good story (see Masterton 1998).

Long-term social, economic and institutional problems, and parties' suggested solutions to them, do not generally score well on the criteria routinely (if subconsciously) employed by television news producers (see Iyengar 1993). For a start, they are rarely very visual. Nor (without risking accusations of bias, anyway) are they easy to present emotively, via, for example, a personalised 'human interest' angle. They are not necessarily as conflictual as might be imagined. They are rarely intense. They are more often than not ambiguous. They are not always of relevance (or even intelligible) to the majority of viewers. They may well be depressingly and/or boringly predictable, as well as seemingly intractable. And – unless they involve some kind of investigative revelations or pseudo-gladiatorial combat with a prominent politician – it is not often that they afford any opportunity for the 'celebrification' of the journalist that increasingly characterises network news (see McGregor 2002). In New Zealand, as in many (though not all) advanced democracies, the news is now 'newszak' (Franklin 1997) – 'cootchie coo news' that has all but abandoned yesterday's 'low-key, authoritative, neutral' tone (where 'the messenger [was] subservient to the message and the message unadorned') in favour of 'sympathy, prejudice and sheer drama', all 'overlaid with sentiment in an attempt to hook the viewer into an emotional response' that will see them safely through the ad breaks (Edwards 2002, p.17).

But the move toward newszak is not the only reason for the lack of focus on policy issues and parties' positions towards them. It also reflects another, wider trend: the tendency of journalists to assert their independence from politicians, in the face of increasingly intense efforts on the part of the latter to control the news agenda and the way they are presented within it. Political parties all over the world have professionalised their media relations (Farrell and Webb 2000). At election time this has seen them seeking, first, to bully journalists into their version of what is and is not important and fair, and secondly, to spoon-feed them with neatly pre-packaged stories based on stage-managed 'pseudo-events' from the so-called 'campaign trail'.[3] As a response to being force-fed with what (ironically) their own coverage had originally indicated to politicians they wanted, journalists and producers the world over have taken to 'disdaining the news' (Levy 1981).

During elections, 'disdaining' boils down to undermining the efforts of politicians, by pointing out to viewers the spinning and the strategic intent behind their statements and pseudo-events, and by revealing the tensions beneath the shows of unity and the fluster and flap beneath the calm and collected exterior (see Blumler, Kavanagh and Nossiter 1996, pp.54–5). Most of the time this is insidious, done routinely (and thus barely consciously) in the course of reportage and comment on substantive stories. But occasionally whole packages – big or small – can be devoted to disdaining. One example from campaign 2002 involved alluding to the fact that the ACT Party, having secured 'a prime spot' in 'the latest game of one-upmanship in the crowded law and order corner' (TV3, 23 July) by putting up a billboard outside the home of crime-crusader Norm Withers, promptly removed it after the cameras had packed up and gone. Another was a biting lament (17 July) by one of TV3's parliamentary reporters on the replacement of traditional political meetings by sanitised, risk-free, invitation-only, no-time-for-questions, fly-in/fly-out photo-opportunities.

Mainstream parties may object to their portrayal as virtual con-artists or conjurers, whose tricks need explaining and exposing lest they put one over on us all. But like parties all over the world who enthusiastically embraced media logic without thinking through its impact on the nature and quality of democracy (see Meyer 2002), they are no less responsible than broadcasters for the downward spiral into which campaign coverage seems to be locked – a spiral which, incidentally, plays right into the hands of entrepreneurial, populist politicians.[4]

If it were simply a case of parties trying too hard to produce what they think the media wants, the resulting shrinkage of issues-based coverage might be more easily reversed. However, other aspects of the professionalisation of campaigning militate against such a switchback. An obvious example is the extent to which, as part of their attempt to ensure equal treatment and balance, parties make it clear to programme-makers that they will be closely monitoring their output. This effectively encourages broadcasters not to home in on particular policy issues (let alone attempt judgement calls on them), since to do so will inevitably court complaints and accusations of bias from those parties for whom that issue is not thought of as a winner. Some will still be covered because they are genuine news stories, whether one party likes it or not: a good example in 2002 was the secondary teachers' dispute, which (presumably much to the chagrin of the government, and albeit in a manner which probably generated more heat than light for viewers) was accorded a great deal of airtime throughout the campaign period.[5] Given the heightened state of awareness among the parties, it is generally 'safer' for the networks to confine the treatment of policies and issues either to short pre-recorded packages (which can be more or less arbitrarily slotted in as back-end filler material in any given news hour) or to non-news election specials or debates. In these formats, broadcasters can more tightly control balance by affording some more or less agreed share of time to each party over a broader (though never deeper) range of (policy or issue-oriented) topics.[6] On the news itself, it is ironically far safer (in terms of both avoiding politicians' complaints, and losing viewers with strong partisan opinions), and of course far cheaper (given the costs of interviewing independent experts and shooting fresh footage), to steer away from the issues and simply declare a half-joking, half-jaundiced plague on both (or under MMP all) the parties' houses.

Something fishy right from the start

That this stance has become standard was evident from the very beginning of the campaign, particularly on TV3. The voiceover provided by its political editor to its first package, which started with a visit by the prime minister to a fish-retailer, began in characteristic fashion: 'Day one of the campaign, and the prime minister's already talking a load of abalone!' Viewers were then told that, after criticising a particular minor party leader, she apparently 'turned her attention to rubbishing' the leader of the Opposition and demonstrating 'her growing disdain for the Greens'. 'Dear me', tutted TV3's news anchor, who'd already told his audience at the top of the hour that the emerging 'battle tactics' of the election seemed to consist largely of the parties calling each other 'nasty names.' After a quick two-way with his political editor on the prime minister (who apparently 'want[ed] it to be a very boring campaign'), he then introduced a package poking fun at National's leader for eating fish and chips before an event designed to publicise the party's position on health – 'a policy launch light on details but huge on calories'. The ensuing two-way, however, centred on the appearance of the leader's wife alongside her husband, with the roving reporter agreeing that:

> she's certainly been prominent . . . It's got a lot to do with this image that National's trying to put out of Bill English: this family man with the common touch. They're looking for good television images and certainly Mary English has been playing the game today.

So far, so predictable. But how much further could it go before it went a little too far? On 3 July, TV3's political editor was asked by a news anchor for her views on a controversial statement by one of the Greens' co-leaders, to the effect that Labour's insistence on lifting the GE moratorium made her wonder whether it was even worth the Greens allowing it to form a government, let alone threatening to bring it down a year or so later. 'The words "naïve, stupid, regrettable" come to mind immediately', she opined.

Right from the beginning, then, New Zealand's television journalists were adopting the 'interpretive reporting' approach that, all around the world, has seen reporters abandon detached scepticism for derisive cynicism, as they move from what one British commentator has recently called 'the age of disdain' into what he calls the 'age of contempt' (Barnett 2002, pp.404–5), or from what American observers have labelled 'watchdog' toward 'junkyard' or 'attack-dog' journalism (Sabato 1991).[7] Central to the style is an all-consuming interest in the *game* rather than the *purpose* of politics, a relentlessly negative tone, and a tendency for the voices of politicians to be drowned out by those supposedly reporting their activities. All of this may ultimately 'rob political leaders of the public confidence that is required to govern effectively' and create 'a politics of shifting standards and fleeting controversies, spurring citizens to demand immediate solutions to stubborn problems, which in turn encourages politicians to pursue short-term and ultimately self-limiting polities and strategies' (Patterson 2000, p.263; see also Robinson 1977, and Capella and Jamieson 1997).

'Traction' over truth

Some will see such high-minded hand-wringing as overblown, and prefer to see in the very same developments 'the emergence of a demystificatory, potentially empowering commentary on the nature of the political process ... which adds to rather than detracts from the stock of useful information available to the average citizen' (McNair 2000, p.175). But this surely ignores the fact that journalists' desire to deconstruct party strategy can actually reduce that stock of information as well. In fact, the 2002 campaign in New Zealand contains a number of examples of the media's instinct to disdain conflicting with its acknowledged duty to inform as well as entertain. On 17 July, for instance, the government released provisional crime figures just as a march arrived on the steps of Parliament to press the case for tougher treatment for violent offenders. The march (unsurprisingly, given the importance of the issue, and the visual impact of the crosses carried by marchers to represent murder victims) was given headline treatment. In a two-way that followed its package on the topic, *One News*'s anchor asked his political editor, 'Do these figures reflect those views, that we are indeed a violent society?' The answer was a classic piece of disdaining deconstruction:

> Well, Richard, what these figures reflect is that Labour is very concerned about its position on law and order – not so much its position as the perception the public has about it – and they're concerned that other parties are getting the jump on them . . . They're worried that, despite the fact that they say they've been tough on the issue, they feel exposed on it, that the public does not recognise that – and that's a big problem for them in the campaign.

Probably – even obviously – true. But it might have been more helpful to viewers-as-voters if they had also been given a chance to see what the government's figures purported to show. The political editor appeared to have them in his hand – they were presumably contained on the sheets of paper he was waving around – but neither he nor the anchor ever let viewers in on the secret. Perhaps time was especially tight that night, possibly due to a three-minute package on the apparently vital part the leaders' spouses were playing in the election. While it was of course fascinating to know that the prime minister's husband saw his role as 'a backroom one, just keeping the house going, making sure it's well stocked, that meals are on the table', it may have been just a tiny bit less relevant than whether the government's response to public concern on crime was indeed as inadequate as protesters seemed to think – especially as TV3 had already run a very similar 'spouse appeal' story ten days previously.

But perhaps the most obvious case of broadcast news failing to deal properly with a politically relevant issue, because of its obsession with strategy and tactics, was its treatment of National's accusation that the government and Air New Zealand were sitting on a plan to sell off a quarter of the latter to Australian rival Qantas – a plan that, as National predicted, did indeed duly emerge fully fledged (to much genuine public interest and debate) after the election. Dismissed by TV1 as the gesture of an opposition leader 'desperate for traction' on 18 July, the story drowned for days as the network concentrated (as did its rival) on Labour's attack advertising and National's inner turmoil, until resurfacing, albeit temporarily, in a story by the network's business editor. Only on the day before the election did it hit the *One News* headlines, accompanied by denials from the government and a 'fuming' head of the airline. Even then things moved swiftly on to a preview (and of course deconstruction) by the political editor of the closing addresses of the party leaders, which any viewers still interested could have spent the evening watching for themselves. The story did even more of a now-you-see-it now-you-don't act on TV3, only popping back up again on the eve of the election – although not, one had the feeling, because it was taken seriously, but rather because it allowed the news anchor (by quoting the airline's head) the thrill of saying in prime time 'It's a load of bollocks'.

'Corngate' – more sinned against than sinning?

By far the most obvious case, however, of the trade-off between information and entertainment, between democratic watchdog journalism and attack-dog celebrity journalism, was 'corngate'. Television coverage of the mid-campaign allegation that the government had covered up the planting, growth and harvesting of GM contaminated corn has to be seen in terms of proximate and ultimate causes. The first of the former was surely what journalists and producers thought (and openly suggested to viewers) were earlier 'heavy-handed' attempts on the part of the prime minister to use threats of legal action to prevent them carrying full details of opposition criticism of her role in the police investigation into 'paintergate' that supposedly saw the campaign get 'down and dirty' (*3 News*, 7 July), and therefore dominated political coverage between July 5 and July 8. Corngate coverage, in other words, was 'round two' of an ongoing bout between the media and the prime minister over the determination of the former to cover what it wanted. Ironically, this determination may have begun as a reaction to whisperings that prior to the election, the media had enjoyed far too cosy a relationship with the woman who 'has turned the cellphone into a powerful tool for both meeting the media's requirements and her own' (O'Leary 2002, p.197).[8]

But television coverage of corngate also has to be seen in the light of more than just increasingly poor relations between a particularly dominant prime minister and a normally compliant set of news providers, newly determined to assert their right to snatch (at least occasionally) the agenda from politicians. It also has to be seen in the context of the product they seek to fashion and the way in which (just as in politics, in fact) that product and its marketing have, rightly or wrongly, come to feed-back on each other. News has to sell and be sold. Since it is available elsewhere and ever-changing, the best way is through a brand. Apart from studio sets and graphics, virtually the only way of branding is via those who present the news, namely the reporters and, most of all, the newsreaders or anchors, who seem compelled to become celebrities – 'personalities' every bit as real and important to viewers as the politicians whom they report on, interact with and, increasingly, go up against. As one international study concludes, broadcast journalists these days 'are functioning less as simple conveyors of information and more as actors involved centrally in the nation's political debate'. These actors 'seek to work their way into the ranks of the favoured few' in their network's 'star system' by 'doing battle with politicians and exposing their personal and political weaknesses – and the higher placed the victim, the more glorious the victory' (Gunther et al. 2000, p.437).

Such words cannot help but bring to mind the journalist who played the biggest part in corngate – a man allowed, indeed encouraged, by his employers to be both a newsreader and an interviewer, thereby 'inviting a confusion between disinterested reporting and aggressive interrogation, which is never entirely disinterested, if only because the interrogator's ego is invariably involved' (Edwards 2002, p.23). The *3 News* special on 10 July was a mess on many fronts. The pre-recorded package – 'what you've never been told is that the shipment [of sweetcorn] was contaminated with genetically-engineered seed'; 'we look in detail at the government's role in covering the entire affair up'; 'they left the plants in the sunlight and kept us in the dark and then they left us to eat the evidence' – was a question-begging travesty. The interview – where the prime minister (having given from memory an off-the-cuff account of what happened that, in hindsight, was not far off the mark) was (a) continually interrupted, (b) quizzed on documents so specific she couldn't have seen them in the first place, let alone recalled them, and (c) all but accused of lying about not recalling them – was even worse. Politicians – and viewers – should expect tough questioning, and perhaps the prime minister had had it too easy for too long. But this was more than tough. This was a man on a mission, a self-appointed people's plenipotentiary so utterly convinced of his role and his cause that he simply didn't know when to stop.

To say this is not to suggest that corngate was just about TV3's John Campbell seeking to recreate the journalistic equivalent of the testosterone high that he got after the famously combative interview he conducted with Jenny Shipley purportedly cost her the leadership of the Opposition. Neither is it to deny that the interview, by exposing Helen Clark's tendency to use the royal 'we' and not to suffer inconvenient fools gladly, brought up some potentially relevant questions of character. Nor is it to deny that her outrage at being 'ambushed' and 'set up' began, as time went on, to smack of an attempt to distract the public from her government's failure to produce a convincing rebuttal for almost a day (which, in today's media-saturated world, is a long time in politics).[9] But it is to suggest that the decision to break the story without the kind of groundwork that might either have contained that outrage, or enabled a more convincing comeback to it, was bound up with a news product that promotes trial by celebrity – in this case, a celebrity who rushed to judgement (or rather to join the prosecution) without doing enough to establish the case for the defence first.

Part of that failure is rooted in practicalities as well as personalities. Enthusiasm for crossing the line between watchdog and attack-dog journalism, between the age of disdain and the age of contempt, is occurring just as increased competitive pressures are giving journalists less time, space and resources either to do investigative reporting in the first place, or to do it in such a way that they can stand the story up under the weight of the reaction of those who stand to lose most by it. Once the sweetcorn story broke, the lack of real homework by those who broke it, and the inability or unwillingness of those who followed up to do any either, became painfully apparent. TV3, with more at stake, worked harder than its rival to find out what had really happened, with political reporter Stephen Parker deserving an honourable mention for his ability to cut through the 'cornfusion' to the core questions of contamination-testing and bureaucratic/political process. But, other than playing off the researcher behind the allegations and the ministers scrambling to rebut them, it had little more to go on than what was in the book that first contained them. This, combined with what has been called 'a much heightened obsession . . . always to be "moving the story on"' (Barnett and Gaber 2001, pp.87–88) almost guaranteed that the latter would be best achieved by speculating on what it might mean for the prime minister's 'credibility' and Labour's vote share ('these sweetcorn could dish up a disaster at the polls' by prompting yet 'another attack on her integrity').[10] In short, both networks moved quickly to focus on the fall-out as much as (and pretty soon more than) the facts.

Of course that fall-out was important, especially inasmuch as it might affect support for and relations between potential coalition partners.[11] Whatever else it was, corngate was a reminder of the inability of Labour and the Greens to work together, and in that sense it probably provided a useful 'cognitive short-cut' that busy, largely uninterested, middle-of-the-road voters needed to make their voting decisions (see Sniderman, Brody and Tetlock 1998). But this was largely a positive byproduct of a decision based primarily on news values and practicality. The lack of ongoing visuals (there are only so many times you can show pictures of the same field of swaying sweetcorn), along with concern that the story's technicalities were beyond the reach of most viewers (reinforced by the government choosing to emphasise 'the science' and taking the constitutionally debatable step of wheeling-out public servants to defend it), made it almost inevitable that the story would be swiftly transformed into a ready-made 'conflict story telling frame' (see Rupar 2002) that was thought most likely to maintain viewer interest and hence audience share. *One News*, notwithstanding its almost obligatory attempt on the second day of the story (11 July) to disentangle what had actually happened, handled the story primarily from the point of view of the potential impact on prime ministerial credibility; on votes ('Has corn contaminated their campaign?' 'No way round it. This is going to be damaging for Labour'); and on the stand-off between a prime minister 'almost incandescent with rage' and the Greens, whom she was now apparently 'accusing . . . of playing dirty'.

But the fact that such speculation won out over a more sustained attempt to research the story itself reflected more than news values alone. It was a matter of media evolution. Like the all-mouth-and-no-homework interview that began it, corngate was rooted in the type of journalist and journalism such values almost inevitably select for. An experienced member of the parliamentary press gallery, which is New Zealand's equivalent of the British system of lobby correspondents, puts it neatly, when he notes (Riddell 2002, p.203) that:

> Old-style reporting of politics used to be by newspapers and radio that . . . reported what happened and who said it at great length and little else. Today, to describe a news medium as 'a journal of record' would be an insult. What is 'news' today is why things are done and said, and a reporter who predicts what is going to happen and why . . . is treasured. News editors want political news that competes with wars, murders, rapes, traffic accidents, corruption, sporting triumphs and disasters . . . Television coverage of politics has had the most dramatic impact on all this.[12]

Three more things were important in that medium's coverage of corngate. The first was the government's highly effective rearguard action, including a classic 'dumping' exercise that saw it (as *One News*, like its rival, felt obliged to inform its viewers) 'swamping the media with information', most obviously in the form of a huge dossier which thudded onto reporters' desks on Friday afternoon.

The second (and related) factor was that it was simply too hard, too resource-intensive and also too politically risky for those reporters to attempt to disentangle the events and the science behind the story, in order to judge whether a breach in biosecurity had occurred, and how appropriate the authorities' response had been. Easier by far to resort to the post-modernist relativism of the *One News* reporter who wrapped up a package on the issue by shrugging, 'The same set of facts, but a different interpretation. And it's unlikely that the two sides will ever agree.'

The third factor reflected the reality that nowadays more media-savvy parties (and governments), recognising that the media will jostle among themselves for access to the sources upon whom they ultimately depend, have less and less compunction about sanctioning (or threatening to sanction) awkward outlets. This they do by, for example, choosing to be more available to their competitors, or by demanding favourable groundrules concerning, for instance, what may and may not be covered in an interview, knowing that there is a competing broadcaster who may be happy to bow to such conditions.[13] Usually these threats are made (or sometimes just implied) in private: public hints that Clark and Labour might engage in some kind of boycott against TV3 were therefore atypical. They may also have been counterproductive, in that they reinforced the impression of bullying intolerance that may have lost Labour votes in the wake of corngate. On the other hand, they arguably achieved what presumably they were intended to achieve, namely to encourage news organisations not to pursue the story as aggressively as might otherwise have been the case. Whether it was this, or the easy-going style of the host, which saw the prime minister given such an easy ride on the issue by TV1's 'flagship' current affairs show, we shall never know.

In the end, television's reluctance to dig deeper into the facts of the story, rather than turn almost immediately to speculation on its ramifications, came down to something that everyone can understand. Quite simply, something newer and fresher (and less difficult to understand, and less risky to communicate) came along to take corngate's place. It is to that event – or was it another pseudo-event? – that we now turn.

Turning the worm to best advantage

The idea that contemporary elections are virtually decided on, if not by, television is commonplace. But it is probably wrong, at least in its full-strength version, which imagines hordes of undecided voters being swung this way and that by fiendishly media-savvy politicians and more or less biased broadcasters. The little academic research there is supporting significant 'media effects' produces results which, in the words of one of its leading practitioners, 'are remarkable for their consistency with research findings from previous decades, which concluded that reinforcement rather than change was the main effect, if any, on vote choice' (Semetko 2000, p.373). In short, watching television, especially non-partisan news broadcasts, during the campaign tends to confirm voter prejudices and preconceptions rather than shift them, if indeed it does anything at all. Even the 'priming' effect of television (the idea that if it cannot tell people what to think, it can suggest to them what to think about and indirectly influence their vote) can be oversold (see Semetko 2000, pp.362–363; Norris et al. 1999; Denemark 2002, pp.679–684).

The idea that televised election debates make a big difference to the result runs counter to a long-held scholarly consensus that, while they are certainly capable of shifting public perceptions of the participants, their impact on subsequent voting choices (although potentially significant in a close race) tends to be small, largely because both perceptions and votes are filtered through pre-dispositions (see Jamieson and Adasiewicz 2000, p.26; Holbrook 1996, pp.98–124).[14] In addition, those people most likely to be swayed (rather than simply confirmed in their belief), namely those without strong preconceived opinions or party loyalties, and with little interest in politics (see Schrott 1990, p.583; Denemark 2002, p.678), are also those least likely to be watching.

However, even those who are sceptical about the impact of debates agree that they can provide voters with substantive information about issue positions (see Lemert et al. 1991; Norris 2000). They also acknowledge that even a marginal effect could prove significant in a close election. Most acknowledge, too, the logic behind the argument that, since fewer and fewer voters have fixed loyalties, and more and more of them make up their minds later and later, election campaigns and campaign coverage may exert increasing influence on electoral outcomes.[15] This influence may be offset somewhat by the fact that the audience for such coverage is fragmenting or dropping, as people get their election news from a greater variety of sources, or else find it easier and easier to find channels which are election-free zones. Yet completely screening out all the information you don't want to see or hear is relatively difficult – as anyone who has ever tried to avoid hearing the result of a football match s/he is hoping to watch on video later will testify. This means that even those who do not watch may well form opinions on which candidate does or does not do well in the debates. Indeed, research suggests that – partly in accordance with the classic 'two-step flow' of political communication, which accords elites a disproportionate role in forming public opinion – it is not just the debate itself that makes a difference, but the post-debate media consensus about who won and who lost (Lanoue and Schrott 1991; Lemert et al. 1991).

All this provides a way to understand the link between the televised leaders' debate and the swift and sudden rise of the United Future Party in the latter stages of the campaign. The TV1 debate itself was unexceptionable: in so far as any discussion with eight participants and a rowdy studio audience could be, it was a reasonable attempt to let each leader have his or her say on some important policy issues, as well as on respective polling performances and possible post-election coalitions. The key event, however, may have been the *One News Late Edition* review of the debate. This was undoubtedly influential in helping to form the opinion, not just of the minority of viewers that watched it, but also of journalists and editors who, over the next few days, helped to form the opinions of the vast majority who did not.

The programme featured TV1's two regular freelance commentators, along with the network's political editor. All three were obliged by programme makers to structure their discussion around selected ups and downs of 'the worm', a computer-generated graphic designed to capture the reactions of an invited studio audience of 100 'undecided' or 'floating' voters.[16] The panel was coming off the back of a package in which a political reporter reminded viewers that 'some believe just how much these people make the worm turn may well dictate the course of this election campaign'. They were also forced to comment on the pre-selected highs and lows of the various participants on the different issues. So the panel almost inevitably kept turning from the substance of the debate to its strategies and styles, and its significance for the parties' poll support. In the course of the discussion, United Future leader Peter Dunne's so-called 'common sense' was brought up time and again by one of the commentators, so that by the end there was little question as to who the 'winner' had been. Any lingering doubts (see Peters 2002) were quickly dispelled. The morning papers may have confined themselves to confirming that Dunne had done well, but by the evening he had become the victor by some margin. To *One News* (understandably keen to extract the last drop of value from its footage from the night before), he was 'the crowd favourite', a positive impression reinforced by its reporter's visit to 'the electorate of [the] worm-conqueror' to produce a vox-pop package crammed to bursting with admiring comments from adoring constituents.

But what was extraordinary in Dunne's case was not just the size of the boost he personally received, but the way that boost translated so directly into a rise in support for his party. New Zealand had seen the transforming effect that a debate (and/or the furore that follows a debate) can have on a party leader before: Helen Clark received a considerable boost after the first 'worm' debate in the 1996 campaign (see Aimer 1997), and presumably remains a big fan of the device.[17] But a stellar campaign performance by a leader does not necessarily net a commensurate return at the ballot box. The boost to Clark's personal ratings in 1996 did not appear to do anywhere near as much for her party's vote share as Dunne's 'win' did for United's in 2002. The difference may have been due to two things. The first is the possibility that leaders are beginning to have more and more impact on how people vote (see Banducci and Vowles 2002, pp.40–42; Banducci 2002, pp.61–65; Mendleson 1996). This is a process to which television is said to contribute, and a thesis which it clearly buys into itself: *3 News*, for instance, spent a great deal of the time it devoted to poll analysis on what it called the 'personal indicators', and its journalist referred again and again to 'presidential-style' campaigning. These may not actually matter as much as people seem to think, but even the most recent and most comprehensive comparative study on the subject, which is highly (and bluntly) sceptical about the electoral impact of leaders (see King 2002), refuses to rule them out entirely.[18]

The second is that the 2002 worm debate occurred both late enough and early enough in the campaign to make a difference. Late on is when research seems to suggest that those most likely to be influenced (the politically uninterested and uninformed) are most likely to make use of the cues picked up from television (or perhaps second-hand reports of it) in deciding how to vote (see Denemark 2002: pp.674–676). But had the debate in question occurred just a day or two before the election (as did the debate between the two main party leaders), the boost for United might have been nowhere near as big. As it was, there was time for Dunne's performance to make a difference to widely reported opinion polls, thereby creating a 'bandwagon effect' which was sufficiently strong not to fade in the few days between their appearance and the election day itself.[19] The *Herald* Digipoll which put Dunne on 6.6 percent – for all the footnotes about its small sample and high margin of error[20] – may have been particularly important in this respect, forcing even TV3 (which had previously paid next to no attention to its rival's worm debate, and normally ignored all but its own polls) to focus on United. The fact that Dunne appeared in a one-on-one interview by the network's political editor on the same night that it ran with his 'meteoric' rise in the polls (22 July) may well have been coincidence (other hitherto ignored minor party leaders were granted the same favour over the next couple of nights). But the civility and time that he (like them) was accorded certainly did him no harm either. Nor, presumably, did TV3's insistence three days later that its own poll, which put United on 4.3 percent and led into a special piece on the party, confirmed, 'we have a new force in New Zealand politics'.

None of this should allow us to forget, of course, that while the rise of United Future may have been media assisted, it had equally (if not more) important foundations in 'real' concerns among many centre and centre-right voters. These concerns presumably centred, first, on whether there was any point voting for a National Party so clearly out of contention; and secondly, on the need to supply a 'safe' (that is, non-Green) coalition partner for a Labour Party no longer likely to win an overall majority. Nor should we forget – given the fact that voters (especially in a country with a Westminster tradition) know they are selecting a government, not just electing a Parliament – that the media would be letting them down if it failed to discuss the impact of movements in support on post-election coalition possibilities. But it would be equally foolish to deny the possibility that, while the media's focus on Dunne may not literally have 'caused' what *One News* (July 24) called United's 'surge of support' in the polls, its coverage of those polls (One News, like TV3, got its money's worth by leading on its own survey a couple of days out from election day) helped the bandwagon on its way, and thus helped to determine the election result.[21]

Dunne was not the only one to benefit from increased media exposure: most of the small parties did, as expected, do better, as voters actually got to hear and see them in a way that they do not between elections. This obviously raises questions about media coverage of politics more generally under MMP. Despite the increased range of voices on offer, most media have continued to concentrate most on the two main parties outside elections. This clearly needs to change, especially when one of the two risks becoming just another minor party. But it will not be easy. It is hard to see how television, given limited time and resources, can cover the whole of the political spectrum, without trading off what little depth there is for a breadth in which only a minority of viewers will be interested. Then there is the sheer inertia that ensures that political culture, of which television is inevitably now a part, often lags behind institutional change. Like an amputee whose reflexes fool him into thinking he still possesses a missing limb, MMP New Zealand may never completely get over its Westminster past. Why should the media be any different? What else – apart from the raucous atmosphere surrounding a debate for eight, and a slightly more convincing case that either Labour or National are likely to end up leading any future government – can explain the decision of both networks to devote their final debate slots exclusively to the prime minister and the so-called Leader of the Opposition?

But since the decision was made and the set constructed, the show simply had to go on, giving each network a vested interest in talking up its importance beforehand (and milking it for everything it was worth afterwards) – so much so, indeed, that news time election coverage risked becoming little more than a teaser. Take this deliciously desperate exchange between a *One News* anchor and his political editor:

> *Political Editor*: The biggest political story tonight will be the long-awaited face-to-face encounter between Helen Clark and Bill English.
> *Anchor*: Yes, Mark, four days to go, both main parties losing ground in the polls. This debate tonight's really taken on an extra edge, hasn't it?
> *Political Editor*: That's right, Richard, and huge significance about what's going to happen in this studio out here.

Worse, far worse – but equally (and unintentionally) self-parodic – was to come, however. Two days before polling, on TV3, television coverage of the election finally ate itself. To start with, journalist John Campbell began many of his questions to Clark and English by inviting them ('X said, and I quote. . .') to react to the opinions of newspaper columnists on their performances so far. No sooner had they begun to answer, than he interrupted. Thus emboldened, he moved on to insults: 'I put it to you [Bill English] that you might as well have had "desperate" tattooed on your forehead'. Finally, when, in what passed for a post-debate discussion, a fellow journalist expressed her disappointment that Helen hadn't really 'gone for' John, he turned to another and asked with genuine interest, 'Why didn't she have a go at me? Have you got a theory?'

But the problem goes deeper than one man who (hopefully only temporarily) allowed his star-performer persona to overcome his considerable intelligence and essential moral seriousness. It is systemic. That is not to say, like some reductionist sociologist, that 'structure' always trumps 'agency', or that a change of personnel will make no difference. At a journalistic level, for instance, it may be that a recent change of political editor at TV3 will bring about some changes. At TV1, the resignation of its head of news and current affairs (worm-champion and so-called tabloid television wunderkind Heaton Dyer) may likewise usher in a new era. But no one should bet on it. TV3's new political editor showed, as a reporter, during the election that he has the grasp and the forensic and presentational skills to do a great job, but whether he can really exercise them fully in a format which demands a conflictual game frame is a moot point.[22] On the other hand, it will be interesting to see whether the new charter for the government-owned TVNZ, which demands that it qualify its pursuit of advertising revenue with a commitment to 'in-depth coverage and analysis of news and current affairs', will herald a move away from the faux (but popular) intimacy and informality of the co-anchored, human interest, 'still-to-come', infotainment style currently on offer, toward what one commentator hopes might be 'a news diet more appropriate to the needs of citizens than the appetites of consumers' (Norris 2002, p.50).

There is overseas evidence of what some would call a 'dumbing down' of political coverage which tends to follow a shift to a more commercial environment (Pfetsch 1996). Whether the process can be reversed by a shift away from commercialism is an experiment we shall watch with interest. Things began promisingly with the decision to give one of the country's finest radio interviewers her own current-affairs slot – an appointment that, she herself acknowledged, could never have occurred without the charter. But the signs since – budgets blown on high-profile overseas interviews with has-been celebrities, and a new orange set which, we are breathlessly informed, allows us to see newsreaders' legs for the first time in years – do not bode so well. We will need to wait until 2005 to see how election coverage is affected. Any real change will inevitably require not only a change in environment, but also some serious self-examination on the part of those individuals who operate within it. As the 2003 contest came to a close, and journalists called in for their final two-ways in order to give their overall judgement, TV3's since-departed political editor confided to her anchor and her viewers alike, 'A lot of the time . . . it was very stage managed. And sometimes I thought "why are we here?"' Not a bad question to start with, perhaps.

23

THE PARTY VOTE, POPULISM AND POLITICAL ADVERTISING IN 2002

Claire Robinson

Not a lot is known about the impact of political advertising on voter decision-making in New Zealand elections. International research suggests that political advertising has the most impact on levels of cognition, affective orientation and behaviour of voters with low levels of campaign involvement, undecided voters, and late deciders (Kaid and Johnston 2001). Given that over 40 percent of New Zealand voters may now make their voting decisions during an election campaign (Vowles 2002a), and might therefore be classed as 'late deciders', it is entirely possible that they could be influenced to some degree by the political advertising they encounter during the modern New Zealand election campaign. Quantification of the extent of influence of a particular advertisement or set of advertisements is difficult to achieve, however, because political advertising does not exist in a vacuum at campaign time. As but one element of a political party's much larger election campaign strategy, political advertising will only ever be one of many messages voters encounter during a campaign, and its impact cannot be easily assessed as a lone variable. Nor can its impact be measured solely on whether an audience has been exposed to an advertisement, as exposure is not the only factor leading to influence. Of far more importance is the visual and verbal content of the message, and the meanings experienced by its target audience over time.

Through the Electoral Commission, New Zealand political parties are allocated a limited amount of public funding and broadcast time with which to convey their campaign messages on television. Political advertisements contain the condensed campaign messages that political parties absolutely want to communicate to voters, before the mediation of journalists and others. They are, in effect, visual and verbal microcosms of parties' wider campaign strategies. Following an election it is possible to analyse the meanings constructed by those advertising messages and so offer a political communications perspective to a particular electoral outcome. This chapter offers such an approach to the 2002 general election.

Although campaigning in an MMP environment is still a relatively new experience for New Zealand political parties, it is clear that there are two fundamental communication requirements that parties need to consider when designing their advertising strategies. These are:
- asking for the party vote; and
- party differentiation – giving voters a reason why they should vote for one party over *all* the others, not just the main opposition party.

This chapter begins with an examination of the party vote advertisements of the two major parties, Labour and National. This leads on to a discussion of populism and the utilisation of populist appeals in the televised political advertising (television commercials and the opening and closing night election broadcasts) of the six electorally successful parties allocated public funding and airtime for election broadcasting – New Zealand First, United Future, Labour, the Greens, ACT and National – as they tried to meet the needs of the electorate and differentiate themselves from the competition in the 2002 election campaign.

The party vote

Asking for the party vote in an MMP electoral system, in which the party vote determines a party's share of the seats in Parliament, is perhaps the most simple and obvious request to make in any political advertising strategy. Most parties contesting the 2002 campaign asked for the party vote in their televised advertising in two ways: verbally by the presenter (or the voiceover), and on an end-of-broadcast visual containing the words 'party vote' and the party's logo (and frequently a tick symbol). Some parties also sprinkled visuals containing their logo and the words 'party vote' throughout their advertisements.

The importance of asking for the party vote seemed to escape National Party campaign strategists, however. Not once in National's 12-minute opening night broadcast were the words 'party vote' spoken. Instead, the main call to action by leader Bill English was for voters to use their vote 'with a warm heart and a large purpose' – a cryptic request, which voters could have taken as an instruction to vote for any party they had nice feelings towards, not necessarily National. Nor did the broadcast end with a visual asking for the party vote. Instead the voiceover and end visual stated

'National. Get the future you deserve'. Not until the party's final week 'I believe' television commercial (TVC) and its closing night broadcast were the words 'party vote' uttered by Bill English in any of National's televised advertising. Even then, the end visual remained unchanged and did not ask for the party vote.

The act of asking for the party vote was never going to be enough for National to win the 2002 election. But when National's efforts are compared to Labour's, a major difference in strategy becomes apparent. Labour was very focused on the party vote, not only in its television advertising, but also in its billboard and print advertising. No one driving along any main road in Wellington or Auckland, for example, could have missed the message on the large billboards asking voters to give Helen Clark and Labour their party vote, with the words 'Labour' and 'Party Vote' standing out in 'black' (heavy bold) sans serif type on a visually arresting red background. The choice of type in any graphic composition conveys many psychological impressions about a message even before any words are read (Spiekerman and Ginger 1993), and Labour's type treatment conveyed a confidence and boldness about its message. Consistent use of colour, type-style and slogan carried through to all of Labour's newspaper advertisements. As in 1999, Labour also manipulated its 2002 campaign image of Helen Clark to full advantage. With wrinkles flattened out, the mole on her chin removed, teeth straightened and whitened and the green of her eyes enhanced, the overall effect was of a flawless, attractive and friendly leader, an image in perfect accord with the caring, compassionate image that Labour had been constructing of her, and through her the party, since 1999.

National did not seem to be playing in the same ball game. The few party newspaper advertisements and billboards produced did not mention the words 'party vote' (although they did contain the party logo alongside 'two tick' symbols, or the words 'two ticks National'). They instructed voters in a condensed sans serif typeface to get the future they deserved – a typographic composition that was much less assertive than Labour's. The image of a grinning, jacketless, Bill English with one hand in his trouser pocket suggested informality, friendliness and approachability. However, given his relative youth and inexperience as a leader, it was perhaps not the most appropriate dress and pose to convey his maturity and readiness for the serious role of prime minister.

Combined with National's failure to ask for the party vote, the perception communicated was that of a leader and party not quite ready to compete in

2002. Even though few expected National to be able to win, its inability to demonstrate the same conviction and single-minded hunger to win the party vote as Labour may have affected public confidence about its will and ability even to fight this election. Ordinarily National-leaning voters may well have translated the party's instruction to get a future they deserved into a vote away from a certain loser (National) and towards the other minor parties occupying the centre-right, who were displaying a greater desire to succeed electorally in 2002. If there was one lesson both major parties would have learned in 2002, it would have been not to take the minor parties for granted. For Labour and National, the competition was no longer simply the other main opposition party, but all the minor parties, and especially the other parties sharing the same side of the political spectrum.

Party differentiation

In any crowded market, products need to differentiate themselves from their competition in order to be noticed. The same holds true for electoral campaigning under MMP, with many parties vying for the attention of voters. Although the central focus of the electoral competition is still between the two 'old' parties, Labour and National, a healthy degree of competition also occurs between parties that are reasonably like-minded on major policy issues on the same side of the political spectrum. Consequently campaign strategists have to become more adept at communicating a range of other reasons why voters should vote for their party. Often these reasons are intangible, coming down to differences in image or perception. In 2002, the parties that differentiated themselves most successfully from their competition on both sides of the political spectrum (and in so doing made significant electoral gains) were those that manipulated their image (by 'manipulated' I mean 'handled with skill'), using a variety of populist appeals in their political advertising.

Populism

Canovan (1999) defines populism in structural rather than ideological terms, seeing it as 'an appeal to "the people" against both the established structure of power and the dominant ideas and values of the society'. Within modern democratic societies, she notes, populist movements often result in challenges and attacks on the 'establishment', on political parties, academics, the news media and those holding elite or 'liberal' values. Populists claim to speak for 'the people', pride themselves on simplicity and directness, and advocate 'common sense' solutions. They denounce complicated bureaucratic procedures and backroom deals, and focus their emotions on charismatic leaders – 'vivid individuals who can make politics personal and immediate instead of being remote and bureaucratic'. Although populism is often associated with the rhetoric of extreme right-wing politicians, Canovan argues that populism can thrive in any established Western democracy where there are tensions between what she calls the 'redemptive' and the 'pragmatic' aspects of democracy. The 'redemptive' aspect of democracy is found in its promise of a better world through action by the sovereign people. At its heart is the notion that people 'are the only source of legitimate authority and salvation is promised as and when they take control of their own lives'. The 'pragmatic' aspect lies in the process of government – the rules, practices and institutions that constitute democratic power and make it effective. She gives an example of this tension in the institution of elections:

> At the pragmatic level, a general election is a nonviolent way of distributing political power. At the same time, however, it is also a ritual of democratic renewal, and unless that ritual is taken seriously by a substantial proportion of voters and politicians, democratic institutions are weakened. If it becomes clear that those involved see in democracy nothing but horsetrading, they, and eventually the system itself, are liable to lose their legitimacy. When too great a gap opens up between haloed democracy and the grubby business of politics, populists tend to move on to the vacant territory, promising in place of the dirty world of party manoeuvring the shining ideal of democracy renewed (Canovan 1999, p.11).

Populism as a discourse is often found residing in political rhetoric – the words and images communicated by politicians. Wells, Duty and Walton (2002) illustrate how Democratic presidential candidate Al Gore employed populist discourse and strategies to align himself with 'the people' in their fight against 'the powerful' during his 2000 presidential campaign. Although Gore's populist campaign did not quite propel him into the White House, the authors see it as evidence that the US populace is currently embracing a dominant populist mindset.

There is evidence of this being the case in New Zealand too. Just over 58 percent of the people who voted in 2002 gave their party vote to the three parties that utilised populist appeals most effectively in their political advertising. Responding to a huge wave of public dissatisfaction in the ability of government and political parties to 'deliver' (Perry and Webster 1999), Labour's articulation of many populist appeals in its 1999 political advertising helped to propel the party to a comprehensive victory in that election. Populism was also reasonably well articulated in Labour's 2002 advertising, helping return the party to government, despite its being entrenched as part of the establishment under attack by the other parties employing strongly populist strategies. Those parties – New Zealand First and United Future – benefited greatly in 2002 from running almost textbook populist advertising campaigns, which helped both parties increase their proportion of the party vote to levels unanticipated at the commencement of the election campaign. That populist appeals had such resonance in the New Zealand electorate in 2002 suggests that the large gap between the promise and the practice of democracy felt at the end of the last decade had not been greatly reduced by the time of the 2002 election.

If the New Zealand electorate was particularly receptive to populism in 2002, it is perhaps not surprising that the parties that did not incorporate populist appeals into their advertising did not succeed electorally as much as they had hoped to do at the start of the campaign. The potential existed for the Greens to exploit the populist moment through its advertising, as a party founded on many 'grass roots' and anti-establishment principles. However, any populist tendencies were neutralised by the Greens' desire to prove that they had journeyed out of the grass roots and into the mainstream, and were ready to become part of the next establishment. ACT's attempts at populist advertising worked to some degree, but liberalism and populism are fundamentally at odds with each other (Canovan 1999), and ACT's populist strategies were always doomed to be in terminal conflict with its elitist underbelly. National made some attempts at articulating populism in its advertising, but suffered from the legacy of being part of the 1990s establishment. It was also severely hampered by its poor promotion of a leader who was not provided with the opportunity to develop the populist charisma needed to attract voters in 2002. A consequence was that the party suffered its poorest election results ever.

New Zealand First

In 1999 Labour differentiated itself from all its competitors by successfully cutting its election manifesto and campaign themes down to seven 'commitments' that were simple enough to be printed on a small card (an idea taken from the British Labour Party.) Inspired by the success of this strategy, New Zealand First ran its own extremely reductionist campaign in 2002, differentiating itself by being the only party to reduce its policy platform down to three key issues. This 'tabloidisation' of policy platforms is characteristic of populist appeals, with politicians claiming the need to simplify issues, so that they can be understood by 'ordinary' people (Canovan 1999).

Running on such a small platform was a risky strategy, especially as the three issues were largely negative, almost extreme, in tenor. But the extreme effects were mitigated by some positive factors in the party's advertising. Clinton campaign strategists James Carville and Paul Begala (2002) maintain that ideas should be communicated in groups of three, as people remember information presented that way. It was certainly a successful formula for New Zealand First. From the start of the campaign through to the end, New Zealand First consistently and steadfastly pushed the three issues in its television, billboard and newspaper advertising, reinforced by an image of party leader Winston Peters holding up three fingers. Each issue had its own 15-second TVC which aired regularly throughout the entire campaign period, often during daytime viewing hours, when many of the party's elderly target audience would have been watching television. The TVCs incorporated symbolic (as opposed to representational) images: a money stacking machine, connoting the greed of lawyers becoming wealthy out of the Waitangi land claim process; a rotating turnstyle, suggesting the ease with which immigrants get into New Zealand; and a revolving door, associated with the speed with which criminals get in and out of prison. Canovan describes the populist rationale in this approach:

> If the government is the people's government, why isn't it looking after the people? Because it is in the hands of corrupt politicians, millionaires, Jews, tools of the IMF, politically-correct patrons of immigrant workers, and so on: the answer is to elect a people's government that will sack those who are feathering their own nests, send the immigrants home, or whatever the local remedy happens to be at a particular time (1999, p.12).

Another mitigating factor, and a populist solution to the problems raised, came in the form of the slogan 'Can We Fix It? Yes We Can' in Winston

Peters' verbal rhetoric. Appropriated from the children's television show Bob the Builder, the slogan became a code shared between New Zealand First and its target audience – an 'in-joke' with grandparents and parents who were familiar with Bob, a kind, resourceful and extremely trustworthy animated character who, although never physically used in the advertisements, became a signifier for Winston Peters in the campaign.

The party's advertising also gave Winston Peters the image of a charismatic elder statesman. In New Zealand First's opening and closing night broadcasts, Peters, formally dressed and speaking direct to camera, was seated at an antique desk surrounded by antique collectables. This offered a domestic but nonetheless formal setting, reminiscent of fireside chat images of Roosevelt or Churchill, and suggested a leader with conservative good taste, surrounded by the rewards of his hard work. At a deeper level, these images communicated a leader and party that identified with, and could be trusted to fight for, the rights and rewards deserved by ordinary conservative New Zealanders, at a time when those rights were allegedly under attack from criminals, immigrants and greedy lawyers. Peters' identification with ordinary conservative New Zealanders in their fight against this 'enemy' was reinforced in his rhetoric. Key to this was his frequent use in the party's advertising of the pronouns 'we' and 'our'. The words are frequently used by populist speakers to establish a personal connection with their intended audience (Wells et al. 2002). In the party's opening night broadcast, Peters spoke of 'our young', 'our citizens', 'our way of life and our values', 'our first duty' and 'our own people'. In so doing he distinguished 'our people' from 'those who don't belong', and identified himself as being firmly on the side of 'right' fighting against those perpetrating the 'wrong' – in particular the Labour and National parties. It was clearly a message that connected with a populist mood in parts of the electorate, as New Zealand First's party vote went up from around 7 percent at the beginning of the campaign to 10.38 percent on polling day.

United Future

If it was a brave move for New Zealand First to reduce its platform down to three issues, it was an even bigger gamble for United Future to shortcut its policy focus to one key platform – the family. However, as with New Zealand First's advertising, any negative ramifications of this were offset by United Future's use of populist rhetoric, as in leader Peter Dunne's frequent appeals to 'common sense'; his identification with popular distrust of politicians: 'for many this election is a bore . . . it's no wonder people are switching off politics in droves'; his denunciation of deals and compromises: 'the tired old parties are too interested in trivia, playing their silly games. United Future has had enough . . .'; his promise of a better government through action by the people: 'soon you have the chance to . . . help bring some much needed common sense to government by giving your party vote to United Future'; his creation of an enemy in the Greens: 'it's time for government to face up to some hard facts, like the fact that every day kids are getting stoned at school. Parties like the Greens seem to have no problem with this, despite the fact that drugs addle young minds and cause depression. Could the fact that youth suicides are up 700 percent in the last 30 years be related?'; and his positioning of the party in the vacant territory between Labour and National: 'we recognise that good ideas come from right across Parliament and we'll work with the major party most committed to helping us achieve our policies . . . we are the sensible middle party New Zealand needs, the logical partner for our next government.'

At a time when other small parties such as ACT and the Greens were trying to broaden their appeal with the aim of appearing more mainstream, United Future successfully differentiated itself from its competition as a simple and uncomplicated 'small' party. This was reinforced through the visual imagery in the advertisements, with a small Peter Dunne positioned well inside the picture frame against a neutral white backdrop, the colour white representing truthful, clean and honest values, cloaking the content of his messages with an aura of respectability – if someone who looked so innocent and sensible was saying these things, they had to be true!

Like Winston Peters, Peter Dunne spoke direct to camera, addressing the audience as equals with his use of the pronouns 'we' and 'our'. The rationale for his 'logical' position was confirmed by what he called 'hard facts' (which were, in fact, a collection of arbitrary and quite extreme statistics), tapping into a collective myth that the sanctity of the New Zealand family had been destroyed by government inattention. Like Winston Peters, he constructed in his rhetoric an 'enemy' in an elitist and uncaring government. The 'facts' were written in a black sans serif typeface on the plain white screen, communicating the impression that they were legitimate evidence, a technique frequently found in US political issue appeals (Johnson-Cartee and Copeland 1997). Communicating the evidence in writing rather than pictures further encouraged viewers to imagine the evidence, and come to the same conclusions as the party about successive governments' alleged neglect.

Canovan has written of populist politics not being ordinary, routine politics, but rather having the 'revivalist flavour of a movement'. This could explain United Future's high levels of popularity in the opinion polls, following Peter Dunne's appearance on the TV1 'worm' debate midway through the campaign, and continuing all the way through to the election. In his television advertising, Dunne appeared sensible, caring and fresh. His was an appeal warmly welcomed by many voters wanting something 'new' to fill the gap between the promise and practice of democracy.

Labour

No party has perfected the art of communicating 'caring' through the image of its leader as much as Labour. In its 1999 political advertising, Labour successfully constructed a populist image of Helen Clark, using a range of quite moralistic myths that forged a strong emotional bond between Labour and middle New Zealand. She was given the image of a self-sacrificing, caring, trustworthy and empathetic samaritan, who visited and listened to the disadvantaged in her spare time, and to whom ordinary 'folk' came flocking to hear her words of wisdom. With the aid of good public relations handling in the subsequent years, the idea of Helen Clark being a caring leader was one that New Zealand voters embraced between 1999 and 2002. She consistently scored highly in opinion polls as 'down to earth' and in touch with the needs of ordinary people, as a capable leader, as a person with sound judgment, and as someone good in a crisis.

Leaders can make good 'cognitive shortcuts' (Shea 1996) — ways of helping voters to make their voting choices with minimal effort — especially at times when the populist mood has tired of bureaucratic structures, and is looking for close personal ties with a charismatic leader (Canovan 1999). Selling one person (a leader) in such times is a more resource efficient process than selling the virtues of all the candidates on a party list, particularly when that person receives a lot of unpaid media coverage by virtue of their position. If voters can bond or develop an emotional attachment to a leader, it is not such a big jump to expect them to develop the same attachment to a party. The image of the leader then becomes the signifier for the party. The challenge for any campaign strategist is to embody in the image of the leader all the brand values of the party, while creating an appropriately realistic persona for the leader, one that voters can relate to without realising that the image is largely artificially constructed.

Labour faced a harder job selling the party through the image of the leader in 2002 than it did in 1999. As the campaign progressed, it became apparent that the earlier image of Helen Clark may have been oversold. Her reactions to 'paintergate', 'corngate' and the ABC and John Campbell media interviews demonstrated to a wider public that there was something of a credibility gap between the 'holier-than-thou' image of 'Helen' the public had consumed up until the start of the campaign, and the more realistic Helen Clark being exposed in the media. The results were reflected in the opinion polls, as support for Labour steadily declined throughout the campaign. The party faced a further difficulty, in that it was now part of an establishment that was under attack by adversaries employing strongly anti-establishment populist messages.

Despite this, Labour still had enough populist strategies in its own bag of campaign tricks to reward the party with a second term. The election was still close enough to the 1990s for Labour to be able to blame much of New Zealand's economic predicament on the old National government, and to argue that Labour had not yet had enough time to fix everything. Labour still needed the support of the people to carry on with the job, as in this excerpt spoken directly to camera by Helen Clark in her office at the end of Labour's campaign opening night broadcast on 28 June:

> When Labour came into government in 1999 New Zealanders were looking for change. The last government had come unstuck. It had taken its hands off the economic tiller and no one knew where the good ship New Zealand was sailing except very close to the rocks. New Zealanders were looking for steady, progressive government and that's what we've committed ourselves to. We put aside the old model of conflict and worked in partnership with others to get things done . . .

Labour also reassured voters in its 'negative' TVC aired over the penultimate weekend of the campaign that it was mindful and disapproving of the backroom deals and compromises expected of the other parties it felt challenged by – particularly New Zealand First and the Greens:

> *Voice-over*: If you're thinking of voting for New Zealand First it would pay to think again. Remember how Winston betrayed you last time and hooked up with Bolger? Remember when his party all fell apart?

If you remember that you should forget them now.

Of course, with the Greens holding the country to ransom over one single issue we'd never get anywhere. It'd be hard to compete in the third world, let alone the first.

It's a serious choice and it's up to you. So this election, do the wise thing and give your party vote to Labour, for strong stable government you know you can trust.

This message was considerably let down by its visuals, which carried little to no symbolic meaning – black lines representing New Zealand First, the colour Green representing the Greens. However, it was a piece of populist rhetoric that might have struck a chord with some voters.

Labour employed other populist tactics with its milking of national pride in a TVC that was regularly broadcast throughout the campaign period. The TVC presented the myth of Helen Clark's single-handed power to achieve great things for New Zealand – from Lord of the Rings to the America's Cup to peace in East Timor and a thawing of relations with the US. It rewarded Labour supporters for their loyalty, making them feel proud for accompanying Helen Clark on her hero's journey. As she says: 'We can take pride in making it happen.' The hero's journey is an important component of populist rhetoric, as 'only the heroic and morally pure . . . can promote necessary change for the betterment of all people' (Wells et al. 2002, p.8). Another key line spoken by Helen Clark in this TVC – 'we believe in looking after the many, not just the few' – reflected the populist idea of the party backing the people against the elite.

Helen Clark's continuing concern for ordinary people was demonstrated in Labour's 'bushwalk' TVC, an advertisement filled with visual symbolism. She spoke to camera as she led a small group of people on a bushwalk and across a stream, a metaphor for moving into a new stage of the hero's journey, though very much a continuation of the journey already started. It was a journey in which Helen Clark would still personally care for others (the word 'caring' is spoken in her voice-over as she helps a grey-haired woman across the stream). It was a responsible journey, not a dangerous one – Helen Clark was predictably dressed in appropriate clothing for bush walking, the team was walking on a well marked track. The underlying message: a vote for Labour would be for continued progress under a caring and risk averse leader – in other words, a vote for the status quo, which was pretty much the result Labour achieved on election day.

The Greens

More than any other party needing to differentiate itself in the 2002 campaign, the Greens had an obvious 'cognitive shortcut' to exploit in the GE issue. But unlike New Zealand First and United Future, who, to their electoral advantage embraced the idea of reducing their policy platform, the Greens' advertising stressed that GE was not its single issue. Instead, the Greens announced their interest in a broad range of issues, using a large number of slogans. This left the door wide open for another party (United Future) to appropriate the single issue position.

The potential existed for the Greens to exploit the populist mood, as a party founded on, and still promoting, many 'grass roots' and anti-establishment principles. However, the Greens had a strong desire to become part of the next government at this election, as confirmed by co-leader Rod Donald in the Greens' opening night broadcast:

> We've proved our worth in the last three years. Now the Greens are ready for the responsibility of government. We'll put the brakes on Labour where we need to, strengthen their resolve where it counts and steer Labour in the right direction on crucial issues.

The party's need to reassure voters it was mature enough to 'get into bed' with Labour meant that it did not attack the establishment in its advertising. Instead, the party concentrated on demonstrating that it had progressed out of the grass roots and into the mainstream sufficiently enough for it to become part of the next government.

Conflicts between the need to mainstream and the need to hold onto its more anti-establishment target audience could be seen in its opening night broadcast. The beginning 1 minute 40 second 'MonstaCo' segment, perhaps the most innovative piece of political advertising seen on television in many elections, was anti-establishment and focused on the GE issue. It was deliberately pitched at the youth audience, and was produced with a healthy sense of irony in its verbal and graphic style, integrating type and image to a sophisticated level. The remaining 6 minutes and 20 seconds of the broadcast, however, were aimed at the more mature 'Values generation' audience. In a documentary format employing bleak and atonal colours and a sombre and conservative tone, the broadcast seemed designed to provoke middle-class guilt on a range of serious issues and images spanning environmental pollution, peace, safe food, television violence, child poverty, vehicle emissions, student loans and organic foods.

Although co-leaders Rod Donald and Jeanette Fitzsimons talked of the 'need for fresh political thinking', the party was not able (or willing) to back this up with a 'fresh' approach to its advertising. The MonstaCo segment was not broadcast again, and the opportunity to shore up the valuable youth audience was missed, in the party's desire to communicate its maturity and readiness for a role in government. The Greens did not lose party votes using this strategy, but neither were they able to make it anywhere near the 12 percent mark they had hoped for at the commencement of the campaign. Nor did they achieve their goal to be part of the post-2002 election's coalition government.

ACT

Populism does not just challenge established parties within democratic systems. It is also resistant to elite political culture, a culture often 'imbued with liberal values of individualism, internationalism, multiculturalism, permissiveness and belief in progress' (Canovan 1999, p.4). In this regard, many aspects of liberalism and populism are fundamentally at odds with each other. ACT, a liberal party priding itself on being a party of elite thinkers, probably faced the greatest challenge of any party in selling a populist message to the electorate. The party went into the election aware that it had a hard job selling its liberal message to people cynical about politicians because they did not deliver, 'people who have no real interest in politics' (Judd 2002). ACT decided to run an 'issue-based election campaign' and, in the populist spirit, simplified its policy platform down to what it called 'issue messages' (Prebble 2002), a handful of short and catchy slogans that appeared on the party's attention-grabbing yellow billboards, newspaper and television advertisements.

It was also aware of the need not to appear elitist. The target audience for its advertising seemed to be anyone but like-minded thinking liberals. At pains to avoid being seen as an exclusive men's club, and to boost its low number of female voters (something it achieved), the party made a special effort to court female voters with a number of TVCs aimed at a female audience, with female ACT MPs, candidates and party members featuring prominently. It also seemed to make a special effort at wooing working class voters. In ACT's opening night broadcast, for instance, MP Rodney Hide was seen talking to builders on a building site:

> *Builder*: I wouldn't mind paying taxes, fair taxes, but this thing is getting out of hand.
>
> *Rodney Hide*: It's getting out of hand. The key to doing better is to get the economy going stronger, to get more jobs, to get more wealth in people's pockets, and the way we believe that we have to do that is to unshackle working people, and that means lower taxes, so that when you're earning you get to keep all . . .
>
> *Builder*: That would be nice.
>
> *RH*: You like lower taxes?
>
> *Other builders*: Yeah yeah.
>
> *RH*: In fact for someone on $40,000 a year we're saying a tax cut will put an extra $670 in their pocket a year, just like that. [In lowered tones and off-camera] These are the people that are the backbone of New Zealand. Here they are, they create everything that we have. It's not politicians, it's not bureaucrats, it's actually working New Zealanders who work hard and create. And what do we do as a government and society? We hammer them!

This was a textbook piece of populist rhetoric. However, while it seems you can take a man out of the office, you can't take the office out of the man! Dressed in a formal suit with white shirt and tie, Rodney Hide looked very much like the bureaucrats he was trying to denounce, and he was not alone. The opening sequence of the broadcast showed party leader Richard Prebble walking along a beach, sharing a leisurely moment with his wife, a child and a dog. When he stopped to talk about his pride in being a New Zealander, he was seen to be wearing a blue and white striped business shirt under his polar fleece. MP Stephen Franks, supposedly being videoed in familiar surroundings on a farm in the same broadcast, was also wearing a blue and white striped shirt under his windbreaker. Their underlying business clothing betrayed any notion that they authentically identified with working class New Zealanders. This was later confirmed in two TVCs, one featuring three ACT MPs (Prebble, Hide and Dr Muriel Newman) striding up an Auckland street, and another with all the members of the parliamentary party, immaculately and formally dressed, striding purposefully up the steps of Parliament, accompanied by the voiceover: 'If you want up front and straight talking MPs, on Saturday party vote ACT, the real alternative.' The verbal and visual messages were unable to deny the party's pride and self-identification as an elite team, different from the rest. ACT's inability to hide its own elitism was countered only somewhat by its decision to simplify its platform and target audience. While its overall percentage of the party vote remained relatively unchanged from its 1999 result, if it had not adopted these populist tactics, things could have been considerably worse for ACT in 2002.

National

The 2002 election was always going to be a hard election for National to win. The electorate was in no rush to forgive or forget National's legacy as part of the establishment of the 1990s. National tried to differentiate itself from the image of the 'old' party by using brighter colours, fresher graphics and images of its younger MPs on its website and in its *National Times* magazine. But it did itself no favours by rehashing some unpopular policies from the 1990s (such as bulk-funding in education) in its platform, serving as a constant reminder that this 'new' version of the party was not so different from the 'old' one. Belatedly the National Party jumped on the populist bandwagon with a few issues – in particular law and order and the Treaty of Waitangi – only to find that vehicle already crowded with the New Zealand First and ACT parties, who had honed their messages in these areas down to simple, catchy slogans with which National could not compete. Bill English's 'I'll settle past Treaty claims by 2008. Then we can all paddle in the same waka' in an early newspaper advertisement simply did not have the same force of conviction as ACT's 'One Law for All' slogan.

National faced a tough challenge constructing an image of Bill English which would be as great and heroic as that already constructed of Helen Clark. Perhaps with their sights more firmly fixed on 2005, National strategists seemed to feel it necessary to go back to basics in 2002. American media researchers Edwin Diamond and Stephen Bates' *The Spot: The Rise of Political Advertising on Television* (1984) identified four phases in any political advertising campaign:

1   ID Spots: ensuring the voters have some sense of the candidate
2   Argument
3   Attack
4   Resolution and Reflection

Although this sort of textbook prescription has long been surpassed internationally by other more creative advertising strategies, National's advertising campaign appeared to adhere closely to it, without much appreciation of how its television spots were going to fit into the shorter time-frame and wider context of the 2002 campaign, or be received by the party's natural constituency. Introducing Bill English in the opening night broadcast, the party located him on stage in a public meeting setting at the focal point of an audience that had (supposedly) gathered there to see and hear him. This occupied almost the entire 12 minutes of the broadcast. The introductory sequence suggested a degree of nervousness before a significant performance, much like his earlier 'Fight for Life' boxing match. The low camera angles and harsh lighting emphasised a degree of gravitas about the event, as well as a professional look to the cinematography. National's primary intent would have been to cement a lasting image of Bill English as a popular, articulate and commanding leader. This was not enough to differentiate him from Helen Clark, however, as her image already had a near-monopoly on these qualities.

The broadcast gave no hint of an awareness of the need to address the audience with a populist message. Bill English rarely looked direct to camera and did not use inclusive pronouns as much as other party leaders. He uttered the word 'I' 33 times, talked of his family six times, and mentioned the name of the National Party only three times. It was a strong empathy appeal: I share your concerns. Vote for me because I am like you. Vote 'with a large heart and a warm purpose' because that's what I have. This type of appeal had been tried by National in 1999, and had not worked well for Jenny Shipley either (Robinson 2002). In contrast, Helen Clark did not mention her family at all in Labour's opening night broadcast, and only used the word 'I' five times. She used 'we', 'our' and 'Labour' more frequently, confirming her and Labour's closer affinity with their audience.

In the TVCs that followed, National almost completely ignored Bill English's natural advantage over Helen Clark in the strong pioneering myths that already surrounded him: that he had descended from an old established true-blue Southland farming family and had real emotional connections with New Zealand's conservative rural heartland. Instead he was rebranded as a smooth urbanite, as 'everyman' – someone who might appeal more to middle New Zealand. 'Everyman' ads work by portraying characters who possess attributes common to all of us, strengths and weaknesses included, in order to engage the 'interest and sympathy' of an audience (Goodman 1961, pp.63–64, cited in Johnson-Cartee and Copeland 1997). Fly-on-the-wall camera techniques familiar to New Zealand audiences watching 'reality' shows such as Big Brother permitted viewers to peek in on selected parts of Bill English's day, in an attempt to expose his 'everyman' qualities. National named the television campaign 'Unguarded Moments'. Unfortunately for National, the images served only to confirm his primary interest in caring for himself and his family over others. While Helen Clark was helping 'old ladies' to cross streams, Bill English was playing computer games with his sons.

Even the last week of the campaign's 'I believe' TVC, an advertisement that Bill English wrested off National's campaign team in an attempt to make an emotional connection with voters by eyeballing them directly and reducing the physical gap by standing beside the lectern rather than behind it (Berry 2002), was focused on establishing his beliefs, rather than identifying with the beliefs of others. It used I-statements to begin each sentence, as in this excerpt:

> *Bill English*: . . . I believe we need to give our schools back to parents and teachers. I believe we can reverse the brain drain by writing down loans for those who can stay and work here. I believe in getting young people off welfare. I believe we need a police force that we can see . . .

Rhetorical analyst Roderick P. Hart asserts that I-statements are important because they 'index a person's feelings and ambitions in especially prominent ways', and that use of a 'great many self-references hint[s] strongly that a special persona is being created in the texts they produce' (1997, pp.225–229). At another time these I-statements may have proved powerful political rhetoric. However, the wholesale rejection of the party at the polls suggests they were not necessarily music to voters' ears in 2002.

National's advertising strategy never reached Diamond and Bates' phases two, three and four. In terms of the election stakes, while all the other party horses had galloped out of the gate as soon as it went up, National was still trying to convince the punters that it had a horse that could run. If phase one goals are to 'ensure voters have some sense of the candidate' (Diamond and Bates 1984, p.302), then National achieved those goals. The last TV3 poll before the election showed that Bill English had improved on most of the personality indicators over the polls taken six weeks earlier. But this was never going to be enough to beat Labour in 2002, and his was not a message that had even a remote chance of being received by voters attracted to the more populist messages of the other centre-right parties.

Conclusion

Is populism empty campaign rhetoric, or a sign of deeper dissatisfaction in the electorate? Just over 58 percent of the people who voted in the 2002 election gave their party vote to the three parties that utilised populist appeals most effectively in their political advertising, despite coming from very different points on the political spectrum (Labour, United Future and New Zealand First), confirming Canovan's assertion that populism is structural rather than ideological. In their visual and verbal rhetoric, these parties challenged and attacked other political parties, constructed enemies, spoke as one with the people, simplified their policy platforms to a few key issues, denounced complicated bureaucratic procedures and backroom deals, and promoted the image of an immediate, personalised, caring and often heroic leader. That populist appeals had such resonance in the New Zealand electorate in 2002 suggests that the large gap between the promise and the practice of democracy felt at the end of the last decade had not been greatly reduced by the time of the 2002 election. Canovan has argued that populism thrives where there are tensions between the 'redemptive' and 'pragmatic' aspects of democracy. Political parties wanting to make electoral progress need to be alert to these tensions, and the need to respond to them, before preparing their campaign messages for the next election, whenever that might be.

24

'READ ALL ABOUT IT!':
NEWSPAPER COVERAGE OF THE GENERAL ELECTION

Janine Hayward and Chris Rudd

Increasingly, election campaigns are seen to be conducted through the medium of television. This would seem to have been confirmed at the 2002 election, with the TV3 John Campbell interview of Helen Clark sparking the 'corngate' issue which came to dominate much of the following campaign news. Then there was the televised leaders' debate that, with the help of the 'worm', thrust Peter Dunne and his United Future Party into the election limelight. These televised events were subsequently taken up and further reported on by the print media.

However, it would be misleading to view newspapers as playing only a secondary role in communicating news about the 2002 election. Newspaper readership in New Zealand is one of the highest in the world, and newspapers are recognised both here and overseas as important sources of political news. It may also be the case that voters derive different things from the two media, with newspapers much more likely to be a source of serious news than television. While television appears to dominate modern election campaign coverage, there is, as this chapter will show, a significant amount of election news (including qualitative news) that a voter can derive from reading his or her morning newspaper.

So how did New Zealand's newspapers cover the 2002 election? We have examined the campaign news of three of the country's metropolitan newspapers: *The New Zealand Herald* (*The Herald*), *The Dominion Post*, and the *Otago Daily Times* (*ODT*).[1] The period of analysis ran from Monday 1 July, following the weekend opening of the major parties' campaigns, until Friday 26 July, the last day on which newspapers were allowed to carry election news.[2]

We were interested in addressing four questions. First, to what extent was the newspaper coverage of the campaign 'presidentialised'? In other words, was the coverage preoccupied with the two main party leaders?

Secondly, how partisan were the editorials? Did editors clearly prefer one party over the others? Thirdly, how was party coverage distributed across the three newspapers? Did the two main parties dominate coverage even in an MMP era? Finally, how much of the campaign coverage was devoted to 'horse race' and 'hoopla' stories, stories about 'who's winning' and 'who's losing' (as exemplified in reporting of opinion polls), the personal traits of candidates, scandals on the campaign trail, and so forth? How did such coverage compare with the amount of space devoted to examining issues and party policy on these issues?

Overview of results

In sheer volume of election news provided by the newspapers, *The Herald*'s dominance is clear and unsurprising given the size and circulation of the paper.[3] It also, however, provided the most election news relative to the size of the newspaper – almost four percent of the overall content of the newspaper was election news, compared with 2.6 percent for both the *ODT* and *The Dominion Post*. *The Herald* also ran the most lead stories (11) and front page stories (21) relating to the election, compared with the other papers. *The Dominion Post* and *ODT* ran six and nine lead stories (respectively), and 10 front page stories each.

The three newspapers shared some common features in their presentation of election news. Each had a logo such as 'Election 2002' and 'The 2002 Campaign' to draw the reader's attention to election stories. For the most part, each paper also dedicated a page (*pages* in the case of *The Herald*) to election news. *The Herald* ran these dedicated news pages right from the start of the campaign, while the other papers picked up this feature in later weeks. Each also provided a daily 'campaign' or 'on the hustings' diary, with goofs, blunders, statements and events from the campaign trail. They also had electorate surveys which scrutinised the candidates and issues, often in key electorates, and usually in the readers' region. *The Herald* dedicated twice the amount of column centimetres to electorate surveys as *The Dominion Post* did, although the latter ran a greater number of surveys. Finally, each newspaper also published a 'guide for voters' to fill in the results on election night.

While sharing some characteristics in their coverage, the papers also had their own style in delivering election news. *The Herald* distinguished itself in the number of feature articles it ran on election issues. The *ODT* distinctively peppered its news with caricatures by cartoonist Murray Webb, and provided more local campaign coverage than the other papers. *The Dominion*'s merger with the *Evening Post* newspaper to become *The Dominion Post* five days into the campaign gave a new look to the entire paper, although it is hard to tell if this also affected the style of election coverage.

Leaders in the limelight

Leaders have long been important, even crucial to election campaigns ('Leader factor is what counts', *The Herald*, 1 July). When the 2002 election campaign began on 1 July, *The Dominion* (as it then was) asserted: '[t]his election is all about who you want to lead New Zealand.... Forget health, education, the economy. This campaign is about Helen Clark and Bill English.' Labour campaign strategists were keen to pit their strength (Helen Clark) against the perceived weakness of the National Party leader. A 'presidential-style' campaign (as in the US), they felt, would be in Labour's favour. The National Party was happy to engage in a head-to-head battle of the leaders also, asserting that 'Bill's our biggest asset' (*The Dominion*, 1 July). Mid-campaign, the National Party announced that '[t]he issue of style – Helen Clark perceived as autocratic versus Bill English as a team player – will be pushed by the [National] party in the coming weeks' ('National sights on Clark', *ODT*, 8 July). As Helen Clark's integrity came under fire with the 'corngate' and 'paintergate' scandals, Bill English seemed all the more determined to focus the campaign on undermining Helen Clark as leader: 'Clark not worthy of trust, English tells party', as the *ODT* reported (8 July).

Readers of any of the three newspapers during the campaign would have encountered many examples of the newspapers reporting the English and Clark head-to-head battle. The *ODT* reported Bill English's description of the election: 'It's law and order, it's education – but it's also Prime Minister Helen Clark' ('PM's leadership "significant issue" ', *ODT*, 13 July). The paper also ran an article entitled 'Champ vs Battler' which emphasised the one-on-one confrontation (13 July). Following English's stint in the boxing ring, this became a favourite analogy for the press to emphasise the 'showdown' between the leaders: 'Boxer Bill delivers blitzkrieg on Clark' (*The Herald*, 8 July), and 'Leaders' gloves come off as election nears' (*ODT*, 20 July). The day before the election, *The Dominion Post* ran a full-page article entitled 'What you're really voting for', which pictured a large cartoon image of the two leaders in the boxing ring (26 July).

There was also no shortage of stories that concentrated on the leaders' characteristics, without necessarily playing them off against each other. One *Dominion Post* article entitled 'The political prime of Miss Helen Clark' described her as '[t]he elegantly tailored woman with the fashionably short haircut' (8 July). In a profile on the National leader the following day, the paper commented that 'Bill English may have southern-man charm, and is no intellectual slouch, but he'll need much more if he is ever to take the throne' (9 July). Even the two leaders' spouses were newsworthy during the campaign: 'PM too busy for kids – husband' (*The Dominion Post,* 12 July) and 'Mary stands by her man' (*The Dominion Post,* 9 July). Spouses were not beyond media comparisons and criticism either; in a story entitled 'An ideal spouse', *The Dominion Post* writer curtly characterised them as '[o]ne immaculately groomed, the other somewhat resembling a muppet' (20 July).

The leaders' debates attracted considerable media attention during the campaign. The newspapers were quick to report these debates, including the Clark and English head-to-head confrontation late in the campaign. Again, there are examples of the style as opposed to the substance of the debate dominating the coverage. *The Herald* offered advice to the leaders under the (rather cynical) sub-headings : 'Preparation: how do I swot for this one?'; 'The look: what should I wear?'; 'Tone: formal or folksy, positive or negative?'; 'Message: how do I do the vision thing?' ('Showdown – how to be a winner', 25 July).

Leaders, therefore, were an important source of election news for the papers. The newspapers themselves appeared at times self-conscious of their focus on leaders. In an article entitled 'Why the election's getting personal', the *Dominion Post* writer stated (presumably with tongue in cheek), '[s]he's strong, she's fearless, she's ruthless, she's Labour leader Helen Clark – and you should vote for her. Oh yeah, by the way, Labour has got some really good policies it thinks you'd like' (22 July). *The Herald* also reflected on the importance of leaders to election campaigns, but commented that 'talk of "presidential" campaigns, as if they were a 1980s invention, is a bit overdone' ('Leader factor is what counts . . .', 1 July). Presidential campaigns refer, of course, to the US presidential elections, which are a head-to-head battle between just two presidential candidates. The inference, therefore, is that despite not having a presidential political system, New Zealand political parties and media focus to an 'inappropriate' extent on the leaders of the two main parties, and that the voters' perceptions of the leaders will influence the way they vote.

Did the newspapers presidentialise the 2002 election coverage? The examples above show tendencies to focus on the two main leaders, but this may be a reflection of the parties' preference to campaign in this fashion. In fact, our results on the amount of coverage devoted to leaders (set out in Table 24.1) revealed interesting results. The papers dedicated a broadly comparable percentage of their overall coverage to the party leaders. Not surprisingly, by far the greatest amount of this coverage was dedicated to the Labour and National Party leaders. As Labour's lead in the polls began to slide, the paper headlines focused on the leader's political ambitions, saying 'PM's dream of absolute power turns to chaff' (*The Herald*, 13 July) and 'Empress is losing her clothes' (*The Herald*, 15 July). The latter was a feature article which noted that the 'crises of the past few weeks have knocked Helen Clark's self-image and that of her party as well'. The National leader received his fair share of negative press also: 'Past sins continue to haunt National's leader' (*The Herald*, 16 July) and 'Time running out for Mr Nice guy' (*The Herald*, 18 July).

Although news on the leaders of the two major parties dominated leadership coverage, this amounted to less than half the total news relating to all party leaders. Winston Peters received more coverage across all three papers than the other minor party leaders, despite his poor showing in the polls. This no doubt reflects the controversial nature of two of his election promises – to 'fix' immigration and the Treaty industry, both of which received considerable attention in *The Herald* and *The Dominion Post*. The ACT leader received the least coverage of all leaders, possibly as a result of his party's strategy to push party policies, rather than have a leader-focused campaign.

In general, the substantial combined coverage of the minor party leaders undermines the suggestion that the newspapers' election coverage is presidentialised; it may be focused on leaders, but not the two main leaders at the expense of all others. This is evident in all the papers. The leaders' debate was widely reported; the *ODT*, for example, ran a story that included photos of each leader framed in a television screen ('Sparks fly in leaders' debte when treaty issues raised', *ODT*, 16 July). *The Herald*'s fashion editor reported on the appearance of all the leaders in a feature story near the end of the campaign. Concluding that Winston Peters' 'gangster chic' style of dress was the best, she also passed judgement that 'An act should be passed

Table 24.1: Coverage of party leaders (as percentage of all coverage)

	New Zealand Herald	Otago Daily Times	Dominion Post	Total
Leaders	28.2	32.6	37.1	31.6
Labour	7.1	8.6	10.3	8.3
National	4.5	7.7	6.9	5.9
Greens	2.0	1.9	2.7	2.2
Alliance	0.6	2.6	1.7	1.4
Progressive Coalition	0.8	2.4	1.1	1.2
NZF	3.9	2.7	3.4	3.5
United Future	1.0	1.9	2.1	1.5
ACT	0.4	1.1	2.2	1.1

immediately preventing Rod Donald from attaching [braces] to his trousers again. They are the biggest fashion crime of the campaign' ('Gangster chic gets our vote', 20 July). The Green co-leaders' attire also attracted attention in a *Dominion Post* article reviewing the leaders' aspirations. Entitled 'Power yes, dressing no', Rod Donald's 'sleeves rolled up and suit pants crumpled' appeared worthy of mention, as did Jeanette Fitzsimons' 'woolly-pully wearing, cosmetic shunning' approach. The newspapers clearly thought the leaders' attire was one quality worth considering in weighing up the leaders' appeal. Although, therefore, the Green leaders did not always get positive press, they were the second most reported minor party leaders, behind Winston Peters.

It is interesting to reflect on the factors that may influence leadership coverage. The electoral system itself should be considered. Recall the dominance of the leadership battle between David Lange (Labour) and Robert Muldoon (National) at the 1984 general election. Did the first-past-the-post system, which encouraged the dominance of two main parties, also encourage presidentialised electioneering? Has proportional representation (MMP) ameliorated this effect? MMP has certainly facilitated the emergence of credible minor parties with leaders who attract their share of the media limelight. MMP may therefore be an obstacle to the 'presidentialisation' of the election campaigns, even though it also produces more newsworthy political leaders. *The Dominion Post* reported the Labour president's comment: 'It's the nature of MMP elections, how do you characterise the party vote, if not by a person?' ('Why the election's getting personal', 22 July). The *ODT* seemed to endorse this sentiment when it commented that the tight travel schedule of the leaders during the campaign reflected 'just how focused on the party leaders New Zealand politics has become' ('A fleeting, flying visit for English', *ODT,* 9 July).

Editorials

Newspaper editorials are particularly interesting during an election campaign, as the part of the newspaper most likely to reflect any partisanship by editors or newspaper proprietors. Up to the 1980s, it was an undisputed fact that daily newspaper editorials 'offered almost unanimous . . . support to the National party' (Cleveland 1980, p.186). Since the 1980s, however, there has been a shift away from this position, and by the 1990s editorial viewpoints had become much more diverse in terms of partisan support. In many cases, editorials had become 'dealigned'; they were as likely to be as critical of *all* parties as supportive of any one of them (and certainly not uncritically supportive, as had been the case in the past).

Table 24.2 sets out the editorials for the three newspapers where the editorial could be identified as relating to a political party. The first thing to note is the small number of editorials on the election which appeared in the three newspapers throughout the campaign. The *ODT,* for example, had over 20 election editorials up to the 1960 election; during the 1990s, this number had fallen by half (Hayward and Rudd 2002). The partisan focus of the 2002 editorials reveals a conspicuous absence of the National Party as a focus of editorial comment. It seems that if editors found little to criticise about National, neither could they find much reason to praise the party; it was simply ignored. The Labour Party, on the other hand, was the focus of a number of editorials, many of them critical. These did not suggest that the electorate should reject Labour, but that the party should amend its policies accordingly (for example, inflation policy in *The Herald,* 5 July), or be more specific about what it would do in a second term of office (*ODT,* 4 July). In fact, editors across the board seemed resigned to Labour winning the election; there was qualified praise for Labour in two of the newspapers' eve-of-election editorials. The major concern was to prevent the Greens from influencing a new Labour administration. Numerous editorials strongly attacked the Greens ('Greens always a danger', 'Greens' GM stand a cop-out'), and on occasion this anti-Green editorial sentiment seemed to spill into news stories (for example, *The Herald's* front page headline on the opening day of the campaign read 'Green spectre stalks leaders at launching').

In fact, none of the minor parties received editorial praise, which reflects an underlying sentiment of the three newspapers that MMP and its consequences – coalition governments – are an undesirable, destabilising factor.

Table 24.2: Editorials

Date	*New Zealand Herald*	*Otago Daily Times*	*Dominion Post*
1 July	Mildly critical of Labour		
2 July	Strongly critical of Greens		
4 July	Critical of Greens	Praises and criticises Labour	
5 July	Mildly critical of Labour	Attack on Greens	
6 July		Critical of Labour	
8 July			
9 July	Critical of Labour leader	Critical of Labour leader	Qualified praise for Labour
11 July		Critical of all parties	
12 July		Attack on Greens	
13 July			Critical of Labour leader
16 July		Critical of Labour	
18 July		Critical of all parties	
22 July			
23 July		Critical of Labour	On the plight of the National Party
26 July	Qualified praise for Labour	Qualified support for Labour	Anti-minor parties

Party coverage

Political parties try to attract as much media attention as possible during election campaigns. Incumbent parties have an advantage in this respect. We investigated the relative coverage of each party by each newspaper.[4] Our results are not able to comment on the *tone* of the coverage; in other words, it might be that a party attracted considerably more coverage than other parties, but some of this might have been negative in tone. Nevertheless, our results regarding the amount of coverage were unequivocal, as shown in Table 24.3. The Labour Party dominated the party coverage across the three newspapers (17.8 percent).[5] This is not surprising – the party was the incumbent, and (as the editorials indicated) was perceived to be the only possible choice of government for the next term. Not all of this coverage would have been positive; the 'paintergate' and 'corngate' scandals were well documented in all papers.

The National Party attracted two-thirds of Labour's coverage (10.5 percent). In terms of minor parties, the Greens at 4.7 percent had the most coverage of any minor party, followed by New Zealand First (3.9 percent). This result is also unsurprising, given the issues that dominated the campaign (as discussed below). The GM scandal mid-campaign generated considerable coverage, and therefore also encouraged coverage of the Green Party. The coverage of New Zealand First is best explained by the very high proportion of New Zealand First coverage which focused on the leader. Winston Peters' campaign style, and his attention to immigration, law-and-order, and the Treaty of Waitangi guaranteed him coverage (although, as noted below, this was not always positive). The Alliance, the Progressive Coalition, United

Table 24.3: Party coverage (as percentage of total coverage)

	New Zealand Herald	Otago Daily Times	Dominion Post	Total
Labour	13.4	23.9	20.5	17.8
National	6.9	13.9	14.3	10.5
Greens	4.5	4.0	5.6	4.7
Alliance	0.8	2.4	4.5	2.1
Progressive Coalition	1.0	1.6	2.5	1.5
NZF	4.4	4.1	2.9	3.9
United Future	1.7	2.6	1.9	2.0
ACT	1.0	4.8	1.9	2.2

Future and ACT captured, on average, between 1.5 and 2.2 percent of the total coverage.

The newspapers demonstrated some interesting anomalies, however, in their coverage of the various parties which are not revealed in Table 24.3. Some parties received much greater coverage in column centimetres in one paper than they did in the other two. For example, the Alliance captured its greatest amount of coverage in column centimetres in the *ODT*, which also gave more space to the Progressive Coalition than other papers. This reflects, perhaps, the dominance of the Labour Party in Dunedin seats, which encourages the paper to pay particular attention to Labour's possible coalition partners. New Zealand First was covered the least in the *ODT*, and received most coverage in *The Herald*. Overwhelmingly, the coverage of New Zealand First focused on its leader, and this coverage was often unfavourable. Referred to in one article as 'Won-ton Winston' (*The Herald*, 20 July), after his suggestion that his Maori heritage also made him Chinese, New Zealand First leader Winston Peters was often criticised in *The Herald*: 'Identikit populist plays same old tune' (23 July) and 'Peters milks fear of one-party rule' (25 July). The *Dominion Post* covered the ACT party more than the other papers did, perhaps a reflection of the strong organisational activity of the party in Wellington, with the party leader formerly holding the seat of Wellington Central.

One unexpected result of this election was the rise of Peter Dunne and the United Future Party. The meteoric rise of the party saw Peter Dunne joined in Parliament by seven United Future MPs, after years of solitude. The story began with the televised leaders' debate mid-campaign, in which Dunne was favoured by the 'worm', which tracked audience reaction to the leaders' statements. The 'worm' is a gimmick which holds a certain appeal for the media; *The Herald*, prior to the 'worm' debate, declared 'Stage set for worm's welcome return' (15 July 2002). But did the media pay too much attention to Dunne's 'worm' performance, and talk up the party's election night result? Our findings gave mixed results. Most news relating to United Future *did* appear after the 'worm' debate on 15 July, although the majority of articles in the *Dominion Post* and *The Herald* were published *after* 23 July, once the opinion polls began showing the rise of Dunne. Nevertheless, *The Herald* deemed his performance as the 'Lollipop king's finest hour', describing the event as an 'unlikely romance between a worm and a political chameleon' (18 July). It announced, following the debate: 'Lone man from the wilderness might finally have Dunne it' (*The Herald*,

17 July). The *ODT* was the newspaper least interested in United Future (even after the debate), publishing fewer stories on the party than the other papers. The most substantial *ODT* report on United Future actually occurred prior to the great 'worm' debate ('Long-serving MP happy to hold middle ground', *ODT,* 11 July). In some respects, the newspapers could be accused of being unusually slow in picking up this story (perhaps because it was a television oriented event). For example, on the same day that *The Herald* reported 'How worm turns up surprise victor', the paper also ran a feature article on the MPs likely to come into Parliament through the lists. United Future was included in 'other parties', with the comment that 'United Future leader Peter Dunne . . . is getting close to getting enough party votes to be joined by his number two. . .' (16 July). It was not until 23 July that the newspaper caught up with the surge of United Future in the polls, and ran a story on all the United Future list members.

Policy vs the 'hoopla and horse race'

Table 24.4 shows that, for all three newspapers combined, 'game coverage' accounted for around two-thirds of total news coverage of the campaign, with over one-quarter devoted to substance. These figures are similar to findings for the 1999 election (Hayward and Rudd 2000, p.95).[6] Of course, it is a subjective assessment as to whether we consider that there was

Table 24.4: Game and substance (as percentage of total coverage)

	New Zealand Herald	Otago Daily Times	Dominion Post	Total
Opinion Polls	7.1	4.1	9.0	6.8
Other Game	68.8	74.3	57.6	67.7
Substance	28.8	21.2	34.9	28.2

'sufficient' substantive coverage of the election issues by the three newspapers. In our opinion, a regular newspaper reader over the four-week election campaign would have had the opportunity to become fairly well informed about the 'real' election issues. However, we have no way of telling if readers opted to focus on the game stories, rather than the substance ones. Game stories were certainly overwhelmingly more likely to appear as front page stories; of 67 front page stories, only 11 were on substance issues.

Game stories
A number of game stories focused, not surprisingly, on 'paintergate': 'PM threatens to sue over paintergate' (*The Herald*, 8 July 2002); 'Paintergate – what Clark wouldn't tell' (*The Dominion Post*, 9 July); and on 'corngate': 'GM scare' (*The Herald*, 12 July); 'Stuff-ups yes, GE no' (*The Dominion Post*, 12 July). A large photo of a defaced Labour election billboard with a GM sweetcorn sticker covering Helen Clark's mouth accompanied both these lead stories on 'corngate'. Other game-related stories concerned possible coalition formations, particularly between Labour and the Greens: 'Green Party to rethink joining govt' (*ODT,* 11 July); 'PM sees red over Greens' threat' (*The Dominion*, 4 July). A Labour and New Zealand First coalition possibility was largely ruled out: 'Black widow steers clear of Peters's web' (*The Dominion Post*, 24 July); 'Peters in Government? Not with us, Clark insists' (*The Herald*, 24 July). The coalition stories were particularly poignant, given Helen Clark's obvious desire from the outset to lead a single majority government. The papers documented the realisation that this would not be the case: 'Slump leaves Clark unhappy as a dog with two tails' (*The Herald*, 15 July); 'Clark will lead minority government, late poll shows' (*ODT*, 26 July).

One aspect of game coverage that epitomises the increasing preoccupation of the media with the horse race nature of elections is opinion polling. As Table 24.4 shows, opinion poll stories made up nearly 7 percent of total coverage. For both the *ODT* and the *The Herald,* there was an average of one opinion poll story for each day of the election campaign. The placement of these stories, however, was not particularly prominent, with just two front page stories on polls each for the *ODT* and *The Dominion Post*, and five for *The Herald*. Front page opinion poll stories, however, often had dramatic headlines: 'Greens lead surge by minor parties' (*The Herald*, 3 July); 'Poll leap turns Dunne into powerbroker' (*The Herald*, 22 July). The lead stories on the eve of the election showed how differently the newspapers interpreted the results of opinion polls. *The Herald* ran the headline 'Labour slump deepens', accompanied by a large photo of a grim-faced Helen Clark, while *The Dominion Post* announced 'Nats in freefall – polls shock' (26 July).

The 'freefalls', 'slumps', 'surges' and 'leaps' reported do suggest that the newspapers used opinion polls to try to dramatise campaign events. Trivialisation was evident in the series of polls run by the *The Herald*, which asked voters which of the party leaders they would 'invite to dinner' (if they had to), or 'would ask to choose their clothes', or 'would buy a used car from'. Can these be the qualities New Zealanders look for in their political leaders?

However, we need to be careful not to assume that dramatic stories on opinion polls or even seemingly trivial topics of opinion polls have a negative educative impact on voters. It may be the case that ordinary citizens are not usually that interested in politics. Opinion polls, with their use of game analogies, may help to stimulate interest, and lead voters to seek more 'serious' information elsewhere in the newspapers. We also found a series of articles appearing in *The Herald* which used polling to produce news stories on issues. 'One man's polls' appeared between 6 July and 12 July and looked at health, education, immigration, and Maori affairs. This showed that polling could be used imaginatively to produce qualitative information, a point that *The Herald* itself noted in an editorial at the start of the second week of the campaign ('Voice of people content', *The Herald,* 8 July).

Policy Issues
The choice of issues that the media considers newsworthy at election time has implications for political parties. Parties want to raise issues and images that reflect favourably upon their party, and avoid raising issues that are favourably associated with opposing parties. In the past, voters generally associated parties of the left with issues concerning social welfare, health, education and beneficiaries. Parties of the right were linked with agriculture, economic management and defence. Since the 1980s, the distinction between issue ownership on the left and right may have become blurred. In a poll reported in *The Herald* on 19 July, people were asked which party was the best to handle the economy, health, education, law-and-order, taxation and Treaty issues. Labour came out as the preferred party not only on its 'own' issues (health and education), but also on the 'National Party' issues of the economy, taxation and law-and-order.

Parties use various devices to try to set the media agenda with regard to 'election issues' with which they are favourably identified, including press releases, press conferences, campaign speeches and political advertisements. The news media, on the other hand, while reliant on these sources of information to fill their news columns and newscasts, are not passive recipients. They also attempt to raise issues they believe are important to the election, often based on their own polling of voters. Is there evidence that the newspapers tried to set the issue agenda during the 2002 election campaign? The *ODT* stated after one week of the campaign (8 July), that the issue of GM was crowding out other issues which the newspaper believed politicians should be addressing, and subsequent articles featured these very issues. All three newspapers, in both editorials and news columns, criticised the parties for not focusing sufficient attention on what they claimed was *the* election issue – the economy (see, for example, the editorials in *The Dominion Post*, 10 July; *ODT*, 16 July; and *The Herald*, 22 July). *The Herald* in particular devoted considerable space in its business section to discussing 'What the election means for business' (a four page spread on 16 July).

All three newspapers had special features on specific election issues. Not surprisingly, the GM issue came in for detailed scrutiny by newspaper journalists, and in feature articles written by outside experts: 'Genetically modified electioneering' (*The Herald*, 5 July); 'Evidence lacking on GE dangers (*The Dominion Post*, 12 July); 'Why are Greens not honest on GM?' (*ODT*, 22 July). The newspaper coverage of greatest value to voters wanting to make an informed decision would, presumably, set out the main parties' policy positions on certain issues. *The Herald* compared party policies in a series of articles on a range of issues, from Air New Zealand ownership to transport. On the eve of the election, the *Dominion Post* also had a full page spread comparing the policies of the five largest parties across 16 issues, suggesting this helped to create an informed voter, with the recommendation 'Happy reading: wise voting'. Close to voting day, the *ODT* also ran a half page spread comparing the party policies on selected issues (25 July).

It is interesting that while all the newspapers made use of opinion polls, they very rarely reported what the public considered the main issues to be. An exception was the story towards the end of the campaign in *The Herald*, 'Health top of wish list', which listed the top 10 most important election issues according to a sample of voters (24 July). The top four – health, crime, education and GM – all featured prominently in the top issues list for each newspaper (see Table 24.5). As the opinion poll was towards the end of the election, however, it is hard to say if the voters were responding to the newspapers' agenda, or vice versa. As for the parties trying to set the media agenda, perhaps the most telling effort was by Winston Peters and his three 'we can fix it' issues: 'fixing our immigration policy', 'fixing the treaty industry' and 'fixing lawlessness and violence in our society'. It would be crediting Winston Peters with too much to say he was responsible for the prominent placing of law-and-order as an issue in all three newspapers – all the other parties gave some priority to this issue, particularly ACT and National. Maori issues were also of some focus for the other parties, although their absence from the *ODT* list would seem to reflect the demographic makeup of its readership rather than any attempt at agenda setting by the newspaper itself. But the immigration issue and Winston Peters' campaign did receive considerable attention in *The Herald* (1, 5, 16 July); this was probably an issue of less relevance to the Wellington and Dunedin based newspapers. Table 24.5 sets out the most covered issues in each paper, by column centimetres.

Table 24.5: Most Covered Issues

New Zealand Herald	cm	*ODT*	cm	*The Dominion Post*	cm
1 Environment	5508	1 Environment	3374	1 Environment	4987
2 Economy	5206	2 Health	2204	2 Education	1556
3 Immigration	3731	3 Education	2033	3 Health	1342
4 Law and order	3232	4 Law and Order	1374	4 Law and Order	1224
5 Education	2990	5 Economy	1289	5 Maori/Treaty	1013
6 Maori/Treaty	2191	6 Taxation	1219	6 Defence	1041
7 Transport	2136	7 Arts, sports, leisure, media	1184		
8 Health	2000				
9 Taxation	1687				

Conclusion

Election campaigns are largely about political parties and their leaders and candidates trying to get their message over to voters. Mostly these messages are communicated indirectly via the media. There is a tendency to view television as the dominant medium of communication in modern campaigns. This ignores the fact that newspapers devote a great deal of resources to reporting the election campaign, and that a great many people still read newspapers. Newspapers' coverage of election campaigns has not been displaced by television, but complements what viewers see on their television screens. Admittedly, not all that was read in the newspapers during the 2002 election would have assisted a voter to make an informed choice between the various parties. But even a casual reader would have had the opportunity to assess the policies of the main parties across a number of issues. Whether they did so, and whether this weighed more heavily in their minds at voting time than the images of 'Empress Helen', 'Boxer Bill' or 'Won-ton Winston' is, of course, another matter.

25

ALL OVER THE PLACE: BILLBOARD BATTLES IN 2002

Nigel S. Roberts

Campaign billboards are probably the most visible manifestation of the fact that elections are being held in New Zealand. Streets and roadsides throughout the country are transformed during an election campaign. An overseas visitor who knew nothing whatsoever about New Zealand's politics could hardly fail to notice the plethora of advertising hoardings that pepper private and public property alike for a period of three to four weeks before a general election.

There is little evidence that campaign hoardings markedly influence voters. Indeed, only 14 percent of the 1,000 people interviewed in the 2002 Victoria University election survey[1] said that billboards and hoardings had been 'particularly important' to them in deciding how to vote. By way of contrast, 39 percent said that televised debates were particularly important; 39 percent said party manifestos were particularly important; 33 percent regarded leaders' speeches on television as particularly important; and 25 percent said meeting politicians was particularly important.[2]

Nevertheless, none of the main parties contesting an election ever feels able to ignore the opportunity offered by billboards and hoardings. During the 2002 campaign, for example, nine of the ten political parties in New Zealand that won at least 1 percent of the party vote mounted extensive, countrywide billboard campaigns. The design and range of the various parties' placards, and the images they presented, were both revealing and significant.

Poles apart: Labour and National

After a few early hiccups (when some Labour candidates displayed hoardings left over from the 1999 general election campaign), the Labour Party's use of billboards in 2002 was impressive. They were simple, striking and straight to the point. All had a bright red background. One Labour billboard, the most widely displayed of the entire election campaign, stressed the party vote. A colour picture of Labour's leader, Prime Minister Helen Clark, was placed prominently in the centre. Below it were the words 'Party Vote' on one line, and the word 'Labour' followed by a red tick in a white circle on the second and final line. The appeal of the billboards was direct and easy to follow. The party was clearly playing the strongest card in its suit – the authoritative personality of the prime minister.

Labour's second set of billboards promoted the party's electorate candidates. They all followed a generic template. They had the same red background as Labour's party vote placards. The left-hand quarter (or sometimes a third) featured a large photograph of the candidate concerned. On the right-hand side there were often only two words: 'Labour', and underneath, the surname of the party's electorate candidate. Both words were preceded by a red tick in a white circle. In most instances, the name of the electorate did not even appear on the billboard, though there were a few exceptions (such as 'Field For Mangere' and 'Goff For Mt Roskill'); but even then, the name of the party's candidate was in type four times larger than the name of the electorate the candidate was standing for. Labour's billboards in the seven Maori electorates were very similar to the party's generic general electorate hoardings, except that they usually stressed the name of the Maori electorate in type about the same size as the name of the party's candidate (for example, 'Turia for Te Tai Hauauru'). In addition, most of Labour's Maori electorate posters had a prominent red, white and black koru strip on their left-hand edge.

The Labour Party's billboards were clear and uncluttered. They reinforced the message all parties need to stress during a Mixed Member Proportional election campaign – the overwhelming significance of the party vote. Labour's advertising hoardings were very well designed. Both the standard party vote billboards and the electorate billboards alike hammered home the need for Labour to win party votes in particular.

By way of contrast, the National Party's billboard campaign was dreadful. It was confused and confusing. For more than half the election campaign, billboards featuring the party leader, Bill English, were conspicuous by their absence. When they finally appeared, just two weeks before polling day, they contained an appealing picture of a semi-casual Bill English (wearing a tie but no jacket, and with his left hand in his trouser pocket). However, the impact of National's leadership billboards was weakened by an anodyne slogan ('Get the future you deserve', a poor throw-back to National's 1975 slogan, 'New Zealand – The Way *You* Want It'), and also by the fact that

National's quest for the party vote was limited to putting two light-grey ticks alongside the party's name on the placard.

The National Party's electorate hoardings were all over the place, but that refers to the fact that they were totally uncoordinated, rather than to their geographic distribution. The party simply did not have a generic model which its candidates could adopt and then adapt to fit their needs. For instance, the National Party's high-profile Coromandel candidate, Sandra Goudie, had an attractive series of billboards with her photograph and name in large type, featuring slogans such as 'Standing up for Coromandel' and 'Here She Comes'. What her posters did not do, though, was stress the need for party votes for National in Coromandel. Sandra Goudie's 'Here She Comes' billboard did not even depict National's logo or contain the name of the party (other than in the candidate's email address). Goudie ran what was in many ways a good campaign, winning 43.6 percent of the electorate votes in Coromandel, and capturing the seat from the Greens' co-leader, Jeanette Fitzsimons, who had won the seat in 1999. In 2002, Fitzsimons received only 22.9 percent of the electorate votes, and came third, 3 percent behind Labour's candidate, Max Purnell. At the same time, however, Goudie's party benefited very little from her work in the electorate, as National won only 22.4 percent of the party votes in Coromandel, compared with Labour's 34.4 percent.

Equally confused were the billboard campaigns by National's candidates in Mana and Napier. Sue Wood, a former president of the National Party,[3] had placards featuring her photograph (which took up about 40 percent of the billboard) alongside the slogan, 'SUE WOOD FOR MANA'. The problem for Wood was that there was no way she was ever going to win the Mana electorate. It is a safe Labour seat and (in its former guise as Porirua as well) always has been. What she needed — and what her party needed — in Mana were party votes for National, not electorate votes. Sue Wood was ranked at 19 on National's party list. National won so few votes in the 2002 general election that only six MPs made it into Parliament via National's list.[4] Sue Wood was not one of them.[5]

The picture presented by Anne Tolley's placards was similar. Initially elected to Parliament as a National Party list MP in 1999, Tolley had also been National's unsuccessful electorate candidate in Napier in that election. She was re-selected as the party's candidate in the Napier electorate for the 2002 election. Labour's Geoff Braybrooke retired from Parliament and vacated the seat at the end of the 2002 parliamentary session. As a result,

Labour's main billboard in 2002: simple, striking and straight to the point.

An example of Labour's generic electorate placards promoting both the party vote and the party's local candidate.

Unlike the vast bulk of its general electorate hoardings, Labour's 2002 posters in the Maori electorates included the name of the seat.

An appealing picture with an anodyne slogan: National's leader, Bill English, put in a late appearance on the nation's billboards in 2002.

A rare example of a good National Party electorate placard.

How not to win an election: despite her dependence on National's party vote, posters for Napier electorate candidate, Anne Tolley, completely neglected to promote the National party vote.

Three fingers for three policies and three slogans: New Zealand First had a simple message in 2002.

ACT promoted a range of policies, tax cuts among them, in 2002.

The Green Party ensured that genetic engineering was at the forefront of its campaign agenda in 2002.

United Future's twin assets – Peter Dunne and a conservative family focus – were paramount on its 2002 placards.

Not surprisingly, the billboards promoting Jim Anderton's Progressive Coalition – the first party in New Zealand to be named after an individual – focused solely on the party's founder and leader in 2002.

A double act with diminished returns: Christian Heritage's long-time leader and the party's new deputy-leader were the choice of only 1.4 percent of New Zealand's voters in 2002.

Double entendre, disastrous result: despite the Alliance's energetic campaign in 2002, the party won fewer votes than the Outdoor Recreation Party whose campaign hoardings were conspicuous only by their absence.

Labour's party vote billboard was cleverly and quickly doctored when the 'corngate' scandal broke.

Taking its cue from Tui's advertisements for beer, a 2002 ACT poster won ironic endorsement.

The unofficial winner of the campaign for the best political billboard in 2002: the Alliance split over differences between party members in connection with the government's response to the war in Afghanistan.

Anne Tolley's lively and attractive billboards cleverly depicted her as 'Napier's ANNE TOLLEY M.P.', implying that she was already the Member of Parliament for Napier. They included the slogan 'carry on Tolley'. However, there was no way that Anne Tolley was ever going to be elected as Napier's electorate MP. The seat has always been solidly Labour.[6] In reality, Anne Tolley's sole route back into the House of Representatives was via National's party list (on which she was ranked at 24). What she desperately needed, both in Napier and throughout New Zealand as a whole, was for electors to cast their party votes for the National Party. Yet Anne Tolley's billboards did not even feature the party's name or logo. There was no indication whatsoever (not even in her website's URL) that Anne Tolley was a National Party MP, and that what she required was party votes for the National Party. Her list ranking and National's poor party vote performance meant that Anne Tolley was not re-elected to the House of Representatives in 2002.

Several National Party candidates did have campaign hoardings that stressed the need for National to win party votes. They included Guy Salmon (a high profile environmentalist and list-only candidate),[7] Dale Stephens (a sacrificial lamb for the National Party standing against the exceptionally popular Peter Dunne in the Ohariu-Belmont electorate),[8] and Greg White (the party's candidate in the Te Tai Hauauru electorate and ranked at 30 on National's list). In the light of National's poor performance at the polls, though, all their pleas were to no avail. None of them was elected to Parliament in 2002.

In brief, the Labour Party's and the National Party's billboard battles in 2002 could not have been more different. Labour's campaign was controlled and coordinated; National's was not. Labour's message was focused – it was simple and strategic; National's was anything but. These differences were reflected in the election results. The Labour Party attracted almost twice the party votes that the National Party acquired, and Labour won 52 seats in Parliament, compared with National's 27. The National Party's president during the 2002 election campaign was Michelle Boag. In the light of the National campaign, it seems hard to believe that she was a public relations expert; it is far less to difficult to understand why she fell on her sword after the election, and resigned from her position as party president.

Putting it in black and white

New Zealand First's 2002 billboards and hoardings were in the party's colours, black and white. Their message was black and white too. They showed Winston Peters holding up the three middle fingers of his right hand,[9] symbolising the party's three-pronged anti-crime, anti-immigrant, and anti-Treaty pitch, accompanied by three slogans. The first was 'Your Country Needs You'. Just in case this Kitcheneresque call was in any danger of being misinterpreted, it was followed by a direct plea to people to 'Give us your party vote'. All the party's hoardings ended with an injunction to voters to '*Keep* New Zealand First'.

In 1999, the New Zealand First party vote fell below MMP's 5 percent threshold for representation. However, because Winston Peters held on to the Tauranga electorate in 1999 (he retained the seat by a margin of only 63 votes), the electoral system's alternative threshold came into force, and Peters brought four additional MPs into the House of Representatives.[10] It was the first time a New Zealand electorate had been a 'trigger' seat in a general election.[11] As a result, Winston Peters and New Zealand First devoted a great deal of attention and effort into shoring up Peters' support in Tauranga in 2002. The city was plastered with placards featuring a colour photo of Peters, and urging electors to 'Re-elect Winston our MP'. It was a simple, direct plea with a personal touch – the use of Peters' first name only, and the use of the word 'our', were clever ways for the party to cement the link between the voters of Tauranga and the New Zealand First leader. Underscoring the significance of Winston Peters' personal appeal for electorate votes in the Tauranga seat is the fact that the party did not mention its request for party votes on Peters' Tauranga posters.

New Zealand First's billboard strategy worked brilliantly: Winston Peters' personal majority in Tauranga increased 164-fold to 10,362 votes, and the party's overall party vote throughout the country as a whole went up from 4.3 percent to 10.4 percent. In the wake of the country's first MMP election in 1996, New Zealand First was the third largest party in Parliament, but its disastrous performance during the 1996–99 parliamentary term saw it plummet in the 1999 general election to being the sixth largest party in Parliament. As a result of the 2002 election, New Zealand First was again third.

Projecting policies: ACT and the Greens

The ACT party's blue and yellow billboards promoted the party's philosophy and policies: 'Act best for small business'; 'Prompt world class healthcare for all'; 'Tax cut for every worker'; 'World class education standards'; and 'Zero tolerance for crime'. All the party's hoardings carried the same message, 'A party vote for ACT sends a message to government.' Every billboard also concluded with the same slogan, 'ACT. SOMEBODY HAS TO.' Making a direct pitch to New Zealand's growing number of Asian immigrants, ACT also included a message in Chinese in the bottom left-hand corner of its posters.

Thanks to the space limitations, the level of political debate on billboards and hoardings must be minimal. While Labour and National scrupulously avoided political arguments on their posters, and New Zealand First merely hinted at what it stood for (by giving voters the three fingers), ACT was not the only party that tried to project an ideology through the medium of advertising hoardings. The Greens also pushed issues on some of its billboards. Unlike ACT, however, the Greens also had general placards. The party promoted the 'GREEN TEAM', exhorting voters to cast their 'Party Vote: Green' and including a picture of the party's (then) seven smiling Members of Parliament. Appropriately, the party also recycled some of its 1999 hoardings, urging electors to 'Make your party vote last for generations. GO Green'. However, Green Party placards also put forward the Greens' views on one of the key issues in the 2002 election – namely, genetic engineering [GE]. 'GE. KEEP IT IN THE LAB' proclaimed bright green billboards. The party also campaigned on the issue in Maori – a distinct rarity in New Zealand politics – with some hoardings saying 'GE. KAUA E WHAKATOI'.

The attempt by ACT and the Greens to engage voters and parties in a political debate was not stunningly successful. Each party won only about 7 percent of the votes to end up with nine MPs apiece. In ACT's case, this was precisely the number the party had had in the previous Parliament. Although the Green Party gained two MPs, this was far below pre-election expectations.

United's family focus

The United Future Party's pre-election expectations were minimal. In 1996 and 1999, Peter Dunne had been elected as the party's sole electorate MP in Ohariu-Belmont, but on each occasion United had not garnered enough party votes throughout New Zealand as a whole for Dunne's win to trigger any other MPs into the House of Representatives.[12] At the start of the 2002 campaign, Dunne was hoping to increase United Future's party vote to a level where he might bring one or possibly even two other MPs into Parliament with him. Part of Dunne's reason for hoping he could do this was that during the 1999–2002 parliamentary term, the United Party had merged with Future New Zealand, formerly the Christian Democrat Party. In 1999, Future New Zealand had won 1.1 percent of the votes. By combining the support bases for both United and Future New Zealand, it was thought that the party could gain one seat, or possibly two, on the back of Dunne's vice-like grip on Ohariu-Belmont.

The influence of Dunne's new allies was reflected on the party's campaign billboards. The generic placard for the party included a picture of Dunne; the party's name, URL and a green fern-leaf; and the slogan 'Your family Our focus'. Quite amazingly for a small party, United Future's main poster did not even include a pitch for the party vote. There was space on the placard, though, for an extra sheet of paper with the words 'Party Vote' to be tacked or pasted onto the poster between Peter Dunne's picture and the party's name! Dunne also campaigned hard in his own electorate and had a special hoarding made for it. It stressed that Dunne was the MP for Ohariu-Belmont, but ignored the party vote.

When Dunne's middle-of-the-road reasonableness appealed to viewers in the first Holmes debate on TV1, and that appeal was rapidly translated into support in the opinion polls, United Future's billboards, with their emphasis on Peter Dunne and on the party's family focus, quickly became an asset for the party. It was, for example, fascinating to see the number of North Island farms that displayed hoardings both for National Party candidates and for the United Future Party. United's share of the party vote in 2002 was 6.7 percent, up from 0.9 percent in 1996 and 0.5 percent in 1999. After being his party's sole MP for two terms in a row, Peter Dunne was joined by seven other MPs as a result of the 2002 election.

Below the 5 percent threshold

The party that came seventh in the election, the only party in 2002 to win seats in Parliament despite falling below the 5 percent party vote threshold, was Jim Anderton's Progressive Coalition. First elected to Parliament in 1984 as a Labour MP, Anderton left his party and established the NewLabour Party during the fourth Labour government's tumultuous second term in office. Anderton held his seat (then known as Sydenham) in the 1990 election, formed the Alliance during the 1990–1993 parliamentary term, and retained his seat (the name was changed to Wigram when new electoral boundaries were adopted for the introduction of MMP) as leader of the Alliance in 1993, 1996, and 1999.

The Labour Party and the Alliance formed a minority coalition government after the 1999 election, with Anderton as deputy prime minister. However, differences in the Alliance – especially over the government's decision to send troops to Afghanistan after the terrorist attacks on New York and Washington on 11 September 2001 – led to increasing tensions within the party. In April 2002, Anderton was removed from the leadership of the party by the Alliance's extraparliamentary council, but he retained the confidence of a majority of the party's Members of Parliament. He thus announced plans to set up a new party and formally did so when Parliament was dissolved for the elections. The basic aim – the *raison d'etre* – of the new party was to provide responsible, stable, continuing support for a Labour-led government. The party also argued that a vote cast for it would not be a 'wasted vote', because Anderton's strong electoral base in Wigram would ensure that the party would cross at least one of MMP's two electoral thresholds.

As a result of Jim Anderton's dominant position in the new party, as well as its singularly narrow pro-coalition focus, the party's election campaign billboards were 2002's simplest political placards. On a red and grey background, they featured only a large colour photograph of Jim Anderton, and four words, 'JIM ANDERTON Progressive Coalition'. The billboards had a dual purpose: they were used both in Wigram (where Anderton was, of course, seeking the electorate vote), and also throughout the rest of New Zealand (where the party was asking electors for their party votes). This accounts for their lack of complexity. They also stood in stark contrast to Anderton's Alliance Party billboards three years earlier, which had stressed education, employment, health, and retirement policies. In 2002, Anderton himself was his party's sole issue.

The Christian Heritage Party has fought the good fight in New Zealand since 1990, when it won 0.5 percent of the votes. In 1993, its vote went up to 2.0 percent. Three years later, in conjunction with the Christian Democrats, the two stood together as the Christian Coalition, which gained 4.3 percent of the party votes in New Zealand's first MMP election. In 1999, the Christian Heritage Party's vote fell back to 2.4 percent. In 2002, as in all four previous elections, the party's leader was Graham Capill, but in an attempt to broaden the party's appeal, a high-profile women's refuge movement activist, Merepeka Raukawa-Tait, was chosen as its deputy leader.

In 1999, Capill was pictured on his party's election placards with his wife. Christian Heritage billboards in 2002 had Ms Raukawa-Tait looking over Mr Capill's shoulder, alongside the slogan, 'family justice choice'. The bottom line was 'CHRISTIAN HERITAGE for your party vote'. However, despite the fact that Christian Heritage's hoardings were clear and visually appealing, the party obviously was not. It won only 1.4 percent of the party votes cast throughout the country as a whole. This was its worst performance since 1990, when the party had contested only 18 out of 97 electorates in New Zealand's second-to-last first-past-the-post election.

After the Alliance split in the run-up to the 2002 election (indeed, the split in the party was a prime reason why Helen Clark opted for an early election), and Anderton was dumped as leader, Laila Harré was chosen as the Alliance Party leader. It was a role she could perform only outside Parliament, but her supporters rallied enthusiastically round her. As soon as the election was called, Alliance election campaign billboards hit the streets: in an impressive display of commitment, dedication and organisation, the Alliance was first cab off the rank. The party's main placard was also impressive. It had a bright red background, and a black-and-white photograph of Laila Harré graced the right-hand third of the billboard. The Alliance's slogan was a clever double-*entendre*: 'the only choice left'. A green stripe near the foot of the billboard pushed a crucial message: 'Party Vote – Alliance'.

However, the Alliance's advertising hoardings also had a cautionary message. Despite a mass of Alliance billboards erected across the entire country, the party polled only 1.3 percent of the party votes cast in 2002. What is more, neither party leader Laila Harré nor deputy leader Willie Jackson won the seats they contested.[13] As a result, the Alliance was out of Parliament. The party that had won 18.2 percent of the poll and come third in its first general election in 1993 virtually disappeared from the New Zealand political map less than nine years later.

Indeed, the Alliance's stunningly poor performance is highlighted by the achievements of the Outdoor Recreation Party. The party was formed not long before the election, qualified for some broadcasting finance, and fronted brief opening and closing campaign statements on TV1. Nevertheless, although I travelled fairly extensively throughout New Zealand during the election campaign period, I did not see a single billboard promoting the Outdoor Recreation Party. The contrast with the Alliance could not have been more striking. Yet despite the Alliance's sea of billboards and the Outdoor Recreation Party's drought, in the end the Alliance won 97 *fewer* party votes than the Outdoor Recreation Party. Counting election posters is clearly no more accurate a guide to the outcome of an election than speaking to hairdressers or taxi-drivers.

Correlations and comparisons

The overall correlation between party placards and election performance is far from negative, however. The message given by Labour's billboards in 2002 was clear, consistent and carefully crafted, and the party's results reflected that fact. Likewise, National's election campaign billboards were chaotic and confused, and, unsurprisingly, the party suffered its worst-ever defeat. It was not surprising, too, that the two parties that are the ideological outliers in the New Zealand Parliament, ACT on the right and the Greens on the left of the country's political spectrum, tried to inject debates about their philosophies and policies into their political advertising hoardings.

By themselves, election campaign billboards and hoardings may not have much of an impact on voters, but they do have an important role to play during an election. For a start, they project and reflect the images that political parties try to create for themselves. Equally important, they reinforce impressions and views created by the other media – television, newspapers, public meetings and the like. They also remind voters (and visitors) that an election is being held. In light of declining voter turnout, this alone is cause enough for two cheers for this aspect of democracy.[14]

New Zealand's political parties have an international reputation for being highly disciplined. This is clearly illustrated in the billboards on display at election time. Parties choose a particular colour scheme and then use it for all their advertising: red for Labour; red and green for the Alliance; green (obviously) for the Greens; blue for the National Party; blue and yellow for ACT. Most parties have a tightly controlled generic format for their election hoardings, which all their candidates use. Although National was a glaring exception to this rule in 2002, it was not an exception in 1999, and almost certainly will not be in 2005.

By way of contrast, American billboards, placards and 'lawn signs' reflect a very different political system. The US party system is much looser than New Zealand's, and election hoardings underscore that fact. Candidates from the same party in the same state use a range of colours – whatever pleases them. One Democrat (such as the late Minnesota Senator Paul Wellstone) may use green, another may use blue, another red, and another brown on their posters. In New Zealand, Margaret Hayward wore a red jacket while campaigning in the Rangitikei electorate, because red is the colour that has been adopted by Labour and Social Democratic parties around the world. In the United States, however, in her 2002 re-election campaign, a Republican member of the Minnesota House of Representatives, Connie Ruth, also wore a red jacket (indeed, her entire advertising campaign was based on the colour red).[15] That would be unthinkable for conservative candidates in Australia, New Zealand, Norway, Sweden or the United Kingdom. Furthermore, American politicians tend to stress their independence rather than their party affiliations. As a result, candidates for office in the United States frequently fail to mention their party allegiance on their campaign billboards.[16] Anne Tolley's hoardings would not have been out of place in New Jersey, New Mexico or New York; they were in New Zealand.

Finally, it should be noted that election hoardings also reflect other wider aspects of different polities and societies. The destruction – often wanton vandalism – that occurs when parties' billboards have holes punched in them or are knocked down is part of a lawlessness and lack of tolerance that are too often exhibited in New Zealand. In Scandinavia, this seldom if ever occurs. Similarly, the fact that there are only a few isolated instances of the intelligent doctoring of political posters in New Zealand[17] is an indication of a society that is somewhat conformist, colourless and humourless.[18]

Election billboards are designed to attract attention, and they deserve to do so. Campaign hoardings and placards provide useful and important insights into the political culture not only of New Zealand, but also of other societies and political systems. When an election is called, billboards spring up like mushrooms after an autumn shower, but they also disappear overnight (in New Zealand this is literally the case: they have to be taken down prior to midnight on election eve). They may be all over the place, but they do not last for long (as a result of vandalism, local body by-laws and electoral law). We need to catch them while we can. It is necessary to document the messages conveyed by election hoardings, and to assess their impact, if we really seek to understand fully the variety and the significance of the multitude of ways in which parties promote themselves, their policies and their candidates.

THE RESULTS

26

REPRESENTATION, SELECTION, ELECTION: THE 2002 PARLIAMENT

Elizabeth McLeay

The 2002 general election again produced a Parliament defined by parties that fit primarily into a unidimensional, left-right policy continuum.[1] Other significant dimensions, however, were represented as well, especially environmental, Maori and religious interests. Further trends that had developed under the new electoral rules were also continued in the 2002 Parliament: the increasingly heterogeneous social composition of the House of Representatives overall; the strengthening of the Maori presence; and a relatively high proportion of new MPs entering Parliament compared with FPP election outcomes. These effects were produced by the systemic characteristics of the MMP rules and the salient cleavages of New Zealand society, as interpreted by party ideology and conditioned by party selection processes.

Party incumbency and the threshold criteria

The first three general elections under MMP delivered an almost monotonous similarity in the number of parties winning seats in Parliament: six in 1996, and seven in both 1999 and 2002. In all three elections, party incumbency was clearly a significant factor in determining which of the parties actually gained parliamentary representation, although the distribution of parliamentary seats among those parties changed, at times quite dramatically. Three of the four parties elected in the last FPP election in 1993 (Labour, National and New Zealand First) survived the first three elections under MMP. The Alliance survived in splintered form, with the Greens splitting off before the 1999 election, the rest of the Alliance dividing into two during 2001–2002, and one faction, the Progressive Coalition, returning two MPs in 2002. United was created by dissidents from within the 1993–1996 Parliament, and only just survived with its one MP until it expanded its representation in 2002. Despite the many other parties formed outside and inside Parliament since 1996, only one, ACT, made its first appearance in Parliament through an MMP election. This pattern of re-electing the incumbent parties has occurred despite the interruption of party proportionality (as determined by the general elections) through party defections and schisms during the first two parliamentary terms, when MPs either transferred their allegiances to other parties or established new ones. In short, the 5 percent threshold has largely protected the parties already in Parliament, by being a substantial barrier to new parties entering Parliament. Yet the alternative, one-electorate threshold has also had an impact on the number and nature of the parliamentary party system, as illustrated again by the 2002 results.

The impact of the 'trigger seats' can be gauged by examining the parties that gained more than 1 percent, but less than 5 percent, of the party vote over the three MMP elections. In 1996, the top runner-up under the 5 percent barrier was the Christian Coalition, with 4.3 percent of the party vote. Having no electorate seats, it failed to get into Parliament. Peter Dunne's United Party gained 0.9 percent, not enough to take colleagues in with him when he won his electorate seat of Ohariu-Belmont, National having stood aside from that particular contest. The Legalise Cannabis Party won 1.7 percent of the party vote and was unable to take its burning issue into the debating chamber.

In 1999, New Zealand First, punished by the voters after its performance in government and Parliament during the preceding term, went from its 1996 party vote of 13.4 percent to a mere 4.3 percent (the same percentage as the Christian Coalition had gained the previous election, although with fewer votes). Despite failing to clear the 5 percent threshold, New Zealand First went back into Parliament with five seats because its leader, Winston Peters, won his Tauranga electorate (albeit by a tiny margin). Without New Zealand First, Labour and the Alliance together would have had a majority in Parliament. Dunne returned to Parliament in 1999, but again, with merely 0.5 percent of the party vote, he had to remain a one-person caucus. Christian Heritage gained 2.4 percent, and Future New Zealand (formerly the Christian Democrats) won 1.1 percent, as did the Legalise Cannabis Party. The Greens, who thought they might have to depend on gaining an electorate seat (Coromandel), managed to win 5.2 percent of the party vote, narrowly hurdling both barriers.

In 2002, it was Jim Anderton's Progressive Coalition that profited from the one-seat threshold. Anderton won his Wigram seat and took one colleague back into Parliament with him. Despite a valiant battle, Laila Harré failed to win Waitakere, and her party, the Alliance, won merely 1.3 percent of the party vote throughout New Zealand. The Outdoor Recreation Party fished up 1.3 percent of the party vote, and the Christian Heritage Party did slightly better with 1.4 percent. Peter Dunne's party, now called United Future to encompass its Christian wing, raised its vote so much that it passed the 5 percent threshold.

So the one-seat threshold has become an important alternative route into Parliament. In the three elections so far under MMP, two parliamentary parties – New Zealand First in 1999, and the Progressive Coalition in 2002 – have been helped by this rule, although they might also have survived had they simply retained one leadership trophy seat, as did Dunne, who had in 1996 and 1999 received insufficient votes to bring colleagues into Parliament with him through the trigger-seat threshold. Should the one-seat threshold be retained? Two of those involved in the Royal Commission have now spoken publicly for its abolition: the commission's chair, Sir John Wallace, and one of the commissioners, political scientist Richard Mulgan. The MMP Review Committee discussed the issue, but decided for the status quo. There were 52 submissions on this topic, 41 opposing the one-seat threshold. The Alliance, the Greens, Labour, National and United all supported keeping the one-seat threshold, while ACT 'supported abolishing it but only if the party vote threshold for parliamentary representation was lowered to 4 percent' (MMP Review Committee 2001, p.50).

The main argument in the rule's favour tends to be that if a party does well enough in one locality, it deserves parliamentary representation in numbers that reflect its nationwide party vote, even when that vote fails to reach 5 percent. The rule allows a party that is struggling to establish itself to break into the system, representing its voters in Parliament and receiving the funding and publicity that follow from achieving incumbency. The trigger-seat rule might particularly help, say, a Maori party, or a regionally based one (a country party, for example). Another justification (one that came up in the public hearings of the MMP Review Committee) is that, without the single-seat threshold, many votes would be 'wasted'. There is no logic to this argument, given that any threshold will 'waste' votes. The 5 percent threshold also 'wastes' votes; for example, the 4.3 percent of the votes that went to the Christian Coalition in 1996. The only way to avoid wastage is to have no threshold at all, suffering the consequences of having perhaps ten parties in Parliament.

The first argument against the alternative threshold concerns the inflated value of some people's votes compared with others. In a 'trophy' electorate, one which is so important to a party that victory or defeat means life or death to it, people's electorate votes are worth more than those of their neighbours in non-'trophy' electorates. Voters in the possible threshold seats not only have to consider who might be their best electorate MP, but also have to vote strategically, considering whether they want that party to be present in Parliament (as well as thinking about the virtues of the particular candidate).[2] In order to calculate whether they want to risk 'wasting' their votes unnecessarily, they need opinion poll data to provide information about the likely winner. This has the effect of inflating the significance of opinion polls, that are not always reliable, especially at the local level, and are generally accurate only as 'snapshots' of views at a particular time rather than being precise predictions of the final result.

More importantly, there is the issue of public understanding of the one-seat threshold rule. The Electoral Commission's polling showed that before the 2002 election 49 percent of their respondents (N=598) knew about the 5 percent threshold, and this rose to 54 percent after that election (N=591). In comparison, the proportions of the population who knew about the one-seat threshold were 34 percent before and 42 percent after the election. Only 27 percent and 34 percent respectively knew about both criteria (Colmar Brunton 2002, p.6). Indeed, this aspect is the least understood feature of the MMP rules.

Party strategy is also affected by the one-seat threshold rule. Parties put disproportionate effort into winning electorate seats when they might be better campaigning nationwide for the party vote. ACT realised this, and in 2002 actively pursued votes across the country rather than trying to capture, for example, the Epsom electorate. The Greens did not, and although they improved their party vote in 2002 (unlike ACT), they might have done even better had they wasted less time on Coromandel. The Coromandel example raises another issue: whether or not accommodations are going to be reached where major parties refrain from standing candidates against potential small party allies (as in Ohariu-Belmont until 2002). This happens when parties are trying to help out possible coalition partners (or parties that will at least support them on votes of confidence). Alternatively, parties can decide to stand a candidate, but encourage vote splitting, to help a minor party into Parliament (as in Coromandel in 1999). This can get quite complicated and devious. For example, rather than fighting for Tauranga in 1999, Margaret Wilson (Labour) could have abandoned the contest in the hope that the National candidate, Katherine O'Regan, would win, making it very difficult for New Zealand First to return any MPs to Parliament.

Trigger seats might make for more exciting elections, but because they involve such tricky decisions, they also make for difficult voting, campaigning and party strategising. Fairness between parties is also an important criterion. Why should some parties get a group of MPs into Parliament through trigger seats while others with more party votes fail to do so? For example, the Greens might have neither won Coromandel nor passed the 5 percent threshold in 1999, yet might have won more party votes than New Zealand First. The Alliance might have won more party votes in 2002 than the Progressive Coalition.

The alternative threshold might exacerbate the proliferation of small parliamentary parties. The more parties there are in Parliament, the more difficult it is to govern. Achieving a majority coalition government becomes harder and minority governing becomes a particularly complicated business. Furthermore, because achieving the one-seat threshold seems an attainable goal, its existence encourages party defections and splits. This happened in both 1996–1999 and 1999–2002. Perhaps Parliament's back door should be made more difficult to enter by installing double doors, that is, establishing a two-seat threshold. (In Germany parties must win three seats to qualify for the alternative threshold.) Alternatively, perhaps that entrance could be boarded up altogether and parties that win just one seat, but do not achieve 5 percent of the party vote, should retain only that solitary place. Perhaps the party vote threshold might be lowered to 4 percent in compensation (thus producing a minimum of five MPs in a caucus), as the Royal Commission on the Electoral System (1986, p.55) recommended.

Multi-party politics, policy influence, and the Opposition role

The switch from a Parliament overwhelmingly dominated by two parties alternating in government to a multi-party Parliament also produced a rise in the number of parliamentary parties that could be classified as 'relevant' or 'significant' to government, either because they are involved in the political executive (as coalition partners), or because they affect government and the policy process, through either co-operation or threats.

Under FPP, between 1935 and 1993, only one party was influential: the party in government. The opposition party or parties had little or no impact on public policy and the views of those who voted for the losing party were not represented in government policy. Because it is so difficult for one party to gain a majority of seats on its own under the MMP rules, power now has to be shared among parties to a much greater extent than before. Table 26.1 sets out the situation since 1996, showing how supporting and coalition parties have been involved in the policy process (although the involvement of the former should not be exaggerated). As Chapter 28 on the government formation process shows, the 2002 election set the stage for an interesting set of consultation arrangements among four political parties.

The 2002 election results also produced a Parliament in which the idea of 'the Opposition' continued to change. New Zealand had inherited from Britain the notion of the monarch's 'loyal Opposition'. The losing party

Table 26.1: Parliament and Government 1996–2002: Number of parties relevant to governing

In Government	Relevant Parties (i.e. coalition parties plus parties that support the government)	Other Parties (Opposition)
National/NZF (Bolger/Shipley) majority govt. 16 December 1996 –28 July 1998	Governing parties (2)	ACT, Alliance, Labour, United
National/NZF (Shipley) minority govt. 28 July 1998 –26 August 1998	Governing parties (2) plus government support party (ACT)	Alliance, Labour, United
National/Mauri Pacific/ Independents (Shipley) minority govt. 26 August 1998–10 December 1999	Governing parties (2) and Independents plus government support party (ACT)	Alliance, Labour, United
Labour/Alliance (Clark) minority govt. 10 December 1999–26 August 2002	Governing parties (2) plus government support party (Greens)	United, NZ First (which sometimes supported the government), National, ACT
Labour/Progressive Coalition (Clark) minority govt. 26 August 2002–	Governing parties (2) plus government support party (United Future)	NZ First, National, ACT, Greens (although the Greens formally agreed to support the government on some issues)

had a duty to oppose the government, but to support the political system that produced that government. The opposing party was tied into the political system partly because it was the 'government-in-waiting'. When the parliamentary *Standing Orders* were rewritten in anticipation of the multi-party chamber that would be produced by MMP, the topic of 'the Opposition' was discussed. It was noted that the existing *Standing Orders* did not recognise political parties, although they did recognise 'a Government and an Opposition' (Standing Orders Committee 1995, p.15) for matters relating to procedural rights. In future, the parties would be recognised and defined. The Standing Orders Committee then addressed the position of Leader of the Opposition, a post that in New Zealand dates back to 1889 (p.16). This position brought with it certain speaking rights and the allocation of a special salary and allowances. 'It is an important constitutional office, marked at the State Opening of Parliament, where the Prime Minister and the Leader of the Opposition flank the Governor-General during the reading of the Speech from the Throne' (p.16). The Committee 'finally decided that the position is still appropriate [under MMP] and should be retained and that it should be held by the leader of the largest opposition party in the House' (p.16).

Thus, since the 1996 election, the position of Leader of the Opposition has continued and has been occupied by either the Labour or the National leader. Nevertheless, the idea of the Opposition itself has become much less defined and probably now simply means those parties that are not part of the government, or are not officially supporting the government. But even this loose and changing definition did not describe the situation after the 2002 general election.

The National contingent was so diminished in numbers after the election that the other non-governing parties, which had improved their shares of seats, contested National's claim to occupy nine frontbench seats, the number it had had between 1999 and 2002. After Parliament had met on the first day, sitting in (more or less) alphabetical order, the re-elected Speaker, Jonathan Hunt, ruled that National would lose two of its frontbench positions but that it would retain the position of Leader of the Opposition. This meant that New Zealand First was allocated three frontbench seats on the opposition benches, while the Greens and ACT were given two seats apiece. United Future occupied one frontbench position on the government side of the crossbenches. Interestingly, this arrangement showed that, despite the formal agreement between the government and the Greens committing themselves to a consultative arrangement, the Greens (who were part of the lobby for the redistribution of the seats) saw themselves as part of the Opposition. They also regarded themselves as an opposition party for the purpose of select committee arrangements. United Future also protected its own independence in its participation on committees. The meaning of 'the Opposition' has therefore continued to change as the MMP Parliaments develop new norms and rules. Certainly, there is no single party that is assuredly the 'government-in-waiting'.

A further consequence of the 2002 general election was that, as a consequence of the interparty negotiations during the government formation process, the opposition parties were awarded more select committee chairs than previously, even when compared with the two preceding MMP Parliaments. National took the chair of the the Regulations Review Committee, which had been chaired by an opposition MP since the 1985 reforms of the select committee system; and United Future, as the support party, was rewarded with an important chair, as parties in similar positions had been since 1996. The two-person Progressive Coalition party did not receive a chair, in contrast to the situation for the junior coalition partner since 1996, nor was ACT allocated a committee chair. Leaving aside the procedural committees, the allocation of chairs as at 21 October 2002 was as follows (Electoral Commission 2002, pp.158–60):

> Labour (9): Commerce; Finance and Expenditure; Government Administration; Health; Justice and Electoral; Law and Order; Maori Affairs; Social Services; Transport and Industrial Relations
> National (2): Primary Production; Regulations Review
> Greens (1): Local Government and Environment
> New Zealand First (1): Education and Science
> United Future (1): Foreign Affairs, Defence and Trade.

As can be seen, Labour retained by far the dominant share of the committee chairs, although these positions were distributed among the parties more in proportion to their relative strengths in the House than in any prior Parliament. It should be noted also that the Labour/Progressive Government did not hold a majority on all the committees, as is inevitable for a minority administration. As with the previous MMP Parliaments, committee membership was distributed across the parties so that their overall shares of committee places reflected their shares of seats. This meant that the committees, as well as the House itself, contained a range of policy perspectives.

Parties and policy dimensions

In 2002, the parliamentary parties represented a range of traditional and new policy dimensions. It has been argued that there are 'one dominant (socio-economic) and three secondary (ethnic, postmaterial, religious) issue dimensions ... present in New Zealand politics' (Aimer 2001, p.277). The 2002 general election confirmed the accuracy of this analysis insofar as the parliamentary party system (as well as the overall party system) is concerned, although several parties represented more than one of these dimensions. The historical, left-right differences regarding the relative roles of the state and the market and the extent of welfare provision were represented by the Progressive Coalition, Labour, National, and ACT, and, to a lesser extent, by United Future and New Zealand First. The Greens, on the other hand, strengthened their presence; Maori became more numerous (especially within Labour and New Zealand First); and the religious gained a foothold in United Future.

Looking at the left-right dimension briefly, what was the overall distribution of seats after the 2002 election? The results altered the ideological parliamentary balance in an interesting way by cluttering the political centre ground. This was due to the revival of New Zealand First and the unpredicted re-creation of United in the form of United Future, which became a real parliamentary party. The left-right composition of Parliament over the three MMP elections is shown in Table 26.2. The Green Party has been placed on the left because, from the time of its origins until 2002, there was no indication that it supported the sorts of ideas about the role of the state, from welfare to regulation, articulated by National and ACT. They have been placed on the far left because in some ways they took the policy position vacated by the Alliance.

Table 26.2: The parliamentary parties after the 1996, 1999 and 2002 elections, arranged according to a left-right dimension

	Greens %	Alliance %	PC %	Labour %	United %	NZF %	National %	ACT %
1996		10.8		30.8	0.8	14.2	36.7	6.7
1999	5.8	8.3		40.8	0.8	4.2	32.5	7.5
2002	7.5		1.7	43.3	6.7	10.8	22.5	7.5

Note: Because of rounding, the figures do not necessarily add up to 100 percent.

Amalgamating the party percentages into three groupings of left, centre and right gives the distribution set out in Table 26.3. After a decisive decision in favour of the left and centre-left in 1999, the ideological profile in 2002 continued to be dominated by the left. However, the centre ground regained some of its 1996 strength, mainly at the expense of National on the centre-right and right but also as a result of the greatly reduced strength of the Alliance/Progressive parliamentary contingent. Two further points are of relevance to the policy profile of the new 2002 Parliament and, of course, the power relationships between the minority government and the other parties: there was the invigoration of the centre party, United Future, with its Christian conservatism and its potential influence on the Labour/Progressive Coalition government in exchange for supporting that government on issues of confidence and supply, through its position as a pivotal and middle party (Hazan, 1996); and, concomitantly, there was the diminished influence of the Green Party, no longer the pivotal party in the House, as it had been in 1999, despite its position on the left of the spectrum.

Table 26.3: Parliamentary representation after the 1996, 1999 and 2002 elections of the left, centre and right

Election Year	Left/ Centre Left %	Centre %	Centre Right/ Right %
1996	41.6	15.0	43.4
1999	54.9	5.0	40.0
2002	52.5	17.5	30.0

Note: Because of rounding, the figures do not necessarily add up to 100 percent.

The MPs: qualifications and attributes

How do these different parties, with their different policy perspectives, represent New Zealand's social groups? What are the characteristics of the parliamentarians?

Those who did not already know the legal stipulations for candidature learned just after the 2002 election that an MP must be a New Zealand citizen, not just a permanent resident, when the apparently newly elected Kelly Chal had to be replaced with the next person on the United Future Party's list. There had been no attempt to mislead the public or the authorities; rather, according to the Chief Electoral Officer, 'Mrs Chal's statement suggests that the way in which she completed the consent form arose from confusion on her part, rather than a deliberate intention to breach the law' (David Henry [Chief Electoral Officer] 2002). At the time of the 2002 election the Electoral Act 1993 (s.47) stated that candidates must be qualified as electors, and must also be either '(a) A New Zealand citizen; or (b) A person who was, on the 22nd of August 1975, registered as an elector'. Interestingly, since 1 February 2003, the alternative entitlement (b) no longer applies (Electoral Commission 2002, p.49), as a consequence of legislative amendment in 2002. Candidates must also be formally nominated.

Apart from being qualified voters and New Zealand citizens, there have been other stated and unstated criteria for becoming candidates for parliamentary election, especially for winnable seats. Historically, the two major political parties selected their aspirants from pools of preferred social groups and interests, a tendency that has not markedly changed since the introduction of MMP. The Electoral Commission's table setting out MPs' previous occupations between 1990 and 2002 shows very few changes in distribution among the categories, except for an increase in the number of teachers, now the second largest group in Parliament (17.5 percent in 2002), and a slight decrease in the number of farmers (8.3 percent), the consequence of Labour's rise and National's fall in parliamentary numbers between 1990 and 2002. The single largest group since 1990 has been those who list themselves as businesspersons (19 percent). The third biggest cluster in 2002 (after those in business, and teachers) were the 12 lawyers (10 percent of the House) (Electoral Commission 2002, p.183).

Labour and National have traditionally demanded a degree of commitment to and experience within the parties. Often local government experience and/or interest group involvement (from trade unions through to trade associations) have also been regarded as pathways to successful candidature. MMP has made little change to these expectations as far as the major parties have been concerned; but the minor parties, lacking history, tradition and behavioural norms, have had to forge their own patterns.

Where MMP has made a discernible difference is in the representation of social and ethnic groups. The arguments in favour of more 'mirror' ('microscopic' or 'descriptive') representation have been put in many publications, including the report of the Royal Commission on the Electoral System; and it is generally agreed that one of the better outcomes of MMP has been its delivery of a more socially representative Parliament. Women,

Figure 26.1: 'Descriptive' representation, 1966–2002

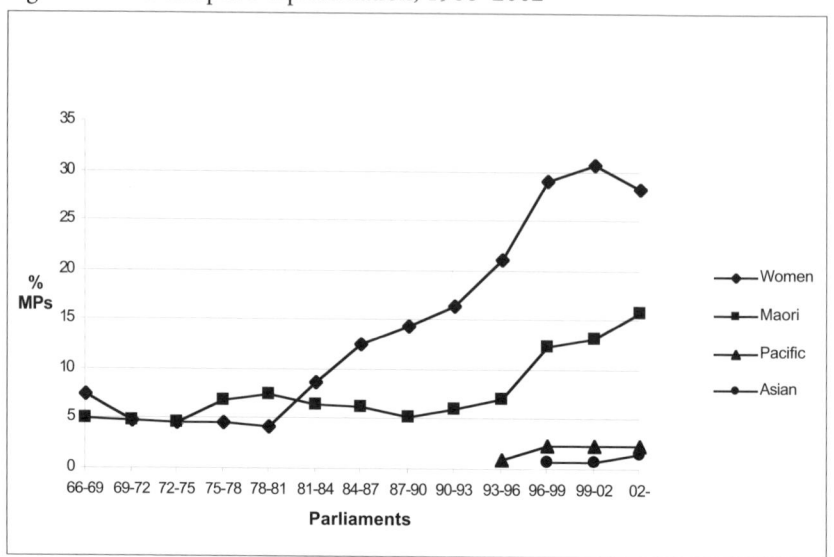

Maori, and non-Maori ethnic minorities have all entered Parliament in larger numbers since the first MMP election in 1996 (see Figure 26.1). A majority of the submissions on these issues to the MMP Review Committee that reported back to Parliament in 2001 argued that MMP had improved legislative representation of women, Maori, and other groups. In the survey commissioned by that committee, 50 percent agreed that MMP had been successful in getting more women MPs into Parliament; 49 percent believed that MMP had been successful in getting more Maori into Parliament; and 45 percent believed that Parliament is now more representative of all New Zealanders. These figures need to be set against the 26 percent, 23 percent and 23 percent respectively who were neutral on this topic, and the remainder who either believed that MMP was unsuccessful in this regard, or were unsure (MMP Review Committee 2001, p.80).[3] Of the 652 opinion leaders surveyed in 2002 by the New Zealand Political Change Project on the effects of MMP, decisive majorities agreed that the effectiveness of Parliament has improved with better representation of women, Maori, and ethnic minority interests. Indeed, the success of MMP in delivering Parliaments that represent peoples and groups more fairly, as well as political opinions as transmitted through parties, appears to have influenced MPs against acting in accordance with the views of electors in 1999, when the overwhelming majority of electors voted in the indicative referendum of that year to reduce the number of MPs to 99 (MMP Review Committee 2001, p.37).

Maori representation has been advanced by the implementation of MMP (see Figure 26.2) to the extent that, by 2002, the proportion of Maori in Parliament was slightly higher than the proportion in the wider population. In part, this has been due to the parties including Maori candidates in their party lists, as anticipated by the Royal Commission (see Figure 26.2). In part, too, the increase has been the fruit of the increased number of Maori seats, as higher proportions of Maori have opted to register on the Maori rather than the General roll – at a time when those seats have attracted much criticism from ACT, New Zealand First, and, after the 2002 general election, National.

However, there is a marked disparity among the parties in their representation of Maori (see Table 26.4). Maori are now well represented in Labour, with a Maori caucus of ten that meets regularly. An interesting feature of Labour Maori candidates is the way in which list MPs have shifted to contest the Maori electorate seats when opportunities present themselves. In 1999, Nanaia Mahuta, elected first as a list MP, shifted to Tainui; and in 2002, Tariana Turia similarly transferred, winning Te Tai Hauauru. Perhaps there is the perception that having a 'direct mandate' is preferable to winning through the list, at least in Labour. The other party with a substantial Maori

Figure 26.2: Pathways to representation: Maori

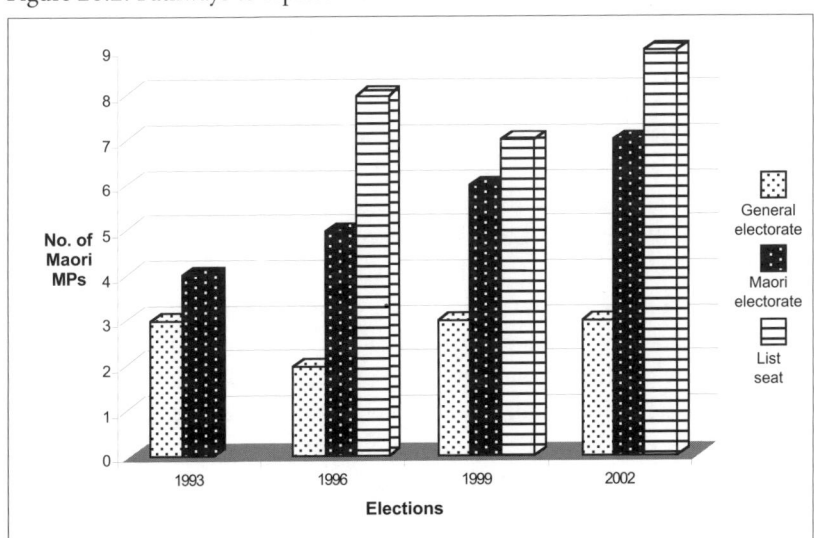

Table 26.4: Parties and Maori representation, 2002

No. of MPs	Greens	PC	Lab	UF	NZF	Nat	ACT	Totals
Maori general electorate	0	0	2	0	0	0	0	2
Maori electorate	0	0	7	0	0	0	0	7
Maori list	1	0	1	0	6	1	1	10
Total Maori MPs	1	0	10	0	6	1	1	19
% Maori MPs	11%	—	19%	—	46%	4%	11%	15.8%

presence is New Zealand First. That party lost all their Maori electorates in 1999, having won them all in the previous election, and did not contest any of them in 2002. However, New Zealand First elected six Maori MPs through the party list in 2002.

National and United First were particularly laggardly in representing Maori in 2002. This is partly a problem of supply. National had relatively few Maori (about seven, it seems) in its list of 65, but it also placed them far too low to be elected – although one, Hekia Parata, might have expected to have entered Parliament had National not performed so poorly in terms of the party vote. For National and, indeed, United Future, the problem is also a matter of adequate recruitment of Maori: the Greens have shown that this can be done. Further research on Maori candidature is urgently needed in order to understand fully the relationship between the parties and Maori representation.

The Royal Commission anticipated that the party lists would be the main routes into Parliament for members of ethnic minorities (see Figure 26.1). In 2002, Pansy Wong was re-elected through the National list, and Ashraf Choudhary entered through the Labour list. However, Taito Phillip Field, Mark Gosche and Winnie Laban (formerly a list MP) won electorates for Labour. Despite the increase in diversity of ethnic representation under MMP, compared with their share of the general population, Pacific and Asian peoples are still under-represented in Parliament. Arthur Anae was placed too low on the National list to be re-elected in 2002, and there were other candidates with Asian and Pacific backgrounds from other parties who missed out on election for the same reason.

There was another, major disappointment with the result of the 2002 election: after years of steadily increasing, the total number of women elected actually went down slightly from 37 (30.8 percent) to 34 (28.3 percent)(see Figure 26.1). Why did this happen? Overall, the percentage of female candidates in 2002 was also lower than in 1999. In 1996, 26.8 percent of all candidates (both electorate and list) were female. In 1999, this proportion went up to 32.9 percent. In 2002, it declined to 28.7 percent, very similar to the proportion actually elected to Parliament (Electoral Commission 2002, pp.176–7).

It is difficult to tell how far the reduced proportions of women who stood and were elected in 2002 can be explained in terms of the numbers of women presenting themselves for nomination for political parties, and/or, in terms of the actual selection behaviour of those parties. At least part of the answer lies in the different views of the parties concerning the desirability or otherwise of women being represented in those parties, and the ways in which those differing preferences were implemented in constructing party lists and choosing electorate candidates. Again, the incentive to create balanced party lists was acknowledged to be an important one for parties' representation of women, an expectation that is in line with comparative analysis on women's legislative representation. In brief, that research demonstrates that where a political culture is already sensitive to women's rights, the nature of the electoral system makes a difference to women's

Figure 26.3: Pathways to representation: Women

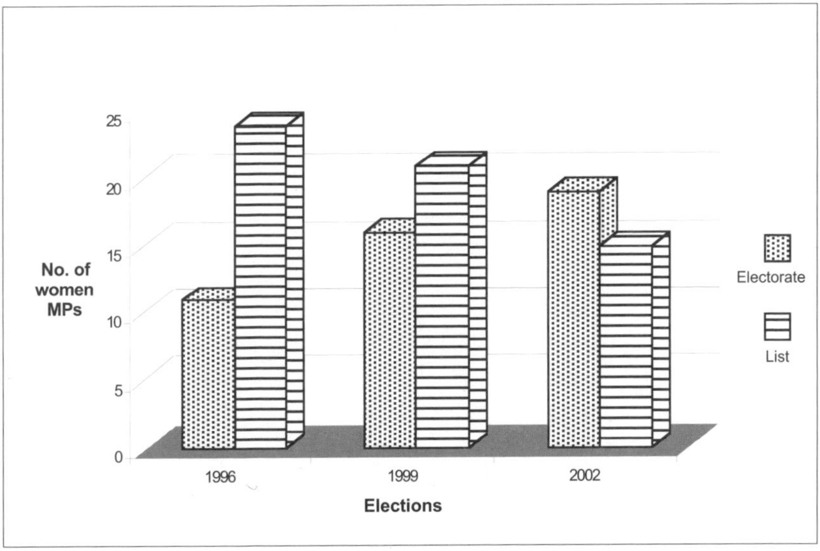

representation. This is mainly related to district magnitude: the more representatives that are to be elected from one constituency, then the more likely it is that women will be elected (see especially McAllister and Studlar 2002; and Norris 1996).[4]

As Figure 26.3 shows, in both 1996 and 1999 the party lists proved to be more reliable pathways to Parliament for women than the (male-dominated) single-member constituencies (Catt 1997; McLeay 2000). In 2002, in contrast, the picture was reversed. How could this be the case? The answer lies in the behaviour of the political parties, always acknowledged by researchers as the gatekeepers to power, whatever particular pathways are designated by the electoral system. Table 26.5 shows women's representation according to party and whether women in 2002 were elected via the electorates or the party lists. The parties are ordered according to their positions on the left-right ideological spectrum, with the Green Party, certainly 'red-green' rather than 'blue-green' or even 'pure green' in New Zealand, again placed on the far left.

Apart from ACT, which has always recognised women's merits as candidates (despite being ideologically hostile to any suggestion of the virtues of 'descriptive' representation), and which has additionally had the advantage of being new and hence relatively unhampered by obligations to incumbents, it has been the Green Party and Labour that have promoted women,

Table 26.5: Parties and women's representation, 2002

No. of women MPs	Greens	PC	Lab	UF	NZF	Nat	ACT	Totals
electorate	0	0 (1)	16 (45)	0 (1)	0 (1)	3 (21)	0 (0)	19 (51)
%	0	0	35.6%	0	0	14.3%	0	37.3%
list	4	0 (1)	2 (7)	1 (7)	1 (12)	3 (6)	4	15 (69)
%	44%	0	28.6%	14.3%	8.3%	50%	44%	21.7%
Total	4	0	18	1	1	6	4	34
%	44%	0	35%	13%	7%	22%	44%	28%

Note: The bracketed figures give the total number of MPs in that party in that category.

especially the former party, and the parties of the centre and the right that have most clearly demonstrated 'blokiness' in their composition. Is this due more to an inadequate supply of women candidates than to the expression of prejudice against female political representatives? Without data on the numbers of women and men who sought candidature, and without in-depth interviews and observation, this question cannot be fully answered.

In the cases of United Future and New Zealand First, however, all but one of the MPs were elected from their party lists, and there were no expectations that those parties would win more than one electorate seat. We can therefore assume that the ambitious wanted places on the list. Were there women on those lists who presumably wanted nomination for a winnable place, but failed to obtain it? The United Future list placed no woman in the top five of its non-successful places, and only one in the following five. There were only 12 women candidates, including Kelly Chal, in the total list of 61. Either there were other women who did not gain list places at all, or else United Future had very few women aspirants. In New Zealand First, there was one woman among the top five unsuccessful candidates, and none in the following five. In the entire list of 22, there were only two women candidates. Again, unless women were excluded from the lists in higher proportions than were men (which is, of course, quite possible), it would appear that there is also a supply problem for New Zealand First. Clearly, these two parties need to develop a more active recruitment campaign among women, although unless they do much better in the next general election, the privileges of incumbency will almost certainly result in male dominance continuing in these parties.

Because the National Party is predominantly an electorate-based one, the situation with this party is more difficult to analyse. Again, there are no available figures on the number of women who tried for winnable electorate candidacies. However, historically women have found it difficult to gain nomination for National constituency candidature. As Table 26.5 shows, the 2002 election showed no reversal of this situation. Of the two National electorate MPs who retired at the 2002 election, Warren Kyd (Clevedon) was replaced by Judith Collins, and Brian Connell replaced Jenny Shipley in Rakaia. Brian Neeson, who was not renominated for Helensville, was replaced by John Key. National did poorly in re-electing its list MPs, as eight of them failed to get back into Parliament. Four of these were women: Marie Hasler, Anne Tolley, Belinda Vernon and Annabel Young. None of these women was in the top five unsuccessful list candidates, having been placed much lower down the list (at 32, 24, 23 and 33 respectively). They were victims of the Party's search for 'new blood'. Yet the top five unsuccessful list candidates did include two high profile women aspirants, Hekia Parata and Sue Wood. Had National done better in 2002, it certainly would have represented women in higher numbers; but it is unlikely that there would have been a huge improvement. Despite evidence of a sufficient supply of women candidates (better than in United Future and New Zealand First), women rarely gain nomination by National for winnable electorates and do not gain many high National list places.

Labour's victories in the battle for the electorates in the 2002 general election, and its consequently low number of allocated list seats, might have resulted in a poor showing for women in the party. As it was, despite the comparatively good performance of Labour compared with National, the figures in Table 26.5 show that it is still difficult for women to gain parity with men. The Labour Party has many constituency seats with male incumbents. Only two electorate MPs retired in 2002, and both were replaced by men: Geoff Braybrooke (Napier) was replaced by Russell Fairbrother, and Judy Keall (Otaki) was replaced by a young parliamentary researcher, Darren Hughes. Labour's women did not fare well in the party list, with three women just missing out because they were placed in the unsuccessful positions of 41, 42 and 43, and the next two places being occupied by men. The experience of Labour women shows that, even when a party is ideologically in favour of women's representation, and there is a reasonably adequate supply of women candidates (28 out of 65), incumbency and electoral mechanics can work against women's equal representation. The impact of incumbency can be counterfactually tested against Green Party representation. With a similar philosophy to Labour regarding women's rights, although with a more explicit recognition of gender equality in the selection process, as a new party the Greens achieved an equal representation of women and men.

One of the many implications of the data presented in Table 26.5 is what it indicates regarding future selection to ministerial positions. If National increases its overall parliamentary representation at the next general election enough to go into government as a single-party minority administration, it will have very few women with parliamentary experience to promote as ministers and to take chairs of select committees. Allying itself with ACT would help, but forming coalitions with either New Zealand First or United Future would not. Indeed, given that posts would have to be awarded to the men of those parties, any Cabinet would be likely to represent women very poorly indeed. An even worse situation would apply concerning Maori ministerial representation were National to become a single-party government or to govern in coalition with ACT. If it formed a government with New Zealand First, there would be a replay of the 1996 situation, at least insofar as the latter party would be able to supply some Maori MPs for ministerial office.

Obviously, the longer the MMP system is in place, the fewer MPs there will be with personal experience of the largely two-party FPP Parliaments. Of all the MPs elected in 2002, 43 (36.8 percent) first entered the legislature before 1996. All of the party leaders except for the Greens are in this group. Unsurprisingly, all but six of the 43 FPP-experienced members represented either Labour or National. Twelve entered in either 1993 or 1994, the years of party defections and party creation. Thus a shrinking minority of MPs has experienced the former single-party majority governments that dominated Parliament. These figures do not, of course, indicate that the post-1996 entrants will favour MMP while the pre-1996 entrants will oppose it, for this is certainly not the case. Nevertheless, it does mean that as new cohorts come in, they will bring different expectations and practices to parliamentary life.

Choosing the 'Right People' (Do their faces 'fit'?)

Section 71 of the Electoral Act 1993 states:

> **Requirement for registered parties to follow democratic procedures in candidate selection** – Every political party that is for the time being registered under this Part of this Act shall ensure that provision is made for participation in the selection of candidates representing the party for election as members of Parliament by –
> a) Current financial members of the party who are or would be entitled to vote for those candidates at any election; or
> b) Delegates who have (whether directly or indirectly) in turn been elected or otherwise selected by current financial members of the party; or
> c) A combination of the persons or classes of persons referred to in paragraphs (a) and (b) of this section.

If parties do not wish to be eligible for party list seats (that is, if they stand candidates for electorate seats only), they are not bound by the requirements set out above. More significantly, given that most parties do wish to register for list seat eligibility, the legal requirements for 'democratic procedures' are restrictive, yet vague. They restrict the entitlement to involvement in party selection to party members, thus consolidating the practice of closed recruitment systems dominant under FPP. At the same time, they are highly non-prescriptive regarding party members' rights, given the flexibility of interpretation of Section 71 (b). This laxness has been exploited by several of the parties.

Under both FPP and MMP, the parties have determined whom they have wanted in Parliament by placing their favourites in winnable positions. Under both systems, the domination of political party over voter choice has ensured that parties are the gatekeepers for electoral success. The ambitious – even a former Reserve Bank Governor – must first become members of political parties if they aspire to legislative office. Yet there are some significant differences between the two electoral systems in terms of candidate selection. These differences help to explain the quite different characters of the 2002 parliamentary parties.

The potential for those at the centre of political parties – the parliamentary leadership and the extra-parliamentary party president and secretary – to influence the selection of candidates to contest the electorates varies. Of the two oldest parties, National has been more democratic and participatory than Labour. This has meant, however, that National's central leadership has been more constrained than Labour in terms of those whom it could place in winnable electorate seats. But despite its participatory selections, National's central leadership could play a dominating role in the candidate selection process, as the then National Party President, Michelle Boag, showed in her influence over locals in the 2002 selections, especially in Hunua and Helensville. And despite some high profile battles in Labour between the desires of the leadership and those of the locals, the latter often got their choice of candidate.

The key difference between FPP and MMP is the added component of selection for the party lists. Naturally, these lists are particularly important for the newer and smaller parties, who will probably win only one electorate seat at most. As well as the discontent aroused by the dual candidature permitted by the new electoral rules, one of the accusations against MMP has been that party list nominations can too easily be manipulated by party leaders, especially as they are closed lists, meaning that voters cannot reorder the candidates. Because the lists are nationwide, however important party members are in constructing regional lists, in the end those lists must be amalgamated in some way; and this gives senior party people the opportunity to exert their influence. The extent to which power can be exerted from the centre varies according to the number of selectors involved in ordering the party list and the formal and informal criteria that guide their choices.

The Greens appeared, at first glance, to have invented a centre-dominated method of nominating their list candidates, for their constitution gives the National Executive the responsibility to select a method. In fact, the Greens adopted the most democratic method of all the parties in 2002. A 'selectorate', comprising all those who wished to be candidates, plus the members of the national executive, ranked the candidates. Then all the party members voted on the list, ranking the candidates using the Single Transferable Vote. Finally, the Candidate Selection Process Committee adjusted the list to ensure it fulfilled the following criteria: geographical and age spread, and gender balance, with at least 40 percent women.

In National, the electorates select up to two list nominees at electorate candidate selection meeting (for a fuller description see chapter 20, also Wood 2001, pp.247–8). This is followed by the creation of regional lists selected through preferential ballot by up to two nominees from each electorate, and by members of the Divisional Council (but not the central organisation). The nationwide list is finally determined by the 31-member List Management Standing Committee in one ballot. The first two list positions automatically go to the Leader and Deputy. The stated criteria are to pay heed to the regional rankings, and also to 'the need to balance across the totality of candidates'. The local voice is present, but the central organisation has the dominant voice in National.

The situation is similar in Labour, although the local voice is rather more muted. Using exhaustive ballots and weighted votes, the six regional conferences elect candidates, the numbers depending on the proportion of the population of the region (for a fuller description see chapter 20, also Miller 2001, pp.234–5). After each group of five candidates is selected, the meeting reviews the overall choice for 'equity' considerations. Then a central, 32-person Moderating Committee selects the final list. It must represent Maori, women, men, ethnic groups such as Pacific peoples, people of different ages and geographic areas, and must also consider under-represented groups with potential parliamentary skills. The final list must also heed regional rankings, although information from the 2002 selection indicates that regional rankings were disregarded in favour of other criteria, especially bringing younger people into Parliament. Again, the selection is reviewed after each five candidates are chosen. As with National, the Leader and Deputy Leader take the first two list positions.

United Future's constitution (the version submitted to the Electoral Commission) is not helpful, as it states that the selection of candidates is 'under consideration' (United Future [undated], p.9). It seems that in 2002, the ten-person Board of United Future, together with some party delegates, selected the electorate candidates. In order to be eligible for a place on the party list, aspirants had to be chosen as an electorate candidate. The list was compiled by the Board, although individuals could make submissions on list composition and order. Thus the process was dominated by the central party organisation and leadership.

New Zealand First's constitution (New Zealand First 1998) states that all prospective candidates are to be approved by the New Zealand First Council, and list candidates must first be selected as electorate candidates. Electorate selection panels, comprising nominees by the Council (up to two), the Regional Committee (up to two), and the Electorate Committee (also up to two), select up to five nominees for final selection. A selection committee, including the Regional Chair and delegates from the electorate membership, vote through exhaustive balloting to choose the candidate. After the regions have ranked their candidates in an indicative ordering (involving, it seems, the electorate chairpersons), the national List Ranking Committee selection college draws up a ballot paper recommending the order of the 65 electorate candidates. This college comprises the Leader, the Deputy Leader, the President, two vice presidents, the regional chairs, and two representatives nominated by the Maori electorates (with substitutes for any of those people who might be candidates, except for the Leader, Deputy and President). In 2002, there were only 22 candidates on New Zealand First's party list. The Leader and Deputy take the first two list places.

ACT's selection method is centre-dominated, although the leadership does not always get its own way. A list of approved potential candidates is sent to all party members, who then nominate in a postal ballot the 20 candidates they most want on the list (see Reid 2001, pp.264–5). The ACT Board (the central governing organisation) ranks the candidates after considering the results of the postal ballot. Secret (non-circulated) nominations can also be considered by the Board. The ACT constitution states that 'merit' is the main criterion.

It is not known how the Progressive Coalition selected its candidates.[5]

Participation of ordinary members in the selection of candidates is a powerful means of involving those members and encouraging people to participate in one of the most important (and most contested) functions of political parties. There is, however, some advantage to having a measure of central control: it allows parties to fulfil their representative criteria and construct 'balanced' lists, and gives them the opportunity to promote potential leaders while also placing others whose faces do not 'fit' so well lower in the rankings. Thus there is some conflict between the goals of member participation and party representativeness. One way in which parties overseas have attempted to solve this problem is through adopting quotas, as the Green Party in New Zealand has done.

The lists can nevertheless be manipulated by leaders to promote favourites and reduce the chances of the unpopular and unfashionable gaining or regaining election.

Bringing in the new . . . throwing out the old . . .

Electoral systems based wholly on party lists are sensitive to quite small shifts in public opinion and are therefore more likely to produce a relatively high turnover of MPs than are single-member constituency, simple plurality systems. In party list systems, incumbency is really protected only in the upper echelons of the party lists, often called the 'mandate' positions. In FPP systems, where elections are won and lost on the basis of often quite a small group of marginal constituencies, turnover tends to be lower, except for the occasional landslide elections when, because FPP systems tend to over-reward the winning party, substantial numbers of MPs can lose their seats to newcomers (who in turn often lose out in the next election). New Zealand's mixed member electoral system would be expected to produce a mid-way result insofar as the entrance of new MPs is concerned. Figure 26.4 demonstrates the entry of new MPs since 1975. It shows the dramatic effects of the landslide elections of that year and of 1990, and the relatively low percentages of newcomers in most other elections held under FPP electoral rules. The 1996 election holds the record for those 10 elections, mainly because MMP opened up the larger Parliament to the new parties with their novice representatives. The two elections since then have reverted to what will probably prove to be a more 'normal' pattern, with exactly 30 new MPs coming into Parliament in 2002. Half of these came from the expanded contingents of United Future (seven out of eight) and New

Figure 26.4: New entrants to Parliament, 1975–2002

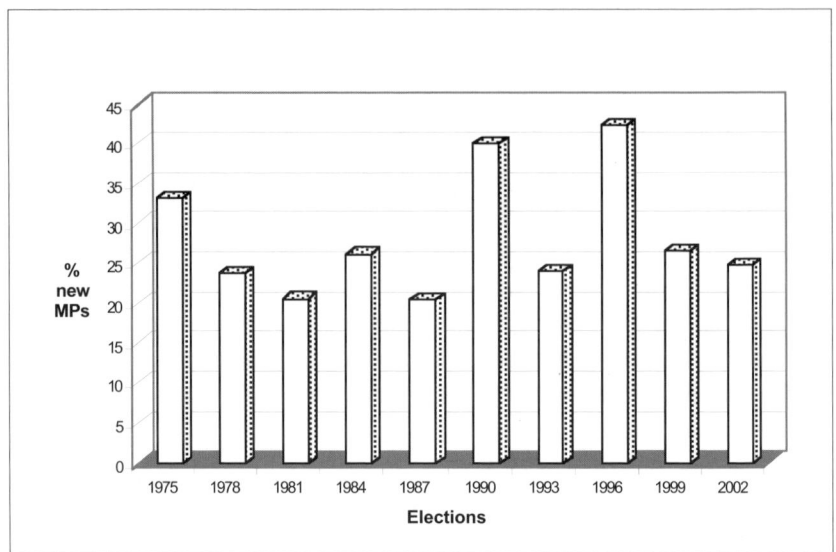

Zealand First (eight out of 13). As one would expect, the majority of new MPs also came from the lists rather than the electorates, with 22 in the first category and eight in the second.

Shifts in voting choice contributed to producing new entrants for Labour (up three seats), and the Greens (two). But voters are not the only political actors who determine which incumbents are returned and how many new MPs enter the legislature: the political parties also play a major role in the process of renewal and consolidation. (For lists of defeats and retirements, see the Electoral Commission 2002, pp.77–8). In 2002, although ACT won exactly the same number of seats as it did in 1999, it managed to bring in two new MPs because it ranked two incumbents, Penny Webster and Owen Jennings, too low in the party list to regain election. The Alliance retained no seats and disappeared from Parliament. The Greens returned their incumbents and added the two already mentioned. Labour's Geoff Braybrooke, Joe Hawke and Judy Keall all retired, allowing new MPs to take their places.

Most controversially, National openly aimed to refresh its team through retirements (voluntary or less voluntary) and deselection. A group of highly experienced MPs resigned: Max Bradford, Wyatt Creech, Doug Kidd,

Warren Kyd, John Luxton and Jenny Shipley. One of the deselected MPs, Brian Neeson, chose to fight for his electorate as an Independent, inevitably, perhaps, losing to his former party's new candidate. The result for National was that, even in an historically disastrous year for the party – when Arthur Anae, Marie Hasler, Gavan Herlihy, Alec Neill, Eric Roy, Bob Simcock, Tony Steel, Anne Tolley, Belinda Vernon and Annabel Young all lost their seats – five new National MPs were elected. Some of them already had a high profile, the most notable being Don Brash, who resigned from his Governorship of the Reserve Bank to take fifth place on the party list. Even if National had managed to do better in 2002, some of the list seats it would have won would have showcased new faces, since some incumbents had been ranked lower. Finally, New Zealand First returned its five incumbents, the Progressive Coalition retained only two seats, both filled by incumbents, and United Future has already been discussed.

Parties, therefore, can play a major role in bringing in the new and discarding the old. Aspirants for political life, however, are not entirely dependent on party and electoral rules. To some extent, those who want to gain or regain political lives are pawns in a larger party contest, but the hopefuls also have the scope to make some decisions on their own. A key one is whether or not to stand for both a party list and an electorate. Of the 2002 intake, 97 MPs took the dual path. Only seven MPs in the 2002 Parliament stood solely for their party lists, while 16 chose to stand only for electorates. Interestingly, the percentages of all candidates who have stood for both the party lists and the electorates have differed quite markedly over the three elections: 54.4 percent in 1996; 49.9 percent in 1999; and 65.4 percent in 2002 (Electoral Commission 2002, pp.174–5). The tactics of the minor parties – for example, whether they choose to stand candidates for all the constituencies – might explain some of the variance. Also, the early election of 2002 might have affected individual and party preparedness and tactics.

The new Parliament

In a sense there is no 'new' Parliament, since every elected House of Representatives contains a high proportion of incumbents, both individuals and parties. Changing party fortunes, however, can produce quite dramatically changing power dynamics within and among the parliamentary parties. In 2002, although Labour remained the key coalition partner in government and although minority government continued, the new Parliament was very different from that of the previous term. The collapse of the Alliance and its vote, the weakening of National's representation, and the regeneration of United Future and New Zealand First, all created a Parliament that was much less of a bipolar institution than between 1999 and 2002, a House in which most of the parties were grasping for the perhaps illusory centre ground. The 2002 Parliament also displayed the continuing forces of social change in New Zealand through the politics of 'presence'. The strength and weakness of those forces were mediated by the various parties according to their own perceptions of voting support, interpretation of the good society, and prejudices and preferences about who they felt would best represent their messages and interests.

27

CONSISTENT PATTERNS AND CLEAR TRENDS: ELECTORAL BEHAVIOUR IN 2002

Stephen Levine and Nigel S. Roberts

The 2002 election result was so predictable that Television New Zealand's election-night commentators successfully predicted the outcome in each of the 69 electorates 10 days before the election. One reason for this was that so many of the electorates were won by the party that already held the seat. Indeed, only three electorates – Coromandel, Hamilton East and Otago[1] – changed hands in 2002. Before the boundary changes for the 2002 election, Labour had held 41 of 67 electorates, and National 22. The remaining four seats were held by the Alliance, the Greens, New Zealand First and United.[2] After the Representation Commission's 2002 report increased the number of electorates by two, Labour's seats (on paper at least) went up to 43. The 2002 election results in the electorates favoured the incumbent parties: Labour held all its 43 seats and gained an additional two from National, which partially offset those losses by taking Coromandel from the Greens.

Electoral prediction was also made easier by the high degree of uniformity in the distribution of the party vote. When party vote results are counted by electorate, Labour won the most pary votes in a staggering 65 of the 69 seats. In the four electorates in which Labour did not win the most party votes, National did so. Three of the seats in which National won more party votes than Labour were the domains of current or former Leaders of the Opposition – Bill English and his predecessors, Jenny Shipley and Jim Bolger.[3] The only other seat where National won a plurality of the party votes was Epsom. (However, this should not necessarily be interpreted as suggesting that its 2002 candidate there, Richard Worth, is guaranteed a future as a leader of the National Party.)

These consistent patterns stem from the aggregate election statistics recording how New Zealanders actually voted (Chief Electoral Office 2002; Electoral Commission 2002). To go beneath the surface – to find out why voters behaved as they did – requires individual (as distinct from aggregate) data: that is, information from survey research that collects and analyses answers by voters to key questions about the election. Here, too, there are clear trends that give greater meaning to the decision of voters on 27 July 2002.

For the third MMP election in a row, the Victoria University pre-election survey interviewed a random sample of 1,000 electors in the week immediately preceding the election.[4] The respondents were drawn from throughout the country.[5] As in 1996 and 1999, the results of the election confirmed the accuracy of the survey: that is, the voting preferences of the survey participants very closely mirrored the actual results of the election. The degree of confidence of the survey organisers was such that they agreed to permit the results of their survey to be shown on television immediately after the close of polls on election night. Figure 27.1 is taken from the graphic displayed by Television New Zealand to show the predicted allocation of seats in the House of Representatives, based on the survey's data on how people intended to cast their party vote.

Figure 27.1: TV1 election night graphic on the expected distribution of seats in Parliament

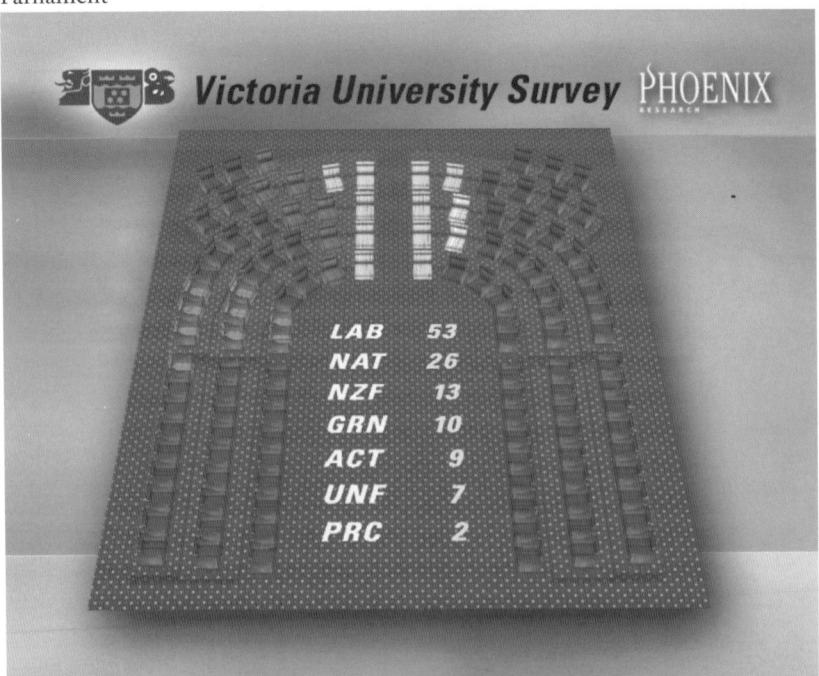

Figure 27.2: Party expected to win the most seats in Parliament in 2002

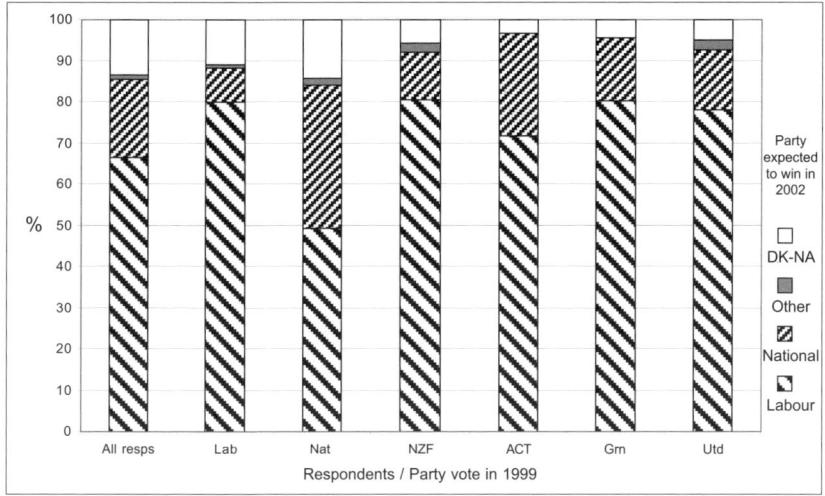

New Zealand First, ACT and the Progressive Coalition each won exactly the number of seats predicted. National and United Future each won one more seat than predicted. Labour and the Greens each won one less seat than predicted. As commentators pointed out on election night, this was an extraordinarily accurate assessment of the final outcome of the election.[6] This independent verification of the accuracy of the survey data therefore means considerable confidence can be placed in the survey's findings on a range of topics relevant to the election.

Expectations about the election

It was not only political scientists and journalists who had a good grasp of the dynamics of the election and were able accurately to foresee the results. Voters themselves had a clear idea of how the election was going to turn out. As Figure 27.2 shows, more than 90 percent of survey participants expected Labour to win the most seats in 2002, as indeed happened. When the expectations of voters are examined according to their party votes, what is striking is that even adherents to the other parties expected their parties to lose. The lowest proportion of voters expecting Labour to do best was the 89 percent of National voters who foresaw a Labour win.

Voters were also asked who they thought would win their own electorate seat. The results for this question were not nearly as lopsided as for the question about the expected nationwide party vote result. Regardless of their own preferences as to candidate or party in their electorate, very nearly half the sample (49.7 percent) thought Labour would win the seat. National electorate candidates were expected to win by 27.2 percent of respondents. Again, this suggests that voters are remarkably realistic: Labour was successful in 45 of the electorate seats, and National won 21 of them. It is interesting to note that 16.4 percent admitted that they did not know who would win their electorate, compared with only 5.3 percent who did not venture an opinion as to which party would do best in terms of party votes throughout the country as a whole. This discrepancy between electorate and nationwide party results in voters' confidence in predicting outcomes reflects the fact that under MMP, much greater attention is given to the party vote by opinion pollsters and party strategists alike, leaving electors somewhat less certain about developments in their own electorates.[7]

Positive and negative party perceptions

While the 2002 election took place against a backdrop of public anticipation of a Labour win, voting patterns in New Zealand have long reflected the fact that more New Zealanders have tended to identify themselves with the National Party than with Labour or other alternatives. However, as we pointed out in our chapter in *Left Turn*, this changed in 1999, when our

Figure 27.3: Party identification in New Zealand, 1996–2002

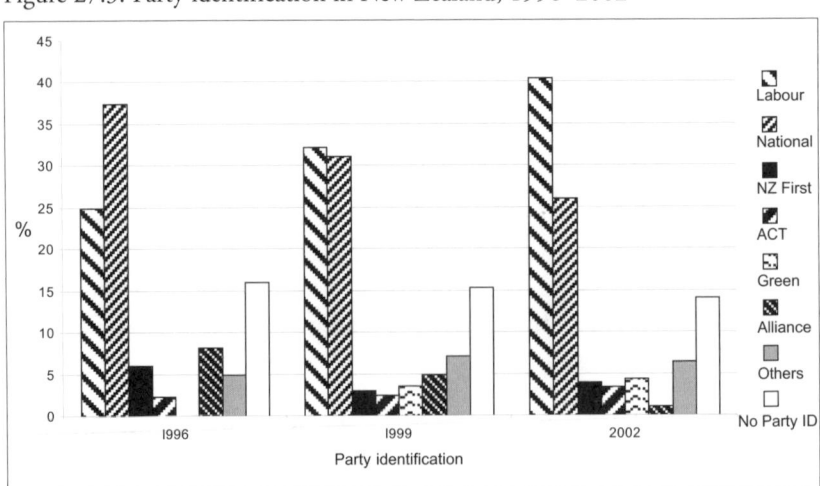

Table 27.1: Pre-election survey data for party identification by party votes in 2002

Party vote in 2002	Party identification (%)							
	Labour	Nat.	NZ First	ACT	Green	United	Prog.	Alliance
Labour	74.6	6.1	2.5	14.7	2.3	3.6	12.5	18.2
National	0.7	57.5	2.5	0.0	2.3	0.0	0.0	9.1
NZ First	4.9	8.1	87.5	0.0	4.5	7.1	0.0	0.0
ACT	0.7	6.1	0.0	70.6	0.0	0.0	0.0	0.0
Green	3.7	1.9	0.0	0.0	75.0	0.0	0.0	0.0
United Future	1.5	3.8	0.0	0.0	0.0	78.6	0.0	0.0
Progressive Coalition	1.5	0.0	5.0	0.0	0.0	0.0	62.5	0.0
Alliance	0.5	0.0	0.0	0.0	2.3	0.0	0.0	45.4
Others	0.2	0.4	0.0	0.0	0.0	0.0	0.0	0.0
Did not vote	11.7	16.1	2.5	14.7	13.6	10.7	25.0	27.3
Total	100.0	100.0	100.0	100.0	100.0	100.0	100.0	100.0
n	405	261	40	34	44	28	8	11

survey data revealed that 'for the first time, more New Zealanders said they usually thought of themselves as Labour than did so for any other party' (Levine and Roberts 2000, p.167). This small but significant shift towards Labour had occurred during the first three years of MMP government (1996–99), while the party was in opposition to an increasingly disparate and desperate National-led government. What would the consequences be for Labour in 2002 of its nearly three years in government as the dominant partner in a two-party coalition? As Figure 27.3 shows, the pattern of party identification first discerned in 1999 was not only confirmed, but also substantially strengthened in 2002. This represents a dramatic turn-around in New Zealand politics.[8] Labour is now 15 percentage points ahead of National, while – as was the case under FPP – the smaller parties generate very low levels of ongoing party identification.

Patterns of party identification are strong predictors of voting behaviour (see Table 27.1). On the other hand, there are some intriguing cross-currents running through the data on voting when it is analysed by party identification. Of those casting their party vote for Labour, 83.7 percent were Labour Party identifiers. By contrast, 94.3 percent of National's party voters were National Party identifiers. While this might seem on the surface to be 'good news' for National, in fact what it underscored was National's inability to reach across party lines and attract a broader range of voters to its fold.

To the right of National stands the ACT Party. Nearly a third of ACT's 2002 party votes came from people who identified with the National Party, and more than a fifth of United Future's party votes came from National identifiers. Of New Zealand First voters, slightly more than a third identified with the party they voted for, but more than 40 percent identified with either National or Labour (in virtually equal numbers).

The position on the left is slightly more complex. More voters for what was known at the time of the election as 'Jim Anderton's Progressive Coalition Party' – subsequently abbreviated to 'the Progressives' – identified with the Labour Party than with Anderton's new vehicle. This is akin to the situation with New Zealand First. However, only about 17 percent of voters for the Alliance – the 'purists' who removed Anderton as their leader and ended up in the political wilderness – were Labour identifiers, and none of the Alliance voters in our survey identified themselves with Anderton or his party. Roughly half the Green vote came from Green Party identifiers, but the party also picked up significant support from Labour identifiers (who made up nearly a quarter of all Green voters), as well as from people identifying with no party (9.4 percent). The comparison with Labour and National on this latter point could not be more striking: only 0.6 percent of National's voters had no party identification at all, and the comparable figure for Labour's voters was 5 percent.

In 2002, for the first time, we followed up our question on party identification with a question which is in some ways the obverse of party identification. Survey participants were asked: 'Which of New Zealand's political parties do you *like the least*?' This recognises that people sometimes cast their vote for essentially negative reasons. They vote for a party not because they favour it, but because they are repelled by one or more of the alternatives. In a sense, people can also be identified by what they dislike, especially in politics, and not only by what they like.

The first thing to note from the responses to this question is, perhaps surprisingly, that New Zealand's major parties – dislike of which led in part to MMP – today attract relatively little opprobrium. On this new and somewhat novel measure, Labour was viewed as the 'least-liked' New Zealand political party in 2002 by only 3.9 percent, and National by a mere 4.6 percent. The parties that came third, fourth and fifth in the election – New Zealand First, ACT and the Greens – together accounted for 59.5 percent of the negative responses by electors to parties. The most unpopular party was the smallest of these three, the Green Party. It was nominated as their least-liked party by 29.6 percent of the entire sample (or by 33.7 percent of those naming a party). ACT was the second most-disliked party, cited by 20.2 percent of respondents. New Zealand First, which (as will be shown) has consistently had its leader named as the country's least-preferred prime minister, had a 'least-liked party' rating of 9.7 percent, thus attracting more negative attention than Labour and National combined, but far less than ACT and the Greens. As for United Future, like its leader, it elicited little antipathy: only 0.2 percent of the sample accorded it least-liked party status. On the left, the schism in the Alliance had its consequences: 5.5 percent regarded Anderton's Progressive Coalition as the worst of the parties, a figure nearly matched by those viewing the Alliance (5.3 percent) the same way. To put this in perspective, these two parties together attracted only 3 percent of the party votes cast in 2002.

The composition of the party vote

Apart from the 9.6 percent drop in support for National, the most dramatic slump between 1999 and 2002 was the 6.4 percent drop in party votes cast for the Alliance.[9] Table 27.2 provides one perspective on what happened to the Alliance vote. Half the vote for Jim Anderton's party – one of the two groups with a claim to being the 'true' heirs to the Alliance's programmes and principles – came from people who had voted for the Alliance in 1999. Put another way, twice as many 1999 Alliance voters preferred Jim Anderton and his new Progressive Coalition Party as preferred the Laila Harré-led group campaigning under the Alliance Party banner. If, for some on the left, the 2002 election was in some sense a mini-referendum on the performance of the Labour-Alliance government, then it is significant that one-third of 1999 Alliance voters changed their vote in 2002 to Labour.[10] Together, the combined Labour and Progressive Coalition vote from people who had previously supported the Alliance constitutes a decisive rejection of their former party in 2002.

Table 27.2 provides an overview of where the party votes in 2002 came from. Several further points in the data shown in the table should be noted. The first is perhaps somewhat paradoxical. An initial glance at the table might suggest that National had, in fact, done very well. After all, the data show that a higher proportion of its vote came from its previous supporters,

Table 27.2: Pre-election survey data for the party vote in the 2002 general election by the party vote in the 1999 general election

Party vote in 1999	Party vote in 2002 (%)								
	Labour	Nat.	NZ First	ACT	Green	United	Prog.	Alliance	Other
Labour	74.8	5.7	15.6	5.7	23.4	8.3	18.8	16.8	0.0
National	4.4	80.5	15.6	28.3	6.3	14.6	0.0	0.0	13.2
Alliance	3.6	0.0	2.1	0.0	6.3	4.2	50.0	33.3	6.7
ACT	1.1	0.6	1.1	49.0	0.0	4.2	0.0	8.3	6.7
Green	1.1	0.6	3.1	1.9	39.1	6.2	6.2	8.3	0.0
NZ First	1.9	1.3	42.7	5.7	1.5	2.1	0.0	0.0	6.7
United	0.0	1.3	0.0	0.0	0.0	6.2	0.0	8.3	6.7
Others	0.6	0.6	2.1	0.0	1.5	43.8	6.2	8.3	40.0
Did not vote	12.5	9.4	17.7	9.4	21.9	10.4	18.8	16.7	20.0
Total	100.0	100.0	100.0	100.0	100.0	100.0	100.0	100.0	100.0
n	361	159	96	53	64	48	16	12	15

people who had voted for National at the previous election. In politics, as in sport, loyalty is a highly prized virtue. However, in fact National's 'success' relative to the other parties masks a much deeper failure. What parties need to accomplish at any election is *renewal*: they need to gain new voters from new sources, while retaining as much of their previous constituency as possible. Viewed in this light, the fact that four-fifths of National's 2002 vote came from 1999 National Party voters underscores the party's inability to win over people who had previously preferred other parties. Likewise, National's 2002 vote sits alongside ACT's in containing the lowest proportion of new voters. By contrast, despite the fact that the Greens increased their overall vote only marginally, more than 20 percent of their vote came from people who had not voted in the previous general election.

The data for United Future also invite closer examination. For a start, the statistics on 'loyalty' for United are by far the lowest for any party – a reflection, of course, of the party's minuscule party vote in 1999. Because the United vote grew so substantially, most of its 2002 vote had to come from other sources. As Table 27.2 shows, to some extent the United vote came from across the board, as might be expected of a self-described 'centre' party. It included significant proportions of votes from 1999 National and Labour voters, as well as from people who did not vote in 1999. However, the most startling statistic in the United column is the nearly 44 percent of its vote which came from people who had, in 1999, opted for 'others' – that is, for parties that had entirely failed to achieve parliamentary representation in 1999. So where did this sizeable segment of United supporters come from? A breakdown reveals that 86 percent of them had been Christian Heritage voters in 1999. In view of United's merger with Future New Zealand (formerly the Christian Democrats, both partners and rivals at various times to Christian Heritage), this preponderance of voting support from Christian Heritage is significant: former Future New Zealand voters contributed only one-sixth of the support that 1999 Christian Heritage voters gave to United in 2002. However, Future New Zealand did allow United to become a viable vehicle for Christian voters frustrated by their parties' inability to gain either electorate or list seats. This voting base will almost inevitably put some pressure on United's leader, Peter Dunne, as he attempts to walk a tightrope between supporting the Labour-Progressive minority government, and satisfying the demands of his largely conservative Christian constituency.

Table 27.3 shows how party voters in 2002 cast electorate votes. Even after three MMP elections, there are still only two parties, National and

Table 27.3: Party votes by electorate votes in the 2002 general election

Electorate vote in 2002	Party vote in 2002 (%)							
	Labour	Nat.	NZ First	ACT	Green	United	Prog.	Alliance
Labour	80.0	5.7	24.0	10.3	36.1	22.3	54.1	39.6
National	5.5	81.8	29.8	54.7	7.7	30.1	5.7	10.1
NZ First	1.4	1.9	22.9	1.8	1.3	2.5	1.4	1.2
ACT	0.9	3.3	3.3	23.8	1.2	2.2	0.7	1.3
Green	3.3	1.0	2.7	1.5	40.3	1.4	2.3	7.3
United Future	2.1	2.5	4.1	3.1	2.0	32.7	1.8	2.1
Progressive Coalition	1.9	0.4	2.0	0.4	1.2	1.0	28.1	2.2
Alliance	1.4	0.5	1.8	0.6	3.2	0.7	1.8	29.9
Others	1.7	1.6	5.7	2.3	4.2	5.9	2.7	4.1
Invalid votes	1.8	1.3	3.7	1.5	2.8	1.2	1.4	2.2
Total	100.0	100.0	100.0	100.0	100.0	100.0	100.0	100.0

Source: Electoral Commission 2002, pp. 148–149.

Labour, that wage a serious and comprehensive nationwide battle for the electorate vote. As noted earlier, these two parties between them won 66 of the 69 constituency seats in 2002. This heritage of two-party hegemony is borne out by the fact that four-fifths of both Labour and National voters cast a 'straight-ticket' pair of votes in 2002. In other words, most electors backing what used to be called New Zealand's two major parties adopted the 'two-ticks' tactic.

The picture is very different when we turn to the behaviour of electors casting party votes for New Zealand's smaller parties. New Zealand First's party voters split almost equally in three distinct ways when it came to casting their electorate vote: Labour, National and New Zealand First each received between 23 and 30 percent support. On the other hand, ACT and Green voters' choices in the electorates were predominantly split between only two parties – their own, and National (in the case of ACT) or Labour (in the case of the Greens).

More than half of those who gave their party vote to ACT cast a vote for a National electorate candidate. On the opposite side of the political spectrum, more than a third of those giving their party vote to the Greens gave their electorate vote to a Labour candidate. It is worth noting that both ACT and the Greens are parties that have won electorate seats under MMP, but have since lost them. In 1999, ACT leader Richard Prebble lost the Wellington Central seat that he had won in 1996; and in 2002, Greens' co-leader Jeanette Fitzsimons failed to hold the Coromandel electorate which she had won for the first time in 1999. In 2002 both parties gave far greater emphasis in their campaigns to the party vote, with ACT in particular virtually abandoning any attempt to win an electorate seat.

As the data in Table 27.3 show, the likelihood that New Zealand voters will 'split' their tickets – giving their party vote to one party, and their electorate vote to another – increases dramatically among those voting for the smaller parties. Across the three MMP elections, the proportions of ticket splitters have been exceptionally stable: 37 percent in 1996; 35 percent in 1999; and 39 percent in 2002 (Electoral Commission 2000, pp.62–64; 2002, pp.68–70). If the rate of ticket-splitting in 2002 for all voters had been the same as that for Labour and National voters, 19.4 percent, it would have been slightly less than half its actual rate, and would also have been little different from the rate of ticket-splitting among voters in Germany (where it averaged 14.5 percent during the six Federal elections from 1980 to 1998) (see, for example, Klingemann and Wessels 2001, p.288).

Leadership – likes and dislikes

The data presented thus far provide perspectives on the sources of the 2002 party vote. What the 2002 Victoria University survey data can also do is to point towards further factors that influenced the outcome of the election. As others in this book have maintained, a principal focus for the election was on leadership and, in particular, the contrast between perceptions of the prime minister, Helen Clark, and the leader of the National Party, Bill English.

In 1999, Helen Clark and the then prime minister, Jenny Shipley, stood virtually equal in voters' assessments of who they 'personally prefer[red] to be prime minister' (Levine and Roberts 2000, p.172). Three years later, the picture could not have been more different. Clark's tenure in office had endowed her with perceived leadership qualities that gave her an enormous, indeed unparalleled, lead over all her rivals. In 2002, more than half of all respondents preferred Clark. Only 11 percent favoured English as prime minister.[11] The leaders of the country's smaller parties registered even lower levels of support.

We first began asking New Zealanders an additional question, focusing on whom they would 'least like to be prime minister', in 1993 (Levine and Roberts 1993, p.150). Accordingly, we have been able to ask representative samples of electors about their most and least preferred prime ministerial choices over all three MMP elections.[12] The leader of the Labour Party in each case was Helen Clark, whereas National had a different leader at each of the three elections. This enables us to examine the comparative performance of Helen Clark over the three elections (see Figure 27.4).

Unlike some of New Zealand's other political leaders, Clark has had a positive differential each time – more people have preferred her as prime minister than have named her as their 'least liked' person for the position. By contrast, New Zealand First's leader Winston Peters and ACT Party leader Richard Prebble, each of whom have, like Clark, led their parties for three successive MMP elections, have always had negative differentials: more people have named them each time as their least preferred prime minister than have preferred them for this post.

From 1996 to 1999, while Clark was in opposition, her positive differential increased somewhat, from +11 percent to +14 percent. Since she became prime minister, it has risen dramatically to +45 percent – the

Figure 27.4: Helen Clark's ratings as most and least preferred prime minister, 1996–2002

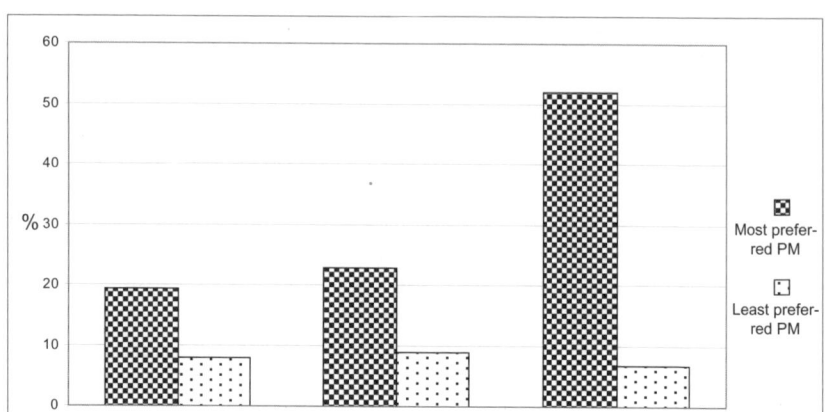

highest positive differential of any New Zealand politician since we began asking this series of questions.

Figure 27.5 summarises the positive and negative responses to seven New Zealand politicians, ascertained by comparing the two survey questions. Several things stand out. The first is that Clark had an insurmountable advantage in the public's perceptions of her and her rivals. Second, even though he was preferred as prime minister by only 5 percent of respondents, Peter Dunne comes second – after Clark and ahead of English – in terms of a positive differential, because very few people disliked him enough to name him as their 'least preferred' prime minister.[13]

Even National Party organisers and strategists concede that there were problems with Bill English's campaign and presentation. The data on preferences with respect to prime ministerial alternatives suggest that English did not evoke an especially strong response, either positively or negatively. As already noted, 11 percent preferred him as prime minister, but this was almost entirely offset by the relatively modest 9 percent who liked him the least – not good, but enviably low compared with the levels of antagonism directed towards Peters and Prebble. Both these leaders have consistently aroused strong feelings from the electorate. With Prebble, there is a clear trend which, both from his point of view and from that of ACT, is not good. In 1996, he had a negative differential of -4 percent. Three years later, it had nearly quadrupled to -15 percent. By 2002, he was at the bottom of the poll with -18 percent.

Peters has had a much more mercurial career. Prior to the formation of the National–New Zealand First coalition in 1996, his negative differential was -19 percent. After three tumultuous years, he was barely able to hold his Tauranga seat and his nationwide negative prime ministerial rating had reached -28 percent.[14] In 2002, when 8 percent of respondents personally preferred him to be prime minister, he was third after Clark and English. On the other hand, he led all other political leaders as the person most frequently named as 'least preferred prime minister' (22 percent). Overall, this did represent an improvement: his negative differential had been halved (to -14 percent).

Jim Anderton's career has also had its peaks and valleys, but generally speaking he has not attracted either the adulation or the antagonism of Peters and Prebble. His overall ratings reflect this. In 1996, he was liked and disliked as a potential PM by more or less equal proportions of electors

Figure 27.5: TV1 election night graphic on 'liked/disliked leaders'

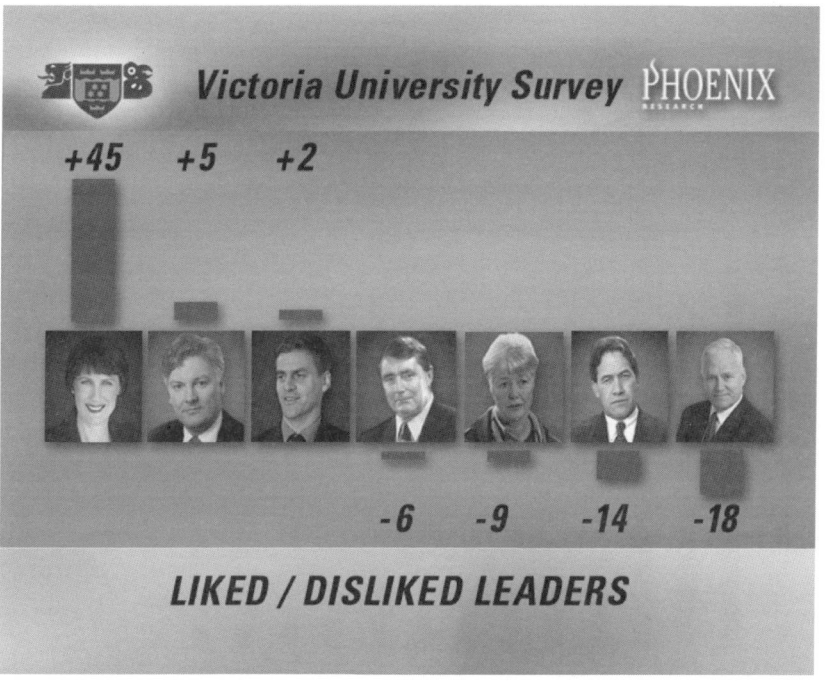

(about 10 percent), and had an overall positive differential of less than 0.5 percent. In 1999, still as leader of the Alliance, his positive differential was +3 percent. After two years and eight months as deputy prime minister, during which time his party split and his own position as Alliance leader became untenable, the proportions preferring him as prime minister had dropped from 9 percent in 1999 to less than 2 percent in 2002, and he achieved an overall negative differential (- 6 percent) for the first time.

Issues and problems

As in all elections, the media's focus on the parties' election prospects and the performance of the party leaders did not entirely eclipse concerns about ongoing issues and problems. The 2002 survey asked questions about both – first, 'When it comes to voting, are there any issues in this election which are particularly important *to you personally?*'; and later, 'What would you say is the *single most important problem* facing New Zealand right now?' As we have noted previously, the two questions are not interchangeable:

> The question dealing with the single most important problem invites participants to name what they consider the most pressing problem facing the country. It does not, of course, ask them to state whether the issue is of any particular personal concern to them. Not surprisingly, therefore, the question generates a smaller set of concerns which more closely coincide

Figure 27.6: Issues of personal concern in 2002

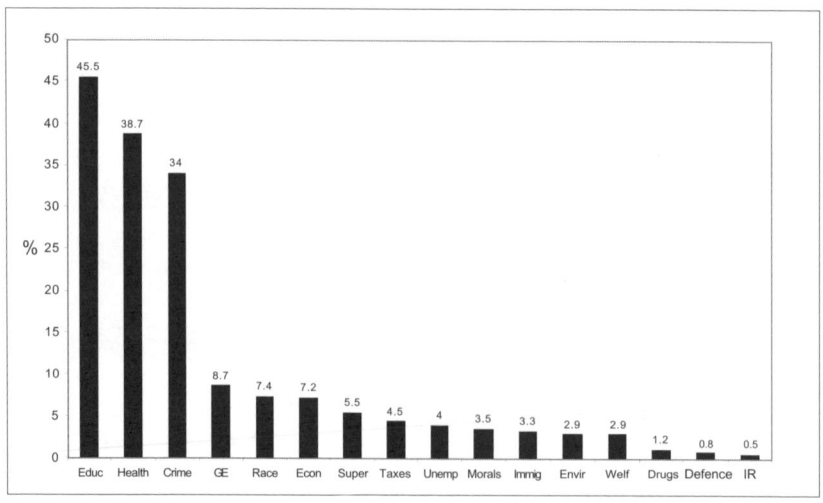

with the sorts of questions most broadly discussed in the media. The question emphasising issues of personal importance, on the other hand, taps a much larger range of apprehensions, anxieties, and aspirations, and successfully evokes comment on matters of individual interest irrespective of their salience for the collectivity (Levine and Roberts 1989, pp.428–429).

Figure 27.6 shows the range of issues of personal concern in 2002. The issue most frequently mentioned in response to this entirely open-ended question was education (mentioned by 45.5 percent of survey respondents). Three years earlier, education had also been a highly salient issue for electors, with over one quarter of that year's sample of survey respondents citing it. At that time, the matter of tertiary student loans was such a visible issue that it was given a separate category of its own, encompassing 18 percent of all respondents. The Labour-Alliance coalition government addressed the issue sufficiently to reduce its salience to electors in 2002, to the extent that it was barely mentioned during the campaign.[15]

The second most frequently cited issue in 2002 was another social welfare policy area, health. Throughout the 1970s and 1980s, it barely featured as an issue of personal concern (Levine and Roberts 1992, p.74). Starting in 1990, in the wake of the fourth Labour government's restructuring of the health system, the issue has consistently been at the forefront of people's personal agendas. When National fell from grace, concerns about the country's health system predominated: the issue was referred to more frequently than any other in our 1999 survey, by 43 percent of respondents. The issue did not go away during the Labour-Alliance government's tenure in office. There was controversy even at the start of the campaign, with the Minister of Health having to intervene personally to maintain a small local hospital's services (and dampen down what could have become a very damaging election issue). It would be difficult to say that Labour's return to power in 2002 was in any way a vote of confidence in its health care policies. The survey data show that the proportion of electors still concerned about the issue fell only slightly. At the same time, despite electors' concern about the state of New Zealand's health system, Labour had clearly managed to contain the issue, winning re-election in spite of not having 'fixed' the matter in quite the same way as it had done with student loans.

What is clear from the data are the strong showings made by New Zealand First (in particular) and ACT (to a lesser extent) in highlighting, or intensifying, voters' concerns about law-and-order. In 1999, the issue came seventh, mentioned by only 12.5 percent of those interviewed. The 2002 survey recorded an almost three-fold increase in the proportion citing the issue. Voters concerned about law-and-order (or 'crime') in 1999 had an opportunity to channel or divert their anger and anxiety over the issue into the citizens' initiated referendum held concurrently with the general election. Three years later, this outlet was no longer available, and the issue proved to be a source of strong support for parties pursuing a populist agenda.

Although interviewees were given three opportunities (by way of follow-up questions) to mention issues, after the first three items – education, health and law-and-order – the numbers of people mentioning any particular issue drop away sharply. Issues that enlivened the debates, the opening and closing addresses, and the election advertising do appear – GE, race relations and Treaty issues, immigration and cannabis – but they were not as 'personally' important for voters as might have been supposed.

Other issues that have been perennials in New Zealand politics – superannuation, taxes, unemployment and industrial relations – have declined significantly. To some extent, these have become dogs that fail to bark: it is their *absence* from voters' consciousness that is now significant. In particular, the unemployment issue, which dominated the 1980s and early 1990s (Levine and Roberts 1992, p.74), is conspicuous by its near-absence, defusing a potentially damaging issue to a remarkable degree.

We have already stressed that the two survey questions, one concerning issues of personal concern, and the other the major problem facing the country, 'tap different aspects of the electorate's perspectives on parties' policies' (Levine and Roberts 2000, p.170). One focuses on a personal connection between electors and the consequences of government policies. The other, on 'the single most important problem', is more cognitive. It does not ask voters whether the problem in question, or the policy to which it relates, affects them personally or directly. It partly reflects an awareness of the topics being stressed by the commentators and spin doctors who, through the media, shape the agenda for political debate. In 1984, voters had been told that the country's accounts were in dire straits, not something that they would have been likely to have felt directly themselves. Accordingly, the balance of payments was cited in 1984 as the single most important problem facing the country by nearly a quarter of those taking part in our pre-election survey (Levine and Roberts 1992, p.79). In 2002, the matter was barely mentioned in the media and on the hustings, and only 1.6 percent cited overseas debt as New Zealand's number one political challenge (see Figure 27.7).

Figure 27.7: The most important problems facing New Zealand in 2002

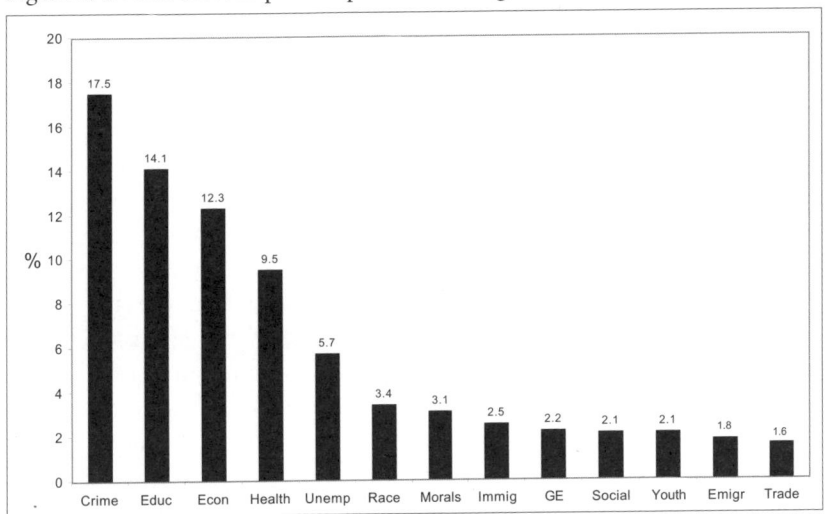

The similarity between the 'issues' and 'problems' cited by survey respondents in 2002 was something of a change from past elections. As others have noted, there was less emphasis on policy during the 2002 campaign. During the first three years of Clark-led government, a process appears to have developed whereby electors' personal concerns became less distinguishable from their perceptions about the major problems facing New Zealand. This in some ways reflects what might be considered as Helen Clark's single most important achievement, namely, establishing herself as a person almost universally regarded as competent, knowledgeable and in command.[16] As a result, her government was increasingly perceived as one that could be trusted to deal with the country's problems; and increasingly, these problems were scarcely distinguishable from 'issues of personal concern when it comes to voting'.

When the issues in Figure 27.6 are compared with the problems in Figure 27.7, what is noteworthy about the 2002 general election is how many of the leading problems also featured as the main issues of concern for voters. Of the top six issues (see Figure 27.6), five were to be found in the first six problems (see Figure 27.7): law-and-order, education, the economy, health, and race relations.

Another sign of the government's control over the campaign agenda was in the relatively low ranking given by survey respondents to the economy.

It was rated as the country's number one problem by only about 12 percent of the sample in both 1999 and 2002. As was the case with the 'issues' question, law-and-order had about trebled in importance, going from 6 percent and fourth position in 1999 to nearly 18 percent and first position in 2002.

Significantly, despite the emphasis given to immigration by New Zealand First, the alleged 'influx' of foreigners to New Zealand (with all that this might imply) was lowly rated both as an issue and as a problem, suggesting that betting a party's future on the potential for intolerance and bigotry among New Zealanders might be decidedly unwise. Likewise, the Greens might have gambled excessively on the impact of the GE issue, which generated probably more media coverage than any other single topic during the course of the campaign. As with immigration, the GE issue can be seen as one which can alter the very character of the country. Yet for most New Zealanders, it was scarcely as compelling as party strategists might have thought. Here was a topic which, for the Greens, was the make-or-break issue: one hoarding claimed that 'the future of New Zealand is the single issue', while another declared of GE, 'Keep it in the lab'. This was the policy area which helped precipitate an early election; and it was also the one on which decisions about whether to join a government or not (or even to allow one to be formed) would be based. Clearly the Greens' view of the centrality of the issue to New Zealand's future was not shared by the vast bulk of the country. No doubt this is partly why the party came to be viewed as 'extreme' by at least a segment of the electorate. Only 2.2 percent of respondents thought that the GE issue really could be regarded as the country's number one problem, and only one in 12 people thought it was an issue of personal importance.

If you ask people specific questions about particular issues and policies, you will, of course, get answers. But this in itself tells you very little about how important (if at all) those issues and policies are in relation to an election. A good example would be the so-called 'Treaty' issue. Here was a topic on which ACT, New Zealand First, and even National sought to make headway. From another question in our survey, we know that almost two in every three people agreed with the view that 'settling Maori claims under the Treaty of Waitangi has gone on long enough and should be discontinued' and that only 27 percent of the sample disagreed. However, despite opposition campaigning, the issue (or 'problem') lacked salience for most voters: they were not going to determine the composition of the next

Parliament on the basis of party policies towards this highly sensitive matter. The Treaty was an 'issue of personal concern' for only 7.4 percent of respondents, and was perceived as New Zealand's major problem (which it undeniably is from one perspective) by only 3.4 percent.

Gender and voting behaviour

The 2002 election was New Zealand's second in a row – and only the second ever – in which the incumbent prime minister was a woman. The 1999 election had been something of a landmark, with women leading each of the major (and one of the minor) parties. Many other countries have yet to reach a point where women have been able to take up leadership positions to this extent. In New Zealand, gender is now no longer an issue at the leadership level.

Gender does remain a factor in other ways, however. Table 27.4 provides evidence about gender voting patterns under MMP. (For reasons of space, the table shows only the proportion of each party's vote coming from women. Obviously the remaining proportion comes from male voters.)

One discernible trend in the data is the decline in the proportion of

Table 27.4: Pre-election survey data on voting by gender in New Zealand, 1996–2002

Party vote	1996 Women (%)	n	1999 Women (%)	n	2002 Women (%)	n
Labour	61.3	*225*	57.1	*326*	56.2	*361*
National	46.3	*283*	50.2	*233*	44.7	*159*
NZ First	50.5	*101*	43.9	*41*	45.8	*96*
ACT	16.4	*61*	21.7	*60*	30.2	*53*
Green	—	—	43.5	*46*	59.4	*64*
United	57.1	*7*	40.0	*5*	50.0	*48*
Alliance	50.8	*128*	47.1	*87*	50.0	*12*
Progressive Coalition	—	—	—	—	37.5	*16*
Christian Heritage	—	—	35.0	*20*	54.5	*11*
Others	13.3	*15*	26.3	*23*	0.0	*4*
Non-voters	57.1	*154*	58.3	*161*	48.9	*176*

Labour's voters who are women. This is, of course, from Labour's point of view, a good thing: the party is no longer so dependent on women voters, and, as Labour was led by Helen Clark at all three elections, the data also underscore her increasing electoral acceptability.

On the other hand, National's appeal to women voters has fluctuated in apparent accord with its successive leadership changes. In complete contrast with Labour, National has had a different leader at each of the three MMP elections. Its appeal to women and men was evenly balanced when Jenny Shipley was leader. In 2002, however, it could very nearly be described as a 'bloke's party', led by a part-time amateur boxer: women constituted a smaller proportion of National's supporters in 2002 than even under Jim Bolger in 1996.

As for New Zealand First, in spite of its leader's assumed appeal to women, the data for all three elections reveal little overall basis for this belief, as male voters predominate. The fourth largest party in 2002 was ACT, which began contesting elections in 1996. At that time, our survey data exposed the party's Achilles' heel: 'five out of six ACT voters were men – an extraordinary result in both New Zealand and international terms' (Levine and Roberts 1997, p.194). Three years later, the picture had improved, but only marginally. In 2002, one of the prime challenges for ACT, recognised by the party's strategists, was to improve its appeal to New Zealand's women voters. Indeed, it was no coincidence that ACT elected Catherine Judd as its new president in 2001.

Did ACT succeed in reducing the extraordinary gender imbalance that characterised its 1996 and 1999 election performances? Has this problem for the party been resolved? The data show some improvement, but it is still the party with the least appeal to female voters. In New Zealand's three MMP elections the proportions of ACT's voters who were men were: 84 percent in 1996; 78 percent in 1999; and 70 percent in 2002. If gender were *not* a factor to be considered in analysing voting behaviour, then all party support would be drawn equally from among women and men. While this may sometimes be the case, the data for ACT – but also for National and Labour – suggest that party, policy and leadership appeals do continue to resonate differently with men and women.

Assessing government and coalition options

The 2002 general election was in many ways an endorsement of the first term of Helen Clark's Labour-led government. Political science is very short of examples of major parties in democratically elected governments increasing their share of votes and seats after a term in office. This is as true for New Zealand as elsewhere. Since the election of the first Labour government (in 1935), this has occurred only three times (in 1938, 1951 and 1987). In that sense, Prime Minister Helen Clark was right on election night to emphasise the historical significance of her party's performance in having become the first party to accomplish this feat since the Lange-led administration in 1987. No overview of the 2002 election ought to ignore this fact.

One reason for Labour's success – all the more remarkable, since it occurred in the wake of the demise of Labour's coalition partner, the Alliance – is in voters' assessments of the coalition government's performance. Ultimately this is the key test of a government, and decisive for its re-election prospects. In 1999, when National fell, its lack of credibility as a competent and coherent government was clearly a principal factor. As we noted in our review of our 1999 nationwide survey data, 'The reason for the rejection of National can be summed up in one sentence. Just over 3 percent of respondents considered the government's performance to have been "very good"' (Levine and Roberts 2000, p.163).

By contrast, in 2002, just over one in five people (20.4 percent) thought that 'the government's overall performance throughout the country as a whole' had been very good. Another way of looking at these figures is to say that in a period of less than three years, from late 1999 to mid-2002, New Zealanders had become much more positive about their government. This is underscored by the fact that a further 67.3 percent judged the government's performance to have been 'reasonable'. In other words, nearly 90 percent of the sample approached the 2002 election with a broadly favourable assessment of the government. Clearly, in the face of such views, opposition parties and leaders would have had to wage a virtually flawless campaign on a multitude of fronts in order to have made much progress.

It has long been argued (with a considerable degree of empirical support) that oppositions do not win elections; governments lose them. In this case, not only was the government in no real danger of losing the election, but the opposition was also far from winning it. Whereas 15 percent of our 1999 sample judged the 1996–99 National-led government's overall performance to have been 'very poor', only a minuscule 2.9 percent took this view of a Labour-led government in July 2002. Put another way, there was simply not enough anger or angst towards Labour to give much force to opposition complaints against the government and its leader.[17]

The data also shed further light on the opposition's woes. National's poor performance can not really be laid exclusively at its leader's feet. Its voters were far less partisan than its MPs in the House in their assessment of the government. Even National's own voters saw the government's record in a positive light: 74 percent of them credited the government with a 'reasonable' or 'very good' performance. A mere 5 percent of National voters saw the government's performance as 'very poor' – not nearly enough discontent to sustain the level of partisanship needed to unseat a government.

It is a commonplace that the ACT Party is a more ideological movement situated to the right of National. Its voters would have been expected to be more critical of a Labour-Alliance coalition that had taken New Zealand on a left turn during the preceding three years. This is obvious – and wrong. Our data show that 87 percent of ACT's voters judged the government's performance to have been 'reasonable' or 'very good', and less than 4 percent labelled it as 'very poor'. Ironically, those most angry with the Clark-Anderton government were Alliance voters. One in twelve thought the government's performance had been very poor.[18]

The overall level of confidence in the government can be even further appreciated by comparing electors' assessments of electorate MPs with their assessments of the government. Respondents were also asked about the 'overall performance' of their MP. In 1999, when (as noted above) electors took an exceedingly dim view of the Shipley-led government's record, they were able in some ways to separate this view from their assessments of their own MP. At that time, 15 percent thought their own MP's overall performance was very good. In 2002, this figure had risen slightly to 18 percent – but, unlike 1999, this was overshadowed by an even more favourable rating for the government. At the other end of the spectrum, only 6 percent of 2002 respondents considered their MP's overall performance to have been 'very poor'; this was still (as we have seen) twice as high as the proportion judging the government in the same terms.

With voters largely comfortable with the government's performance, and expecting Labour to win the election, the question that came increasingly to dominate the campaign was one of coalition options. Various scenarios rose and fell during this period, as the relationships between the parties (and the parties' fortunes) fluctuated. At the start of 2002, the Greens had been willing to take part in a coalition, and it appeared that Labour would have been willing to have them. This all came undone before the calling of the election, and the election campaign itself did nothing to bring the two closer together – indeed, quite the opposite. During the course of the campaign, as New Zealand First's popularity in the opinion polls rose, questions about Winston Peters' potential as a 'kingmaker' (as he had so dramatically been in 1996) came to the fore. However, Labour's distaste for his use of the immigration issue meant that the prime minister was loathe to consider any such proposition. The Alliance was obviously unavailable; and National and ACT were wholly unsuitable.

Just as the campaign seemed gradually to narrow down (for commentators and voters alike) to the question of which party would be Labour's next coalition partner, so too did our survey. Electors were told that 'each MMP election has resulted in a coalition government'. This was followed by a question asking them for their coalition preference: 'which [party do] you think would be the *best* coalition partner for Labour?' The results are a further endorsement of Labour's overall strategy and another indication of how well informed (and rational) New Zealand's voters can be. Despite having been in existence as a party for only a few weeks, the party known at the election as 'Jim Anderton's Progressive Coalition' was the choice of more people than any other party as Labour's preferred coalition partner. The data suggest that voters largely approved of Labour's choice of a coalition partner, even though that party was – to be blunt – little more than an insignificant remnant of a once much more meaningful political movement. Overall, 28 percent of those who had a view on the matter thought that Anderton's Progressives were Labour's best choice. Looking only at the coalition preferences of those who cast their party vote for Labour, fully one-third backed a coalition with Anderton – by far the most popular choice.

As chapter 28 details, the election was followed not only by the coalition agreement with the Progressives, but also by relationships negotiated with United Future ('support') and the Greens ('consultation'). In all, of those with an opinion, 58 percent preferred a 'coalition' – the only relationship given to them as an option – with one or other of these three parties. Again, the government seems to have read public opinion accurately.

Conclusion

The ending of one election campaign is always the start of another, at least for those immersed in politics (be they the opposition, the government, or the media). Although the 2002 election did not give Helen Clark the majority that she initially sought (and that had seemed possible at the start of the campaign), the minority coalition government that was achieved (with 54 of 120 MPs) has so dominated the political landscape since the general election that, more than at any time since December 1999, it has seemed, to all intents and purposes, to be simply a Labour government. The correct descriptions – either that New Zealand has a Labour-led government or, even more accurately, that there is a Labour-Progressive minority government – are very seldom if ever used. United Future and the Greens are there, but they (especially United) remain very much in the background. In short, what the election produced was virtually the functional equivalent of what the prime minister desired from the very beginning. New Zealand has a government almost wholly identified with the Labour Party.

What remains to be seen is whether Labour can win again, or even improve on its performance as a government. If it can, and consequently goes on to a third term in office, then its position in New Zealand politics will have been consolidated and, perhaps with it, the MMP electoral system. All this and more depends largely, if not almost entirely, on the ability of one person to control – or at least successfully manage – events and people. That person is the incumbent prime minister, Helen Clark. It is a remarkable outcome for a democratic polity that it should be possible for a system to have, in effect, come down in some ways to rule by one person. That this has been achieved with so little discontent – or, to put it another way, with such ease and such high levels of public satisfaction – makes this development all the more extraordinary.

28

GOVERNMENT FORMATION AFTER THE 2002 GENERAL ELECTION

Jonathan Boston and Stephen Church

As in late 1999, but in sharp contrast to the situation in late 1996, the process of government formation following the general election on 27 July 2002 was concluded in short order. Within two weeks of the election, on 8 August, a brief coalition agreement between Labour and the Progressive Coalition Party (now more commonly referred to simply as the Progressives) was signed by the respective party leaders, Helen Clark and Jim Anderton. On the same day, the reconstituted minority government also signed a support agreement with the broadly centrist United Future Party, thus giving it an assured parliamentary majority on issues of confidence and supply. The new Cabinet was subsequently sworn in by the Governor-General on 15 August. A little later, on 26 August (the day before the formal state opening of Parliament), the Labour-Progressive government signed a cooperation agreement with the co-leaders of the Green Party, Jeanette Fitzsimons and Rod Donald. Thus, within a month of the election, the basic framework of the new governing arrangements had been crafted, and the government had resumed the legislative agenda that had been put on hold in mid-June when the prime minister called an early poll.

This chapter explores the political context for government formation following the 2002 general election, discusses the governing options, and outlines the strategic considerations that influenced the pattern of interparty bargaining.[1] Particular attention is given to the reasons that led the Labour-Progressive coalition to forge a support agreement with United Future, rather than with the Greens. The chapter then explores the nature of the various interparty agreements that were negotiated during August, and compares and contrasts these with previous coalition and support agreements. Finally, consideration is given to the composition of the reconstituted government, the nature of its policy programme and its likely durability. It should be noted that the discussion which follows is based on interviews with some of those directly involved in the government formation process, together with a variety of secondary sources.

Before proceeding, it is worth noting that there is a small but steadily expanding literature on the process of government formation in New Zealand under proportional representation.[2] This includes analyses of the institutional context (including constitutional conventions) within which the process occurs, and how this context compares with other parliamentary democracies.[3] Some attention has also been given to the theoretical issues surrounding government formation.[4] These include factors that affect the behaviour of parties during coalition negotiations, and why certain bargaining outcomes (such as minimum winning coalitions of ideologically connected parties) are more likely than others (such as ideologically disconnected or oversized coalitions). Since these topics have been well canvassed elsewhere, they will be largely omitted from the following analysis.

The political context immediately after the 2002 election

The party composition of the legislature is obviously critical in determining the nature of the governments that will be established in parliamentary democracies such as New Zealand. In this respect, the results of the 2002 general election had a number of important parallels with the situation almost three years earlier. For instance, it was evident on election night, as in late 1999, that the parties of the centre-left (i.e. Labour, the Progressives and the Greens) enjoyed a clear majority in Parliament, albeit reduced from twelve to four seats. This majority subsequently increased to six seats after the counting of special votes (see Table 28.1). There was thus no question of a change of government. Likewise, Labour was again the largest party, increasing its share of the party vote, and securing almost twice as many seats as its long-term rival, National. More importantly, as in 1999, the election results left Labour strategically placed, both as the party representing the 'median voter' on the all-important socio-economic dimension, and as the party holding the 'pivotal' position in the legislature (i.e. it is a necessary member of all the potential winning coalitions that are ideologically connected).[5] Given the current composition of Parliament, therefore, no stable coalition was possible without Labour as an active participant; it was thus in a very strong bargaining position.

Similarly, as in 1999, pre-election commitments made it almost inevitable that Labour would form a coalition rather than seeking to govern alone.

There was, however, at least an element of doubt over whether Labour would form a two-party *minority* coalition with the Progressives (which had broken away from the Alliance several months before the election), or whether it would seek a three-party *majority* coalition, either with United Future or with the Greens. If the former strategy were adopted, then Labour would need to forge a *legislative* (rather than an *executive*) coalition of some kind with United Future and/or the Greens, to ensure that it had a majority on issues of confidence and supply.

But while the political context following the 2002 general election had some striking similarities to the situation after the second MMP election, there were also at least three notable differences. First, the Progressives, with only two seats, were in a much weaker strategic position than had been the case with respect to the Alliance (with 10 seats) in late 1999. That said, the mathematics of the party configuration in Parliament meant that Labour needed the active support of the two Progressive MPs if it were to build either a legislative or an executive coalition with United Future (but not with the Greens).[6]

Second, and more important, whereas the party system had been predominantly unidimensional during the first two terms of MMP, with

Table 28.1: The state of the parties after the 1999 and 2002 general elections

Party	1999	2002
ACT	9	9
National	39	27
United (1999) United Future (2002)	1	8
New Zealand First	5	13
Labour	49	52
Alliance	10	—
Progressives	—	2
Greens	7	9
Governing Options		
Labour + Alliance/PC	59	54
Labour + Alliance/PC + Greens	66	63
Labour + PC + United Future	—	62
Centre-Left Majority	12	6
Total Number of Seats	120	120

the traditional socio-economic (or left-right) ideological dimension strongly in the ascendancy (see Brechtel and Kaiser 1999; Kaiser and Brechtel 1999), other issue dimensions had grown in political salience during 2002. This had complicated the pattern of interparty relationships, especially on the centre-left of the political spectrum. Crucial in this context were the contrary positions that Labour and its support party, the Greens, had come to adopt on the highly controversial issue of genetic modification. Whereas Labour was committed to lifting the (temporary) moratorium on the commercial release of genetically modified organisms when it expired in October 2003, the Greens were implacably opposed to such action. Indeed, their hostility to the lifting of the moratorium was such that in May 2002, they had declared that they would not support on issues of confidence and supply any government – centre-left or centre-right – that allowed the release of genetically modified organisms into the environment. Prior to this, the Greens had offered the Labour-Alliance government unconditional support on confidence and supply (see Bale and Dann 2002; Boston 2000a).

The positions adopted by Labour and the Greens inevitably created tensions during the months leading up to the election. These tensions were much exacerbated during the campaign following the publication of a book, *Seeds of Distrust*, by the veteran activist Nicky Hager, which claimed that the Labour-Alliance government had failed to inform the public about an unauthorised planting of genetically modified sweet corn seeds in late 2000. Although Clark and other senior ministers strenuously denied Hager's allegations, the Greens were quick to exploit the apparent inconsistencies in the government's policy position, and sought to use the book's findings to boost support for their campaign to extend the moratorium. In the event, the acrimony between Labour and the Greens over this issue not only undermined the relationship between the parties' leaders, but also highlighted the Greens' threat to withdraw support on confidence and supply if the moratorium were lifted. In so doing, it called into question the willingness and capacity of the two parties to cooperate satisfactorily after the election. Both parties suffered electorally as a consequence: support for the Greens fell from about 9–10 percent to 7 percent during the latter part of the campaign, while support for Labour declined from over 50 percent to about 41 percent. In short, the controversy over the moratorium highlights the problems that can arise in a context of multidimensionality, particularly where parties with shared policy affinities on the left-right dimension are deeply divided on another issue dimension of high political salience.

Third, and related to this, the conflict between Labour and the Greens contributed to a significant surge in electoral support for the United Future Party during the final weeks of the campaign. Led by a former Labour MP, Peter Dunne, United Future represented an amalgam of several rather different political groups and traditions. On the one hand, it contained the remnants of the socially liberal, market-oriented MPs and their supporters from Labour and National who had established United in 1995, with the aim of building a viable centrist party that could hold the balance of power in the new MMP environment. Of the original seven MPs, only Peter Dunne had retained his seat in 1996 (partly as a result of an electoral accommodation with National). On the other hand, United Future incorporated Future New Zealand, a party that started life as the Christian Democrats (formed in 1995 by a National MP, Graeme Lee). The Christian Democrats were largely centre-right in orientation, conservative on social and economic issues, and strongly committed to family values (see Boston 2000b). Having failed to win any seats in either 1996 (under the banner of the Christian Coalition in alliance with the Christian Heritage party) or 1999 (campaigning on its own), Future New Zealand had joined forces with United in late 2000, believing that this represented the best means of securing parliamentary representation.

In the event, this strategy met with remarkable success: United Future secured nearly 7 percent of the party vote in 2002, thereby winning eight seats (an increase of seven). As noted, an important factor in explaining United Future's emergence as a significant political force was the bitter conflict between Labour and the Greens. Also relevant, however, was Dunne's unequivocal declaration during the election campaign that his party would be prepared, on certain conditions, to support a Labour-led government.[7] By making this offer, United Future positioned itself closer to the centre of the political spectrum, at least from the perspective of many voters. The subsequent dramatic boost to the party's electoral fortunes had the effect of altering the nature and dynamics of the party system, replacing the largely bipolar (or two-bloc) model that had characterised much of the previous parliamentary term with a balancing-centre model of the kind more common, certainly until recent times, in countries such as Denmark and Norway. Strategically, the main beneficiary of this change was Labour: given the mathematics of the election results, and assuming that an acceptable deal could be forged with United Future, Labour would no longer be wholly dependent upon the Greens for support on confidence and supply. Equally comforting for Clark, Labour would have little need to seek the backing of New Zealand First and its mercurial leader, Winston Peters, for legislative initiatives that the Greens would not support.

Governing options

In terms of the composition of the new administration, several matters were relatively apparent within a short time of the election-night results being declared. First, the Progressives would remain within the Cabinet, and thus there would continue to be a coalition, rather than a single-party government. Labour's preference for a coalition, rather than a support arrangement, with Jim Anderton's small, fledgling party can be explained largely on the basis of 'path dependence' (see Bale et al. 2002; Pierson 2000).[8] Clark and Anderton had worked extremely closely over the preceding parliamentary term, and had established a cordial and constructive relationship. During the testing times surrounding the break-up of the Alliance in early 2002, Clark had lent her full support to Anderton and made it abundantly plain that she preferred a political relationship with his new Progressive Party rather than with the more radical elements that had remained faithful to the Alliance. Further, throughout the election campaign Clark had emphasised her firm intention to forge a coalition with Anderton's party, assuming that Labour was in a position to form a government (which seemed highly probable), and that the Progressives succeeded in retaining parliamentary representation (which also seemed very likely, given the personal support for Anderton in his Wigram constituency). Having given such commitments, and having invested substantial political capital in the relationship with Anderton, there would have been significant costs for Clark if she had chosen to govern alone after the election. By contrast, the costs of negotiating another coalition deal with Anderton were modest, in terms of both policy concessions and Cabinet places: realistically, the Progressives could only expect one ministerial post, given their poor electoral performance. Similar considerations of path dependency help explain why it is so common, in multiparty systems, for junior coalition partners to remain in office after an election, even in circumstances where they are not needed to ensure that the government retains a parliamentary majority.

But what of the prospects of a three-party *majority* coalition? After all, the theoretical literature on coalitions suggests that parties have strong incentives to build majority executive coalitions, because of the greater control over the legislature that this ensures. But, as in 1999, elements of path dependency contributed to Labour's preference for another minority government. Clark had declared repeatedly during the election campaign that if Labour and the Progressives failed to secure a parliamentary majority, she would favour a two-party minority government, with support on confidence and supply from a third party. Evidently, she regarded minority government as a preferable option under these circumstances, partly because it gave Labour greater control over the executive (and thus more Cabinet places for its caucus members), and partly because it would increase the government's bargaining options when it came to securing parliamentary support for its legislative initiatives (as it had the previous term with New Zealand First on occasion). Additionally, by August 2002, Clark had had almost three years of experience in the art and craft of leading a minority government. As with her Social Democratic counterparts in countries such as Denmark, Norway and Sweden, she had found this to be a relatively satisfactory mode of governance.

But whatever the prime minister's predilections, there were other important considerations which rendered a majority government unlikely. Given the stance of the Greens over the moratorium on the release of genetically modified organisms (and especially the threat to withdraw support on confidence and supply), and given Labour's unwillingness to change its own position on the issue, a coalition involving the Greens was politically untenable. In any case, the Greens had failed to secure the level of voter support that they had previously indicated would be necessary if they were to enter office (i.e. close to 10 percent).

A coalition with United Future was equally problematic, albeit for different reasons. With the exception of Dunne, none of the party's MPs had previous parliamentary experience. The party was thus ill-prepared for immediate entry into a Labour-led government. Partly for this reason, and partly because of the serious political and electoral difficulties encountered by the junior partners in all the coalitions since 1996, the new caucus of United Future, at its first meeting several days after the election, rejected any idea of seeking Cabinet positions in the new government. The caucus also rejected the potential option of maintaining a more equivocal or oppositional stance in Parliament, preferring instead to adopt the role of a support party (as the Greens had done during the previous term).

Following the election, therefore, the main question was not over the composition of the government, but rather over the nature of the support

arrangements that would be entered into by the government with its potential parliamentary allies. There were, in effect, three main possibilities:
1. A formal support agreement with United Future
2. A formal support agreement with the Greens
3. Formal support and/or cooperation agreements involving both United Future and the Greens.

Within a day or so of the election, the second of these options appeared the least likely. As previously noted, the Greens' stance on genetic modification, coupled with Labour's unwillingness to bend, meant that the government could not rely on the Greens for support on confidence and supply after the moratorium was lifted in late 2003. Understandably, Labour was not willing to entertain a short-term agreement: it wanted guaranteed support for the whole parliamentary term. During the interparty negotiations in the weeks immediately following the election, various options were advanced for resolving the disagreement over genetic modification, or at least enabling the two parties to develop a conditional support agreement. For instance, one possibility was for the Greens to support the government on confidence issues, except for the first confidence motion following the lifting of the moratorium. In this instance, the government would need to rely on United Future to maintain its parliamentary majority. However, for various reasons such an option was not considered by either party to be politically viable.

In the absence of guaranteed, medium-term support from the Greens, Labour and the Progressives had little alternative but to seek the backing of United Future. From the government's perspective, such an arrangement – assuming it could be negotiated – offered a number of advantages. Over the short to medium term, it would significantly increase the likelihood of being able to secure the backing of United Future for important elements of the Cabinet's legislative programme, thereby reducing the previous heavy dependence upon the Greens. Put differently, it would enhance the government's flexibility in terms of building majorities in the House, and thus extend the range of legislative measures that were likely to secure parliamentary backing. Equally important, Labour was mindful of the likely need for support from United Future for procedural motions, such as urgency. Without this, and given the Greens' reluctance to support urgency except for bills that they supported, the government would have difficulty making progress on its legislative agenda.

Aside from such considerations, there was also a longer-term strategic calculus: by securing the support of United Future on issues of confidence and supply, and by drawing the party more fully into the policy-making process, there was the possibility of forging a relationship that would last beyond the current parliamentary term. In other words, if United Future became accustomed to working with the parties of the centre-left, then it might become more favourably disposed to the idea of backing a Labour-led government over the longer term. Equally, a successful working relationship between Labour and United Future might well reduce National's electoral appeal at the next election, thereby enhancing the prospects of a continuing centre-left majority in the House. Strategically, therefore, a deal with United Future offered important attractions.

United Future, for its part, was keen to replace the Greens as the government's main support party. This would give it a privileged role (in terms of access to Cabinet ministers, their advisers and official papers) and a degree of political leverage that it would otherwise lack. It would thereby increase its chance of influencing the government's policy agenda and winning support for key elements of its own policy programme. More generally, there was the prospect of shifting the government towards a more centrist and socially conservative position. Significantly, too, the experience of the Green Party (which had increased its share of the vote in 2002) indicated that there were relatively few political risks for small parties that adopted a formal support role – unlike the evident electoral costs associated with full incumbency.

Given such considerations, there was every prospect after the election that the government would negotiate a formal support arrangement with United Future. The main questions, therefore, concerned the precise terms of the agreement, and whether any kind of deal might also be struck with the Greens, albeit something less than a full support agreement. On the latter issue, both the Greens and Labour had reasons for wanting to heal the wounds of the election campaign and re-establish a constructive working relationship. On the one hand, Labour knew that it would need the support of the Greens if it were to enact reforms that United Future was likely to oppose. On the other hand, the Greens wished to retain their previous access to ministers and information, and hence their capacity to influence policy formulation within the executive. At a strategic level, both parties were also acutely aware, based on the gruelling experience and disappointing results of the 2002 campaign, that a collaborative relationship was likely to be to their mutual electoral advantage. After all, if the centre-left vote declined any further in 2005, and if United Future imploded or changed its allegiances, then both parties risked being left out in the cold. Accordingly, while the disagreement over genetic modification ruled out a formal support agreement (at least in the short term), it did not prevent the two parties reaching an accommodation to work in a cooperative manner on a host of other matters (especially environmental issues and those typically categorised as left-right issues).

The negotiations

As in 1999, the negotiations between the various parties were conducted by relatively small teams of people, comprised mainly of the party leaders and senior advisers. Thus, in the case of Labour, the key participants were Helen Clark, Dr Michael Cullen (Deputy Leader) and Heather Simpson (the prime minister's Chief of Staff and long-serving senior adviser); the Progressives were represented by Anderton and his Chief of Staff, Dr Andrew Ladley; the United Future team consisted of Dunne, Mark Stonyer (the head of the party's parliamentary unit), Anthony Walton (the party's deputy leader), and Inky Tulloch (the party president); while the Greens were represented by their co-leaders (Jeanette Fitzsimons and Rod Donald), two party members (Gordon Jackman and Olivier Mitchell), and the head of the party's advisory unit in Parliament, Deb Moran. Consistent with previous experience, most of the detailed discussions on specific issues were conducted by the key advisers, who then reported the results of their deliberations to their respective colleagues.

Again, as in 1999, all the negotiations were handled on a bilateral (rather than a multilateral) basis, with Labour holding separate (and parallel) negotiations with the Progressives, United Future, and the Greens. To be sure, Labour kept its coalition partner informed about the outcome of its discussions with the two potential support parties, but neither Anderton nor Ladley were involved directly in the bargaining process.

Interestingly, United Future and the Greens chose not to hold any joint discussions, and thus did not develop any agreed negotiating positions on specific issues (notwithstanding the potential advantages of so doing). While the Greens were open to the possibility of a dialogue with United Future – both on issues where the parties shared similar policy positions, and in relation to matters of mutual concern (such as the management of Parliament and the allocation of select committee chairpersonships) – Dunne rebuffed the Greens' informal approaches immediately after the election. Accordingly, the opportunity to apply joint pressure on Labour was missed. Equally, the lack of any dialogue between the two parties, coupled with the strict confidentiality surrounding the negotiations, meant that neither party knew what Labour was offering the other until the conclusion of the process.[9] Strategically, such an arrangement served to strengthen Labour's bargaining position. There are some interesting parallels here with the government formation process in 1996, although in the latter instance it was New Zealand First that enjoyed the pivotal bargaining position, and Labour and National that chose not to collude (see Boston and McLeay 1997).

By international standards, the negotiating process was remarkably brief (see Boston 1998; Müller and Strøm 1997). The text of the coalition agreement between Labour and the Progressives was more-or-less complete within a few days of the election, while the text of the support agreement between the government and United Future was effectively completed within a week. Only the cooperation agreement with the Greens took a while to negotiate, but even this was finalised within four weeks of the election. Apart from the usual political imperatives for an expeditious process, the speed with which the new government formed in 2002 can be attributed to three main factors. First, the bargaining context was relatively uncomplicated. Matters may well have been different if Labour had not been able to turn so readily to United Future for support on confidence and supply. Secondly, the leaders and advisers of the respective parties were, for the most part, experienced negotiators and were on relatively good terms (although the relationship between the prime minister and the Greens' co-leaders was certainly in need of repair). Thirdly, there was a broad consensus that the various agreements should be relatively brief and focus primarily on procedural rather than detailed policy matters. Accordingly, the number of issues requiring in-depth discussion was limited. Assisting the process, too, was the fact that the parties could draw on previous documents as a guide, including the coalition agreement negotiated in December 1999, and the subsequent unsigned support agreement between the Labour-Alliance government and the Greens; there was thus no need to start from scratch.

As in 1996 and 1999, the government formation process in 2002 was conducted in relatively stable, tranquil and benign economic conditions. There was no obvious anxiety in financial markets concerning the likely outcome, and thus no significant movement in equity or currency markets.

To be sure, various business and union leaders expressed certain preferences, with business leaders arguing that Labour should negotiate a support agreement with United Future and union leaders preferring a deal with the Greens. There is no evidence that such views had any bearing on the outcome of the negotiations. Against this, the disquiet among certain Labour backbenchers concerning a support arrangement with United Future no doubt contributed to the political pressures on Clark to repair her relationship with the Greens, and negotiate another medium-term deal.

The agreement between Labour and the Progressives

The Labour-Progressive coalition agreement is the fourth significant document of its type since the referendum on MMP in 1993, the other three being those between National and United in late February 1996, National and New Zealand First in mid-December 1996, and Labour and the Alliance in early December 1999. Table 28.2 summarises the key features of these four agreements, and highlights their similarities and differences. As will be evident, the latest agreement has much in common with the Labour-Alliance agreement, and is also similar in many respects to the deal between National and United. The National-New Zealand First agreement, by contrast, was radically different.

The latest coalition agreement, at about 430 words, is even more concise

Table 28.2: Coalition agreements: comparisons and contrasts

	National and United (Feb 1996)	National and New Zealand First (Dec 1996)	Labour and the Alliance (Dec 1999)	Labour and the Progressives (Aug 2002)
Length	553 words	17,000 words (approx)	486 words	431 words
Statement of Priorities and Objectives	Extremely brief	Reasonably detailed	Extremely brief	Extremely brief
Policy Coverage	No policy content	Very comprehensive; policy agreements in at least 37 areas	No policy content	Very limited policy content
Agreed Fiscal Parameters	No	$5 billion extra expenditure over 3 years (1997–2000)	No	No

Commitment to Consensual Decision Making	Yes	Yes	Yes	Yes (but no formal requirement for the Progressives to be present at Cabinet meetings for there to be a quorum)
Coalition Management Mechanisms	Dealt with generally	Dealt with explicitly and in detail; Coalition Management Committee mentioned	Dealt with generally; Coalition Management Committee mentioned	No mention of specific coalition management mechanisms
Dispute Resolution Procedures	Mentioned: disagreements to be referred to a Disputes Group	Fundamental Disputes to be referred to a Coalition Dispute Committee	Disputes to be handled by Coalition Management Committee	No mention of procedures for handling disputes
Provision for Public Disagreements	Yes, within limits	No	Yes; party 'distinction' provision	Yes; party 'distinction' provision, but wording modified from 1999 coalition agreement
Collective Cabinet Responsibility	Endorsed	Endorsed	Endorsed	Endorsed
Confidence Issues	United agreed to support issues nominated by the PM as ones of confidence	Taken as read that the two parties would vote together on matters of confidence	Taken as read that the two parties would vote together on matters of confidence	Taken as read that the two parties would vote together on matters of confidence
Composition of Executive	Provided for United to have one position in the executive	Set out the composition of the executive in detail, and provided for mid-term changes	Provided for a Cabinet of 20 with 16 Labour and 4 Alliance members	Provided for the Progressives to have one Cabinet position
Electoral Accommodations	Stated that National would not contest the seat of Ohariu-Belmont at the 1996 general election	No	No	No
Term of Agreement	Until the next general election	Until the next general election unless terminated earlier	Not mentioned, but assumed to last until next general election	Not mentioned, but assumed to last until next general election

than the one between Labour and the Alliance; in fact, it would have been some 50 words shorter, had the paragraph summarising the two parties' objectives not been inadvertently repeated! Interestingly, the document is also shorter than the support agreement with United Future, which in turn runs to fewer words than the cooperation agreement with the Greens. In terms of content, there are significant parallels between the Labour-Alliance and Labour-Progressive agreements. For instance, both documents are concerned primarily with managing interparty relationships, rather than with enunciating agreed policy positions. Having said this, the Labour-Progressive agreement contains slightly more policy material than its predecessor, with a commitment by Labour to recognise:

> the Progressive Coalition's general priorities of employment, support for low income families, health and education and its wish to make specific progress on:
> - ensuring better co-ordination and integration of industry assistance.
> - implementation of a comprehensive drug strategy aimed at protecting young people and educating them on the dangers of drug use.
> - policy to promote a better balance of work and family responsibilities.

No doubt Anderton would have sought, and probably obtained, more significant policy concessions from Labour, had his party secured a much stronger electoral mandate. But with less than 2 percent of the party vote, he could not reasonably expect (and was in no position to demand) more than a brief mention of his core political concerns.

As with the previous Labour-Alliance deal, the latest agreement enables the two governing parties, under certain conditions, to take different policy positions in public and in Parliament, without compromising the doctrine of collective Cabinet responsibility. However, the provisions of the so-called 'agree-to-disagree' clause have been amended. Under the 1999 agreement, there was provision for either party leader to identify a particular policy matter as being 'of importance to the party's political identity'. In these circumstances, the issue would be considered by the Coalition Management Committee, which could, if it so chose, declare the matter to be one of 'party distinction', thus enabling the two parties to take different positions in Parliament. When the 1999 agreement was signed, it was recognised that the 'agree-to-disagree' clause was designed primarily for the benefit of the junior coalition partner, the Alliance, and that in practice it would only be the junior partner that would seek to invoke the provision (see Boston 2000a). Furthermore, there was a widespread acknowledgement that, for political as well as constitutional reasons, any use of the provision would have to be infrequent. The 2002 agreement recognises these political realities. In particular, it explicitly refers to the need for the smaller party to be 'able to maintain a separate but responsible identity', and states that when the 'agree-to-disagree' provisions apply, 'the Progressive Coalition will be free to express alternative views publicly and in Parliament'. For obvious reasons, no reference is made to the possibility of Labour wishing to differentiate itself from its tiny coalition partner. Nor is there any mention of a Coalition Management Committee: in the event, the previous committee met only once; and with Anderton's new party having only two MPs, there is less need for formal interparty structures.

As with the 1999 agreement, the 2002 document affirms that 'decision-making will be by consensus' and that the 'parties . . . will operate in government on a good faith and no surprises basis'. Mindful of the huge imbalance in the relative size of the two parties, the document states, unsurprisingly, that with regard to Cabinet procedures, 'quorum rules relating to the need to have at least one member from each coalition party present for a quorum will not generally apply'. For similar reasons, although not explicitly stated in the agreement, the system of coalition consultation that ministers put in place in late 1999 has been abandoned. But in order to facilitate participation by the Progressives in the policy-making process, Anderton has the right to attend any or all Cabinet committees. Indeed, since the 2002 election he has continued his previous practice of attending most Cabinet committees.

The agreements with United Future and the Greens

From a comparative perspective, perhaps the most interesting and indeed novel feature of the government formation process in August 2002 was the drafting and formal ratification of both a *support* agreement and a *cooperation* agreement. Minority governments in other countries do often seek the backing of parties both to their left and to their right. They may also negotiate understandings with more than one parliamentary party, if the circumstances so require. But such formal agreements are not typically signed (or even made public). Nor is it common for there to be separate types of agreements, of the kind negotiated by the Labour-Progressive government. In fact, the dual nature of the formal accords with United Future and the Greens may well be without precedent.

The first substantive support agreement in New Zealand since the electoral referendum in 1993 was negotiated between the Labour-Alliance government and the Greens in late 1999 and early 2000 (Bale and Dann 2002; Boston 2000a). Although the relevant document was never signed, it provided the basis of the operating arrangement between the respective parties for over two and a half years. Under the accord, the Greens agreed to provide more or less unconditional support for the government on confidence and supply for the parliamentary term, and to cooperate in good faith to ensure stable and effective government. In return, the government agreed to consult the Greens on its policy intentions and priorities (including budgetary matters), to provide opportunities to contribute to policy development (especially in those areas of most concern to the party, such as conservation, employment, the environment, energy, social welfare and transportation), and to give serious consideration to the party's policy proposals, including those with fiscal implications. With the exception of confidence motions and budgetary matters, it was accepted that Green support for particular legislative measures would be negotiated on a case-by-case basis.

As outlined in Table 28.3, the deal negotiated with United Future in August 2002 is broadly similar in nature. It is, however, rather more exacting in the obligations it places on the government (e.g. in relation to the nature and degree of consultation with United Future over policy-making). Moreover, unlike the previous agreement with the Greens, it contains specific policy commitments. For instance, the document includes four explicit pledges by the government: to develop proposals for a Commission for the Family (one of United Future's pivotal policy goals); to pass legislation before the end of 2002 to strengthen victims' rights and increase support for victims' support groups; to enact new transport legislation (including provision for alternative ways of funding new roads); and to 'implement a comprehensive drug strategy aimed at protecting young people and educating them on the dangers of drug use'. In the whole scheme of things, of course, these concessions to United Future were modest. In fact, only the commitment to create a Commission for the Family represented a clear departure from the government's previous policy position, and at the time of writing, it remains to be seen what kind of commission will ultimately be agreed to, at what cost, and to what effect.

The only other notable difference from the earlier support agreement with the Greens was a provision under the heading of 'collective responsibility'. This reads as follows:

> Although United Future will not be bound by collective responsibility on government decisions, where there has been full participation in the

Table 28.3: Support and cooperation agreements: comparisons and contrasts

	Operating arrangement under which the Green Party supported the Labour-Alliance Government (Dec 1999)	Agreement for Confidence and Supply between the Labour-Progressive Government and United Future (Aug 2002)	Cooperation Agreement between the Labour-Progressive Government and the Green Party (Aug 2002)
Publicly ratified	No, partly due to objections from the Alliance	Yes, 8 Aug 2002	Yes, 26 Aug 2002
Support for the government on confidence and supply	Yes	Yes	No
Good faith	Agreement that the parties would operate on a good faith and no surprises basis	Explicit agreement for the parties to operate on a good faith and no surprises basis	Explicit commitment by the parties to having a constructive relationship based on good faith
Contribution of the support/cooperating party to the government's policy programme	Agreement that the Greens would be given the opportunity to contribute to policy formulation and priority setting, especially in areas of importance to the support party	Agreement that the government's policy programme will take account of the policy priorities of the United Future Party	Agreement that the government and the Greens will co-operate on agreed areas of policy development and legislation in order to facilitate the implementation of a shared agenda
Specific policy agreements	No	Agreement by the government to give priority to four specific initiatives promoted by the United Future party, including the establishment of a Commission for the Family	Agreement by the government to review certain aspects of the Environmental Risk Management Authority, and to consult with the Greens over the scope of the review

Budgetary matters	Agreement by the government to consult the Greens on the annual Budget, and give the party an opportunity to advance budgetary proposals	Agreement by the government to consult United Future on broad budgetary parameters, and give the party an opportunity to advance budgetary proposals	No provision for consultation on budgetary matters
Consultation arrangements	Agreement by the government for relevant Ministers to meet with designated Green spokespersons on a regular basis, and for the Greens to be given advance notice of important government initiatives	Agreement by the government to consult with United Future, in a timely fashion, on a range of matters including the legislative programmes, key legislative measures, and major policy issues; provision for ongoing relationships between relevant portfolio Ministers and United Future spokespersons	Agreement by the government to consult the Greens on a range of issues including: the legislative programmes and the priorities within it, key legislative measures, and major policy issues. Three categories of engagement identified: full participation in the policy process; consultation on the broad direction of policy; and information sharing.
Leadership meetings	Provision for meetings on an approximately quarterly basis and additionally as required	Provision for regular (approximately monthly) meetings with the Prime Minister	Provision for quarterly meetings with the Prime Minister
Confidentiality	Agreement that government information provided to the Greens prior to public release should be treated confidentially	Agreement that briefings and government papers provided to United Future will be confidential, unless otherwise agreed	Agreement that briefings and government papers provided to the Greens will be confidential, unless otherwise agreed
Collective Responsibility	Assumed that the Greens would not be bound by collective responsibility for government decisions	Where there has been full participation by United Future in the development of a policy initiative and an agreed position has been reached, all parties to this agreement will be expected to support the process and the outcome	Assumed that the Greens would not be bound by collective responsibility for government decisions

Procedural motions in Parliament	Agreement that the Greens will support all government procedural motions unless there is specific notice to contrary in advance	Agreement that United Future will support the government on procedural motions in the House and in Select Committees unless the party has previously advised that such support is not forthcoming	Not mentioned
Select Committees	Not mentioned	Agreement that United Future and the government will develop an agreed position on the make-up and operation of select committees	Not mentioned
Legislative programme	Support for legislative measures which do not relate to confidence or supply to be negotiated on a case-by-case basis	Support for legislative measures which do not relate to confidence or supply to be negotiated on a case-by-case basis	Not mentioned, but it is assumed that support for legislative measures will be negotiated on a case-by-case basis
Term of agreement	For the parliamentary term	For the parliamentary term	For the parliamentary term

development of a policy initiative, and that participation has led to an agreed position, it is expected that all parties to the agreement will publicly support the process and the outcome.

This is a rather curious provision. After all, when parties negotiate over a particular matter and reach agreement, it is normal for them to support the outcome, both publicly and privately. Such support, however, may be lukewarm, and a party may perceive that it is in its interests to let it be known that it has backed the proposal in question only with great reluctance. A case in point was the very tepid endorsement that senior Labour ministers gave to the Cabinet's decision in 2000 to establish Kiwibank (a key Alliance initiative). Likewise, the agreement between National and New Zealand First to hold a referendum on the controversial issue of superannuation in 1997 was vigorously opposed within the National caucus, with many MPs publicly challenging the coalition government's preferred policy option during the ill-fated referendum campaign. United Future's leadership was plainly mindful of such instances, and was particularly keen to avoid situations where the party's hard-won policy victories were subsequently damned with faint praise by senior ministers. For various reasons, Labour's negotiators shared this desire to build a greater degree of discipline into the consultation process. In particular, they wished to ensure that United Future publicly endorsed those policies that were the subject of detailed negotiations and explicit interparty agreements. Whether the inclusion of the relevant wording in the support agreement will achieve its desired effect obviously remains to be seen.

The terms and conditions of the cooperation agreement between the Labour-Progressive government and the Greens have many parallels with the party's previous support agreement and the deal with United Future. The fundamental difference, of course, is the absence of any pledge from the Greens to provide support on confidence and supply. Instead, the agreement states that the respective parties 'are committed to having a constructive relationship based on good faith for this term of Parliament', and that they 'will co-operate on agreed areas of policy development and legislation in order to facilitate the implementation of a shared agenda'.

Most of the other differences from United Future's support agreement are minor. For instance, the support agreement states that the leaders of the government and United Future will meet regularly '(approximately monthly)', while the cooperation agreement commits the government to 'quarterly meetings between the Prime Minister and the Green Party Co-Leaders'. Likewise, while the support agreement commits the government to consulting with United Future on its 'legislative programme and priorities', 'key legislatives measures', 'major policy issues', and 'broad budget parameters', there is no explicit mention of the Budget in the cooperation agreement (presumably because of the Green's unwillingness to provide unconditional support on supply). Whether the Greens will be excluded in practice from any participation in the annual Budget round is another matter. While they may not be given the opportunity to put in specific bids, as happened during the Budgets of 2000–02, their prior involvement in the budgetary process will have various ongoing implications. To illustrate, budgetary allocations are frequently made for out-years (i.e. the years beyond the fiscal year for which the Budget is prepared), with the implementation of the relevant policy decisions occurring over an extended period. As a result, the Greens will have a continuing role with respect to specific ministers and programmes arising from some of the budgetary allocations that were announced during the 2000–02 period. This provides another example of the importance of 'path dependence' in the political process.

On the subject of consultation between the government and the Greens, the cooperation agreement distinguishes between three different levels or degrees of engagement: full participation, consultation, and the sharing of information. To quote the agreement:

Category A
- Full participation of Green Party spokespeople in the development of policy positions with the expectation of developing joint positions.

Category B
- Consultation on the broad direction of policy, and the development of related legislation, with the aim of achieving support for legislative measures and/or policy proposals.

Category C
- Consultation for the purposes of information sharing without any particular expectation of developing agreed positions.

Issues will be assigned to a category by agreement and the procedures which will be followed will be dependent on that assignment.

The cooperation agreement includes an appendix setting out in some detail the nature of the minimum consultation expectations under each of the three categories.

It remains to be seen how the universe of issues will be divided between these categories and, in particular, which matters will be assigned to Category A. Potentially, however, the Greens may be in a position to have as much involvement – and influence – in the policy process as United Future, at least in those portfolio areas where their policy positions are closer to the government than those of United Future (and all the more so if and when the moratorium issue is resolved). Significantly, a Cabinet Office Circular (see Cabinet Office 2002) outlining consultation arrangements in the wake of the support and cooperation agreements makes no substantive distinction between United Future and the Greens (in terms of how they will be treated by the government), and assumes that the nature and extent of their involvement 'in the development of issues will vary according to subject'. This means, in effect, that the three categories of engagement will be applied to United Future in much the same way as they are applied to the Greens. Viewed from this perspective, the only substantive difference in the government's relationship with the two parties might be that United Future is favoured in terms of the number of issues that are handled under the provisions of Categories A and B. Having said this, there is another dimension which should not be ignored, namely the government's assurances that it will treat United Future as its 'preferred partner', and thus its first port-of-call when seeking legislative support. If such assurances are not fulfilled, the relationship between United Future and the government is bound to come under strain.

Only one specific policy matter is mentioned in the cooperation agreement. Given the respective parties' concerns about the performance of the Environmental Risk Management Authority (ERMA), especially its handling of matters relating to genetic modification, it was agreed that there should be a review of 'certain aspects of ERMA's . . . operation to ensure it is capable of providing a robust mechanism to fully implement those parts of the HSNO (Hazardous Substances and New Organisms) Act relevant to new organisms, in a manner consistent with the purpose of the Act'. The government agreed to consult the Greens over the scope of the review and who would conduct it. Labour's quick acceptance of the idea of holding an independent inquiry into the very matter that had precipitated its heated conflict with the Greens during the election campaign is significant. Presumably, it reflects the fact that senior ministers shared at least some of the Greens' concerns about the way ERMA had managed the events surrounding the possible release of genetically modified sweet corn seeds several years earlier.

Whatever the impact of the support and cooperation agreements hammered out in August 2002 on the conduct of policy making under the Labour-Progressive government, and whatever their impact on the relative political influence of United Future and the Greens, the decision to negotiate and sign such documents is bound to set a lasting precedent. Not only will minority governments be expected – for political and constitutional reasons – to have formal support agreements, but henceforth potential support parties are also likely to regard a suitably worded accord – with governmental concessions on their key policy goals – as an essential condition for any commitment on confidence and supply. Equally, any party such as the Greens that has ideological affinities with the governing parties, yet for one reason or another is unwilling to offer unconditional support on confidence and supply, can be expected to seek an appropriately worded cooperation agreement. For a government to refuse to negotiate such an accord might well be seen as an act of bad faith. The events of August 2002, therefore, seem destined to influence the nature and pattern of interparty relationships in the MMP environment for many years to come.

The Labour-Progressive Cabinet

The Labour-Alliance coalition formed in December 1999 consisted of 20 Cabinet ministers, five ministers outside Cabinet, and one undersecretary, giving a total of 26 office holders. This was comparable to that of the National-New Zealand First ministry formed three years earlier, although that had six ministers outside Cabinet, and no undersecretaries. The Labour-Progressive government, sworn in on 15 August 2002, consisted of 20 Cabinet ministers, six ministers outside Cabinet, and two undersecretaries. In total, therefore, the executive numbered 28, among the largest in the country's history. Additionally, the prime minister appointed three parliamentary private secretaries (PPSs) to assist some of the busier ministers. Of the 28 members of the ministry, there are eight women (three fewer than in late 1999), five Maori (one more than in 1999, but only two inside Cabinet), and two with Pacific Island backgrounds. As expected, the Progressives secured one Cabinet post, with Anderton retaining his responsibilities for economic development, industry and regional development (and becoming Associate Minister of Health). But he ceased to be Deputy Prime Minister, as that post went to Cullen.

Clark's decision to increase somewhat the size of the executive was influenced by several factors. First, her caucus included a significant number of MPs who believed themselves to be deserving of promotion. To thwart too many ambitions might provoke internal dissent and prove politically costly. Second, pressure from United Future and the Greens meant that Labour would chair fewer select committees than in the previous Parliament. There were thus a number of senior backbenchers who needed to be found alternative avenues for channeling their energies. But whatever the justifications, the result gave over 50 percent of Labour's MPs positions of some kind within the executive, thereby ensuring that the Cabinet maintained, if not enhanced, its dominance of the parliamentary party.

As for the allocation of portfolios and overall structure of the ministry, there were few significant changes. All the senior ministers retained their major areas of responsibility. Likewise, as in the past, no significant portfolios were allocated to ministers outside Cabinet. The prime minister signalled her clear intention, however, to make more substantial changes later in the parliamentary term, once the government had more fully implemented its major policy reforms in areas such as tertiary education, social assistance and health care.

Clark's decision to appoint three PPSs represented a significant departure from previous New Zealand traditions. Prior to this, there had been only one instance of a prime minister appointing a PPS, namely David Lange's recruitment of Noel Scott in the mid-1980s to assist him with the Education portfolio. Those appointed as PPSs in 2002 were: Tim Barnett (who assists the Minister of Justice on human rights issues, the Minister for the Community and Voluntary Sector, and the Minister of Social Services and Employment); David Cunliffe (who assists the Ministers of Finance, Revenue and Commerce); and Nanaia Mahuta (who assists the Ministers of Local Government and Education). It is expected that one or more of these MPs will be elevated to ministerial status as and when positions become available (as a result of retirements or resignations). In some other jurisdictions, most notably Britain, it has been a long-standing practice for Cabinet ministers to have PPSs. Whether such an arrangement becomes well-established in New Zealand remains to be seen. Even if it does, however, the small size of the House, together with the limited pool of available talent, means that PPSs are likely to remain relatively few in number.

The coalition's policy programme

The new government's policy programme was negotiated during mid-August and enunciated by the Governor-General, Dame Silvia Cartwright, in the Speech from the Throne on 27 August. In keeping with the approach adopted in late 1999, the 2002 statement outlined a moderate programme of reform, designed to achieve the government's core objectives: increasing economic growth, reducing inequality, and improving the social and economic well-being of New Zealanders and their families, in a manner which is environmentally, socially and economically sustainable. Key commitments included:
- Achieving a rate of economic growth over the medium to longer term sufficient to improve New Zealand's GDP per capita, not merely in real terms, but also relative to the OECD average
- Maintaining fiscal surpluses (to help pay for the Superannuation Fund and keep gross government debt at manageable levels)

- Adopting a more flexible approach to monetary policy management
- Ratifying the Kyoto Protocol
- Extending eligibility for student allowances, and developing a system of maximum fees within the tertiary education sector
- Enhancing infrastructure investment, foreign direct investment, and the funding of research
- Lifting the moratorium on the commercial release of genetically modified organisms, and conducting a review of the effectiveness of ERMA
- Simplifying and reforming social assistance programmes
- Implementing the primary health care strategy enunciated in early 2002
- Developing an integrated and balanced family-friendly work/life programme
- Improving the process for the settlement of claims under the Treaty of Waitangi.

Given the government's commitment to maintaining a relatively tight fiscal strategy, and the very limited amount of additional expenditure which is available over the medium term, there will be little scope for large-scale policy initiatives to alleviate family poverty, or a rapid expansion of existing social, education or health services. In all likelihood, therefore, the government can be expected to adopt an incrementalist approach, with any costly initiatives being implemented over a relatively long timeframe.

Government durability

Since the electoral referendum in 1993, New Zealand has experienced a marked decline in government durability (see Boston, Church and Bale 2002).[10] Indeed, thus far no Cabinet has survived with exactly the same party configuration for a full three-year parliamentary term. In one case (February 1996), another party joined the government. In other case (August 1998), the junior coalition partner split in two, with half the party leaving the government. In yet another case (April 2002), the junior coalition party divided after months of internal wrangling. While both factions remained in the government, the events surrounding the party's disintegration contributed to the calling of an early election. Given this track record, can there be much confidence that the Labour-Progressive government will survive a full three-year term? In our view, an affirmative answer is plausible.

First, New Zealand is very likely to retain a centre-left government for at least the next three years. The three centre-left parties are all relatively stable internally, and enjoy an adequate parliamentary majority. In effect, they can afford to lose at least two MPs as a result of by-election losses or defections before there could be any possibility of an early election or a change of government. Second, it is unlikely that the prime minister will be tempted to call another early election, at least not in the absence of compelling reasons. Third, it is doubtful whether United Future will make a determined bid to join the government during the current parliamentary term, and even if it did, Labour is unlikely to favour such an initiative. Equally, the risk of United Future withdrawing support for the government is low: for one thing, the party has given a three-year commitment; for another, it has made much of its role as a responsible centre party that can be relied on to act in a 'common sense' fashion, and in the interests of political stability. In view of this, it would need very strong reasons for reneging on the support agreement. Moreover, even if it did, the Greens are unlikely to precipitate an early election, notwithstanding their previous threats. For all these reasons, the Labour-Progressive government probably has the best chance of any government since the early 1990s of surviving a three-year term.

But what are the prospects of a centre-left government continuing beyond the next election? There are two circumstances under which a Labour-led government might be possible beyond 2005: the retention by the centre-left parties of a parliamentary majority, or a willingness on the part of United Future (or another possible centrist party) to support the centre-left rather than the centre-right, in circumstances where the two blocs were both in a position to accede to office.

Empirical studies consistently indicate that close to two-thirds of governments in parliamentary democracies lose votes at elections (Müller and Strøm 2000, p.588). Overall, their net losses average around 2 percent of the total vote. However, minority governments, on average, lose only around 1 percent (Strøm 1990, p.124). If the combined voter support for Labour and the Progressives were to fall by only 1 percent in 2005, and if the Greens were – at the very least – to maintain their share of the party vote, then there is a reasonable prospect that the centre-left would retain a small parliamentary majority. If, on the other hand, the centre-right (including United Future) secured a majority, the shape of the government would depend on the nature and configuration of the centre-right parties, and whether United Future, if it held the balance of power, preferred to support a Labour-led government, or a government of the centre-right. If the parties of the centre-right were to remain relatively fragmented, it is certainly possible to envisage a situation in which United Future might consider that a less fractionalised centre-left government would be both in its own and in the national interest.[11] However, at this juncture one can do little more than speculate.

Conclusion

As in 1999, the 2002 election delivered a clear majority to the parties of the centre-left, thus enabling the main elements of the previous coalition government to remain in office, albeit with Anderton's new party having a much reduced role and influence relative to that of the Alliance almost three years earlier. Again, as in 1999, the various negotiations between the parties were conducted swiftly and expeditiously, thereby demonstrating that proportional representation is not inimical to the rapid formation of governments – at least if the parties in question are prepared to act in a cooperative fashion, and are willing to eschew detailed agreements.

The formation of yet another *minority* administration – technically the seventh in New Zealand since 1995 – should not be regarded as a surprising result, notwithstanding the expectations of many coalition theorists. Minority governments are common in countries with proportional representation; in fact, in some European democracies, especially in Scandinavia, they are the norm (see Lijphart 1999; Strøm 1990). Given the mathematics of the 2002 election results, Labour's conflict with the Greens over genetic modification, and the relative inexperience of United Future, a *majority* executive coalition was not a politically attractive outcome for any of the four parties most directly involved.

For the reasons outlined in the preceding discussion, there is every likelihood that the new minority government will survive for a full three-year term. To be sure, Labour will face the challenge of simultaneously balancing the interests and policy preferences of three other parties – a coalition partner, a support party and a cooperating party. This will not always be easy, but two of these parties (the Progressives and the Greens) have a vested interest in ensuring the survival of a centre-left government, and the other (United Future) has an equally strong interest in building its reputation as a reasonable, common sense party committed to political stability and moderation. Given these considerations, the government can expect to secure majority support for most of its legislative initiatives, and will have only itself to blame if it mishandles the art and craft of coalition management.

NOTES

Preface

1. The chapters by party officials and organisers (in the second section of the book) are presented in alphabetical sequence by party name (i.e. the ACT chapter comes first and the United Future chapter comes last). The same applies to chapters 12 to 15 (i.e. the chapters by various party candidates in general electorates).
2. The Progressive Coalition was not formed in time to qualify for the allocation of broadcasting funds and time from the Electoral Commission and, as a result, had neither television advertisements nor opening and closing campaign statements.

1 New Zealand Votes: An Overview

1. For an overall treatment of 'mixed' electoral systems, see Shugart and Wattenberg 2001. The New Zealand experience is considered in Denemark 2001 and in Barker, Boston, Levine, McLeay and Roberts 2001.
2. A brief exception to this otherwise uninterrupted flow of first-past-the-post elections occurred in 1908 and 1911, when New Zealand introduced a 'second ballot' system for parliamentary elections. The system proved to be only a brief experiment: see Royal Commission on the Electoral System 1986, pp.A-50 to A-53.
3. There was a majority government for less than 20 months of the first six years of MMP. Since mid-1998, New Zealand has been governed by a succession of minority governments.
4. The Labour Party was quick to refute any suggestion that a 'snap election' had been called. Use of the term was discouraged, in favour of 'early election'.
5. Anderton was clearly an exception to this, which in turn generated criticism of him from within his own party.
6. See, for instance, Hunn and Smith 2000.
7. For instance, the turnout at the British General Election of 2001 was 59.4 percent (http://www.electionworld.org/errors/404.html). Turnout at the 2002 New Zealand election was probably influenced by expectations about the election result. Labour's return to power in both countries had been accepted as virtually a foregone conclusion.

2 Going Early

1. Under the new law Anderton would have been able to contest a by-election, since he held an electorate seat.

2   Even if the three Alliance MPs who identified with the anti-Anderton group were to split away, the government would still have had 56 votes, plus seven from the Greens.
3   The Greens are philosophically opposed to the taking of urgency. In practical terms, minority governments have to be sure of their parliamentary support for their legislative tactics to be successful. Thus the Greens were in a powerful position procedurally.
4   During the campaign the police announced that there was prima facie evidence of forgery but that there was not a sufficient case to warrant prosecution.
5   After the 1981 election National had 47 seats, Labour 43, and Social Credit 2. By the end of that Parliament, two Labour MPs had become Independents, but National MPs Waring and Mike Minogue had crossed the floor several times.
6   This would have required co-operation between Labour and Social Credit, plus either Waring and Minogue or the two Independent ex-Labour MPs, John Kirk and Brian MacDonell.
7   The correspondence between Bowen and Stafford is recorded in *Parliamentary Debates* 1872, pp.580–582. It should be noted that it was relatively common for governments to lose the confidence of the House in this period, and they were often replaced mid-term rather than resorting to an election. For example, the second Fox government resigned after losing a vote relating to the control of native affairs (*Parliamentary Debates* 1861–1863, p.476), while the third Fox government lost three consecutive votes relating to the implementation of public works and immigration schemes (*Parliamentary Debates* 1872, p.156).
8   In June 1884 the Atkinson Government tied and lost two votes relating to supply, which led Atkinson to request an early dissolution to settle the matter (*Parliamentary Debates* 1884, p.4; *Parliamentary Debates* 1884, pp.193, 312). Similarly, in 1887 after defeats in the House on tariff legislation and other financial proposals of the government, the Stout ministry considered its position and sought a dissolution (*Parliamentary Debates* 1887, pp.535, 540).

3 Two Million Voters in Search of a Rationale

1   The policy reforms after 1984 coincided with the assumption of independence, in the sense that in that period the nation developed a much more distinctive voice in an explosion of literature, music of all forms, film and graphic arts, as a generation born after 1945, not sharing its parents' sentimental attachment to Britain and with sharply different values, came to maturity and made itself felt. The period should thus be seen as the independence revolution, the emergence from colony.
2   Tactical voting of the sort seen in the party vote in 2002 had been seen in embryo in electorate voting in the late 1970s and early 1980s. In seats where the third party, Social Credit, reached a certain critical mass, supporters of the underdog main party (usually Labour in safe National seats, but it did happen also to National in some safe Labour seats) would move to Social Credit as the more credible option to unseat the enemy. In three seats, all National-held, this won Social Credit the seat. In the one seat where Social Credit did well but where neither main party could be considered weak, there was a three-way fight and Social Credit could not quite win the seat.
3   That voters grasped the importance of the party vote is born out by the *Herald* DigiPoll post-election poll of 500 taken on 30 and 31 July: 79 percent said the party vote was more important (17 percent said the electorate vote); 92 percent of United Future voters, 90 percent of Greens and 84 percent of ACT voters were clear it was the party vote.
4   Clark and Anderton campaigned for the return of a government which explicitly contained both.

5   Discussion on 7 August with Wyatt Creech, former Deputy Prime Minister, with special reference to the Wairarapa electorate.
6   The TV1 Colmar Brunton pre-election 'issues survey', showing a drop in distrust of politicians and the government from 75 percent in 1999 to 66 percent, might be partly due to Clark's perceived authority and her message that she had done during the term what she had promised to do in 1999.
7   This in itself was a most unusual event. At Science Minister Pete Hodgson's request, State Services Commissioner Michael Wintringham convened a press conference of officials from the Ministry for the Environment, the Ministry of Agriculture and Forestry and the Environmental Risk Management Authority. Hodgson introduced the officials and remained in the room. While the officials conducted themselves properly, sticking to facts and events, that they did so on a matter of high importance to the course and outcome of the campaign has raised important issues for future consideration if the political neutrality of the public service is not to be jeopardised in the public's eyes.
8   After the election, Labour ministers were angry at media coverage of Labour in the campaign. Helen Clark is reported to have spent a good part of the first meeting of the new Labour caucus lambasting the media. Apart from the 'corn' and the 'worm', ministers complained at a style of television interviewing that constantly and intrusively interrupted answers to questions.
9   This was in answer to the questions 'which one of these [nominated] issues do you personally believe is most important to you, your family and your life personally right now?' and 'which other four issues do you personally believe . . .', etc. Similar, though slightly different, results were recorded to near-identical questions as to which issues were 'most important to New Zealand as a country'. Likewise, the rankings were similar, though again slightly different, when the question was phrased as 'issues . . . you personally believe will have the most influence on your decision of which party to vote for'.
10 However, only 16 percent told the *Herald* DigiPoll post-election poll that they expected 'a year from now that either they or their family will be better off', 2 percent more than expected to be worse off. To this needs to be added, however, the 64 percent who expected things to be the same.
11 This was a significant finding from a panel of 50 Kapiti electorate voters, who were interviewed periodically on issues of the day for six months leading up to the election. The survey, which I organised, was funded by, and periodically reported on in, the *National Business Review*.
12 It should be noted, however, that in March 2003 the Health Select Committee's report on the Smoke Free Environments (Enhanced Protection) Amendment Bill recommended removing exceptions in the original legislation that allowed smoking in bars.
13 Clark's policy repositioning, her own cautious (conservative) style of prime ministership and the reduction in the temperature of political debate may have been factors in the TV1 Colmar Brunton pre-election issues survey's finding that only 35 percent agreed strongly with the proposition that 'you cannot trust politicians or the government' compared with 50 percent in 1999; 31 percent agreed, compared with 25 percent in 1999. Some 87 percent agreed that 'New Zealand is the best country to live in' (60 percent in 1999); 93 percent agreed that 'New Zealand is a great place to raise a family'; 70 percent disagreed that 'New Zealand does not offer a lot of opportunities' (48 percent); and 53 percent were 'happy with the direction New Zealand is moving in' (30 percent).

14 The TV1 Colmar Brunton pre-election 'issues survey' recorded 49 percent agreeing strongly with the proposition that 'people don't put enough effort into families and relationships any more' and another 27 percent agreeing slightly.
15 The *Herald* DigiPoll post-election poll found 54 percent preferring MMP to 30 percent FPP, with predictably higher pro-MMP ratings among Labour, Green and United Future voters. Some 71 percent said the 'MMP system of two votes worked well on Saturday', again with higher positive figures among Labour, Green and United Future voters. Notably, however, only 55 percent thought the result would produce a stable government (Labour voters were 73 percent confident).
16 Helen Clark's opportunistic calling of an early election against tradition means that, quite apart from possible instability among her partners, no confidence can be placed in the present Parliament running full term. It is perhaps interesting that some ministers are sympathetic to the idea of a fixed term for Parliament.

4 Leadership and the Campaign

1 For the purposes of this paper, the following definition of political leadership is made:
Political leadership is a dynamic interaction that occurs between an elected leadership (whether individual or group based) and its citizenry. It is mediated to varying degrees by situational constraints and opportunities. A leader or leaders combining power and purpose to achieve certain shared objectives with the citizenry characterises the leadership interaction.
2 The TV3 NFO poll was at one extreme among the various polls, generally giving Labour its highest levels of support when compared with other polls. Like many other analysts, I have generally used a poll average drawn from the TV1 Colmar Brunton, *Herald* DigiPoll, TV3 NFO and the NBR HP-Invent polls. The polls had last converged during the so-called 'winter of discontent,' when business confidence slumped and the government's flagship 'Closing the Gaps' policy was sapping its popularity. While Labour recovered, and never dropped below National again, the gap between the two old parties grew dramatically after the events of September 11 and the government's response in support of 'The War Against Terror.'
3 Weller's six factors influencing the relative power weightings between a prime minister and their Cabinet ministers were: the right to select and dismiss ministers; the right to control Cabinet's structure and proceedings; the development of disciplined parties supporting the prime minister; the increased direct influence of the media; an increase in the levels of prime ministerial patronage; and new processes of co-ordination providing greater intelligence and manipulative potential for the prime minister to control the bureaucracy.
4 Lincoln's journey to the presidency was built on the back of considerable perseverance in overcoming continued setbacks throughout his career. He was defeated in his various attempts to win public office six times during his political career, before finally winning the presidency at age 51. As for Clark, her political setbacks and disappointments include her being overlooked for Cabinet in 1984; continued poor poll performance as Labour leader while in opposition; having her leadership challenged prior to the 1996 election; and seeing New Zealand First decide to coalesce with National in 1996, thereby failing to become New Zealand's first woman prime minister. More generally, it took a great deal of perseverance and skill for Clark to endure the rise of the neo-liberals during the two terms of the fourth Labour Government and the disastrous defeat that ensued in 1990.

5   To elaborate, the 14 questions and the four leadership categories comprise: integrity (is more honest than most politicians); competence (is a capable leader, would be good in a crisis, has sound judgement, understands the economic problems facing New Zealand); positive image (is down to earth, has a lot of personality, is in touch with the needs of Maori); and negative image (has more style than substance, tends to talk down to people, is rather narrow minded, is too inflexible, is rather inexperienced, and is out of touch with ordinary people).

6   The material in this section has been drawn from TV3's leaders' debates on 4 and 25 July, Sky News election debates conducted by Bill Ralston with respective party leaders, TV1's 'worm' debate held on 15 July, and Kim Hill's interview with Bill English on 19 July 2002.

7   The term 'negalitarian' is my label for the longstanding cultural strand referred to popularly as the 'tall poppy syndrome'. Leslie Lipson described the cultural strand as a 'perverted equalitarianism' in *The Politics of Equality*, going on to write: 'In its anxiety to raise minima, the country has deemed it necessary to lower maxima' (Lipson 1948, p.491).

8   Labour's seven new pledges were quite non-specific, its targets vague and inexact. The pledges were:
    - Work with all sectors to create an innovative economy with more jobs
    - Better access to primary health care so problems can be tackled early
    - Keep tertiary education affordable. Get more teachers into schools
    - Put government funds aside now to guarantee current super for everyone in the future
    - Double the number of modern apprenticeships
    - Tougher sentences for the most serious offenders. More support for proven programmes to cut youth offending
    - No rise in rates of income tax, GST or company tax.

9   Michelle Boag said publicly (and rather unwisely) that National would not mind if some of its Epsom voters wanted to give ACT their party vote and National candidate Richard Worth their electorate vote.

5 The Electoral Commission and the 2002 General Election

1   The views expressed in this article are those of the author and are not necessarily those of the Electoral Commission.

2   Since this article was written, the terms of reference for the Justice and Electoral Select Committee's inquiry into the 2002 general election have been announced, and include the current election broadcasting regime.

6 ACT III

1   ACT averaged 4.4 percent in *One Network News* surveys, 5.0 percent in *National Business Review* surveys, and 4.0 percent in TV3 surveys from November 1999 to July 2002.

2   Of course, this ignores the possibility that an effective party can exert a (limited) degree of influence over a government from opposition. However, it appears that this possibility is not a strong attraction to floating voters in the political centre.

3   Many of those interested in health policy recognised that government cannot afford a comprehensive health system and believed that no party offered a credible solution to this problem. Further, voters didn't have a clear picture of anyone's (not just ACT's) health policy. A party's health policy tended to be remembered by those who supported them,

though the causal relationship between recall and support is unclear.
4   These figures are somewhat extreme as they are daily figures. The tracking poll used a small daily sample size which is not statistically significant on its own.
5   For further details on the gender division among ACT voters, see chapter 27.
6   Webcasting is the broadcasting of sound or images over the web. ACT webcast all daily press conferences during the campaign live so that they could be watched by commentators, supporters, and members anywhere around the country or the world. Our international campaign launch in Auckland also featured a webcast address from ACT's London coordinator.
7   Readers may be interested to note that ACT has announced its intention to contest electorates and seek electorate votes at the next general election (*Dominion Post* 2 September 2003, p.2) – Eds.

13 Being a Green Candidate

1   In 1999 Nandor Tanczos won 3,057 electorate votes (9.4 percent) in Auckland Central; in 2002 he received 6,212 electorate votes (20.2 percent).

15 'Out of my Comfort Zone'

1   As the chapter in *From Campaign to Coalition* on the 1996 ACT campaign noted: 'The closing act of this drama occurred two days before the election when Prime Minister Jim Bolger, speaking on national television, picked a Prebble victory in Wellington Central.' (Fraser and Zangouropoulos 1997, p.56.)

19 Window on Wairarapa

1   This chapter draws heavily on interviews with Labour Party members in Wairarapa, as well as from accounts in the *Wairarapa Times-Age* and in regional economic publications.
2   It might be noted that Social Credit polled reasonably well in Wairarapa, with a high of 19.5 percent achieved in 1981.
3   This section is based both on Georgina Beyer's biography, *Change for the Better*, and on time spent with her as an intern for six weeks in October–November 2001, and briefly again during the election campaign in June–July 2002.
4   The three times previously that Labour had won the Wairarapa seat involved substantially smaller margins than were achieved by Beyer: 1969 saw a 3.4 percent margin of victory; in 1972 Labour won by 6.1 percent; and in 1984, Labour won by 1.8 percent. Georgina Beyer's margin in 1999 was 9.3 percent.

20 Choosing Candidates

1   Personal interviews were held with: Michelle Boag (President of the National Party); Gill Boddy-Greer (Labour candidate for Ohariu-Belmont); Darren Hughes (Labour MP for Otaki); Glenda Hughes, (National candidate for Rongotai); Annette King (Labour MP for Rongotai; Minister of Health); Neil Miller (Director of the National Party parliamentary research unit); Hekia Parata (National candidate for Wellington Central); Grant Robertson (Senior Adviser in the Office of the [Labour] Prime Minister); Dale Stephens, National candidate for Ohariu-Belmont; Sue Wood (National candidate for Mana; former President

of the National Party); and Mike Williams (President of the Labour Party).
2 It should be noted, however, that none of these independent MPs was initially elected as an independent. Rather, these were MPs elected under the banner of one party who subsequently left that party while in Parliament.
3 If the contested spot is below number 20 on the regional list, however (in practice meaning that the spot is of no importance), it is dealt with by a single vote over a block of five list slots (NZLP 2001, s.258).
4 One National Party observer did note, however, that the extra-parliamentary party has lost considerable financial and political power to the party's MPs over the last 20 years.
5 It should be noted, however, that some National Party interviewees also cited a poor speech at the regional conference, a reliance by Hughes on the power of her previous publicity, and a naiveté on her part as to the realities of the voting process and the consequent need for lobbying by candidates.
6 A rare instance of New Zealand political science focusing on candidate selection can be found in the research carried out by Simon Sheppard on the influence of competing Labour Party factions in the 1987–1993 period (see Sheppard 1998).
7 It should be noted that the rise in ACT's vote was minimal – from 7.0 percent in 1999 to 7.1 percent in 2002. On both occasions, the party won nine seats in the House of Representatives.

22 News, Newszak, New Zealand

1 Talk of crowding out, however, should not stop us acknowledging the possibility that viewer interest sparked by the 'horse race and hoopla' may facilitate viewer interest in issues (Zhao and Bleske 1998).
2 Those who determine the content of broadcast news seem to pay very little attention to these public issue preferences – even though their own polling, as, for instance, TV3 acknowledged in its eve-of-poll news programme, makes them plain as day. If 'public journalism' (the attempt by news organisations to give their consumers a role in setting the news agenda, and to provide a problem-solution frame rather than simply a conflict frame in their coverage) has a foothold in New Zealand, it would appear to be in the print rather than in the broadcast media (see Venables 2002; McGregor, Comrie and Fountaine 1999). This is not the case elsewhere: in recent years, for instance, the BBC has made serious attempts to structure its election coverage around the public's professed interests (Blumler and Gurevitch 2001, p.389). Given the overseas research which suggests that people actually prefer to watch coverage which focuses on analysis of what they regard as real issues rather than 'horse-race news' (see Just et al. 1996, p.240), broadcasters might ask themselves whether rebalancing their output may in fact make financial as well as 'civic' sense.
3 Much of what parties serve up and the media more or less digest during campaigns is pre-cooked. Whether, however, this renders such media events somehow fake or unreal, is another matter. As Fiske (1996, p.2) points out: 'The term media event is an indication that in a postmodern world we can no longer rely on a stable relationship or clear distinction between a 'real' event and its mediated representation. Consequently, we can no longer work with the idea that the 'real' is more important, significant, or even 'true' than the representation. A media event, then, is not a mere representation of what happened, but it has its own reality, which gathers up into itself the reality of the event that may or may not have preceded it.'

4   Mancini and Swanson (1996a, p.273), having touched on the way the 'spiraling fashion' of counter-responses between politicians and journalists leads to both becoming so 'preoccupied with their escalating struggle within a closed circuit of discourse' that voters' concerns almost disappear from view, observe that the resulting negative atmosphere suits politicians who characterise themselves as outsiders who can clean up politics. They may well have been thinking of Ross Perot, but there are politicians in New Zealand who also spring to mind. See Bale (2002b).

5   Coverage of the dispute merits a case study of its own. Suffice to say that it was served up on both networks with conflict rather than content in mind, by reporters who apparently thought viewers so clueless that they needed to be reminded day after day that the government wanted it settled, since it gave it 'a chance to try to score some campaign points' (*One News*, 18 July).

6   With the possible exception of TV1's current affairs show *Sunday* (during which party representatives were given a grilling by invited panels of journalists, or members of the public) and the late-evening, one-on-one interviews conducted on the same channel by the redoubtable Kim Hill, most of television's election efforts outside news broadcasts and leader's debates, were, to coin a phrase from an analysis of such programming in the UK, little more than 'low-budget, non-peak-time public service fig-leaves' (Barnett and Gaber 2001, p.85). There was no equivalent in 2002 of the *Decision 99: The Issues* programmes, each of which was devoted to the topics that survey research indicated were of most concern to voters (see Church 2000a) – perhaps because these had garnered low ratings, even for the Saturday evening graveyard slot they were allotted.

7   Barnett makes the point that in the UK, the tabloid press is at the cutting edge of the tendency to see politicians not as for the most part 'honest, honourable individuals doing their damnedest to make their country a better place' but rather (in the words of a *Sun* editorial) as 'sad, sordid, pathetic, inadequate wimps with private lives that make ordinary people's stomachs churn' (Barnett 2002, p.405); but he also notes the tendency of television to follow such a lead. Possibly the absence of a tabloid culture – as well as the familiarity between what are inevitably small numbers of journalists and politicians – will insulate New Zealand from the full impact of such a development.

8   Perhaps the prime minister's ferocious response was not so much proof that she'd been caught out, as some opponents alleged, as simply anger that journalists were for a second time biting the hand that had fed them so well for the previous two-and-a-half years: surely she had not spent all that time becoming the acme of accessibility, only to be ambushed by tough questions on topics not submitted to her team in advance? One can't help but wonder as well whether she felt let down by her own team whose job it was to anticipate questions and assist her in preparing responses, as they had done on other stories (O'Leary 2002, p.194)?

9   The guru behind the UK Labour Party's media operations urges those who would learn from the party (a group which definitely includes Labour in New Zealand) that 'You must always rebut a political attack.-. ...And you must do it instantly, within minutes at best, within hours at worst, and with a defence supported by the facts' (Gould, 1998, p.295)

10 Those interested in the impact of intra-media imperatives and the 24-hour news cycle would do well to consult Kovach and Rosenstiel 1999.

11 As someone who hastened (nay rushed!) into print on the politics of the matter (see Bale 2002a), the only thing which prevents me issuing my own shamefaced *mea culpa* is a residual

belief in a division of labour between newspaper columnists and reporters and editors. In any case, although political scientists appearing in the media admittedly risk augmenting rather than arresting its tendency to focus on the game of politics rather than its substance, it would be blowing their importance out of all proportion to suggest that they are one of the drivers behind it!

12 Some, of course, argue that the premium put on opinion makes more sense than ever in the age of the internet, since information is now easily available, but risks drowning out the interpretations that make sense of it. On the other hand, the premium, one suspects, predates the net!

13 'Denial of access is a relatively minor nuisance for a newspaper but for a broadcaster it is potentially disastrous, depriving the medium of the voice or picture of the central characters being reported' (Barnett and Gaber 2001, p.101; see also pp.7–8, 113).

14 A few scholars are more persuaded of the effect of the debates, with Schrott's work on Germany (see Schrott 1990) and Johnston's on New Zealand (see Johnston 1998) being obvious examples. But even so, most of them acknowledge the consensus view that any impact may best be put down to predisposed voters being mobilised rather than the neutral or the hostile being converted (see Johnston 1998, p.78). They are also forced to make a leap from correlation to causation – a problem that plagues most of the literature devoted to showing 'campaigning makes a difference'. But most is not all: one study of debate effects that persuasively overcomes the problem focuses on Spain in 1993, an election in which it seems enough of the (admittedly huge) audience for the (admittedly serious and substantive) final television debate between the leaders of the two biggest parties were swung by what they saw to keep the charismatic prime minister Felipe Gonzalez in office against predictions (see Gunther, Montero, and Wert 2000, pp.68–69).

15 For a summary of the arguments for and against the idea that campaigns make a difference (and a conclusion that the evidence is mixed, but that they just might in a close race) see Holbrook (1996, pp.5–20).

16 These lucky few were equipped with dials which they had to turn to one of four positions as they watched the leaders – the choices were *good*, *very good*, and (believe it or not) *dull*, or *very dull*!

17 Ever the no-nonsense pragmatist, Clark maintains 'that in the consumer age where political choice differs little in nature from the making of other product choices, the use of the worm to measure likes and dislikes was appropriate. . . . A device like the worm . . . is these days an entirely relevant tool to apply to the measuring of political performances.' See Clark 2000, p.127.

18 For the record, King (2002, p.216) concludes: 'In other words,. . .the almost universal belief that leaders' and candidates' personalities are almost invariably hugely important factors in determining the outcomes of elections is simply wrong. [They] usually count for something – of course they do – but not for nearly so much as is generally supposed. A traditional piece of lore thus turns out to be folklore, unable to withstand scientific scrutiny.'

19 The putative ability of opinion polls which show a rise in popularity to amplify that rise and translate it into actual votes is known by political scientists as a 'bandwagon' effect. In fact, most research evidence does little to support the idea that polls make much of a difference. For every bandwagon effect, one can also posit an 'underdog' or sympathy effect that cancels it out (see Ceci and Kain 1982). If, for instance, one party appears to be doing badly or to be slipping under the 5 percent threshold, as many voters may move to support

it as might jump on the bandwagon of a party that, by contrast, is doing well. But that is not to say that they never make a difference or that the difference, even if small, will not be important. Research suggests, for instance, that in 1999 opinion polls had no effects (positive or negative) on National, Labour, NZ First or ACT, but that the poll which first showed Jeanette Fitzsimons had a good chance of winning Coromandel might have added a crucial 1 percent to the Greens' final party vote (Vowles 2002).

20 The poll released on 22 July was taken over a weekend; it had a sample of only 512, and a margin of error of +/- 4.3 percent.
21 This should not be taken to suggest that the publication of opinion polls should be prohibited. Free speech arguments apart, they provide relevant information to voters looking to make strategic decisions, and they would be conducted in private (and then leaked) anyway (see Bale 2002c).
22 On 17 July, *3 News* asked rhetorically (though hardly self-reflectively) why the economy had been 'strangely absent' from the campaign, before leading into a package by the reporter in question which began 'Ten days out from polling day, now finally the political parties are beginning to trade insults over the economy' and focused so much on partisan costings of the various programmes that he left himself no room to tell us about their respective contents – not because he was in any way personally incapable of doing it, but because it just would not have fitted the conflictual game frame that the format (for which read producers) routinely demands.

24 'Read All About It!'

1 Wellington's morning daily, *The Dominion*, merged with the city's evening newspaper, *The Evening Post*, to become *The Dominion Post*, with the first issue of the new paper appearing on 8 July 2002.
2 We would like to thank those people who dutifully collected the newspapers for us throughout the election campaign.
3 The total column centimetres of election news for the papers were as follows: *The Herald*, 108,004; *The Dominion Post*, 56,426; *Otago Daily Times*, 49,625.
4 This included articles which exclusively covered one party – many articles that covered 'all parties' or a majority of the parties were not included.
5 Party coverage included coverage of the party leader.
6 The remaining coverage was on editorials which were not coded as either 'game' or substance.

25 All Over the Place

1 See chapter 27 for further details of the 2002 Victoria University survey.
2 Clearly e-democracy is still some way off in New Zealand – party websites were the most lowly rated medium of communication. Only 9 percent of respondents considered them to be particularly important.
3 Sue Wood was president of the National Party when Sir Robert Muldoon called the 1984 'snap election'. The pictures of her at the time, standing alongside a prime minister much the worse for drink, are some of the most poignant and memorable television images from the last quarter of the twentieth century in New Zealand.
4 See Table 1.2 in chapter 1 of this book.

5   After the MMP Sainte Laguë formula was used to allocate all the parties' seats in Parliament in the wake of the 2002 election, Katherine Rich, ranked at 14 on National's list, was the last National list MP to be elected. She was also the last list MP of *any* party to be elected – she won the last seat in the 120-member Parliament.
6   In 1999, for example, Braybrooke won 60.0 percent of the electorate vote in Napier, while Tolley won only 23.9 percent.
7   Salmon was ranked at 20 on National's list.
8   Stephens was also ranked at 46 on National's list.
9   The hand with three raised fingers in the centre looked oddly detached from Mr Peters' body in the billboard photo, but one can only assume that it was, indeed, Peters' hand.
10 New Zealand First won 4.3 percent of the party votes in 1999. It was a fascinating instance of lightning striking the same place twice, because in 1996 the Christian Coalition had also won 4.3 percent of the party votes. However, because the Christian Coalition did not win any electorate seats in 1996, it won no seats in the House of Representatives at that election (nor has it won any since).
11 In 2002, Wigram became the country's only other trigger seat in an MMP election. Jim Anderton won the seat, and although his Progressive Coalition Party (literally *his* party: for the purposes of the election it was called Jim Anderton's Progressive Coalition!) won only 1.7 percent of the party votes cast in the election, Anderton's election triggered the elevation of a second Progressive Coalition MP (list MP Matt Robson) into Parliament.
12 As a result, Peter Dunne became the closest in both 1996 and 1999 to being an 'overhang' MP.
13 Their electorates were Waitakere and Tainui respectively.
14 For more on the phrase 'two cheers for democracy', see Forster 1951.
15 Connie Ruth wore red on the campaign trail and in all her campaign photographs. All her advertisements, bumper stickers, leaflets and posters had a red background, and her campaign staff often wore red t-shirts.
16 For example, Connie Ruth's advertisements and posters completely avoided the fact that she was a Republican Party candidate for office. These observations arise out of an opportunity I had to study aspects of US political campaigning during a research visit to Minnesota in November 2002.
17 Two of the few good New Zealand instances of this form of political debate were (i) a corn-cob sticker placed over Helen Clark's mouth on Labour Party posters in 2002, after campaign accusations that the government had covered up the accidental planting of a genetically modified corn crop (an incident that was inevitably dubbed 'corngate' by the news media), and (ii) a 1999 ACT poster that was modified by the addition of a picture of Montgomery Burns, the wealthy entrepreneur and nuclear power station owner in *The Simpsons* television programme. See Hager 2002; and Boston, Church, Levine, McLeay and Roberts 2000, p.128e.
18 See McLauchlan 1976.

26 Representation, Selection, Election

1   I am grateful to Tim Bale and Jonathan Boston for their helpful comments on this chapter, and to Tim Bale and the Electoral Commission for their help with material on candidate selection.

2   Note that the nationwide 5 percent threshold can also involve electors in casting strategic votes. For example, they might be considering whether it is worth choosing a party that is at risk of falling below that threshold.
3   The survey was conducted by UMR Insight Ltd, and 750 people were surveyed. See also the data and discussion in Karp 2002.
4   This paper concentrates on comparative opportunities, rather than on whether or not representative groups make a difference to policy. On women and the issue of how many women legislators are needed before they can affect legislatures, see Grey 2002, and Studlar and McAllister 2002.
5   Despite a number of requests to the Progressive Coalition party, no information had been received on its selection method by the time of writing.

27 Consistent Patterns and Clear Trends

1   In Coromandel the Greens' co-leader, Jeanette Fitzsimons, was defeated by National's Sandra Goudie; in Hamilton East, Labour list MP Dianne Yates captured the seat from National's Tony Steel; and in Otago, National's Gavan Herlihy lost to Labour's David Parker.
2   These electorates were, respectively, Wigram, Coromandel, Tauranga, and Ohariu-Belmont.
3   The three electorates were Clutha-Southland, Rakaia, and Taranaki-King Country.
4   The survey was part of the New Zealand Political Change Project, a multi-faceted research programme into the consequences of MMP for New Zealand's government and politics funded by the New Zealand Foundation for Research, Science and Technology (FRST). We acknowledge with thanks the support given to the survey (and the overall project) by FRST. The interviews were conducted by Phoenix Research Limited.
5   Each of these nationwide MMP election surveys was complemented by a special study of a key electorate. In 1996, this was Wellington Central (which might have been needed to be won by the ACT Party in order to win representation). In 1999, it was Coromandel, which might have been necessary as a 'trigger' seat for the Greens, had they been unable to win more than 5 percent of the party vote. The electorate chosen for special study in 2002 was Tauranga, which had been won narrowly in 1999 by New Zealand First leader Winston Peters. His party had then won only 4.3 percent of the party vote, thus failing to clear the 5 percent threshold required to gain parliamentary representation. In 2002 Tauranga was thus potentially the key to the party's survival.
6   See, for example, the website of Phoenix Research, which includes statistical comparisons between the Victoria University pre-election survey and three other main polls, concluding: 'Careful attention to detail in the design and execution of the Victoria University survey conducted by Phoenix Research made it by far the most accurate forecast of the election result' (http://www.phoenix.co.nz/about/articles/phoenix_delivers.html).
7   Paradoxically this was also the case under FPP, when New Zealanders only had one vote for an electorate MP, and the overall result of an election was the aggregate of the separate constituency contests. Even then, reflecting the emphasis given by the media to nationwide polls, New Zealanders both felt more confident and were more accurate in predicting which party would win the election throughout the country as a whole, compared with the result in their own seat (Levine and Roberts 1991).
8   For details of National's earlier predominance with respect to party identification, see Levine and Roberts 1992a, p.53.

9   On the other hand, the two most significant gains were by New Zealand First (whose vote rose by 6.1 percent) and by United (with a rise of 6.2 percent).
10 In addition, the proportion of 1999 Alliance voters opting for the Greens in 2002 was roughly the same as those remaining with the 'official' Alliance remnant.
11 Since 1978, pre-election surveys by the authors of this chapter have also asked a series of questions designed to elicit New Zealanders' preferences for prime minister ultimately from among the leaders of the Labour and National parties only. In 2002 these questions produced the following result: Helen Clark was the choice of 66.4 percent of *all* respondents for the position of prime minister, Bill English of 28.4 percent. Unlike other opposition leaders in the past – notably Labour's Bill Rowling in 1978 and David Lange in 1984 – English was unable to close the gap with Clark in the sequence of questions gradually excluding other politicians and minor party leaders, so as to narrow the choice simply to the only two people with a real chance at the position after the election. For comparative data on prime ministerial preferences since 1978 (and a more elaborate explanation of the methodology), see Roberts 1980, p.243; Levine and Roberts 1987, pp.11–12; Levine and Roberts 1989, pp.425–428; Levine and Roberts 1991, pp.132–134; Levine and Roberts 1994, p.150; Levine and Roberts 1997, pp.192–193; and Levine and Roberts 2000, pp.171–173).
12 For the 1996 results on these questions, see Levine and Roberts 1997, pp.191–193; and for 1999, see Levine and Roberts 2000, pp.171–172.
13 He was named by only four out of the 1,000 survey respondents.
14 Peters' rating as 'least preferred prime minister' by 33 percent of respondents in 1999 remains the highest such score since we began surveying electors about this topic.
15 Reflecting this, only 5.6 percent of electors still regarded student loans as a particularly important personal issue. As a result, in 2002 the topic was not categorised separately and was included as part of an overall education category, along with people who mentioned the teachers' strike, teachers' pay and the National Certificate of Education Achievement (NCEA).
16 For much of the 1999–2002 term, Clark was ably assisted in developing the image of a government (and prime minister) in control through the efforts of her deputy prime minister, Jim Anderton, and her finance minister, Michael Cullen, the latter of whom had succeeded in cultivating improved links between the government and the business community after the government's somewhat shaky start in this area.
17 The contrast between assessments of the Clark-led government and the Labour government ousted in 1990 could not be more striking. In 1990 more than 20 percent of electors viewed the Fourth Labour government's performance as 'very poor' (Levine and Roberts 1992b, p.499).
18 Fewer than 1.3 percent of the electorate voted for the Alliance in 2002. This was accurately reflected in our sample, which means that the total number of Alliance voters unearthed by our interviewers was very small. The data thus need to be interpreted with caution.

28 Government Formation after the 2002 General Election

1   The authors wish to thank Natalie Baird, Dr Tim Bale, Rod Donald, Peter Dunne, Dr Chris Eichbaum, Dr Andrew Ladley, Deb Moran and Helen Patterson for their invaluable assistance with the preparation of this chapter.

2   For instance, see Boston (1997, 1998, 2000a), Boston and McLeay (1997), Hardie Boys (1998) and Miller (1998, 2002).

3   For analyses of the influence of institutional variables on the process of government formation, see Bergman (1995), Budge and Keman (1990), De Winter (1995), Laver and Schofield (1990), Laver and Shepsle (1996), and Strøm, Budge and Laver (1994).

4   See Boston (1994), Brechtel and Kaiser (1999) and Kaiser and Brechtel (1999).

5   For an analysis of the issues surrounding the 'median voter' and 'pivotal parties', see Budge and Keman (1990) and Laver and Shepsle (1996).

6   The election night results gave United Future nine seats and Labour 52. Thus, the two parties enjoyed a parliamentary majority of two seats, excluding the Progessive Coalition. It was recognised, however, that the results might change marginally once special votes were counted. In the event, United Future ended up with only eight seats. Accordingly, Labour was no longer in a position to rely solely on United Future for parliamentary support. By contrast, the Greens increased their final tally of seats from eight on election night to nine once special votes had been counted. As a result, Labour and the Greens enjoy a parliamentary majority.

7   This statement was based on some informal contacts between United Future and Labour during the previous few months.

8   The concept of 'path dependence' refers to the causal relevance of preceding stages in a temporal process, and hence the conclusion that the particular sequencing of events or processes may be a critical factor in explaining certain decisions or outcomes. More specifically, it is the idea that preceding steps in a particular direction tend to induce further steps in the very same direction (perhaps because the costs of changing direction become all the larger the further one proceeds down a particular path).

9   United Future was informed of progress in Labour's negotiations with the Greens once the support agreement had been concluded. Prior to this, United Future had correctly assumed, based on the demeanor of Labour's negotiators, that the government's relationship with the Greens was strained.

10 For the purposes of this discussion, the definition of a change of government includes a change in the party composition of the Cabinet, and a change in the parliamentary basis (or numerical status) of the government from a majority to a minority government and vice versa. While government durability has declined significantly since 1993, the degree of change in relation to the personnel serving in the Cabinet has been much less marked. In some cases, the same people have remained in office, but as members of a different party.

11 Interestingly, in the final stages of the 2002 election campaign, National implored United Future not to rule out a centre-right coalition (presumably embracing ACT, National, New Zealand First and United Future). This proposition, however, was rejected by United Future on the grounds that Labour was likely to remain the largest political party (by some distance) and because of the likely difficulties of governing when the support of four parties was required to secure a parliamentary majority.

REFERENCES

Aimer, Peter 1997, 'Leaders and Outcomes: The Clark Factor in 1996', in Jonathan Boston, Stephen Levine, Elizabeth McLeay and Nigel S. Roberts (eds), *From Campaign to Coalition: New Zealand's First General Election Under Proportional Representation*, Dunmore Press, Palmerston North.

Aimer, Peter 2001, 'The Changing Party System', in Raymond Miller (ed), *New Zealand Government and Politics*, Oxford University Press, Auckland, pp.271–82.

Aldrich, J. 1993, *Why Parties*, Chicago, University of Chicago Press.

Alley, Roderic 1992, 'The Powers of the Prime Minister,' in Hyam Gold (ed), *New Zealand Politics in Perspective* (3rd ed.) Auckland, Longman Paul, pp.174–193.

Apter, David 1991, 'Institutionalism reconsidered' in *International Social Science Journal*, vol. 8.

Bagnall, Austin G. 1976, *Wairarapa; An Historical Excursion*, Wright and Carman, Trentham.

Bale, Tim 2002a 'Lousy politics puts nation's trust at risk', *New Zealand Herald*, 12 July 2002.

Bale, Tim 2002b 'Identikit Populist Plays the Same Old Tune', *New Zealand Herald*, 23 July 2002.

Bale, Tim 2002c 'Restricting the Broadcast and Publication of Pre-election Opinion Polls: Some Selected Examples', *Representation*, vol. 39, no. 1, pp.15–22.

Bale, Tim and Dann, Christine 2002, 'Is the grass really greener? The rationale and reality of support party status: a New Zealand case study', *Party Politics*, vol. 8, no. 3, pp.349–365.

Bale, Tim, Boston, Jonathan and Church, Stephen 2002, 'Explaining the obvious: 'normal science', the new institutionalism, and the New Zealand government of 1999'. Paper presented to the workshop 'Government Formation: A Theoretically Informed Inductive Approach' at the ECPR Joint Sessions in Torino, March 22–27.

Banducci, Susan 2002, 'Gender and Leadership', in Jack Vowles et al., *Proportional Representation on Trial: the 1999 New Zealand General Election and the Fate of MMP*, Auckland University Press, Auckland.

Banducci, Susan and Vowles, Jack 2002, 'Elections, Citizens and the Media', in Jack Vowles et al., *Proportional Representation on Trial: the 1999 New Zealand General Election and the Fate of MMP*, Auckland University Press, Auckland.

Barker, Fiona, Boston, Jonathan, Levine, Stephen, McLeay, Elizabeth and Roberts, Nigel S. 2001, 'An Initial Assessment of the Consequences of MMP', in Matthew Shugart and Martin Wattenberg (eds), *Mixed-Member Electoral Systems: The Best of Both Worlds?*, Oxford University Press, Oxford, pp. 297–322.

Barnett, Steven 2002, 'Will a Crisis in Journalism Provoke a Crisis in Democracy?', *Political Quarterly*, vol. 73, no. 4, pp.400–408.

Barnett, Steven and Gaber, Ivor 2001, 'Westminster Tales: the 21st Century crisis in political journalism', *Continuum*, London.

Bartels, Larry M. 1993, 'Messages Received: the Political Impact of Media Exposure', *American Political Science Review*, vol. 87, pp.267–285.

Bean, Clive 1992, 'Party Leaders and Local Candidates,' in Martin Holland (ed), *Electoral Behavior in New Zealand*, Oxford University Press, Oxford, pp.141–168.

Bergman, Torbjorn 1995, *Constitutional Rules and Party Goals in Coalition Formation: An Analysis of Winning Minority Governments in Sweden*, Umea, University of Umea Printing Office.

Berry, Ruth 2002, 'English to see eye-to-eye with you', *The Dominion Post*, 22 July 2002, p.2.

Beyer, Georgina 2000, 'Address in Reply – Georgina Beyer', *New Zealand Parliamentary Debates (Hansard)*, Wellington, Government Publishers.

Beyer, Georgina 2002, Transcript of Interview. Tuesday, 8th October.

Bille, L. 2001, 'Democratizing a democratic procedure: Myth or Reality? Candidate selection in Western European Parties, 1960–1990', *Party Politics*, vol. 7, no. 3.

Blumler, Jay G. and Gurevitch, Michael 2001, ' "Americanization" Reconsidered: U.K.-U.S. Campaign Communication Comparisons Across Time', in W. Lance

Blumler, Jay G., Kavanagh, Dennis, and Nossiter, T.J. 1996, 'Modern Communications versus Traditional Politics in Britain: Unstable Marriage of Convenience', in Paolo Mancini and David L. Swanson (eds), *Politics, Media and Modern Democracy*, Praeger, Westport, CT.

Boston, Jonathan 1994, 'Electoral Reform in New Zealand: The Implications for the Formation, Organization and Operations of the Cabinet', *Australian Quarterly*, vol. 66, pp.67–90.

Boston, Jonathan 1997, 'Coalition Formation', in Raymond Miller (ed), *New Zealand Politics in Transition*, Auckland, Oxford University Press.

Boston, Jonathan 1998, *Governing Under Proportional Representation: Lessons from Europe*, Wellington, Institute of Policy Studies.

Boston, Jonathan 2000a, 'Forming the Coalition between Labour and the Alliance', in Jonathan Boston, Stephen Church, Stephen Levine, Elizabeth McLeay and Nigel S. Roberts (eds), *Left Turn: The New Zealand General Election of 1999*, Wellington, Victoria University Press.

Boston, Jonathan 2000b, 'Christian Political Parties and MMP' in R. Ahdar and J. Stenhouse (eds), *God and Government: The New Zealand Experience* Dunedin, Otago University Press.

Boston, Jonathan, Church, Stephen and Bale, Tim 2002, 'The Impact of Proportional Representation on Government Effectiveness: The New Zealand Experience', unpublished manuscript.

Boston, Jonathan, Church, Stephen, Levine, Stephen, McLeay, Elizabeth and Roberts, Nigel S. 2000 (eds), *Left Turn: The New Zealand General Election of 1999*, Victoria University Press, Wellington.

Boston, Jonathan, Levine, Stephen, McLeay, Elizabeth and Roberts, Nigel S. 1996, *New Zealand Under MMP: A New Politics?*, Auckland University Press, Auckland.

Boston, Jonathan and McLeay, Elizabeth 1997, 'Forming the First MMP Government: Theory, Practice and Prospects', in Jonathan Boston, Stephen Levine, Elizabeth McLeay and Nigel S. Roberts (eds), *From Campaign to Coalition: The 1996 MMP Election*, Palmerston North, Dunmore Press.

Brechtel, Thomas and Kaiser, André 1999, 'Party System and Coalition Formation in Post-

Reform New Zealand', *Political Science*, vol. 51, no. 1, pp.2–26.

Budge, Ian and Keman, Hans 1990, *Parties and Democracy: Coalition Formation and Government Functioning in Twenty States*, Oxford, Oxford University Press.

Cabinet Office 2002, 'Coalition, Support and Co-operation Agreements: Administrative Arrangements', *Cabinet Office Circular*, CO(02)11, 3 September.

Campbell, A. 2002, 'Poll puts Heritage second.' *Wairarapa Times-Age*, 25 July 2002, p.1.

Canovan, Margaret 1999, 'Trust the People! Populism and the Two Faces of Democracy', *Political Studies*, vol 67, pp.2–16.

Cappella, Joseph N. and Jamieson, Katherine Hall 1997, *Spiral of Cynicism: the Press and the Public Good*, Oxford University Press, New York.

Cargill, Thomas F. and Hutchison, Michael M. 1991, 'Political Business Cycles with Endogenous Election Timing: Evidence from Japan', *Review of Economics and Statistics*, vol. 53 no. 3, pp.733–39.

Carlyle, Thomas 1841, *On Heroes, Hero-Worship and the Heroic in History*, John C. Winston, Chicago.

Carville, James and Paul Begala 2002, *Buck Up, Suck Up . . . and Come Back When You Foul Up: 12 Winning Secrets From the War Room*, Simon & Shuster, New York.

Casey, Cathy 1999, *Change for the Better: The Story of Georgina Beyer*, Random House, Auckland.

Catt, Helena 1996, 'New Zealand' in Norris, Pippa (ed), *Passages to Power: Legislative recruitment in advanced democracies*, Cambridge University Press, Cambridge.

Catt, Helena 1997, 'Women, Maori and Minorities: Microrepresentation and MMP', in Jonathan Boston, Stephen Levine, Elizabeth McLeay, and Nigel S. Roberts (eds), *From Campaign to Coalition: The 1996 MMP Election*, The Dunmore Press, Palmerston North, pp.199–206.

Ceci, Stephen J. and Kane, Edward L. 1982 'Jumping on the Bandwagon with the Underdog: the Impact of Poll Results on Electoral Behaviour', *Public Opinion Quarterly*, vol. 46, no. 2, pp.228–242.

Chief Electoral Office, 1997, *The General Election 1996*, E9, Chief Electoral Office, Wellington.

Chief Electoral Office, 2000, *The General Election 1999*, E9, Chief Electoral Office, Wellington.

Chief Electoral Office, 2002, *The General Election 2002*, E9, Chief Electoral Office, Wellington.

Chowdhury, Abdur R. 1993, 'Political Surfing over Economic Waves: Parliamentary Election Timing in India', *American Journal of Political Science*, vol.37 no.4, pp.1100–18.

Church, Stephen 2000a, 'Crime and Punishment: The Referenda to Reform the Criminal Justice System and Reduce the Size of Parliament', in Jonathan Boston, Stephen Levine, Elizabeth McLeay and Nigel S. Roberts (eds), *Left Turn: the New Zealand General Election of 1999*, Victoria University Press, Wellington.

Church, Stephen 2000b, 'Lights, Camera, Action: the Television Campaign', in Jonathan Boston, Stephen Levine, Elizabeth McLeay and Nigel S. Roberts (eds), *Left Turn: the New Zealand General Election of 1999*, Victoria University Press, Wellington.

Clark, Helen 2000, 'The Worm that Turned: New Zealand's 1996 General Election and the Televised "Worm" Debates', in Stephen Coleman (ed), *Televised Election Debates: International Perspectives*, Macmillan, Basingstoke.

Clark, Rt. Hon. Helen 2002, Press Release, 11 June.

Cleveland, Les 1980, 'The Mass Media', in Howard Penniman (ed), *New Zealand at the Polls*, American Enterprise Institute, Washington DC.

Cohen, M. et al (forthcoming), *Beating Reform: The Resurgence of Parties in Presidential Nominations 1980 to 2000*.

Colmar Brunton 2002, 'MMP Monitor Post-election Results 2002: Summary Report', Prepared for the Electoral Commission, Wellington.

Denemark, David 2001, 'Choosing MMP in New Zealand: Explaining the 1983 Electoral Referendum Reform', in Matthew Shugart and Martin Wattenberg (eds), *Mixed-Member Electoral Systems: The Best of Both Worlds?*, Oxford University Press, Oxford, pp.70–95.

Denemark, David 2002, 'Television Effects and Voter Decision Making in Australia: a Re-examination of the Converse Model', *British Journal of Political Science*, vol. 32, no.4, pp.663–690.

De Winter, L. 1995, 'The Role of Parliament in Government Formation and Resignation', in H. Döring (ed), *Parliaments and Majority Rule in Western Europe*, St. Martin's Press, New York.

Diamond, Edward and Stephen Bates 1984, *The Spot: The Rise of Political Advertising on Television*, MIT Press, Cambridge, Massachusetts.

Dick, R. G. 1960, *A Descriptive Atlas of New Zealand*. R. E. Owen, Government Printer, Wellington.

Diermeier, Daniel, and Stevenson, Randolph T. 2000, 'Cabinet Terminations and Critical Events', *American Political Science Review*, vol. 94 no. 3, pp.627–40.

Donald, Rod 2002, 'Why Settle for Less', speech given at Green Party Election Campaign Opening, http://www.greens.org.nz/searchdocs/speech5419.html.

Duverger, Maurice 1954, *Political Parties*, Wiley, New York.

Edwards, Brian 2002, 'The Cootchie Coo News Revisited', in Judy McGregor and Margie Comrie (eds), *What's News: Reclaiming Journalism in New Zealand*, Dunmore Press, Palmerston North.

Electoral Commission 1997, *Annual Report for the year ended 30 June 1997* (E.57).

Electoral Commission 1997a, *The New Zealand Electoral Compendium*, Electoral Commission, Wellington.

Electoral Commission 2000, *The New Zealand Electoral Compendium*, 2nd edn, Electoral Commission, Wellington.

Electoral Commission 2002, *The New Zealand Electoral Compendium*, 3rd edn, Electoral Commission, Wellington.

Evening Post 27 May 2002.

Evening Post 7 June 2002.

Farrell, David and Webb, Paul 'Political Parties as Campaign Organisations' in Russell J. Dalton and Martin P. Wattenberg (eds), *Parties without Partisans: Political Change in Advanced Industrial Democracies*, Oxford University Press, Oxford.

Fiske, John 1996, *Media Matters*, University of Minnesota Press, Minneapolis.

Forster, Edward M. 1951, *Two Cheers for Democracy*, Arnold, London.

Fowler, L. and McClure, R. 1989, *Political Ambition: Who Decides to Run for Congress*, Yale University Press, New Haven, Connecticut.

Franklin, Bob 1997, *Newszak and News Media*, London, Edward Arnold, 1997.

Fraser, Liz and Zangouropoulos, Nik 1997, 'The ACT Campaigns: Wellington Central and Beyond' in Boston, Jonathan, Levine, Stephen, McLeay, Elizabeth and Roberts, Nigel S. (eds), *From Campaign to Coalition: The 1996 MMP Election*, Dunmore Press, Palmerston North.

Gallagher, Martin 1988, 'Conclusion' in Gallagher, Martin and Marsh, M. (eds), *Candidate Selection in Comparative Perspective: The Secret Garden of Politics*, Sage Publications, London.

Ganley, Marcus 1997, 'Waipareira: A Four-Way Fight', in Boston, Jonathan, Levine, Stephen, McLeay, Elizabeth and Roberts, Nigel S. (eds), *From Campaign to Coalition*. Palmerston North, Dunmore Press, pp.96–112.

Gardner, H., with Laskin, E. 1995, *Leading Minds: An Anatomy of Leadership*, Basic Books, New York.

Go Wairarapa 2002, *2002–2007 Regional Economic Strategy*, Go Wairarapa: 1–30.

Gomibuchi, Seichi 2001, *Followers and Leadership Durability: An Analysis of Leadership Support in the New Zealand Labour Party – 1990–1996*, University of Canterbury, Unpublished PhD Thesis.

Gould, Philip 1998, *Unfinished Revolution: How the Modernisers Saved the Labour Party*, Little, Brown, London.

Grey, Sandra 2002, 'Does Size Matter? Critical Mass and New Zealand's Women MPs', *Parliamentary Affairs*, vol. 55, pp.19–29.

Gunther, Richard, Montero, José Ramón and Wert, José Ignacio, 2000, 'The Media and Politics in Spain: from Dictatorship to Democracy', in Gunther, Richard and Mughan, Anthony (eds), *Democracy and the Media: a Comparative Perspective*, Cambridge University Press, Cambridge.

Hager, Nicky 2002, *Seeds of Distrust: The Story of a GE Cover-Up*, Craig Potton Publishing, Nelson.

Hardie Boys, Michael 1998, 'The Role of the Governor-General Under MMP', in A. Simpson (ed), *The Constitutional Implications of MMP*, Occasional Publication No. 9, School of Political Science and International Relations, Victoria University of Wellington.

Hart, Roderick, P. 1997, *Modern Rhetorical Criticism*, 2nd ed., Allan and Bacon, Needham Heights, Massachusetts.

Hayward, Janine and Chris Rudd 2000, 'Metropolitan Newspapers and the Election', in Jonathan Boston, Stephen Church, Stephen Levine, Elizabeth McLeay and Nigel S. Roberts (eds), *Left Turn: The New Zealand General Election of 1999*, Victoria University Press, Wellington.

Hayward, Janine and Rudd, Chris 2002, 'The Coverage of Post-War Election Campaigns: The Otago Daily Times', *Political Science*, vol. 54, no. 2, pp.3–20.

Hazan, Reuven 1996, 'Does Centre Equal Middle? Towards a Conceptual Delineation. with Application to West European Party Systems', *Party Politics*, vol. 2, pp.209–28.

Heifetz, Ronald A. 1994, *Leadership Without Easy Answers*, Harvard University Press, Cambridge.

Henry, David 2002, 'Statement by the Chief Electoral Officer on Kelly Chal, United Future Candidate, Wellington, 19 August 2002. http://www.elections.org.nz/elections/news/020819.html.

Holbrook, Thomas M. 1996, *Do Campaigns Matter?*, Sage, Thousand Oaks, California.

Hunn, Don and Smith, Mel, 2000, *Review of the General Election Process 1999*, Ministry of Justice, Wellington.

Iyengar, Shanto 1991, *Is Anyone Responsible? How Television Frames Political Issues*, University of Chicago Press, Chicago.

James, Colin 1992, *New Territory: The Transformation of New Zealand 1984 – 92*, Bridget Williams Books, Wellington.

James, Colin 1996 (ed), *MMP Elections: A Guide for Journalists*, New Zealand Journalists Training Organisation, Wellington.

James, Colin 1998 (ed), *MMP Elections: A Guide for Journalists*, (2nd ed), Wellington, New Zealand Journalists Training Organisation.

Jamieson, Katherine Hall and Adasiewicz, Christopher 2000, 'What Can Voters Learn from Election Debates', in Stephen Coleman (ed), *Televised Election Debates: International Perspectives*, Macmillan, Basingstoke.

Johansson, Jon 2002a, *Political Leadership in New Zealand: Theory & Practice*, Unpublished PhD Thesis, Victoria University of Wellington, Wellington.

Johansson, Jon 2002b, 'Past sins continue to haunt National's leader,' in *The New Zealand Herald*, 16 July, p.A15.

Johnson-Cartee, Karen S. and Copeland, Gary A. 1997, *Manipulation of the American Voter: Political Campaign Commercials*, Praeger Publishers, Westport, Connecticut.

Johnston, Richard 1998, 'Issues, Leaders and the Campaign', in Jack Vowles et al. (eds), *Voters' Victory: New Zealand's First Election Under Proportional Representation*, Auckland University Press, Auckland.

Johnston, Ron and Pattie, Charles 1999, 'Constituency Campaign Intensity and Split-Ticket Voting: New Zealand's First Election Under MMP, 1996', *Political Science*, vol. 51, no. 2, pp.164–181.

Jones, Nicholas 2001, *The Control Freaks*, Politicos, London.

Joseph, Philip A. 1993, *Constitutional and Administrative Law in New Zealand*, The Law Book Company, Sydney.

Judd, Catherine 2002, 'Communicating the Liberal Vision', speech to ACT 2002 Annual Conference, Auckland, http://www.act.org.nz/item.jsp?id=22197.

Just, Marion R. et al. 1996, *Crosstalk: Citizens, Candidates and the Media in a Presidential Campaign*, University of Chicago Press, Chicago.

Kaid, Lynda Lee and Johnston, Anne 2001, *Videostyle in Presidential Campaigns: Style and Content of Televised Political Advertising*, Praeger Publishers, Westport, Connecticut.

Kaiser, André and Brechtel, Thomas 1999, 'Party System, Bargaining Power and Coalition Formation after the 1999 New Zealand General Election, *Political Science*, vol. 51, no. 2, pp.182–6.

Karp, Jeffrey 2002, 'Members of Parliament and Representation', in Jack Vowles, Peter Aimer, Jeffrey Karp, Susan Banducci, Raymond Miller, and Ann Sullivan, *Proportional Representation on Trial: The 1999 New Zealand General Election and the Fate of MMP*, Auckland University Press, Auckland, pp.130–145.

Kayser, Mark 2000, 'Election Timing under Alternate Electoral Structures', paper presented to the Annual Meeting of the American Political Science Association, Washington DC, 30 August – 3 September.

Keith, Kenneth 1994, 'On the Constitution of New Zealand', *Political Science*, vol. 44, no.1, July, pp.30–31.

King, Anthony 2002, *Leaders' Personalities and the Outcomes of Democratic Elections*, Oxford University Press, Oxford.

Klingemann, Hans-Dieter and Wessels, Bernhard 2001, 'The Political Consequences of Germany's Mixed-Member System: Personalization at the Grass Roots?' in Matthew Shugart

and Martin Wattenberg (eds), *Mixed-Member Electoral Systems: The Best of Both Worlds?*, Oxford University Press, Oxford.
Kovach, Bill and Rosenstiel, Tom 1999, *Warp Speed: America in the Age of Mixed Media*, Century Foundation, New York.
Langdon, Christine 2002, 'Beyer accused of putting gays first', *The Dominion*, 23 January 2002.
Lanoue, David and Schrott, Peter 1991, *The Joint Press Conference*, Greenwood, New York.
Laver, Michael and Schofield, Norman 1990, *Multiparty Government: The Politics of Coalition in Europe*, Oxford University Press, Oxford.
Laver, Michael and Shepsle, Kenneth 1996, *Making and Breaking Governments: Cabinets and Legislatures in Parliamentary Democracies*, Cambridge University Press, Cambridge.
Lemert, J. et al. 1991, *News Verdicts, the Debates, and Presidential Campaigns*, Praeger, New York.
Levine, Stephen and Roberts, Nigel S. 1987, 'Parties, Policies, and Personalities: A Study of Two Electorates in the 1984 General Election in New Zealand', *Political Science*. vol. 39, no. 1, pp.1–16.
Levine, Stephen and Roberts, Nigel S. 1989, 'Parties, Leaders, and Issues in the 1987 Election', in Hyam Gold (ed), *New Zealand Politics in Perspective*, 2nd edn, Longman Paul, Auckland, pp.423–445.
Levine, Stephen and Roberts, Nigel S. 1991, 'Elections and Expectations: Evidence from Electoral Surveys in New Zealand', *Journal of Commonwealth and Comparative Politics*. vol. 29, no. 2, pp.129–152.
Levine, Stephen and Roberts, Nigel S. 1991a, 'A Mirror for Miramar? The 1990 Election in Perspective', in Elizabeth McLeay (ed), *The 1990 General Election: Perspectives on Political Change in New Zealand*, Department of Politics, Victoria University of Wellington, Occasional Publication No. 3, Wellington, pp.119–150.
Levine, Stephen and Roberts, Nigel S. 1992, 'Policies and Political Perspectives: The Importance of Issues and Problems in New Zealand Electoral Behaviour', in Martin Holland (ed), *Electoral Behaviour in New Zealand*, Oxford University Press, Auckland, pp.71–93.
Levine, Stephen and Roberts, Nigel S., 1992a, 'Sore Labour's Bath? The Paradox of Party Identification in New Zealand', in Margaret Clark (ed), *The Labour Party After 75 Years*, Department of Politics, Victoria University of Wellington, Occasional Publication No. 4, Wellington, pp.50–72.
Levine, Stephen and Roberts, Nigel S. 1992b, 'National to Power: Voter Choice in 1990', in Hyam Gold (ed), *New Zealand Politics in Perspective*, 3rd edn Longman Paul, Auckland, 3rd edition, pp.493–512.
Levine, Stephen and Roberts, Nigel S. 1994, 'The Last Hurrah: The New Zealand General Election of 1993 — What Happened and Why', in Jack Vowles and Peter Aimer (eds), *Double Decision: The 1993 Election and Referendum in New Zealand*, Department of Politics, Victoria University of Wellington, Occasional Publication No. 6, Wellington, pp.141–161.
Levine, Stephen and Roberts, Nigel S. 1997, 'Surveying the Snark: Voting Behaviour in the 1996 New Zealand General Election', in Jonathan Boston, Stephen Levine, Elizabeth McLeay and Nigel S. Roberts (eds), *From Campaign to Coalition: New Zealand's First General Election Under Proportional Representation*, The Dunmore Press, Palmerston North, pp.183–197.
Levine, Stephen and Roberts, Nigel S. 2000, 'Voting Behaviour in 1999', in Jonathan Boston, Stephen Church, Stephen Levine, Elizabeth McLeay, and Nigel S. Roberts (eds), *Left Turn:*

The New Zealand General Election of 1999, Victoria University Press, Wellington, pp.161–176.

Levy, Mark R. 1981, 'Disdaining the News', *Journal of Communication*, Vol. 31, no. 3, pp.24–31.

Lijphart, Arend 1994, *Electoral Systems and Party Systems: A Study of Twenty-Seven Democracies 1945–1990*, Oxford University Press, Oxford.

Lijphart, Arend 1999, *Patterns of Democracy: Government Forms and Performance in Thirty-Six Countries*, Yale University Press, New Haven.

Lippman, Walter 1922, *Public Opinion*, Free Press, New York.

Lipson, Leslie 1948, *The Politics of Equality*, University of Chicago Press, Chicago.

Lupia, Arthur, and Strom, Kaare 1995, 'Coalition Termination and the Strategic Timing of Parliamentary Elections', *American Political Science Review*, vol. 89 no. 3, pp.648–65.

M. B. E. Incorporated 2001, *Wairarapa: Economic Development in a Lifestyle Environment*, Masterton Business Enterprise, Masterton.

M. B. E. Incorporated 2002, 'Economic Activity At An All Time High', *Wairarapa Business Review*, pp.1–4.

McAllister, Ian and Donley T. Studlar 2002, 'Electoral Systems and Women's Representation: A Long-Term Perspective', *Representation*, vol 39, pp.3–14.

McGregor, Judy 2002, 'Terrorism, War, Lions and Sex Symbols: Restating News Values', in Judy McGregor and Margie Comrie (eds), *What's News: Reclaiming Journalism in New Zealand*, Dunmore Press, Palmerston North.

McGregor, Judy, Comrie, Margie and Fountaine, Susan 1999, 'Beyond the Feelgood Factor: Measuring Public Journalism in the 1996 New Zealand Election Campaign', *Harvard International Journal of Press/Politics*, vol. 4, no. 1, pp.66–77.

Mackie, Thomas T., and Rose, Richard 1991, *The International Almanac of Electoral History*, Congressional Quarterly, Washington DC.

McLauchlan, Gordon 1976, *The Passionless People*, Cassell, Auckland.

McLeay, Elizabeth 1995, *The Cabinet and Political Power in New Zealand*, Auckland University Press, Auckland.

McLeay, Elizabeth 2000, 'The New Parliament', in Jonathan Boston, Stephen Church, Stephen Levine, Elizabeth McLeay, and Nigel S. Roberts (eds), *Left Turn: The New Zealand General Election of 1999*, Victoria University Press, Wellington, pp.203–216.

McNair, Brian 2000, *Journalism and Democracy: an Evaluation of the Political Public Sphere*, Routledge, London.

McRobie, Alan 1989, *New Zealand Electoral Atlas*, Government Printing Office, Wellington.

McRobie, Alan and Roberts, Nigel, S. 1978, *Election '78; The 1977 Electoral Redistribution and the 1978 General Election in New Zealand*, John McIndoe, Dunedin.

McWhinnie, Toni 1995, 'Same Street, Different Worlds: Secondary School Years in Masterton, 1945–1960', *History*, Wellington, Victoria: 88.

Mancini, Paolo and Swanson, David L. 1996, 'Introduction', in Paolo Mancini and David L. Swanson (eds), *Politics, Media and Modern Democracy*, Praeger, Westport, Connecticut.

Mancini, Paolo and Swanson, David L. 1996a, 'Patterns of Modern Electoral Campaigning and their Consequences', in Paolo Mancini and David L. Swanson (eds), *Politics, Media and Modern Democracy*, Praeger, Westport, Connecticut.

March, James and Olsen, Johan 1984, 'The New Institutionalism: Organizational factors in political science' in *American Political Science Review*, vol. 78.

March, James and Olsen, Johan 1996, 'Institutional perspectives on political institutions' in *Governance*, vol. 9, no. 3.

Masterton, Murray 1998, 'A Theory of News' in Myles Breen (ed), *Journalism: Theory and Practice*, Macleay Press, Sydney.

Mendelson, Matthew 1996, 'The Media and Interpersonal Communications: the Priming of Issues, Leaders, and Party Identification', *Journal of Politics*, vol. 58, no. 1, pp.112–125.

Meyer, Thomas 2002, *Media Democracy: How the Media Colonize Politics*, Polity Press, Cambridge.

Miller, Raymond 1998, 'Coalition Government: The People's Choice?' in Jack Vowles, Peter Aimer, Susan Banducci and Jeffrey Karp (eds), *Voters' Victory? New Zealand's First Election Under Proportional Representation*, Auckland University Press, Auckland, pp.120–134.

Miller, Raymond 2001, 'Labour', in Raymond Miller (ed), *New Zealand Government and Politics*, Oxford University Press, Auckland, pp.226–241.

Miller, Raymond 2002, 'Coalition Government: The Labour-Alliance Pact', in Jack Vowles, Peter Aimer, Jeffrey Karp, Susan Banducci, R. Miller and Ann Sullivan (eds), *Proportional Representation on Trial: The 1999 New Zealand General Election and the Fate of MMP*, Auckland University Press, Auckland, pp.114–129.

Miskin, Sarah 2002, 'New Zealand Election: 27 July 2002,' *Parliamentary Library of Australia*, Research Note no. 9.

MMP Review Committee 2001, 'Report of the MMP Review Committee: Inquiry into the Review of MMP', *Appendices to the Journal of the House of Representatives*, I.23A.

Müller, Wolfgang and Strøm, Kaare (eds), 1997, *Koalitionsreierungen in Westeuropa. Bildung, Arbeitweise und Beendigung*, Wien, Signum Verlag.

Müller, Wolfgang and Strøm, Kaare 2000, 'Coalition Governance in Western Europe', in Wolfgang Müller and Kaare Strøm (eds), *Coalition Governments in Western Europe*, Oxford University Press, Oxford.

New Zealand First 1998, *Constitution of New Zealand First*.

New Zealand Herald 14 May 2002.

New Zealand Herald 23 May 2002.

New Zealand Labour Party 2001, *Constitution and Rules*.

New Zealand National Party 2000, *Party Constitution*.

Norris, Paul 2002, 'News Media Ownership in New Zealand', in Judy McGregor and Margie Comrie (eds), *What's News: Reclaiming Journalism in New Zealand*, Dunmore Press, Palmerston North.

Norris, Pippa 1996, 'Legislative Recruitment', in Lawrence LeDuc, Richard G. Niemi, and Pippa Norris (eds), *Comparing Democracies: Elections and Voting in Global Perspective*, Sage, London, pp.184–285.

Norris, Pippa 2000, *A Virtuous Circle: Political Communications in Postindustrial Societies*, Cambridge University Press, Cambridge.

Norris, Pippa et al. 1999, *On Message: Communicating the Campaign*, Sage, London.

Norton, Clifford 1988 (ed), *New Zealand Parliamentary Election Results – 1946–1987*, Department of Political Science, Victoria University, Wellington.

O'Leary, Eileen 2002, 'Political Spin', in Judy McGregor and Margie Comrie (eds), *What's News: Reclaiming Journalism in New Zealand*, Dunmore Press, Palmerston North.

Parliamentary Library, New Zealand House of Representatives 2002, 'Final Results 2002 General Election and Trends in Election Outcomes 1990–2002', *Background Note, Information Briefing Service for Members of Parliament*, 20 August 2002.

Parliamentary Debates 2002, vol. 599.

Parliamentary Debates 1861–1863, vol. 4.

Parliamentary Debates 1872, vol. 13.

Parliamentary Debates 1884, vol. 47.

Parliamentary Debates 1884, vol. 48.

Parliamentary Debates 1887, vol. 57.

Parliamentary Library 2002, *Wairarapa Electorate; Electoral/Statistical Profile*, Wellington, Parliament, pp.1–15.

Patterson, L. 2002. Transcript of interview. 8 October.

Patterson, Thomas E. 2000, 'The United States: News in a Free-Market Society' in Gunther, Richard and Mughan, Anthony (eds), *Democracy and the Media: a Comparative Perspective*, Cambridge University Press, Cambridge.

Patzelt, W 1999, 'Recruitment and Retention in Western European Parliaments' in *Legislative Studies Quarterly*, vol. 24, no. 2.

Perry, Paul and Alan Webster 1999, *New Zealand Politics At The Turn Of The Millennium*, Alpha Publications, Auckland.

Peters, Winston 2002, 'Fourth Estate or Fifth Column? The Media and Politics in New Zealand', *Political Science*, vol. 54, no. 2, pp.69–72.

Pfetsch, Barbara 1996, 'Convergence through Privatization? Changing Media Environments and Televised Politics in Germany', *European Journal of Communication*, vol. 11, no. 4, pp.427–451.

Pierson, P. 2002, 'Increasing Returns, Path Dependency, and the Study of Politics', *American Political Science Review*, vol. 94, no. 2, pp.251–67.

Prebble, Richard 2002, 'ACT Campaigning on the Real Issues', speech to ACT Campaign Opening, Auckland, http://www.act.org.nz/item.jsp?id=22820.

The Press 22 April 2002.

Reid, Bradford G. 1998, 'Endogenous Elections, Electoral Budget Cycles and Canadian Provincial Governments', *Public Choice*, vol. 97, pp.35–48.

Reid, Nicola 2001, 'ACT' in Raymond Miller (ed), *New Zealand Government and Politics*, Oxford University Press, Auckland, pp.262–270.

Representation Commission 1995, *Report of the Representation Commission*, Government Printer, Wellington.

Riddell, Oliver 2002, 'A Gallery of Rogues?', in Judy McGregor and Margie Comrie (eds), *What's News: Reclaiming Journalism in New Zealand*, Dunmore Press, Palmerston North.

Riker, William 1986, *The Art of Political Manipulation*, Yale University Press, New Haven.

Roberts, G. 1988, 'German Federal Republic: The two-lane route to Bonn' in Gallagher, Michael and Marsh, Michael (eds) *Candidate selection in comparative perspective: The secret garden of politics*, Sage, London.

Roberts, Nigel S. 1980, 'The Outcome', in Howard R. Penniman (ed), *New Zealand at the Polls: The General Election of 1978*, American Enterprise Institute for Public Policy Research, Washington, D.C., pp.215–249.

Robinson, Claire 2002, 'Supermodel or Saint? The Selling of Helen Clark through Advertising Imagery in the 1999 General Election' in *3:1 Writing and Research from the College of Design, Fine Arts and Music*, vol. 1, pp.83–98.

Robinson, Michael J. 1977, 'Television and American Politics', *The Public Interest*, vol. 48, pp.3–39.

Rowe, S. 2002, 'No Regrets for a Details Man', *Wairarapa Times-Age*, 20 July 2002, p.3.

Royal Commission on The Electoral System 1986, *Report of the Royal Commission on the Electoral System: 'Towards a Better Democracy'*, Government Printer, Wellington.

Rupar, Verica 2002, 'Keeping our Options Closed: The Dominance of the Conflict Story-Telling Frame in Media Coverage of the Royal Commission's Report on Genetic Modification in New Zealand', *Political Science*, vol.54, no. 2, pp.59–67.

Sabato, Larry J. 1991, *Feeding Frenzy: How Attack Journalism has Transformed American Politics*, Free Press, New York.

Scarrow, S., Webb, P. and Farrell, David 2000, 'From Social Integration to Electoral Contestation: The Changing Distribution of Power within Political Parties' in Dalton, R. and Wattenburg, Martin (eds), *Parties Without Partisans*, Oxford University Press, Oxford.

Schattschneider, Elmer E. 1942, *Party Government*, Rinehart, New York.

Schrott, Peter R. 1990, 'Electoral Consequences of 'Winning' Televised Campaign Debates', *Public Opinion Quarterly*, vol. 54, no. 4, pp.567–585.

Semetko, Holli A. and Canel, María José 1997, 'Agenda-Senders versus Agenda-Setters: Television in Spain's 1996 Election Campaign', *Political Communication*, vol. 14, pp.459–79.

Semetko, Holli A. 2000, 'Great Britain: The End of News at Ten and the Changing News Environment', in Richard Gunther and Anthony Mughan (eds), *Democracy and the Media: A Comparative Perspective*, Cambridge University Press, Cambridge.

Sharpe, M. 2002, 'Joint Effort', *Wairarapa Times-Age*, 31 July 2002, p.3.

Shea, Daniel M. 1996, *Campaign Craft: The Strategies, tactics and Art of Political Campaign Management*, Praeger Publishers, Westport, Connecticut.

Sheppard, Simon 1998, 'The Struggle for the Agenda: New Zealand Labour Party Candidate Selections 1987–93', *Political Science*, vol. 49, no. 2, pp.198–229.

Shugart, Matthew and Wattenberg, Martin 2001 (eds), *Mixed-Member Electoral Systems: The Best of Both Worlds?*, Oxford University Press, Oxford.

Sky News Australia 2002, *The Election Debates*, 16 July.

Sky News Leaders Debates 2002.

Skowronek, Stephen 1997, *The Politics Presidents Make: Leadership from John Adams to Bill Clinton*, Harvard University Press, Cambridge.

Smith, Alastair 2000, 'Election Timing in Majority Parliaments', paper presented to the Annual Meeting of the American Political Science Association, Washington DC, 30 August–3 September.

Sniderman, Paul, Brody, Richard, and Tetlock, Philip 1998, *Reasoning and Choice: Exporations in Political Psychology*, Cambridge University Press, Cambridge.

Sowry, Roger 1997, 'The National Campaign: Tactics and Strategies', in Jonathan Boston, Stephen Levine, Elizabeth McLeay and Nigel S. Roberts (eds), *From Campaign to Coalition: New Zealand's First General Election Under Proportional Representation*, The Dunmore Press, Palmerston North, pp.25–32.

Spiekerman, Erik, and Ginger, E. M. 1993, *Stop Stealing Sheep and Find Out How Type Really Works*, Adobe Press/Prentice Hall, Englewood Cliffs, New Jersey.

Standing Orders Committee 1995, *Review of Standing Orders*, New Zealand House of Representatives, Wellington (I.18a).

Strøm, Kaare 1990, *Minority Government and Majority Rule*, Cambridge University Press, Cambridge.

Strøm, Kaare, Budge, Ian and Laver, Michael 1994, 'Constraints on Cabinet Formation in Parliamentary Democracies', *American Journal of Political Science*, vol. 38, no. 2, pp.303–335.

Strøm, Kaare and Müller, Wolfgang 1998, 'Coalition Government in Parliamentary Democracies', paper prepared for the International Conference on Opportunities and Dilemmas of Parliamentary Leadership, Ljubljana, Slovenia, 6–9 July.

Studlar, Donley T. and McAllister, Ian 2002, 'Does a Critical Mass Exist? A Comparative Analysis of Women's Legislative Representation since 1950', *European Journal of Political Research*, vol. 41, pp.233–253.

TV1 2002, *Holmes Leaders Debate*, 17 July.

TV3 2002, *NFO Opinion Poll*, 10 June.

TV3 2002, *Leaders Debate*, 4 July.

TV3 2002, '*Leaders Debate*, 25 July.

United Future New Zealand (undated), *Constitution of United Future New Zealand*.

Van der Eijk, Cees 2000, 'The Netherlands: Media and Politics between Segmented Pluralism and Market Forces', in Gunther, Richard and Mughan, Anthony (eds), *Democracy and the Media: a Comparative Perspective*, Cambridge University Press, Cambridge.

Venables, David 2002, 'Public Journalism', in Judy McGregor and Margie Comrie (eds), *What's News: Reclaiming Journalism in New Zealand*, Dunmore Press, Palmerston North.

Vowles, Jack 2002 'Did the polls influence the vote? A case study of the 1999 New Zealand General Election', *Political Science*, vol. 54, no. 1, pp.67–78.

Vowles, Jack 2002a, 'Did the Campaign Matter?', in Jack Vowles, Peter Aimer, Jeffrey Karp, Susan Banducci, Raymond Miller, Ann Sullivan (eds), *Proportional Representation on Trial*, Auckland University Press, Auckland.

Vowles, Jack, Aimer, Peter, Karp, Jeffrey, Banducci, Susan, Miller, Raymond and Sullivan, Ann 2002, *Proportional Representation on Trial*, Auckland University Press, Auckland.

Warwick, Paul 1994, *Government Survival in Parliamentary Democracies*, Cambridge University Press, New York.

Weller, Pat 1985, *First Among Equals: Prime Ministers in Westminster Systems*, George Allen & Unwin, Sydney.

Wells, Scott D., David M. Duty and Justin D. Walton 2002, 'Al Gore and Election 2000: Populist Discourse and Strategies', paper presented to the 2002 American Political Science Association, Boston.

Wills, Garry 1992, *Lincoln at Gettysburg: The Words That Remade America*, New York, Simon & Schuster.

Wood, Antony 2001, 'National', in Raymond Miller (ed), *New Zealand Government and Politics*, Oxford University Press, Auckland, pp.242–251.

Zhao, X. and Bleske, G. 1998, 'Horse-Race Polls and Audience Issue Learning, *Harvard International Journal of Press/Politics*, vol. 3, no. 4, pp.13–34.

APPENDIX 1

Coalition Agreement between the Labour and Progressive Coalition Parties in Parliament

The Labour and Progressive Coalition parties in Parliament agree to form a government with the objective of:

Providing stable government over the next term of Parliament, so as to implement a comprehensive policy programme aimed at increasing economic growth, reducing inequality and improving the social and economic well-being of all New Zealanders and their families in a manner which is environmentally, socially and economically sustainable.

Objective
To provide stable government over the next term of Parliament so as to implement a comprehensive policy programme aimed at increasing economic growth, reducing inequality and improving the social and economic well-being of all New Zealanders and their families in a manner which is environmentally, socially and economically sustainable.

Good faith and no surprises
Both parties to this agreement will operate in government on a good faith and no surprises basis.

Maintaining identity
The coalition partners will work in good faith to further the objectives of government, while accepting the need for distinctive party political identities within government, especially in relation to the smaller party being able to maintain a separate but responsible identity. Agree to disagree provisions will apply where necessary and in such circumstances the Progressive Coalition will be free to express alternative views publicly and in Parliament.

Cooperation with other parties

The government will enter into agreements with other parties to secure confidence and supply and to facilitate the implementation of the preferred legislative programme in Parliament.

Policy Programme

The manifestos of Labour and the Progressive Coalition have much in common with both parties being committed to a progressive social democratic policy programme. Reflecting its electoral mandate, Labour will lead the broad policy programme, recognising the Progressive Coalition's general priorities of employment, support for low income families, health and education and its wish to make specific progress on:

- ensuring better co-ordination and integration of industry assistance.
- implementation of a comprehensive drug strategy aimed at protecting young people and educating them on the dangers of drug use.
- policy to promote a better balance of work and family responsibilities.

The detail of the policy programme for this term of Parliament will be set out in the Speech from the Throne.

Cabinet Government

Cabinet positions will be allocated by the Prime Minister after appropriate consultation. The Progressive Coalition will have one Cabinet position. The Cabinet Manual provisions will apply to the cabinet process and decision-making will be by consensus.

It is accepted that because of the relative numbers in the coalition, quorum rules relating to the need to have at least one member from each coalition party present for a quorum will not generally apply.

Signed in Wellington this 8th day of August 2002.

Helen Clark
Leader of the Labour Party

Jim Anderton
Leader of the Progressive Coalition

APPENDIX 2

Agreement between the Labour/Progressive Government and the United Future Parliamentary Caucus

Agreement for Confidence and Supply between the Labour/Progressive Government and the United Future Parliamentary Caucus.

The United Future parliamentary caucus agrees to provide confidence and supply for the term of this Parliament, to a Labour/Progressive Government with the objective of:

Providing stable government over the next term of Parliament, so as to implement a comprehensive policy programme aimed at increasing economic growth, reducing inequality and improving the social and economic wellbeing of all New Zealanders and their families in a manner which is environmentally, socially and economically sustainable.

Good faith and no surprises

All parties to this agreement will operate on a good faith and no surprises basis for the term of this Parliament.

Policy Programme

It is agreed that the detail of the policy programme will be based on the manifestos of the Government coalition partners and will take account of the policy priorities of the United Future Party.

It is acknowledged that policy initiatives advanced by United Future during this parliamentary term will be considered by the Government and resolved according to the procedures set out in this agreement.

In particular the Government will, as immediate priorities, in consultation with the leader of United Future,

- By the end of this year develop proposals for a Commission for the Family which will have regard to the United Future policy platform, and relevant parts of the Labour Manifesto, including the Parenting Council initiative, with a view to implementation in the 2003/04 financial year.
- Pass, by the end of this year, strong victims rights legislation, including increased support for victim support groups.
- Ensure that new transport legislation is introduced and passed that includes provisions for alternative funding options to facilitate the accelerated development of new roading infrastructure.

The government will not introduce legislation to change the legal status of cannabis and will implement a comprehensive drug strategy aimed at protecting young people and educating them on the dangers of drug use.

Consultative arrangements

The government will consult with United Future on a range of issues including:
- The broad outline of the legislative programme and the priorities within it.
- Key legislative measures.
- Major policy issues.
- Broad budget parameters.

That consultation will occur in a timely fashion so that the views of United Future can be incorporated into final decision making.

Formal consultation will be managed between the Prime Minister's Office and the Office of the Leader of United Future, and there will be ongoing relationships between relevant portfolio ministers and United Future spokespeople.

Regular leadership meetings (approximately monthly) will be scheduled between the Government and United Future.

Briefings

It is agreed that relevant spokespeople within United Future will be briefed on significant issues which are likely to be politically sensitive before any public announcements are made.

Confidentiality

It is agreed that where briefings are provided to United Future, or where United Future is involved in a consultative arrangement with regard to legislation, policy or budgetary matters, all such discussions shall be confidential unless otherwise agreed.

In the event that Government papers are provided to United Future in the course of consultation or briefings they shall be treated as confidential and shall not be released or the information used for any public purpose without the express agreement of the relevant minister.

In the event that Cabinet or Cabinet committee papers are provided to United Future for the purposes of consultation they shall be provided to a designated person within the Office of the Leader who will provide a formal receipt and take responsibility for ensuring they are accorded the appropriate degree of confidentiality.

All papers provided to United Future shall be copied to the Prime Minister's Office.

Collective Responsibility

Although United Future will not be bound by collective responsibility on Government decisions, where there has been full participation in the development of a policy initiative, and that participation has led to an agreed position, it is expected that all parties to this agreement will publicly support the process and the outcome.

Procedural Motions

United Future agrees that it will support the Government on procedural motions in the House and in Select Committees unless United Future has previously advised that such support is not forthcoming.

The Government agrees that it will operate a no-surprises policy in terms of procedural motions it intends to put before the House or a select committee.

Select Committees

United Future and the Government will develop an agreed position on the makeup and operation of select committees.

Legislative Programme

Support for particular legislative measures which do not relate to confidence or supply will be negotiated on a case by case basis.

Signed in Wellington this 8th day of August 2002.

Rt Hon Helen Clark
Prime Minister

Peter Dunne
Leader of United Future

APPENDIX 3

Co-operation Agreement between the Labour/Progressive Government and the Green Parliamentary Caucus

The Green Party Parliamentary caucus (Green Party) and the Labour/Progressive government are committed to having a constructive relationship based on good faith for this term of Parliament.

The commitment of the Labour/Progressive government is to:

1. Provide stable government over the next term of Parliament, so as to implement a comprehensive policy programme aimed at increasing economic growth, reducing inequality and improving the social and economic well-being of all New Zealanders and their families in a manner which is environmentally, socially and economically sustainable.
2. The Green Party is committed to building an ecologically sustainable, socially just, participatory and peaceful society.
3. The Government and the Green Party share many similar goals and will co-operate on agreed areas of policy development and legislation in order to facilitate the implementation of a shared agenda.

Co-operation on Policy and Legislation

The Government will consult with the Green Party on a range of issues including:

- The broad outline of the legislative programme and the priorities within it
- Key legislative measures
- Major policy issues

The Government and the Green Party will engage on the detail of policy via a number of categories:

Category A
- Full participation of Green Party spokespeople in the development of policy positions with the expectation of developing joint positions.

Category B
- Consultation on the broad direction of policy, and the development of related legislation, with the aim of achieving support for legislative measures and/or policy proposals.

Category C
- Consultation for the purposes of information sharing without any particular expectation of developing agreed positions.

Issues will be assigned to a category by agreement and the procedures which will be followed will be dependent on that assignation. The initial procedures are set out in the attachment to this agreement.

Formal consultation will be managed between the Prime Minister's Office and the Office of the Co-Leaders of the Green Party.

Other co-operation will include:
- Access to relevant Ministers by designated Green Party MPs
- Quarterly meetings between the Prime Minister and the Green Party Co-Leaders
- Advance notification to the other party of significant announcements by either the Government or the Green Party
- Briefings by the Government on significant issues before any public announcement.
- Ongoing input by the Green Party into the implementation of previously agreed budget initiatives

Both parties agree that it is desirable to review certain aspects of ERMA's (Environmental Risk Management Authority's) operation to ensure it is capable of providing a robust mechanism to fully implement those parts of the HSNO (Hazardous Substances and New Organisms) Act relevant to new organisms, in a manner consistent with the purpose of the Act. The

Government intends to initiate such a review and will consult with the Green Party on the terms of reference and personnel.

Confidentiality

It is agreed that where briefings are provided to the Green Party or where the Green Party are involved in a consultative arrangement with regard to legislation or policy, (i.e. Category A or B issues), all such discussions shall be confidential unless otherwise agreed.

In the event that government papers are provided to the Green Party in the course of consultation or briefings they shall be treated as confidential and shall not be released or the information used for any public purpose without the express agreement of the relevant Minister.

Once confidential information is in the public domain, the Green Party is able to make comment on the information.

In the event that Cabinet or Cabinet committee papers are provided to the Green Party for the purposes of consultation they shall be provided to a designated person within the Office of the Co-Leaders who will provide a formal receipt and take responsibility for ensuring they are accorded the appropriate degree of confidentiality.

All papers provided to the Green Party shall be copied to the Prime Minister's Office.

Signed this 26th day of August 2002

....
Rt Hon Helen Clark   Rod Donald   Jeanette Fitzsimons
Prime Minister   Green Party Co-Leaders

Minimum consultation expectations

Category A

Category A policy areas and legislation will be specified and jointly agreed by the parties at quarterly meetings of Green Party Co-Leaders and the Prime Minister.

Where the Green Party and government have agreed to work together on Category A policy areas and legislation it is expected that the parties will work in good faith towards an agreed outcome that advances the policies of both parties.

To this end there will be:
- full participation by the Green Party in the policy development process and development of legislation with the aim of developing jointly agreed positions
- access to relevant Cabinet Ministers and, through the Minister to officials where appropriate, for designated Green Party MPs
- access to relevant papers
- public acknowledgement of the Green Party's contribution through measures such as: press releases; speeches; or supporting agreed Green Party amendments to legislation
- agreement on the timetable for policy development and passage of legislation through Parliament
- advance notification of any significant announcements by either party
- support from the Green Party for procedural motions in the House or select committees on any legislation coming out of this process
- full confidentiality, in line with the provisions in the agreement

Where a policy and/or legislation has been developed within the guidelines set out above, and both parties have agreed on the outcome, both parties will publicly support the process and the outcome.

Category B

Category B policy areas and legislation will be specified by agreement between the offices of the Prime Minister and the Green Party Co-Leaders.

In Category B areas both parties will:
- act in good faith towards achieving a legislative outcome able to be supported in the House.

The Green Party spokesperson can expect to
- be briefed on policy development and consulted on options before decisions are taken.
- be invited to make submissions into the policy process.
- be consulted on legislation drafting.
- be consulted on the timeframe and timetabling of legislation and policy.

The Green Party will:
- in relation to agreed legislation coming out of this process, support

government procedural motions in the House and in select committees unless previously advised otherwise.

The Government will:
- operate a no surprises policy in terms of procedural motions it intends to put before the House or a select committee in such circumstances.

Category C

Category C will include all other issues. On these issues the parties will act in good faith to provide each other with sufficient information on issues to allow for informed responses, and to maximise co-operation.

APPENDIX 4

MPs in the 47th Parliament

Labour

Rick Barker (Tukituki)
Tim Barnett (Christchurch Central)
David Benson-Pope (Dunedin South)
Georgina Beyer (Wairarapa)
Mark Burton (Taupo)
Chris Carter (Te Atatu)
Steve Chadwick (Rotorua)
Ashraf Choudhary (list)
Helen Clark (Mt Albert)
Clayton Cosgrove (Waimakariri)
Michael Cullen (list)
David Cunliffe (New Lynn)
Lianne Dalziel (Christchurch East)
Helen Duncan (list)
Harry Duynhoven (New Plymouth)
Ruth Dyson (Banks Peninsula)
Russell Fairbrother (Napier)
Taito Phillip Field (Mangere)
Martin Gallagher (Hamilton West)
Phil Goff (Mt Roskill)
Mark Gosche (Maungakiekie)
Ann Hartley (Northcote)
George Hawkins (Manurewa)
Dave Hereora (list)
Marian Hobbs (Wellington Central)
Pete Hodgson (Dunedin North)

Parekura Horomia (Ikaroa-Rawhiti)
Darren Hughes (Otaki)
Jonathan Hunt (list)
Graham Kelly (list)
Annette King (Rongotai)
Luamanuvao Winnie Laban (Mana)
Janet Mackey (East Coast)
Steve Maharey (Palmerston North)
Nanaia Mahuta (Tainui)
Trevor Mallard (Hutt South)
Damien O'Connor (West Coast-Tasman)
Mahara Okeroa (Te Tai Tonga)
David Parker (Otago)
Mark Peck (Invercargill)
Jill Pettis (Whanganui)
Lynne Pillay (Waitakere)
Mita Ririnui (Waiariki)
Ross Robertson (Manukau East)
Dover Samuels (Te Tai Tokerau)
Jim Sutton (Aoraki)
Paul Swain (Rimutaka)
John Tamihere (Tamaki Makaurau)
Judith Tizard (Auckland Central)
Tariana Turia (Te Tai Hauauru)
Margaret Wilson (list)
Dianne Yates (Hamilton East)

National

Shane Ardern (Taranaki-King Country)
Don Brash (list)
Gerry Brownlee (Ilam)
David Carter (list)
John Carter (Northland)
Judith Collins (Clevedon)
Brian Connell (Rakaia)
Bill English (Clutha-Southland)
Sandra Goudie (Coromandel)
Phil Heatley (Whangarei)
Paul Hutchison (Port Waikato)

John Key (Helensville)
Wayne Mapp (North Shore)
Murray McCully (East Coast Bays)
Simon Power (Rangitikei)
Katherine Rich (list)
Tony Ryall (Bay of Plenty)
Lynda Scott (Kaikoura)
Clem Simich (Tamaki)
Lockwood Smith (Rodney)
Nick Smith (Nelson)
Roger Sowry (list)
Georgina te Heuheu (list)
Lindsay Tisch (Piako)
Maurice Williamson (Pakuranga)
Pansy Wong (list)
Richard Worth (Epsom)

New Zealand First
Peter Brown (list)
Brent Catchpole (list)
Brian Donnelly (list)
Bill Gudgeon (list)
Dail Jones (list)
Ron Mark (list)
Craig McNair (list)
Pita Paraone (list)
Edwin Perry (list)
Jim Peters (list)
Winston Peters (Tauranga)
Barbara Stewart (list)
Doug Woolerton (list)

ACT
Donna Awatere Huata (list)
Deborah Coddington (list)
Gerry Eckhoff (list)
Stephen Franks (list)
Rodney Hide (list)
Muriel Newman (list)
Richard Prebble (list)

	Heather Roy (list)
	Ken Shirley (list)
Green	Sue Bradford (list)
	Rod Donald (list)
	Ian Ewen-Street (list)
	Jeanette Fitzsimons (list)
	Sue Kedgley (list)
	Keith Locke (list)
	Nandor Tanczos (list)
	Metiria Turei (list)
	Mike Ward (list)
United Future	Paul Adams (list)
	Marc Alexander (list)
	Larry Baldock (list)
	Gordon Copeland (list)
	Peter Dunne (Ohariu-Belmont)
	Bernie Ogilvy (list)
	Murray Smith (list)
	Judy Turner (list)
Progressive	Jim Anderton (Wigram)
	Matt Robson (list)

APPENDIX 5

The Government†

Ministers in the Cabinet

1 Helen Clark	Prime Minister
	Minister for Arts, Culture and Heritage
	Minister in Charge of the NZ Security Intelligence Service
	Minister Responsible for Ministerial Services
2 Michael Cullen	Deputy Prime Minister
	Minister of Finance
	Minister of Revenue
	Leader of the House
3 Jim Anderton*	Minister for Economic Development
	Minister for Industry and Regional Development
	Minister Responsible for the Public Trust
	Associate Minister of Health
4 Steve Maharey	Minister of Social Services and Employment
	Minister of Broadcasting
	Minister Responsible for the Transition Tertiary Education Commission
	Associate Minister of Education (Tertiary Education)
5 Phil Goff	Minister of Foreign Affairs and Trade
	Minister of Justice

† As announced on 15 August 2002.
* Anderton (Progressive) is the sole member of the Cabinet appointed from outside the Labour parliamentary caucus.

Appendix 5 – 403

6 Annette King	Minister of Health
	Minister for Food Safety
7 Jim Sutton	Minister of Agriculture
	Minister of Forestry
	Minister for Biosecurity
	Minister for Trade Negotiations
	Minister for Rural Affairs
8 Trevor Mallard	Minister of Education
	Minister of State Services
	Minister for Sport and Recreation
	Minister for the America's Cup
	Minister Responsible for the Education Review Office
	Minister for Adult and Community Education (CRRCT)
	Associate Minister of Finance
9 Pete Hodgson	Minister of Energy
	Minister of Fisheries
	Minister of Research, Science and Technology
	Minister for Crown Research Institutes
	Convenor of the Ministerial Group on Climate Change
	Associate Minister for Industry and Regional Development
	Associate Minister of Foreign Affairs and Trade
10 Margaret Wilson	Attorney-General
	[The portfolio of Attorney-General also includes responsibility for the Serious Fraud Office]
	Minister of Labour
	Minister in Charge of Treaty of Waitangi Negotiations
	Minister for Courts
	Associate Minister of Justice
11 Parekura Horomia	Minister of Maori Affairs
	Associate Minister of Social Services and Employment
	Associate Minister of Education (Employment)

	Associate Minister of Fisheries
	Associate Minister of Forestry
12 Lianne Dalziel	Minister of Commerce
	Minister of Immigration
	Minister for Senior Citizens
	Minister Responsible for the Law Commission
	Associate Minister of Justice
	Associate Minister of Education (Special Education)
13 George Hawkins	Minister of Police
	Minister of Internal Affairs
	Minister of Civil Defence
	Minister of Veterans' Affairs
14 Mark Burton	Minister of Defence
	Minister for State Owned Enterprises
	Minister of Tourism
	Deputy Leader of the House
15 Paul Swain	Minister of Transport
	Minister for Information Technology
	Minister of Communications
	Minister for Small Business
	Associate Minister of Finance
	Associate Minister of Revenue
	Associate Minister for Economic Development
16 Marian Hobbs	Minister for the Environment
	Minister for Disarmament and Arms Control
	Minister with Responsibility for Urban Affairs
	Minister Responsible for the National Library
	Minister Responsible for Archives New Zealand
	Associate Minister of Foreign Affairs and Trade (Official Development Assistance)
	Associate Minister for Biosecurity
	Associate Minister of Education
17 Mark Gosche	Minister of Corrections
	Minister of Housing
	Minister of Pacific Island Affairs
	Minister for Racing
18 Ruth Dyson	Minister for ACC
	Minister of Women's Affairs

19 John Tamihere	Minister for Disability Issues
	Associate Minister of Social Services and Employment
	Associate Minister of Health
	Minister of Youth Affairs
	Minister of Statistics
	Minister for Land Information
	Associate Minister of Maori Affairs
	Associate Minister of Commerce
	Associate Minister for Small Business
20 Chris Carter	Minister of Conservation
	Minister of Local Government
	Minister for Ethnic Affairs

Ministers outside Cabinet

21 Judith Tizard	Minister of Consumer Affairs
	Minister with Responsibility for Auckland Issues
	Associate Minister for Arts, Culture and Heritage
	Associate Minister of Transport
	Associate Minister of Commerce
22 Tariana Turia	Minister for the Community and Voluntary Sector
	Associate Minister of Maori Affairs (Social Development)
	Associate Minister of Health
	Associate Minister of Social Services and Employment (Social Services)
	Associate Minister of Housing
23 Rick Barker	Minister of Customs
	Associate Minister of Justice
	Associate Minister of Social Services and Employment
24 Dover Samuels	Minister of State
	Associate Minister of Tourism
	Associate Minister for Economic Development
	Associate Minister for Industry and Regional Development

25 Damien O'Connor Minister of State
                              Associate Minister of Agriculture
                              Associate Minister for Rural Affairs
                              Associate Minister for Racing
                              Associate Minister of Immigration
                              Associate Minister of Health
26 Harry Duynhoven Minister of State
                              Associate Minister of Energy
                              Associate Minister of Transport (including Civil Aviation)

Parliamentary Under-Secretaries

Taito Phillip Field	Parliamentary Under-Secretary to the: Minister of Pacific Island Affairs; Minister of Justice; Minister of Social Services and Employment
Mita Ririnui	Parliamentary Under-Secretary to the: Minister of Corrections; Minister of Conservation; Minister in Charge of Treaty of Waitangi Negotiations

Parliamentary Private Secretaries

Tim Barnett	Parliamentary Private Secretary to the Minister of Justice on human rights issues, and the Minister for the Community and Voluntary Sector
David Cunliffe	Parliamentary Private Secretary to the Minister of Finance and of Revenue, and the Minister of Commerce
Nanaia Mahuta	Parliamentary Private Secretary to the Minister of Education and the Minister of Local Government

CONTRIBUTORS

Tim Bale is a senior lecturer in political science at the University of Sussex. Until mid-2003 he taught comparative politics at Victoria University of Wellington. His most recent work focuses on the Green Party, on anti-party sentiment in New Zealand, on the British Labour Party, on EU diplomatic cooperation and on the European centre- and far-right. His publications on the media and politics include 'The symbolic agenda of a British satellite broadcaster's 1997 General Election coverage' (with Karen Sanders), *Journal of Broadcast and Electronic Media*; and 'Managing sleaze: Prime Ministers and news management in Conservative Great Britain and Socialist Spain' (with Karen Sanders and Maria-José Canel), *European Journal of Communication*.

Jonathan Boston is professor of public policy at Victoria University of Wellington. He has published widely on various aspects of New Zealand politics, public management, higher education and social policy. He is a member of the New Zealand Political Change Project, a research project funded by the Foundation for Research, Science and Technology [FRST] from 1995 to 2003. The project has been examining the impact of proportional representation on New Zealand's political institutions and policy processes. He was a co-author/co-editor of each of the project's principal book-length publications: *New Zealand Under MMP: A New Politics?*; *From Campaign to Coalition: New Zealand's First General Election Under Proportional Representation*; *Electoral and Constitutional Change in New Zealand: An MMP Source Book*; and *Left Turn: The New Zealand General Election of 1999*. During 2000–01 Professor Boston was a member of the Tertiary Education Advisory Commission.

Stephen Church is a political adviser, based in Parliament, for the United Future Party. He was previously a research fellow for the New Zealand Political Change Project based at Victoria University of Wellington, where he also taught political science and public policy from 1999 to 2002. He was a co-editor of *Left Turn* and was a contributor to four of the book's chapters.

Eamon Daly, at the age of 16, incurred a high level spinal injury as the result of a trampoline accident. Now 34, he is heavily involved in party politics, with current positions including being an elected member of the Labour Party Policy Council and Deputy Chair of the Canterbury Labour Regional Council. In 2002 he was a list-only Labour candidate for Parliament. During the time leading up to the 2005 general election campaign, he has taken up the opportunity to complete his PhD in Philosophy at the University of Canterbury, where he is a current holder of the University's Doctoral Scholarship for Students with Disabilities. Eamon Daly also works part time as a member of the government-appointed Bioethics Council, and as a Human Rights Trainer under the auspices of the Human Rights Commission.

Brian Donnelly entered Parliament in 1996 as a New Zealand First list member. He subsequently became a Minister in the New Zealand First-National coalition government but resigned his portfolio when that coalition came to an end. He was re-elected to Parliament in 1999 and 2002 as a list member. He is chairperson of New Zealand First's policy committee, was New Zealand First's campaign co-ordinator for the 2002 election, and is chairperson of Parliament's Education and Science Select Committee. He contributed the chapter on the New Zealand First campaign in *Left Turn: The New Zealand General Election of 1999*.

Cate Faehrmann arrived to manage the New Zealand Green Party's campaign from South Australia, after coordinating the Greens' state election campaign and running as lead Senate candidate for the 2001 Australian Federal election. After the 2002 New Zealand election, she crossed the Tasman once again to coordinate media for the Greens during the Victorian and then the New South Wales state elections. Cate Faehrmann has a background in student politics and campaigning, and is an Arts graduate majoring in cultural politics and gender studies.

Stephen Franks is an ACT MP who first entered Parliament as a list member in 1999. Re-elected in 2002, he is Deputy Chairman of the Justice and Electoral Select Committee and a member of the Regulations Review Select Committee. Before entering Parliament he was a senior partner in the Wellington law firm of Chapman Tripp, with 20 years of commercial law experience.

Paul Gibson is a partially blind disability consultant and National Policy Manager for CCS. He has been involved in a number of community, education and disability organisations, and has served as President of the Disabled Persons Assembly, an organisation led by disabled people, and representing the diversity of disabled people, their families and whanau, and the many organisations providing services for them; and as President of the Students Association at Victoria University of Wellington. He has a Bachelor of Science, majoring in physics, and is completing a Master of Public Policy. In 2002 he was a list-only Labour candidate for Parliament.

Tim Grafton is National Party Leader Bill English's Chief Advisor. He has almost 20 years' political experience. He was a parliamentary press gallery journalist during Labour's two terms in office in the 1980s. After the 1990 election, he joined Sir William Birch's office as his senior media adviser and his representative on the Bolger government's communications strategy and 1993 campaign committees. In 1994, he joined the private sector, advising major corporations and organisations on government relations and strategic communications. In 2000, he joined Jenny Shipley's senior staff, advising on strategy, and was retained by Bill English on the change of leadership.

Paul Harris was appointed the first Chief Executive of the New Zealand Electoral Commission in 1994. Prior to that he was a senior lecturer in the school of political science and international relations at Victoria University of Wellington and was Deputy Dean of the Faculty of Arts. He served as the Principal Research Officer for the Royal Commission on the Electoral System in 1985–86. He wrote the introduction to *From Campaign to Coalition: New Zealand's First General Election Under Proportional Representation*.

Janine Hayward is a senior lecturer in New Zealand politics at the University of Otago. In addition to her research on political campaigning and the media, she has a particular interest in the Treaty of Waitangi and indigenous politics in other Commonwealth nations. Together with Chris Rudd, Dr. Hayward wrote the chapter on 'Metropolitan Newspapers and the Election' in *Left Turn: The New Zealand General Election of 1999*.

Margaret Hayward is completing her doctoral dissertation at Victoria University of Wellington on *Political Leadership in New Zealand from 1984–2000*. She worked as a private secretary to Prime Minister Norman Kirk and is the author of the award-winning *Diary of the Kirk Years*, which records his brief but pivotal period in office. Subsequently she spent many years teaching business communication and public relations, and also wrote a number of books on rose gardening. She has since contributed articles and chapters on political leadership and on women as political leaders to a range of publications. In 2002 Margaret was the Labour candidate for the National-held seat of Rangitikei.

Colin James is a political journalist of 30 years' experience. He writes columns in the *New Zealand Herald* and in *Management Magazine*, is an occasional political commentator on radio and television, runs a forecasting group for business, and directs a programme on the state sector at the Institute of Policy Studies. He has written several books, including *The Quiet Revolution* and *New Territory*, as well as three on New Zealand elections. Colin James wrote chapters on the 1996 and 1999 elections for *From Campaign to Coalition* and *Left Turn* respectively.

Jon Johansson is a lecturer in political science at the school of history, philosophy, political science and international relations at Victoria University of Wellington. He completed his doctoral dissertation entitled *Political Leadership in New Zealand: In Theory and Practice* in 2002. His teaching and research interests include political leadership, political psychology, and New Zealand and US politics.

Tomas Kriha is a freelance public affairs consultant. A member of ACT since 1994, he has been involved in all of the party's general election and by-election campaigns. During the 2002 election campaign he worked in ACT's 'war room' on media strategy. A graduate of Victoria University of Wellington, he served as ACT's research and policy advisor during its first term (1996–1999) in Parliament.

Matt Lamason completed an honours degree in political science and international relations at Victoria University of Wellington in 2002. In addition to his interests in New Zealand politics and the parliamentary process, he has a keen interest in social justice and the politics of third world development. In the near future he hopes to write an MA thesis on the global trade in coffee, a topic brewed out of four years of making coffee in the Wellington café scene.

Stephen Levine is professor and head of the school of history, philosophy, political science and international relations at Victoria University of Wellington. He has published widely on voting behaviour and constitutional issues in New Zealand and the Pacific Islands. He served as director of the New Zealand Political Change Project (1995–2003), examining the implications of New Zealand's proportional representation electoral system for New Zealand's government and politics. In addition to co-authoring/co-editing the project's four main books, he is the co-editor of *The New Zealand Politics Source Book: Third Edition* and co-author of *From Muldoon to Lange: New Zealand Elections in the 1980s*.

Elizabeth McLeay is an associate professor in political science at Victoria University of Wellington. She has published on Cabinet government, the political representation of Maori and women, comparative public policy, housing and policing policy. She helped to establish the New Zealand Politics Research Group and has been a co-editor of the journal, *Political Science*. Between 1995 and 1998 she was Deputy Dean of Victoria University of Wellington's Faculty of Humanities and Social Sciences. In 2001 she was a Fulbright visiting professor in New Zealand Studies at Georgetown University. As a member of the New Zealand Political Change Project, she was a co-author/co-editor of the project's four main books. In 1999 Professor McLeay edited *New Zealand Politics and Social Patterns: Selected Works of Robert Chapman*.

Al Morrison is a former teacher and journalist. He is a graduate of Dunedin Teachers College and Otago and Canterbury Universities, and in 1978 spent a year doing post-graduate research at the University of Columbia, Missouri, on a Rotary scholarship. He was political editor at Radio New Zealand for five years, leaving after the 2002 election to take up a general manager's position at the Department of Conservation.

Brian Nicolle is a partner at Awaroa, a Wellington-based public relations firm. He has acted as ACT's campaign manager in all three MMP elections and was also involved in the 1993 referendum on MMP. He has a background in retail banking, public affairs, political and event management, as well as a strong personal involvement in the voluntary and not-for-profit sectors.

Hekia Parata is a founding partner and the executive director of Gardiner Parata since 1995, a Wellington-based consultancy company devoted to Maori development. She is a graduate of Waikato University and has attended the Kennedy School of Government at Harvard University. She has been a senior public servant in Foreign Affairs, the Prime Minister's Office, the Housing Corporation, and the Ministry of Maori Development, and was the Crown's Chief Negotiator for the Taranaki claims in 2000. She stood unsuccessfully for National in Wellington Central in the 2002 election, and would be the first to enter Parliament from National's party list in the event of a National list MP leaving the House before the next general election.

Nigel S. Roberts is an associate professor of political science at the Victoria University of Wellington. His teaching and research interests include New Zealand government and politics, Scandinavian government and politics, comparative electoral systems and voting behaviour. As a member of the New Zealand Political Change Project, he co-authored or co-edited the project's principal publications, and was the author of the chapter on New Zealand's elections and electoral system in the recent Oxford University Press volume *Elections in Asia and the Pacific*. He has been an election-night analyst and commentator for TV1 since 1987.

Claire Robinson is programme leader of graphic design and advertising at Massey University's college of design, fine arts and music. She is a former New Zealand foreign service officer (1985–1990) and former Private Secretary to the Minister of Women's Affairs (1991). In pursuit of creativity she gained a Bachelor of Design degree from the Wellington School of Design in 1995. Her passion for visual communications design has merged with a fascination with elections, carrying on a family tradition – her father was Dr Alan Robinson, who specialised in the study of parties, elections and voting behaviour at the school of political science and public administration at Victoria University of Wellington. She is presently completing a PhD on political advertising in the 1999 and 2002 general elections.

Chris Rudd is a senior lecturer in political studies at the University of Otago. His major research interests are New Zealand politics and the welfare state, as well as New Zealand elections and the media. He is co-editor of *The Political Economy of New Zealand*, and a contributor to *The Decent Society*, *Electoral Behaviour in New Zealand*, and *Left Turn*.

Rob Salmond is a PhD student in the department of political science at the University of California, Los Angeles. A graduate of the school of political science and international relations at Victoria University of Wellington, he now specialises in comparative political institutions, New Zealand politics and American legislative politics. His most recent publication was 'Democratic Reform in Tonga: Towards an Alternative Electoral System' in *Revue Juridique Polynesienne*.

Mark Stonyer served for eight years as Chief of Staff of United Future New Zealand's parliamentary unit and was the election co-ordinator for the party during the 2002 general election. Prior to this he was parliamentary chief advisor to party leader Peter Dunne, MP for Ohariu-Belmont. He graduated from Victoria University of Wellington with a degree in political science and public policy. He contributed chapters on United's 1996 and 1999 campaigns to *From Campaign to Coalition* and *Left Turn*. He left United Future in February 2003 and is now self-employed as a government relations consultant.

John Tamihere was elected as the Labour MP for Hauraki in 1999 and re-elected in the Tamaki Makaurau electorate in 2002. During the 46th Parliament he served as chairperson of the Maori Affairs Select Committee. He also served as a member of the Finance and Expenditure Select Committee. Following the 2002 election, he was elevated to Cabinet, where he holds the Land Information, Statistics and Youth Affairs portfolios. He is also Associate Minister of Maori Affairs, Small Business and Commerce.

Nandor Tanczos was elected in 1999 and 2002 as a list MP for the Green Party and is the Greens' spokesperson for Drug Law Reform, Justice, Education, Treaty Issues, Urban Affairs and Youth Affairs. He is a member of the Justice and Electoral Select Committee. He is co-owner/director of the Hempstore Aotearoa, a small retail business. He has a Bachelor of Social Sciences degree from the University of Waikato.

Graham Watson is the party manager of ACT New Zealand and was involved in co-ordinating ACT's 2002 election campaign, including running its research programme. A graduate of the University of Auckland with an MA in political philosophy, his background has included hosting talkback radio, political/market research, and a longstanding involvement in political campaigning and activism.

Mike Williams took 15 months away from his information technology and marketing consultancy to act as campaign manager for the Labour Party in the 1999 general election, and published a chapter on the campaign in *Left Turn*. He joined the Labour Party in 1967 and worked as a political organiser for the Australian and New Zealand Labour parties in the 1980s. Subsequently he set up his own companies specialising in market research, software development, and direct database, telephone and internet marketing. In 2000 he was elected President of the Labour Party.

INDEX

ACT 22, 24, 43, 47, 51, 130-1, 135, 154, 203, 243, 284, 285, 288, 289, 290, 291, 300, 315, 318, 330, 331; advertising 94-6, 100-1, 219, 236, 240, 248, 274-5, 279; and early election 34, 93; and Maori 54, 295-6, 301, 326; and media 90, 94-5, 219, 259, 262-3; and women 93, 248, 298, 326-7, 328; candidates, selection of 304; leadership 62, 70, 92, 94-5, 109, 319-20; party vote 89, 97, 250, 286, 313-14, 316-17, 318; policies 54, 70, 91, 92, 96-7, 119, 137-8, 139, 185, 215, 248, 250, 268, 274, 323; polls 90-3; results 25-6, 70, 188, 306, 311, 318, 335; *see also* Prebble, Richard

ACT campaign 54-5, 57, 70, 87-97, 105, 135-9, 185, 187, 248-50, 258

advertising, electoral and party 100, 103, 114, 126, 129-30, 137, 148, 235-53, 247, 252, 253; hoardings and billboards 94-6, 107, 129, 146, 148, 237, 241, 270-80; mail out 94, 96, 101-2, 127, 129, 144, 147; posters 101, 142; websites and email 21, 97, 99, 128, 131, 164, 172, 250, 273

Alliance 20, 22, 23, 24, 27, 46, 47, 51, 130, 140, 154, 185, 186, 276-7, 287, 288, 291, 292, 309, 314, 316, 317, 351; and Labour 31, 34, 39, 50, 104, 288; and media 259, 262-3; and women 327; collapse of 16-17, 31-2, 36, 37, 38, 39, 40, 71, 118, 128, 211, 278, 308, 315, 329, 338; leadership 31-2, 71, 213, 214, 322; reaction to early election 43; reaction to US war on terror 31; results 25-6, 188, 283-5, 306, 315,

335; *see also* Harre, Laila *and* Labour-Alliance Coalition

Anae, Arthur 296, 307

Anderton, Jim 16, 23, 24, 31-32, 34, 37, 38, 46, 60, 71, 188, 211, 276-7, 278, 285, 314, 315, 321-2, 330, 331, 333, 338, 342, 346, 347, 355; *see also* Progressive Coalition

Aotearoa Legalise Cannabis 25-6, 188, 284

Asian MPs 294, 296

Asian vote 55, 95-6, 123, 275

Atkinson, Harry 42

Auckland Central 101, 140, 144

Barnett, Tim 356

Beattie, David 42

Beetham, Bruce 145, 148

Beyer, Georgina 147, 175, 178, 180-1, 182-4, 185-6, 187, 188, 189-90

Blair, Tony 64, 138

Boag, Michelle 35, 38, 194, 198-9, 201, 203, 205, 302

Bolger, Jim 69, 245, 288, 309, 328

Bowen, George 42

Bradford, Max 306

Brash, Don 39, 302, 307

Braybrooke, Geoff 272, 300, 306

Broadcasting Act 1989 76, 77

Brooks, Brian 202

Brown, David 124

- 415 -

Brown, Peter 121
Buchanan, Ian 184, 185, 186, 188, 189
Buchanan, W.C. 179
Bunny, H. 179
Burton, Mark 147

Campbell, John 50, 69-70, 107, 210, 225-6, 233, 245, 254
candidates, selection of 192-206, 301-5; *see also* ACT *and* Greens *and* Labour *and* National *and* New Zealand First *and* United Future
Capill, Graham 131-2, 277-8
Cartwright, Dame Sylvia 63, 356
Chal, Kelly 292-3, 299
Choudhary, Ashraf 296
Christchurch Central 169
Christian Coalition 23, 25-6, 284, 285, 337
Christian Democrats 26, 124, 276, 277, 284, 317, 337
Christian Heritage 25-6, 37, 57, 131, 181, 185, 188, 191, 277, 285, 317, 327, 337
Clark, Helen 23, 45-6, 57, 58, 104, 121, 148, 171, 288, 325, 329, 330, 333, 339, 342, 355; and Bill English 24, 35, 48, 65-6, 69-70, 115, 233, 251. 319-20; and 'corngate' 49, 50, 107-8, 210, 224-8, 245, 254, 256, 265, 336; and early election 15, 28, 31-4, 38-41, 43, 62-4, 184, 278; and Greens 33, 40, 48, 71, 93, 100, 227, 265, 335-6, 344; and media 24, 46, 48-51, 68-9, 212-13, 221, 223, 224, 225-6, 228, 231, 233, 254, 265, 269; and MMP 36; and New Zealand First 24, 55, 328; and 'paintergate' 37, 48-9, 209-10, 224, 245, 256, 265; and United Future 131; and 2002 campaign 67-8; image 17, 49-50, 55-6, 57, 64, 74, 110, 237, 246, 256-7, 258, 269, 320; leadership 48-50, 56, 59-60, 61-2, 64-6, 67-9, 105, 110, 115, 231, 244-6, 250-2, 256-7, 319-20, 321, 325, 328, 332; *see also* Labour
Clevedon 299
Clifton, Jane 119
coalition government 15, 16, 17, 29, 89, 109, 111-12, 116, 261, 287, 330-1, 332, 333, 334-5, 338-9, 343-7, 356, 360
Collinge, David 126, 132
confidence and supply 123, 286, 336, 337, 339, 340-1, 343, 345
Connell, Brian 299
Cooper, Garth 53
cooperation agreement 333, 340, 346, 347-55, 359
Coromandel 98, 103, 109, 140, 213, 272, 284, 286, 287, 309
'corngate' 46, 49-50, 57, 61, 71, 93, 103, 106-8, 109, 115, 210-11, 224-8, 254, 262; *see also* Clark, Helen
Creech, Wyatt 177-8, 179, 180, 181-2, 306
Cullen, Michael 39, 342, 355
Cunliffe, David 356

Daly, Eamon 162, 164, 168-74
debate 114, 136-7, 152-3, 220, 229-30, 270; law and order debate 142-3; leaders' debate 23, 50-1, 56, 66, 69-71, 93, 121, 128, 130-2, 142, 214, 230-3, 244, 254, 257, 258-9, 263-4, 276; *see also* media
Dennis, Renetta 147, 148
Devoy, Susan 53
disabled community 161-7, 168-4
Donald, Rod 71, 100, 247, 248, 259, 333, 342
Douglas, Roger 56, 70
Dunne, Peter 23, 24, 27, 47, 56-7, 70-1, 109, 123, 124, 125, 126, 128, 129, 212, 254, 263-4, 265, 273, 284, 285, 315, 317, 320, 339, 342-3; leadership 51, 74, 130-1, 132, 230-2, 242-4, 275-6, 337; *see also* United Future
Dyer, Heaton 234
Dyson, Ruth 164, 171, 172

early election 15-18, 27, 28-44, 62-4, 65-6, 76, 278, 333, 358; constitutional rules for 41-3, 63; effects of 37-8, 65, 76, 147, 184, 191, 194; in contrast with 1984 16, 28; reactions to 18, 119-20; reasons behind 28, 31-3, 37, 46, 104, 278; theories

Index – 417

behind 28-31, 43-4; *see also* ACT *and* Alliance *and* Clark, Helen *and* English, Bill *and* Greens *and* Labour *and* National *and* New Zealand First *and* Progressive Coalition *and* United Future
Electoral Act 1993 15, 19, 75, 77, 78, 94, 178-9, 293, 301
electoral administration 19-20
Electoral Commission 19, 20, 21, 26, 36, 75-84, 101, 125, 129, 178, 235, 286, 290, 293, 297, 304, 309
Electoral Integrity Act 2001 17, 31, 75
electoral boundaries, changes in 18-19, 177-80, 187, 190, 276, 309
electorate seats 19, 21-2, 24, 25-6, 81, 83, 98, 125, 128, 181, 311-12
electorate vote 81, 317-18
Elworthy, Sir Peter 53
Employment Relations Bill 112
English, Bill 24, 39, 52, 69-70, 74, 92, 114-15, 215, 236-7, 309; and debates 131, 233; and Helen Clark 24, 35, 65-6, 69-70, 115, 233, 251; and media 221, 251, 269; image 69-70, 91, 250, 251-2, 256-7, 258, 269, 271; leadership 35, 47, 48-9, 62, 64-6, 91, 106, 109, 111-12, 117, 159, 237-8, 250-2, 256, 319, 320, 321; reaction to early election 40, 43; *see also* National
Epsom 89, 90, 286, 309
ERMA 349, 354, 357
'ethnic' vote 21, 126, 303

Fairbrother, Russell 300
Falloon, John 178, 180
Field, Taito Phillip 271, 296
Finlayson, Chris 201
Fitzsimons, Jeanette 24, 71, 98, 102, 248, 259, 272, 333, 342
FPP 15, 18, 21, 25, 27, 33, 44, 45-6, 58, 161, 213, 259, 283, 288, 301, 302, 305
Franks, Stephen 135-39, 142, 143, 249
Fraser, Ian 183
Fraser, Peter 64

fundraising 126, 136, 147, 153-54
Future New Zealand 25, 26, 124, 125, 276, 284, 317, 337

Gallagher, Martin 173
Gardiner, Wira 154
genetic engineering/modification (GE/GM) *see* Clark, Helen *and* 'corngate' *and* Greens *and* issues
GE moratorium 33, 38, 53, 102-3, 108, 109, 211, 221, 336, 339, 356
Gibson, Paul 161-7, 171, 172
Goff, Phil 142, 271
Gosche, Mark 296
Goudie, Sandra 272
government formation 333-60
Greens 15, 22-3, 24, 27, 48, 51, 55, 56, 67, 87, 88, 93, 105, 106, 122, 127, 154, 185, 186, 209, 210, 240, 243, 285, 287, 288, 289, 290, 291, 292, 318, 334, 335, 340, 344, 359; advertising 95, 100-1, 142, 236, 240, 247-8, 275, 279; and GE 33, 38, 40, 46, 47, 50, 53-4, 67, 71, 99-100, 102-3, 108, 109-10, 112, 211-12, 221, 247, 260, 267, 275; and Labour 32-3, 36, 37, 38, 40, 46, 49, 50, 54, 57, 89, 93, 98-100, 108, 115, 116, 123, 140, 211, 226, 245-6, 247, 265, 289-90, 331, 336-7, 339, 341, 342-3; and Labour-Alliance Coalition 100; and Labour-Progressive Coalition 89, 332, 333, 352-3; and Maori 141, 296; and media 50, 98, 99-100, 142-3, 221, 247-8, 259, 260, 261, 262; and New Zealand First 118-19, 120, 121; and women 298-9, 300, 301, 303, 327; candidates, selection of 100, 303, 305; CD 101, 102, 142; global party 102-3; leadership 49, 62; party vote 144, 248, 275, 286, 316, 318, 358; policies 53-4, 99, 100, 101-3, 109, 212, 247, 326; polls 99, 105; reaction to early election 43; results 25-6, 71, 93, 103, 144, 188, 284, 291, 306, 309, 311, 314, 315, 317, 339
Greens campaign 71, 98-103, 109, 140-4, 247-81

Grey Power 183
Grey, George 42

Hager, Nicky 49, 50, 53, 102, 107, 210, 336
Hamilton East 173, 309
Hamilton West 173
Harding, Graham 120
Harre, Laila 49-50, 71, 213, 214, 278, 285, 315
Hasler, Marie 299, 307
Hauraki 156
Hawke, Joe 306
Hayward, Margaret 145-9, 150, 279-80
Hazardous Substances and New Organisms Bill/Act 99, 100, 354
Helensville 299, 302
Henderson, Bill 185, 188
Herlihy, Gavan 307
Hide, Rodney 90, 109, 248-9
Hill, Kim 131
Hirschfeld, Michael 202
Hobbs, Marian 152, 154, 202
Holland, Sid 28, 42
Holmes 'worm' debate *see* debate *and* media
Horomia, Parekura 158
Hosking, Mike 123, 136-7, 142
Hughes, Darren 300
Hughes, Glenda 200
Hunt, Jonathan 289
Hunterville 302
Hunua 302

Independents 158, 288, 307
issues of 2002 election 51-7, 72, 137-8, 186, 218, 322-7; abortion 167; animal welfare 102; cannabis decriminalisation 55-6, 121, 143-4, 212, 243, 324; children 102; commonsense and family 56, 71, 129, 212, 243, 276; drug strategy 346, 348; ecological tax reform 102; economy 52, 56, 57, 64, 66, 92, 101, 105, 114, 116, 117, 187, 189, 212, 215, 218, 266, 267, 268, 324, 325-6, 356; education 37, 51, 52-3, 70, 92, 102, 105-6, 113, 114, 115, 116, 117, 189, 215, 218, 250, 252, 256, 266, 268, 277, 323, 324, 325, 346, 356; employment 277, 324, 325, 346; energy 348; environment 47, 99, 268, 283, 348, 356; family 57, 125-7, 131-2, 212, 242-3, 275-6, 348, 356; foreign and defence policy 72, 266; free trade agreement with US 38-9, 47; gay marriage 121; gender 167; genetic engineering 33, 38, 39, 40, 46-7, 49, 50, 53-4, 57, 67, 71, 89, 99, 100, 101, 102-3, 106-8, 112, 119, 185, 186-7, 189, 247, 260, 267, 275, 324, 325, 326, 336, 340, 342, 356; health 51, 52, 92, 101, 102, 105, 113, 114, 116, 117, 181-2, 189, 215, 218, 266, 267, 268, 277, 323, 324, 325, 346, 356; human rights 164; immigration 23, 33, 47, 54-5, 57, 61, 66-7, 70, 106, 212, 215, 241, 258, 262, 267-8, 274, 324, 325, 326; industrial relations 324; inequality 162-3; law and order 66, 97, 113, 114, 115, 137-8, 215, 218, 219, 222, 250, 256, 262, 266, 267-8, 274, 323-4, 325, 326; Maori issues 23, 47, 51, 54-6, 73, 100, 153, 157-8, 159, 212, 268; privatisation 139; prostitution reform 55, 121; race relations 74, 92, 97, 324, 325; religion 291; retirement 277; social policy 56; social welfare 47, 116, 139, 348, 356; superannuation 72-3, 74, 119; taxation 51, 70, 92, 102, 139, 266, 268, 324; transport 102, 181-2, 185, 267, 268, 348; Treaty of Waitangi 23, 51, 54, 55, 66-7, 68, 72, 73, 106, 114-15, 116, 119, 137, 141, 157, 185, 215, 241, 250, 258, 262, 266, 267, 268, 274, 324, 326-7, 356; violence and crime 23, 51, 54, 70, 92, 95, 96, 106, 116, 117, 138, 185, 187, 215, 222, 241, 324, 325, 348

Jackman, Gordon 342
Jackson, Willy 278
Jennings, Owen 306
Judd, Catherine 328

Keall, Judy 148, 202, 300, 306
Key, John 198, 299
Kidd, Doug 306
Kyd, Warren 299, 307

Laban, Winnie 296
Labour 22, 24, 37-8, 56, 71, 73-4, 88-9, 118, 119, 121, 138, 139, 154, 192, 209, 232, 233, 242, 243, 253, 284, 285, 290, 291, 293, 301, 306, 307-8, 312-14, 315, 316, 329, 334, 341, 342, 345, 346, 356, 358-9; advertising 122, 126, 236, 237, 240, 244, 253, 270-1, 273, 279; and ACT 138-9; and Alliance 31-2, 34, 46; and disabled 161-7, 168-74; and Greens 32-3, 38, 46-7, 54, 57, 93, 98-100, 106, 115, 116, 118-19, 140, 210-11, 226-7, 232, 245-6, 331, 336-7, 340, 348-51, 353-4; and Maori 56, 68, 156-60, 271, 294-5; and Maori MPs 295-6; and media 38, 174, 212-13, 216, 222-3, 228, 244-5, 259, 260, 261, 262, 263, 336-9, 340, 343, 347-55; and National 32, 40, 52, 62, 105, 198, 202, 238, 329-30, 334; and New Zealand First 338; and United Future 337, 341-2, 348-51; and women 298-9, 300, 327-8; candidates, selection of 145-6, 161-2, 169, 183-4, 192, 194-6, 197-8, 201-2, 293, 302, 303-4; election manifesto 241; electoral vote 185, 187, 271, 317-18; Kirk Branch 169, 174; Labour Electoral Council 84; lead up to 2002 election 46, 62, 64; leadership 33, 62, 105, 117, 156, 214, 244-5, 256-60, 271, 289, 302, 327; list MPs 295, 296; party list 162, 166, 169-70, 195, 196, 202; party vote 149, 156, 185, 187, 237-8, 271, 313, 316; policies 51-2, 56, 74, 105, 114-15, 164-5, 171, 172-3, 216, 222, 260, 266, 323, 356; polls and ratings 18, 33-4, 36, 43-4, 49, 51, 62-3, 87-8, 90, 98, 111-13, 115, 329-30; readiness for 2002 election 37, 39, 66, 104-5, 184; results 25-7, 45, 129, 188, 309, 311; safe seat 45, 175, 272-3; 1935 election 329; 1938 election 329; 1951 election 329; 1984 election 177; 1987 election 108-9, 177, 329; 1996 election 24-5, 194, 231, 343; 1999 election 25, 26, 45, 56, 109, 177, 245, 277, 283-4, 349-55; *see also* Clark, Helen
Labour campaign 67-8, 72-3, 104-10, 145-9. 156-60, 163-5, 168-74, 180, 184-6, 209, 237, 241, 244-6, 256
Labour-Alliance Coalition 15, 16, 31, 34, 38, 39, 55, 56, 100, 104, 123, 277, 288, 315, 323, 329, 330, 335, 336, 343, 346, 348, 355
Labour-Progressive Coalition 15, 23, 24, 46, 60, 71, 89, 211, 288, 290, 292, 332, 333, 335, 336, 343, 344-7, 349, 355-6, 357-8
Ladley, Andrew 342
Lange, David 259, 329
leadership 24, 48-50, 59-74, 94-5, 105, 111-13, 156, 157-8, 189, 193, 214, 231, 242, 244, 254, 255-60, 319-22, 328, 332; *see also* ACT *and* Alliance *and* Clark, Helen *and* Dunne, Peter *and* English, Bill *and* Greens *and* Labour *and* National *and* New Zealand First *and* Peters, Winston *and* United Future
Leay, Barrie 45
Lee, Graeme 337
Life Sciences Network 103
list candidates 21-2, 161-7, 168-74, 181, 194
list MPs 18, 166, 181, 188-9, 295
Luxton, John 307

majority government 15, 18, 23, 24, 27, 33, 36-7, 38, 44, 46, 60, 63, 73, 89, 106, 156, 332, 339, 359
Mahuta, Nanaia 295, 356
Mana 200, 272
Mana Maori 188
Maori candidates 150-5, 156-60, 303
Maori representation 158, 161, 195, 294-6, 355
Maori roll 156-7, 295
Maori seats 19, 24, 156-60, 161, 271, 283, 291
Maori vote 79, 82-3, 126, 156-8
marginal seats 145
Mauri Pacific 158, 288

McCarten, Matt 31, 140
McCully, Murray 38, 209
MacFarlane, Ian 185, 188
MacKenzie, Denise 181
McVicar, Garth 187
media 19, 38-41, 71, 94-5, 96, 102, 110, 114, 115, 142, 148, 151-2, 171, 174, 190, 209, 324, 332; accessibility of 164; allocation of election broadcasting 75-8, 80, 94, 100-1, 129-30, 236, 278; effect of 40-1, 44, 50-1, 52, 57, 61-2, 66, 88, 89, 107, 143, 189, 210-11, 212, 228, 231; journalism 110, 209-11, 213, 224-8; newspapers 95, 148-9, 254-9, 279; radio 95, 102, 130, 159, 210; responsibility of 143, 216, 218; television 50, 107-8, 114, 129-30, 136-7, 138, 141, 210, 214, 217-34, 235, 250-1, 254, 268, 270, 279; 'worm' 23, 50-1, 56-7, 71, 121-2, 128, 189, 214, 230-1, 234, 244, 254, 263-4
Millington, Sarah 184, 188
MMP 15, 16-17, 19, 21, 22, 33, 36, 44, 58, 60, 75, 76, 77, 87, 89, 105, 109, 117, 126, 156, 161, 166, 167, 177, 183, 192, 193-4, 213, 216, 220, 232-3, 236, 238, 255, 259, 261, 271, 274, 277, 283, 285, 286, 289, 290, 291, 293, 294, 295, 301, 302, 312, 313, 314, 317, 318, 327, 328, 331, 332, 334, 335-6, 337, 344, 355; compared with FPP 21, 45-6, 156, 161, 180, 283, 287-8, 302, 305, 313; effects of 19, 20-3, 27, 36, 180-1, 188-9, 190, 192, 213, 261, 276, 284, 289, 293; information campaign on 21, 75, 76, 78-84; MMP Review Committee 36, 294, 285, 295; public understanding of 21; views on 18, 20
minority government 15, 46, 71, 109, 277, 308, 339, 347, 358, 359-60
Mitchell, Oliver 342
Moran, Deb 342
Morrison, Al 154-5, 209-16
Muldoon, Robert 16, 23, 28, 42, 64, 67, 69, 259
Mulgan, Richard 285
Mullins, Koro 184

Napier 272-73, 300
National 22, 24, 31, 45, 56, 71, 73, 89, 104, 105, 109, 118, 119, 130, 144, 147, 180, 184, 186, 189, 192, 212, 232, 233, 242, 243, 284, 285, 290, 291, 292, 293, 295, 301, 323, 331, 337, 341, 345, 351; advertising 114, 126, 236, 240, 250-2, 261, 262, 271-2, 273, 279, 308, 309, 312-14, 323, 331, 337, 341, 345, 351; and Labour 36, 52, 112, 113, 114, 198-201, 237, 238; and Maori 47, 54, 114-15, 153, 159-60, 296, 326; and media 112, 114, 151-2, 209, 223, 236-7, 251-2, 259, 260, 262; and women 298-301, 327-8; candidates, selection of 150-5, 192, 194, 196-201, 202, 203, 204, 205-6, 293, 302, 303, 304, 306-7; challenges to Alliance leadership by 31-2; electorate-based party 299; electorate votes 149, 155, 272, 317-18; in opposition 31-2, 34-6, 112, 116, 225; leadership 35, 62, 69, 91, 111-13, 114-15, 117, 159, 197, 203, 205, 206, 240, 250, 251, 256-60, 271, 289, 302, 319-22; lead-up to 2002 election 52-3, 54, 62, 64-5, 111-14; party list 146, 155, 178, 194, 197, 201, 203, 206, 272, 299, 301-2; party vote 114, 236-8, 272-3, 313, 315-16; policies 40, 47, 52-3, 54, 70, 111, 113-15, 116-17, 159, 187, 215, 250, 266, 268; polls and ratings 35-6, 47, 49, 87-8, 105, 112, 113, 114, 115, 209; reaction to early election 18, 20, 39-40, 43, 65-6, 111, 113, 150; results 25-7, 45, 108-9, 129, 188, 203-4, 309, 311, 315-16, 334, 336; safe seats 145-6, 149, 175, 177, 180, 187, 189; scandal in 35-6; supporters 36, 45, 47, 57, 69, 70, 88, 117; 1951 election 16, 28; 1978 election 45; 1981 election 54; 1984 election 16, 28, 42, 43; 1993 election 283; 1996 election 24-5, 343; 1999 election 25, 26, 36, 45, 116, 194, 329-30; *see also* English, Bill
National campaign 69-70, 72-3, 105, 111-17, 150-5, 159, 236-7, 250-2, 256
National-New Zealand First Coalition 15, 17, 26, 56, 66, 118, 288, 321, 344-5, 355

National-United Coalition 344-5
Neeson, Brian 198-9, 205, 299, 307
Neill, Alec 307
Neill, Sam 53
Nelson 98
New Zealand First 20, 22, 47, 50, 62, 66-7, 70, 71, 88, 89, 90, 93, 94, 103, 114, 185, 203, 245, 246, 283, 284, 285, 287, 289, 290, 291, 295, 314, 331; advertising 114, 121, 236, 240, 241-2, 253, 273-4; and Greens 47, 67, 118-20, 121; and Labour 24, 66-7, 119, 121, 242, 338, 339; and Maori 24, 54, 66, 67, 119, 158, 215, 296, 301, 326; and media 89, 94, 119, 259, 262-3, 265; and National 17, 343, 351; and women 298-9, 300, 327-8; candidates, selection of 119, 299, 304; leadership 24, 51, 62, 109, 120, 262, 319, 328, 331; party vote 274, 299, 316; policies 54-5, 70, 119-20, 187, 241-2, 247, 250, 323, 326; polls 17, 119, 121; reactions to early election 119-20; results 25-6, 122, 158, 188, 305-6, 307, 309, 311, 317, 318, 335; return from oblivion 24, 105, 122, 308; *see also* Peters, Winston
New Zealand First campaign 66-7, 118-22, 212, 241-2
New Zealand Political Change Project 66, 67
Newman, Muriel 249

Ohariu-Belmont 123, 125, 129, 198, 213, 273, 275-6, 284, 286, 345
One NZ 188
opposition 16, 17, 23, 24, 31-2, 35, 39, 46, 61, 110, 112, 223, 225, 287-90, 329-30, 332
O'Regan, Katherine 287
Otago 309
Otaki 145, 202, 300
Outdoor Recreation 17, 26, 278, 285
Owen, Frank 185
Owens, Adam 185, 188

Pacific Island representation 195, 294, 296, 303, 355
Pacific Island vote 55, 79, 82-3
Pahiatua 175, 179
'paintergate' 37, 48-9, 115, 209-10, 245, 256, 262, 265-6; *see also* Clark, Helen
Parata, Hekia 150-5, 198, 296, 300
Parker, Stephen 226
party hopping 31, 34
party lists 18, 21-2, 24, 26, 79, 82, 83, 100, 102, 128, 161-7, 168-74, 180, 181, 185, 193, 194, 197, 206, 244, 298, 299, 301-3, 305, 306, 307; *see also* Alliance *and* Labour *and* list candidates *and* list MPs *and* National
party vote 20, 24, 25-7, 36-7, 45, 81-2, 83, 84, 87, 89-90, 97, 98-9, 102, 103, 114, 120, 123, 125-6, 144, 155, 156, 174, 185, 187, 188, 193, 213-14, 236-8, 239-40, 243, 259, 264, 272, 274, 278, 284, 286, 309, 312, 315-18; *see also* ACT *and* Greens *and* Labour *and* National *and* New Zealand First *and* United Future
Perry, Edwin 185, 188
Peters, Winston 17, 51, 55, 57, 66-7, 70, 71, 74, 109, 118, 120, 121, 122, 131, 142, 212, 215, 241-2, 243, 245, 258, 259, 265, 267-8, 269, 284, 319, 320, 321, 328, 331, 338; and Helen Clark 24; leadership 24, 47, 62, 66-7, 109, 274, 320-1; personal style/image 24, 66-7, 118, 212, 241-2, 258, 263, 269; *see also* New Zealand First
Pillay, Lynne 49, 214
polls/surveys 18, 31, 33-6, 37, 43, 44, 47-8, 49, 58, 61, 62, 81-4, 92-3, 104, 113, 119, 121-2, 128, 132, 138, 195, 209, 211, 214, 231, 244, 255, 258, 264, 265-7, 286, 330-1; Engineers Union 214; *Herald* Digipoll 40, 48, 51, 53, 57, 131, 138, 214, 231, 265-6, 267; National Business review poll 36, 138; One Network News/Colmar Brunton poll 39, 48, 51, 52, 286; telepolling 160; TV3 NFO Opinion Poll 62, 65, 131, 231-2, 252; UMR Insight 36, 129; Victoria University survey 18, 19-20,

41, 270, 309-32; *see also* ACT *and* Greens *and* Labour *and* National *and* New Zealand First *and* United Future
populism 88, 105, 109, 238-42, 245-6, 248-50, 252-3, 263
Potton, Craig 49, 103, 211
Power, Simon 145, 146, 149
Prebble, Richard 24, 55, 70, 71, 92, 94-5, 109, 131, 249, 258, 318, 319, 320-1
preferred leaders 319-22
presidential-style election 61-2, 102, 105, 112, 114, 138, 189, 254-8
Progressive Coalition 23, 24, 46, 60, 71, 185, 211, 259, 262, 263, 276-7, 283, 285, 287, 290, 291, 292, 296, 298, 304-5, 307, 311, 314, 315, 316, 317, 327, 331, 334, 336, 338-9, 342, 346, 347, 355, 358; policies 346, 359; reaction to early election 43; results 26, 188; *see also* Anderton, Jim *and* Labour-Progressive Coalition
Purnell, Max 272

Raikaia 299
Ralston, Bill 130
Rangitikei 145-49, 280
Raukawa-Tait, Merepeka 181, 185, 187-8, 277-8
Richardson, Ruth 56, 69, 70, 182
Robson, Matt 143
Rodney 98
Rongotai 200
Roy, Eric 307
Royal Commission on the Electoral System 19, 21, 78, 181, 285, 287, 293, 295, 296

safe seats 21, 126, 156; *see also* Labour *and* National
Salmon, Guy 273
Scott, Noel 356
seating arrangement in Parliament 289-90, 310
Select Committees 46, 190, 290, 351
September 11 2001 72, 74, 112-13; *see also* US-led war on terror

Serious Fraud Office 36, 113
Sheppard, Mike 125
Shipley, Jenny 35, 57, 225, 251, 288, 299, 307, 309, 319, 330
Simcock, Bob 307
Simich, Clem 199
Simpson, Heather 342
single-member districts 193
single party government 338
smaller parties 16-17, 22, 24, 26, 27, 32-3, 36, 38, 93, 94, 95, 105, 109-10, 180, 193, 232, 238, 243, 258, 259, 261, 286, 287, 293, 302, 307, 313, 318
Social Credit 145
Stafford, Edward 42
Steel, Tony 307
Stephens, Dale 198, 273
Stewart, Alex 145
Stonyer, Mark 123-32, 342
Stout, Robert 42
support agreement 15, 58, 331, 333, 338, 339-40, 341, 344, 346, 347-55, 359
Sustainability Council 103

tactical voting 45-8, 57, 58, 61, 88-9, 90-1, 181, 191, 203, 209, 232, 286-7, 318
Tainui 295
Tait, Gerald 185, 188
Tamaki 199
Tamaki Makaurau 156
Tamihere, John 156-60
Tanzos, Nandor 101, 140-4
Taranaki-King Country by-election 1998 96
Tauranga 118, 120, 213, 274, 284, 287, 321
Te Heuheu, Georgina 159
Te Tai Hauauru 273, 295
Teahan, Peter 184
Tizard, Judith 140
Tolley, Anne 272-3, 280, 299, 307
'trigger' seats 284, 286-7
Tulloch, Inky 342

Turei, Metiria 101
Turia, Tariana 55-6, 295

United New Zealand 22, 24, 25, 123-5, 283-4, 288, 291, 309, 316, 336, 337
United Future 15, 23, 24, 48, 55, 88, 94, 121-2, 185, 203, 240, 247, 253, 285, 288, 289, 290, 291, 292, 300, 305, 307, 314, 315, 316-17, 331, 332, 337, 343, 344-5, 352, 355; advertising 126-32, 236, 240, 242-3, 275-6; and cannabis 143-4; and Greens 47, 127, 143, 243, 342-3; and Labour-Progressive Coalition 89, 333; and Maori 296; and media 51, 70, 89, 93, 94, 95, 123, 129-32, 231-2, 254, 259, 262-4; and women 299; candidates, selection of 128, 299, 304; emergence of 27, 47, 56-7, 70-1, 105, 108, 115, 121, 123-5, 212, 230-2, 263, 308; leadership 51, 124, 126, 128-9, 132, 231, 242-3, 276, 352; party vote 123, 276, 316-17; policies 57, 70-1, 127, 212, 247, 276; polls 129, 131, 213, 231, 244; reaction to early election 127; results 26, 93, 129, 188, 311, 335, 337; *see also* Dunne, Peter
United Future campaign 70-1, 123-32, 242-4
US-led war on terror 16, 23, 31, 39, 112-13, 212; *see also* September 11 2001

Vernon, Belinda 299, 307
volunteers 135-36
voter turnout 20-1, 25, 26, 84, 101, 103, 158, 160, 184, 189, 279

Wairarapa 175-91; *see also* Beyer, Georgina
Waitakere 198, 205, 213, 214, 285
Wallace, Sir John 285
Walton, Anthony 124, 126, 129, 343
Waring, Marilyn 42
Webster, Penny 306
Wellington Central 89, 90, 101, 135, 150-55, 198, 200, 202, 205
White, Greg 273
White, Jill 147
Wigram 213, 276, 277, 285, 338
Williams, Gary 163
Williams, Mike 39, 104-10
Wilson, Bruce 147
Wilson, Margaret 166, 287
Withers, Norm 219
women candidates 29, 180, 200, 293-4, 298-300, 303
women MPs 93, 161, 293-4, 296-301, 327-8, 355
women voters 79, 82, 93, 195, 243, 327-8
Wong, Pansy 296
Wood, Sue 272, 300
'worm' *see* media
Worth, Richard 309

Yates, Dianne 173
Young, Annabel 198, 299, 307
young voters 21, 79, 82-3, 101, 140-2, 157-8, 195, 247, 248

CONTENTS OF THE *NEW ZEALAND VOTES* CD

A ACT's 'One law for all New Zealanders' television commercial
B ACT's 'Tax cut for every worker' television commercial
C ACT's 'Zero tolerance for crime' television commercial
D The Alliance's party vote television commercial featuring Laila Harre
E The Christian Heritage Party's television commercial featuring Graham Capill and Merepeka Raukawa-Tait
F The Christian Heritage Party's television commercial featuring Merepeka Raukawa-Tait pitching for the Wairarapa electorate vote
G The Green Party's 'Keep GE in the lab ...' television commercial featuring Jeanette Fitzsimons
H The Green Party's mock MonstaCo television commercial, that was part of its opening party political broadcast
I The Labour Party's party vote television commercial featuring Helen Clark in tramping gear
J The Labour Party's 'When the country needed leadership ...' television commercial
K The National Party's education television commercial featuring Bill English
L The National Party's 'I believe' television commercial featuring Bill English
M New Zealand First's 'Fixing the Treaty' television commercial featuring Winston Peters
N An extract from New Zealand First's campaign closing statement by Winston Peters
O Outdoor Recreation's party political broadcast featuring party founder Stuart Mirfin
P The United Future Party's television commercial featuring Peter Dunne
Q Extracts from the Radio New Zealand party leaders' debates broadcast on 30 June, 7 July, and 14 July 2002
R Excerpts from Helen Clark being interviewed by John Campbell on 9 July 2002 and broadcast on TV3 on 10 July 2002
S Excerpts from TV1's worm-assisted analysis of the 15 July 2002 party leaders' debate chaired by Paul Holmes (the analysis section also features Mark Sainsbury, Chris Trotter, Colin James, and Peter Williams)